JUDICIAL REVIEW

IN THE

ENGLISH-SPEAKING

WORLD

Edward McWhinney

Barrister-at-Law and Solicitor
Professor of Law
University of Toronto

THIRD EDITION

UNIVERSITY OF TORONTO PRESS

BY THE SAME AUTHOR

Comparative Federalism: States' Rights and National Power

Constitutionalism in Germany and the Federal Constitutional Court

Föderalismus und Bundesverfassungsrecht

"Peaceful Coexistence" and Soviet-Western International Law

JUDICIAL REVIEW IN THE ENGLISH-SPEAKING WORLD

TO JULIUS STONE

FOREWORD

Nothing in the law books is more commonplace than the statement that the common law, the law of the English-speaking world, is essentially "judge-made" law. Indeed, this is usually made the point of contrast with civil law jurisdictions in which the statutory origin of modern law is stressed and the role of the judge as law-maker, in theory, denied. Paradoxically, many of the law books that stress the creative or dynamic role of the common law judge relegate this activity to past history and present the modern common law judge as a slave to the "law" of his predecessors on the bench or to the growing volume of legislation emanating from a sovereign legislative body.

The notion of a complete and perfect body of law worked out in the past and waiting only to be found and applied has had and still has an appeal and a vogue out of all proportion to its naïveté. Man, in his yearning for certainty, for a system that will operate mechanically and objectively, for the rule by "law" rather than "men," finds comfort in the idea. At a time when the function of law was conceived as a mere policing of individual actions in the interest of general security, self-denying statements of the judges to the effect that they merely "administered" the law as they "found" it undoubtedly enhanced the already high reputation and prestige of the English bench. It is strange that the very denial of their creative role, together with the development of the doctrine of *stare decisis*, helped preserve for the English (and later Commonwealth) judges the position of dignity and importance they had gained as a truly creative branch of government—a position which far transcends the civil service status of the continental judiciary.

Accepting the predominance of the "judge" in the common law legal system, it is not surprising that increased attention has, during the last thirty years, been given to the nature of the judicial process. Even in the field of judge-made private law, it has become increasingly apparent that under the guise of "applying" existing law a considerable amount of creative work is inevitable. After all, it is only the fringe cases that reach the courts. Where the law is clear and socially accepted, there is little need for court participation. In the numerically small but qualitatively important cases that reach the court, the law is far from clear and conflicting analogies or interpretations—call them what you will—compel the courts to face the necessity of choosing. It is in this inevitability of choice that the creative role inheres. To cover it up under the guise of a rule of law dictating an inevitable result undoubtedly preserves the dignity of a court as an institution (a value not lightly to be disregarded) in permitting it to lay blame on something other than itself for a given decision. On the other hand, constant repetition of this fiction obscures the necessity for choice and prevents a clear statement of the reasons, philosophies, postulates, ideals—in short, the value judgment—that are involved, and consequently issues may be decided unwittingly on an "inarticulate premise."

In the growing field of modern legislation and its increasing concern in regulating and directing human actions according to varying ideals of social good, it is becoming increasingly evident that, despite protests of many judges to the contrary, courts are much more than mere judicial "slot-machines" administering the sovereign will of Parliament. Here again we see a paradox. Whereas in the field of private, and largely judge-made law, the courts deny any policy-making role and do their creative work under the guise of explaining or developing what they themselves (or their predecessors on the bench) have said on other occasions, in the realm of legislation they are faced with intruders in a field traditionally theirs. Here policy-making is more clearly demonstrable and frequently takes the form of open hostility. "A statute in derogation of the common law shall be strictly construed." "The sovereignty of Parliament is an ever-present danger to the supremacy of law." Obviously a court cannot nullify a statute merely because it considers the legislation to be contrary to values expressed by the courts in their centuries-long exposition of the common law. What is possible, of course, is a restrictive "interpretation" of the statutes. Because statutes use words, and because words are not self-operating, it is well to remember that despite our theory of the sovereignty of Parliament, a statute will have only the effect that a court may say it should. Any one who has read decisions in which courts "construe" privative clauses attempting to prevent judicial review of administrative bodies must recognize that, despite protests to the contrary, under the guise of interpretation courts do take sides on "burning issues."

In many cases of this kind, it is difficult to believe that courts are not conscious of their power to act in opposition to legislative policies repugnant to the values of the common law of an earlier era. It is arguable that courts perform a valuable service in so acting since in that way the values of the past can at least be placed in opposition to the newer values declared by what may be hasty legislation. In these instances, moreover, the legislative body can always restate more clearly its objectives and expressly overrule, if it chooses, the judicial opposition. The difficulty here is that many judges honestly believe that they are not participating in policy-making or policy enunciation in these cases. As a result, the choices open to them are neither clearly seen nor articulated, and decisions are worded in the language of "black-letter" law and "inevitability." Thus the reasoning and evaluation processes are neither as informative nor as well informed as they otherwise might be.

If the courts in a country like England can, in this way, restrict or expand legislative policy, it is obvious that in a country such as Canada, for example, with a written constitution dividing legislative power between federal and provincial authorities, the courts have a doubly important and creative role in the growing scope of direct judicial review of legislation. Here, because decisions may result in complete nullification of legislative policy with no opportunity for changing those decisions save through cumbersome procedures of constitutional amendment, the courts have in fact a powerful and controlling veto power. The growth of written constitutions in other countries of the Commonwealth, whether those constitutions be in the form of statutes or otherwise, and whether they divide legislative power on some basis of federalism, or whether they create directly or indirectly restrictions on legislative competence, raises serious and far-reaching questions concerning the role of the courts in constitutional development.

It is this modern phenomenon of written constitutions and the courts' work of interpreting these constitutions that furnish the basis for Professor McWhinney's study. For many years Canadians have become accustomed to reading statements of the Privy Council that the B.N.A. Act was "just" another statute to be considered according to the ordinary canons of interpretation. This complete denial of the role of judicial statesmanship has been widely accepted in professional circles in Canada, along with a fairly general acceptance of the "black-letter," or what Professor McWhinney styles the "positivist," approach to law generally. In an atmosphere of that kind, to study legal developments in other jurisdictions has usually been considered as either a waste of time or an academic exercise in fatuity. The only important thing to be studied was what judges—especially English judges, since the Privy Council's word was "law"—had said, to the exclusion of any consideration of what might have been done or what could still be done, or what had already been done in other jurisdictions with a common law background or a constitution with similarities or differences.

For some years many of the law faculties in Canada have been attempting to break down this unrealistic and insular approach to law. There are, of course, dangers in a complete and uncritical acceptance of the "policy-making" role of the judges even as there are dangers in perpetuating the belief that courts merely apply existing rules and have nothing to do with the shaping of those rules in accordance with some philosophy. What is required, of course, is a study of the merits and demerits, the difficulties and pitfalls of either approach. Concentration on the passive and inactive role of the judge has, however, had a profound and melancholy effect on both legal scholarship and legal administration in countries where that belief is paramount. In Canada, for example, as a recent committee of the Canadian Bar Association has reported, legal research and legal scholarship are at an all-time low. The judgments of our courts cannot, by the widest stretch of imagination, be styled as enlightening or enlightened and in the main consist of a dreary collection of unrelated extracts from judgments of other judges. The abolition of appeals to the Privy Council provides some hope that Canadian courts may take a broader view of their functions than that of "following" something already handed down from above in an existing and complete ready-made form.

Professor McWhinney's examination of the role of English-speaking courts faced with diverse written constitutions brings together material for comparison from the United States as well as all the Commonwealth courts. He thus affords the reader an opportunity of re-examining his own beliefs concerning the proper function of courts in constitutional issues by providing comparisons and analogies without which sound evaluation is impossible. The fact that the author advocates greater and more dynamic participation in policy-making by the courts may or may not find general acceptance. An avowed exercise of a policy-making power with no criterion of values other than an individual judge's own preferences and philosophies may be as dangerous as a policy-making function which is obscured by the "judicial positivism" which the author attacks. The fact that courts do participate in creative activity does, however, need to be emphasized, and this activity is by no means confined to constitutional issues. Indeed, one criticism of the present work might well be the assumption of the author that in realms of private law such as property and equity there is assumed to be an absence of a dynamic or creative role. This is apparent in the author's criticism of many judicial appointments being made from the ranks of the practising profession rather than from persons who have, presumably, participated largely in public affairs. This is open to argument: it may be that persons trained in weighing the value of competing interests in the private law field may well be the best qualified persons for developing slowly but none the less surely a hierarchy of values on public law issues. What is important in both fields, of course, is an appreciation of the job to be done, an understanding of its inherent difficulties, and a conscious effort to meet those difficulties by supporting the right of legislatures to experiment and at the same time examining such experiments against the values (of which we talk so much and understand so little) basic to our concept of freedom under law.

The importance of the present book lies not only in the broad issues it discusses in constitutional law but in the hope it raises for the future of legal scholarship in Canada. In departing from the law-in-books approach, and the mere cataloguing of judicial dicta which has characterized so much of lawyers' writing on constitutional matters, McWhinney furnishes further evidence of a growing sense of maturity in Canadian legal writing. The work of Professors Bora Laskin, V. C. MacDonald (now Hon. Mr. Justice MacDonald), and Frank Scott has been concerned with investigating the creative role of Canadian courts in constitutional development. Professor McWhinney has now drawn on the experience of the United States and other Commonwealth countries as bearing on the same problem. It is this wide sweep that makes the present study of additional value to the student of constitutional law. No system of law is self-sustaining, even as today no country by itself can stand alone. To understand his own country and his own laws, the lawyer of today and of tomorrow can afford neither the luxury of self-complacency nor the sense of security engendered by a belief in law as a static and sure guarantee of the *status quo*. The world moves, and with it the law. The lawyer's task is not that of a mere observer. He must direct and guide the path of the law consciously and with knowledge and wisdom. Books like the present should make us realize the difficulty of our task and help us in its better performance.

CECIL A. WRIGHT

Faculty of Law
University of Toronto

PREFACE TO SECOND EDITION

The very gratifying response, both in Canada and in other countries, to the First Edition of this book, which appeared in 1956, has necessitated a further printing. I have been very conscious of the sage counsel of my old friend and former colleague on the Yale Law School faculty, the late Judge Jerome Frank, who used to warn against writing new editions. It was Judge Frank's opinion that by the time the occasion for a second or third edition should arrive, the author would be quite a different person to the author of the first edition—wiser, perhaps, but certainly older and with rather different intellectual attitudes, demands, and expectations. A later edition, in Judge Frank's view, was thus inevitably condemned to be a hodgepodge blend of two different personalities, and doomed to disappointment like so many joint, collaborative writing undertakings.

Nevertheless, there have been good and sufficient reasons why this should be made a Second Edition rather than a mere Second Impression. Major constitutional developments in the Union of South Africa since the time of first writing in 1956 suggested the need for the addition of a special chapter (chapter X), since the tragic resolution of the controversy between court and executive-legislative authority in South Africa has a constitutional importance and interest that quite transcends that country. In addition, recent events in Pakistan, plus the availability for the first time in North America of the official law reports for Pakistan and other public records, have permitted a complete rewriting of the section on Pakistan in the light of these authoritative source materials. I have also, in the new final chapter (chapter XI), essayed some more comprehensive study of the interaction and interplay of factors of judicial personalities, values, and techniques, in the implementation of the decision-making role of a Supreme Court exercising judicial review. This has, I think, facilitated the examination, on a comparative basis, of the function of the final appellate tribunal as policy-maker in the modern state, and also of the major intellectual problems besetting the individual judge who aspires to be a liberal activist. Beyond this, I have tried as far as possible to confine the changes to minor textual ones, so as both to retain as much of the original flavour of the First Edition as possible, and also to keep the book to about the same length. In particular, I have resisted the temptation to include additional chapters taking account of Continental European experience with judicial review —an area in which I have been working increasingly in recent years— feeling that this material should be saved as far as possible for special treatment in its own right at some later stage.

Some words, perhaps, as to basic research methodology. Though, as I said in my Preface to the First Edition, this work tends to straddle the fields of constitutional law and jurisprudence, I regard it as being, on balance, more of a study in jurisprudence—of the judicial process, judicial habits and specialized thought-ways, and judicial philosophy. I therefore feel no special responsibilities to attempt any exhaustive, case-by-case canvassing of the constitutional law of each one of the countries selected for study. In some instances, where such case law lends itself to comparative analysis, through time, in terms of changing trends in judicial philosophy, I have made such examination in detail: in other instances I have preferred to concentrate on a few *causes célèbres*, which, to the extent that they are, in fact, *leading cases*, seem to me fairly to illustrate the particular national system of jurisprudence from which they are drawn.

In emphasizing, in the full tradition of the American Legal Realist movement, the need for studying what judges actually do in deciding cases as well as what they say they do in their official opinions in support of the decision, I should stress that I am not to be taken as an enemy of judicial power as such, or certainly as implying any necessary disrespect for the judiciary, as one Commonwealth reviewer of the First Edition tended perhaps too quickly to assume. Likewise, though I have criticized certain English decisions, of the turn of the century, in which the economic predilections of the judges seem to be exposed more nakedly than is usual, this is certainly not a work written with any "left-of-centre" partisan political orientation, as an English reviewer mistakenly concluded. The best answer to this particular impeachment may be the countervailing criticism by the distinguished Socialist legal theoretician, Stefan Rozmaryn, writing in *Państwo i Prawo* (*State and Law*) that I have not given adequate emphasis, in interpretation of appellate court decisions, to economic deterministic theories of judicial motivation and judicial behaviour. I am appreciative of the intellectual worth of Professor Rozmaryn's brilliant analysis of my main thesis, coming as his comments do from the rather different intellectual vantage point of a jurist in a Socialist country; but, in truth, as one schooled in large measure in the American Pragmatist and Sociological approaches to law, I could not myself regard economic motivation as amounting to any more than one (and not necessarily the most important one) among a number of significant variables to be taken into consideration in the scientific appraisal of judicial decision-making.

Actually, readers familiar with my more general writings on law will have little difficulty in identifying me as one of the affirmative supporters of judicial power at the present day. It has been one of my main theses, in fact, that the immense complexity of executive government in the eras of the planned and welfare states (and also of the garrison state that now, fortunately, seems *passé*); plus the general attrition of the legislative process; the breakdown of the constitutional amending power in so many countries; the problem of the frequent lack of a trained decision-making élite in the case especially of the newly independent and self-governing (ex-colonial) countries—all render both necessary and inevitable a widespread expansion of judicial power. But it is my position also that it is a judicial power that needs to be exercised with public candour and frankness, with much of the wide-ranging intelligence and intellectual curiosity of the social scientist, and above all with a sense of humility and personal self-restraint. The measure of wise judicial statesmanship may well be the recognition by the judges of the necessary limits—institutional, societal, and intellectual—to the carrying on of their policy-making role.

I have benefited by a great number of stimulating and thoughtful reviews of the First Edition, and without wishing to appear in any way to discriminate among these, will note specifically, in addition to the review by Professor Rozmaryn already referred to, especially the reviews by Dennis Lyons in the *Harvard Law Review*; E. C. S. Wade in the *Canadian Bar Review*; William Anderson in the *American Political Science Review*; and André Tunc in the *Revue Internationale de Droit Comparé*; Barna Horvath in the *American Journal of Comparative Law*; Helmut Rumpf in the *Archiv für Rechts- und Sozialphilosophie*; George W. Stumberg in the *Journal of Public Law*; and Francis H. Heller in the *Annals of the American Academy of Political and Social Science*.

In the First Edition, I recorded my very great personal and intellectual obligations to my former colleagues and teachers, Julius Stone, Filmer Northrop, Myres McDougal, Harold Lasswell, Eugene Rostow, and the late Judge Jerome Frank; and I also acknowledged invaluable criticisms of the manuscript by Paul A. Freund and by Vincent C. MacDonald; and of sections of the work by Erwin N. Griswold, Hessel Yntema, and George V. V. Nicholls. To these names, I would like to add, now, particularly Edmond Cahn, Harry Jones, Carl Friedrich, and Alexander Brady, to each of whom I am indebted for the opportunity for fruitful intellectual exchange, through correspondence or personal conversations, in the past years.

I am indebted to Francess Halpenny and Jean Houston of the University of Toronto Press for editorial advice and guidance in connection with this Second Edition. Breta M. Fuller, Librarian of the University of Toronto Law Library, has assisted me in ensuring access as far as possible to the law reports, statutes, and public records of the various countries dealt with in the present volume. Carole Harris of the staff of the University of Toronto Law School typed all of the manuscript for the new sections and otherwise helped me in the organization of the materials for the Second Edition.

Finally, I have to thank the *Canadian Bar Review* for granting me permission to draw freely, in the writing of the new sections, on articles I have published in that journal from time to time.

EDWARD MCWHINNEY

Max-Planck-Institut
für Auslandisches Öffentliches Recht
und Völkerrecht,
Heidelberg
August, 1960

PREFACE TO THIRD EDITION

The extraordinarily widespread interest which, as already noted in the Preface to the second edition of this work, is now being taken in the idea of judicially-based control of constitutionality, has necessitated yet a further printing. Judging from the range of the published reviews and also from the personal comments and criticisms made directly to me, this interest is by no means confined to the essentially English-speaking, Anglo-Saxon Common Law-influenced, countries covered by the present book. For the contemporary interest in judicial review extends also, it is clear, to the countries of Continental Europe, to the "emergent" (newly independent and self-governing), countries of South-East Asia and Africa, and not least perhaps to the Socialist countries of Eastern Europe where the concern, in scientific legal circles, with the institutional moderation of power, has increased markedly with the attempts at effectuation, in legal terms, of the policy of liberalisation and de-Stalinisation generally.

Following on the publication of the second edition, a number of friends and correspondents suggested to me the possibility of expanding the scope of the volume to include those countries of Continental Europe where judicial review actually exists today as part of the working machinery of government. The advantages, in terms of testing of hypotheses and general propositions otherwise formulated too easily on the basis of the experience of the Anglo-Saxon Common Law-influenced countries alone, of further comparative study directed, this time, to legal systems where the public law institution of judicial review exists on a Civil Law, as distinct from a Common Law, general legal base, are clear. This need may perhaps be met in part by my recent book, *Constitutionalism in Germany and the Federal Constitutional Court* (1962), which attempts to examine the shifting balance between judicial activism and judicial self-restraint against a distinctively Continental European legal background of Court specialisation, judicial anonymity, and the collegial principle of judicial decision-making and judicial opinion-writing. It is hoped to expand on the range and scope of this particular study in Continental European judicial review, at some later stage.

In addition, I have had some further requests made to me that I should discuss in some more considerable detail the constitutional experience of the "new" countries of South-East Asia and of Africa. From my own contacts, over the years, with professors and graduate students from these countries, and also from more recent, first-hand discussions with Indian constitutional experts on the occasion of my giving various lectures in New Delhi to the Indian Law Institute, the Indian School of International Studies, and the Indian Society of International Law, I am conscious of the innate richness and variety of the experience of these countries. I feel, however, that extended coverage in depth of these countries might better be reserved for some autonomous study, in its own right, of the process of reception of Western public law institutions and Western basic legal values in non-Western societies; and of the independent constitutional growth and development and refinement, and ultimately constitutional novation, that thereby has ensued in these same non-Western societies. I have therefore, for purposes of the present edition, tried to leave the treatment of democratic constitutionalism in South-East Asia essentially as it appeared in the second edition. The recently published studies in Indian constitutionalism on the part of Dr. M. P. Jain, presently the Research Director of the Indian Law Institute, and also of Dean Ramaswamy of the Delhi Law Faculty, have helped to persuade me that the discussion of the conflict between judicial positivism and judicial policy-making on the Supreme Court of India advanced in the second edition still remains essentially true today, so far, at least, as concerns its delineation of the dilemmas of philosophic choice in an Indian judicial context.

While it would be unfair to single out any jurists in particular among the many who have helped with their reviews, or else with their various personal comments and criticisms, in regard to the second edition, I will take the opportunity of mentioning, in addition to those already indicated above, the late Lord Birkett, writing in the *Law Society's Gazette*; Professor Hans Spanner, writing in the *Archiv des öffentlichen Rechts*; and finally Sir Ian Lewis, Attorney-General of Northern Nigeria.

The new material in the present edition, contained in the final chapter of the volume, derives in part from a hitherto unpublished paper that was delivered to a special seminar on Legal Philosophy and Legal Positivism, held under the auspices of the Rockefeller Foundation (Division of the Social Sciences) at Villa Serbelloni, Lago di Como. Responsibility for views expressed in the new edition, as in the two earlier editions, remains, of course, that of the writer personally.

Edward McWhinney

University of Toronto
January, 1965

CONTENTS

JUDICIAL REVIEW IN THE ENGLISH-SPEAKING WORLD

1

CONSTITUTIONAL LAW IN GREAT BRITAIN AND THE COMMONWEALTH COUNTRIES

Constituent power in the old British Empire was exercised very simply, in terms of strict juridical theory. The constitutions of Canada, Australia, the Union of South Africa, and New Zealand were not of popular origin at all, according to this particular conception, but imposed from above, through enactment of the sovereign United Kingdom Parliament, and are thus to be found in British statutes. Yet this fact of formal enactment by the United Kingdom Parliament does not explain altogether, or even substantially, the ultimate form and content of these constitutions: for the action by the United Kingdom Parliament was generally preceded by the holding of representative local conventions which agreed on the essentials and frequently on the details of the principles subsequently embodied by the United Kingdom in its legislation. The fundamentals of the governmental systems established under these new constitutions were thus essentially due to the efforts of the local political leaders, and each constitution may thus be said to have in effect, apart from its formal, juridical, imperial origins, a local or popular root.[1]

Among the key features of these constitutions of the pre-Commonwealth era, we may note, first, a certain harmony of language and style—notwithstanding their being spread over a period of fifty years or so—

---

[1]"The fact that our constitution is the creature of the British Parliament seems to me a fortuitous circumstance which is quite irrelevant; so too is the fact that we have a written constitution. I would have been of the same opinion if it had been framed by a constituent assembly of the people, made by Solon or extracted from the law of Hammurabi. It seems to me immaterial whether one adheres to the mandatory theory of legislative power or any other. The fact remains that the South Africa Act is our constitution and apart from the constitution there are no organs of state and no powers. If you will, call the cohesive force what Jellinek used to term 'die normirende Kraft des Factischen.' " *Per* van den Heever J., concurring, *Minister of the Interior* v. *Harris*, [1952] 4 S.A.L.R. 769 (A.D.); the second *Harris Case*.

And see also F. R. Scott, "The Re-distribution of Imperial Sovereignty," (1950) 44 *Royal Society of Canada Transactions* (Series III, Section 2) 27.

which a common subjection to correction, in their final versions, by the British parliamentary draftsman no doubt partly explains.[2]

Secondly, although the constitutional instrument is not the sole source of constitutional power in each of these countries, being supplemented also by custom and convention,[3] nevertheless to a very considerable extent what is unwritten law only in the case of the United Kingdom has been concreted in the case of these countries into formal rules set out in the constitutional instrument itself—for example, the structure of government and the relationship *inter se* of the various arms of government. This tendency is in keeping, in theory anyway, with the basic condition of countries which had only recently emerged from dependent, colonial status to full self-government and which were, no doubt, not fully experienced as yet in the practice of representative government.

Thirdly, putting to one side for the moment the question of federalism, these constitutional instruments are all quite skeletal in their drafting apart from the detailing of the functional machinery of government, that is, the minimum framework necessary for the conduct of government within the country. In particular, the written portions of the constitution do not contain anything corresponding to the elaborate bills of rights or other systems of fundamental limitations on legislative power that have characterized constitutional drafting in Continental Europe especially since World War I. Partly, I think, this particular fact is due to the pervasive influence (in the preliminary drafting by local leaders as well as the final drafting by the United Kingdom Parliament) of English constitutional ideas, which strongly opposed the elaborations of the Continental constitution-makers as being unrealistic and mere paper affirmations— see the strictures in this regard advanced by Professor Dicey at the end of the nineteenth century;[4] partly to the widespread notion that even the more limited guarantees contained in the American Bill of Rights were always substantially part of the common law of England, carried as such

[2]Until 1949, amendments to the Canadian Constitution had to be effected by Act of the United Kingdom Parliament, owing to the absence of amending machinery in the British North America Act, 1867. The procedure actually operative over the last forty years was for the amendments to be drafted by the Canadian government and then formally enacted by the United Kingdom Parliament; but throughout, the British parliamentary draftsman insisted, partly no doubt for reasons of sheer pedantry, in making verbal changes and correcting the language, style, and even the punctuation of the texts submitted by the Canadian government. Cf. F. R. Scott, "The British North America (No. 2) Act (1949)," (1950) 8 *U. of Toronto L.J.* 201.

[3]See generally A. V. Dicey, *The Law of the Constitution* (1st ed., 1885), 341 *et seq.*

[4]*Ibid.*, 109 *et seq.*

by English settlers to the various colonies,[5] and presumably gaining very little in import by being written down in a constitutional instrument; partly to the temper of the times, for laissez-faire was still politically at its height, manifesting itself in notions of self-help that brooked no sympathy for (much less, indeed, recognized) those social and economic rights that are so popular with constitution-makers of the present age.

In the cases of Canada and Australia, some extra complexity in the basic structure of government in comparison with that of the United Kingdom was made inevitable by the fact that their constitutions, and for that matter South Africa's too, were to be built, like the United States Constitution, on a number of existing states which had an autonomous constitutional history and development of their own. It is not to be wondered that the Canadian constitution-makers, faced with the problem of devising an appropriate form of government for two distinct and differing nationalities, should seize upon the American federal form as the best constitutional arrangement for those who wanted to form a common government and to act as one people for some purposes but to remain independent and to retain their own national identity in all other respects. Likewise, the Australian constitution-makers at the close of the nineteenth century, though they had the good fortune, in comparison with Canada, to be dealing with an unusually homogeneous racial group, selected the federal form as the best means of combining six existing states that had been settled separately around the littoral of a vast and sparsely settled continent. In the case of South Africa, however, in spite of differences between the two main European races in language, culture, religion, and history that might surely have seemed at the time as deep-seated and compelling as the divisions in Canada had appeared in 1867, the federal form was not employed, primarily because it was realized in 1909 that the central problem for the new Union of South Africa would be how to regulate the affairs of the native (African) population, and because it was thought, rightly or wrongly, that a single European policy on native affairs could only be devised in a unitary, as distinct from a federal, state.

The existence of the federal form in the case of Canada and of Australia introduces additional problems to their constitutional law, in view of the need for special machinery in the constitutional instrument governing the relationship *inter se* of the national government and of the member states of the federal system. This machinery is provided for in both Canada and Australia (as in the United States) by the inclusion of provisions setting

[5]"It is clear law that in the case of British Colonies acquired by settlement, the colonists carry their law with them so far as it is applicable to the altered conditions." *Per* Griffith C.J., *R. v. Kidman*, (1915) 20 C.L.R. 435.

out the allocation of legislative powers to the nation and to the states respectively. The Australian arrangements in this regard are very simple, involving the specific spelling out of the powers of the nation, with the residue necessarily belonging to the states; the Canadian arrangements are slightly more complex; but it still seems correct to say in the case of both these constitutions that the use of the federal form by itself (and for the moment without considering the interposition of judicial review) has not unduly burdened the machinery of government.

The constitutions of the Commonwealth countries drafted since the Statute of Westminster, 1931, present something of a contrast to the earlier constitutional instruments. There is an attempt, first of all, formally to assert a local, popular root for the constitution in opposition to the old strictly juridical notion of the constitution deriving its binding authority and legal efficacy through the fact of enactment by the United Kingdom Parliament. The first instance of this is in the case of Ireland. The Constitution of 1937, from the opening words of the preamble onwards, demonstrates a clear purpose to eschew English constitutional forms and patterns as a means of strengthening the break with the imperial past.[6] It is manifested also in the case of the Constitution of the new Republic of India, which was the product, formally and actually, of the three years of deliberations of a locally selected Constituent Assembly, and in the case of the "Constitution of the Islamic Republic of Pakistan," finally adopted in 1956 after nine years' work by local constituent assemblies.

Secondly, the new constitutions not merely represent a polar extreme to the completely unwritten Constitution of the United Kingdom, but also contrast sharply with the fairly skeletal, functional constitutions of the Commonwealth of the pre–Statute of Westminster era. The modern cult of prolixity in constitutional drafting as expressed through the proliferation of detail is carried to its logical extreme perhaps in the case of the new Indian Constitution, and to a less extent in the case of the Pakistan Constitution also; but the present constitutions of Ireland and Ceylon also are as long as, or longer than, even the constitutions of Canada and Australia without having the extra complication of a federal form and the consequent need for allocation of powers between nation and component member states that the drafters of the latter two instruments had to consider. The explanation in the case of Ireland seems to lie in the conscious recourse of the constitutional drafters to Continental European forms and even phraseology, with consequent loss, for better or worse, of the terse-

---

[6]Strictly speaking, the Irish Constitution of 1937 simply continues and extends policies begun in the Constitution of the Irish Free State (Saorstat Eireann) of 1922.

ness of expression that normally characterizes British legal drafting. In the case of India and Pakistan, the desire (which seems also, as we have noted earlier, to have been not without a degree of influence in the drafting of the pre–1931 constitutions) to provide an elaborate, all-foreseeing blueprint for a people not yet experienced in the practice of representative, democratic government appears to have operated very strongly. And Ireland, India, Pakistan, and Ceylon have each broken new ground, in comparison with traditional English constitutional ideas, in inserting formal limitations on governmental (executive and legislative) authority in the constitutional instrument itself. In the case of India, Pakistan, and Ceylon, the inclusion of a bill of rights was made logical by the presence of racial and religious minorities within the territorial borders; Ireland felt the need, in view of the essentially Roman Catholic composition of its society, to give special emphasis to those cardinal institutions recognized in scholastic legal thought, the Family and the Church. And Ireland, India, and Pakistan take note, in differing ways however, of the swing from laissez-faire towards collectivism, and the current conflict over the adjustment of individual and public claims to property, by including specific constitutional provisions as to the "right to property." The Irish looked directly to Continental European legal thought for guidance here, especially, so far as technical forms were concerned—see the "Directive Principles of Social Policy"—to the Spanish Republican Constitution of 1931. The Indian constitution-makers, even more broadly eclectic than those in Ireland, borrowed from Ireland and wherever else they could, through most assiduous culling of the assorted constitutional texts.

In terms of functional organization of government, notwithstanding some surface differences of nomenclature—see the institution of a "President" in the case of Ireland, India, and Pakistan—the post–1931 constitutions all hew to the fundamentals of English constitutional organization, namely, the institution of representative government as expressed through a parliamentary executive (the cabinet) formally responsible to and controlled by the legislature. The only qualification that needs be made relates to the institution of judicial review, which will form the subject of detailed comment at a later stage.

Of the post–1931 constitutions, only those of the Republics of India and of Pakistan are expressly federal in form. Generally speaking, the organization and arrangements of the member states within the new Republic of India accord with the political and administrative arrangements under British rule. But the constitutional instrument accords wide powers to the national legislature in relation to the states; by simple legislative enactment, the national legislature may form new states out of existing states, increase or diminish the area of a state, or alter its boundaries;[7] and on proclamation of an emergency by the national executive, it may legislate on any matters within state legislative powers,[8] such national legislation to prevail over earlier or later inconsistent state legislation.[9] Such drastic powers for the national legislature suggest that the federal form in the case of India is rather less a response to well-articulated claims to autonomy at the local level than a recognition of considerations of administrative expediency by a nationally minded constituent assembly. It is true that the problem stemmed originally from the very unevenness, and also the differences in point of time, in the development of institutions of representative, democratic government in the various component states: some of these, being historically more directly associated with the British government, acquired experience in representative government fairly early; others, like the princely states, lagged further behind; and still others, the territories, had almost no such experience. Hence the need to provide for a sort of staggered federalism, with appropriate adjustment in the powers and responsibilities of each category of state according to degree of political advancement. The trouble has been that, to make such a complex arrangement viable, it has seemed necessary to the Indian constitution-makers to make the national legislature substantially omnipotent in relation to the member states of the federation.

The federal nature of the Constitution of the Republic of Pakistan[10] rests on two constituent units, the provinces of East Pakistan and West Pakistan, corresponding to the two main, and widely separated, geographical units of the country.[11] The principal guarantee of the maintenance of a federal character must be the formal guarantee in the Constitution of parity of representation for each of the two provinces in the unicameral federal legislature, the National Assembly.[12] This provision should at least insure that regional interests are brought to bear in the processes of governmental policy-making at the centre, a prime demand of the East Bengal separatist movement that has been most active in the province of East Pakistan in recent years.

Principal Agencies of Constitutional Change

There are four generally accepted agencies of constitutional change. First is constituent power itself, whether expressed forcibly, as in the rup-

[7]Republic of India Constitution, article 3.

[8]Article 250.

[9]Article 251.

[10]Republic of Pakistan Constitution, article 1 (1): "Pakistan shall be a Federal Republic to be known as the Islamic Republic of Pakistan, and is hereinafter referred to as Pakistan."

[11]Article 1 (2) a.   [12]Article 44 (1) and (3).

ture of the American colonies with Britain in 1776 and on some views, perhaps, in the establishment of the Constitution of the Irish Free State (Saorstat Eireann) of 1922, or whether expressed more peaceably, in full conformity to the pre-existing legal situation, as indeed has been the general case with the establishment of the constitutions of the Commonwealth countries. Thus, though the Constitution of the Republic of India of 1949 is expressed in its preamble to have a local popular root, from the strict legal viewpoint it is still true that the attainment of Indian independence was also achieved in full conformity with the theory of the sovereignty of the United Kingdom Parliament in relation to India up to that time; for it was an Act of the United Kingdom Parliament, the Indian Independence Act of 1947, which formally partitioned India into two separate dominions, India and Pakistan, and also invested constituent assemblies in each country with plenary powers to draw up and adopt a constitution.

A second means of constitutional change is through developing custom and convention. Thus, to take a classic example, though the constitutions of the Commonwealth countries that were enacted before the Statute of Westminster were all, in their ultimate juridical origins, statutes passed by the United Kingdom Parliament and therefore, in theory, liable to repeal or amendment by subsequent inconsistent statutes, there was in practice no risk of any such action by the United Kingdom Parliament; for the powers of the United Kingdom Parliament in this regard soon became hedged in by a well-accepted convention to the effect that such power would not be exercised except at the request and with the consent of the countries concerned, a convention that was finally written into positive law form in section 4 of the Statute of Westminster. Other examples of the operation of custom and convention in the Commonwealth are the effective disappearance, through desuetude, of the prerogative (or reserve) powers of the British Crown in relation to the countries of the Commonwealth; even the Crown's power of appointment of the titular executive of those countries (that is, the Governor-General) has now to be exercised in strict compliance with the wishes of the governments of those countries.

A third agency of change is direct amending power. All the constitutions of the Commonwealth countries with the exception of Canada contain provisions establishing procedures for their own amendment, and it is by these procedures that formal amendment was clearly intended, historically, to be effected.

Since the Constitution of Canada, as enacted by the United Kingdom Parliament in 1867, contained no provision for its own amendment, any amendments have accordingly had to be effected over the years by resort to the United Kingdom Parliament. In fact there developed over the years an elaborate set of conventional rules governing the making of such amendments. The United Kingdom Parliament, it was said, would act only at the request of the national Parliament of Canada, though there was considerable conflict of authority and practice as to what degree, if at all, the national Parliament of Canada was bound to consult the provinces prior to making requests to the United Kingdom Parliament for amendments. In 1949, moves began for the devising of a procedure for amendment of the Canadian Constitution, to be located and operated wholly within Canada. These moves were partially realized by a constitutional amendment passed by the United Kingdom Parliament in 1949 at the request of the Canadian government, but the successful completion of the whole project seems now to have been postponed indefinitely, owing to difficulty in obtaining any agreement between the national government and the provinces as to the exact nature of the final procedure for amendment to be adopted for the future.

In the case of the Australian Constitution, proposed amendments must be approved by each House of the national Parliament, and then subsequently approved at a popular referendum by a majority of the electors throughout Australia and also by a majority of the electors in a majority (four) of the six member-states.[13]

The Constitution of the Union of South Africa, in terms of section 152 of the South Africa Act, may, with certain exceptions only, be amended by simple enactment of the Union Parliament. The exceptions concern the provision for equality of the English and Dutch languages[14] and also the provision preserving the special voting rights of the so-called "coloured" voters in the Cape Province of the Union.[15] These provisions (the "entrenched clauses" of the South Africa Act) can be amended only by a two-thirds majority of the total number of members of both Houses of the Union Parliament, at a joint sitting.

By section 2 of the New Zealand Constitution (Amendment) Act of 1857, the Parliament of New Zealand was given power to amend or repeal by ordinary legislative enactment any of the provisions of the Constitution, subject to certain exceptions only. These exceptions were removed by the New Zealand Constitution (Amendment) Act of 1947, passed by the United Kingdom Parliament at the request of the New Zealand government, so that all of the provisions of the New Zealand Constitution can now be amended or repealed by ordinary legislative enactment of the New Zealand Parliament.

[13]Commonwealth of Australia, Constitution, s. 128.
[14]South Africa Act, s. 137.
[15]S. 35.

Under the new Republican Constitution of India, coming into force in 1950, the general rule as to amendments is that these may be effected by a two-thirds majority vote in each House of Parliament.[16] In respect to certain matters, mainly relating to the federal structure of the Constitution (for example, the Supreme Court, the distribution of legislative powers between the union and the states, representation of the states in Parliament), an additional requirement of ratification of amendments by the legislatures of one-half of the member states exists. As against this, however, a large number of provisions of the Constitution are open to alteration by the national Parliament by a simple majority, in so far as they are not to be classified as "amendments to the Constitution" and therefore not to be subjected to the special procedures required under article 368 for the making of amendments; and in addition, under the "emergency provisions" of the Constitution,[17] the national government is given drastic powers to suspend, during emergencies, the "fundamental rights" guarantees contained in the Constitution,[18] including the right of free speech.[19]

The Ceylon Constitution may, under section 29 of the Ceylon (Constitution) Order-in-Council, 1946, be amended by vote of a two-thirds majority of the total number of members of the legislature of Ceylon.

The Pakistan Constitution may be amended by vote of the unicameral federal legislature, the National Assembly, provided that the proposal for amendment is approved by both a majority of the total number of members of the Assembly and also a two-thirds majority of the members actually present and voting, and finally assented to by the President.[20] A small number of provisions, principally having to do with the relations of the two constituent provinces, East Pakistan and West Pakistan, to the federal government and *inter se,* and including the special provision guaranteeing East Pakistan and West Pakistan parity of representation in the National Assembly,[21] require also approval by a resolution of each provincial Assembly affected.

In spite of the hopes and expectations of the constitutional drafters, the machinery for amendment of the constitution, in the case at least of those Commonwealth countries where there has been any extended experience of its working operation over a period of years, has not been very productive of actual changes. The Canadian and Australian constitutions were each drafted at the time of the political dominance of laissez-faire, and one might have expected that there would be attempts to supplement the existing, rather skeletal, constitutional provisions with guarantees of social and economic welfare as social democratic ideas increasingly became

[16]Republic of India Constitution, article 368.   [17]Articles 352–60.
[18]Articles 12–35.   [19]Article 19.
[20]Republic of Pakistan Constitution, article 216.   [21]Article 44 (1) and (3).

received opinion in the United Kingdom and the overseas Empire. But any attempts in this direction have been largely abortive to date, owing in part perhaps to the nature of the machinery available for direct constitutional amendment. For example, the Canadian government, following the Privy Council ruling in 1937[22] that legislation creating a national scheme of unemployment insurance was *ultra vires,* spent three years in obtaining the acquiescence of all the provinces to a constitutional amendment conferring on it the necessary legislative power and then securing its formal enactment by the United Kingdom Parliament. This experience has hardly been such as to encourage the Canadian Parliament in the belief that large and urgent demands of social policy can readily be effected through the formal machinery for amendment of the constitutional instrument. The urgent moves by the Canadian government, so far unsuccessful, to obtain self-operating amending machinery for the Canadian Constitution become understandable in this light. Likewise, the many attempts formally to amend the Australian Constitution, especially in the direction of conferring "planning" powers on the national government, have almost all come to nought. The public referendum, which has been so productive of constitutional changes in the case of Switzerland, has been the principal rock on which the national government's hopes in Australia have foundered.

These difficulties give rise, of course, to some reservations as to the full wisdom of the more enthusiastic forms of constitutional eclecticism. The referendum works well (in the sense of easily) in Switzerland where people have had some considerable experience over the years in its use as part of the general machinery of government. Is that, however, any necessary guarantee of its success when transplanted abruptly to Australia where it had not previously had any roots? The Australian experience with the referendum as part of the constitutional machinery of government, indeed, tends to support the historical school's general thesis that positive law forms, to be viable in action, must be based on and grow out of a people's past experience. But it may perhaps also be suggested that the practical break-down of the formal amending machinery in the case of Australia, and perhaps in the case of Canada too, at least where it concerns the failure to augment the existing constitutional instrument by a bill of rights and provisions for social welfare, once more is due to the survival of English-derived attitudes in favour of confining the constitutional instrument so far as possible to the detailing of the bare functional arrangements of government and no more.

[22]*Attorney-General for Canada* v. *Attorney-General for Ontario,* [1937] A.C. 355.

That the constitutions of Canada and of Australia, in spite of the effective failure to produce changes through the normal amending machinery, have nevertheless undergone considerable modification and even transformation over the years since they first came into being, is due, above all, to a fourth agency of constitutional change, judicial interpretation of the constitution. Apart from the experience of judicial interpretation of the constitutions of Canada and of Australia, it is submitted, the record in regard to the Constitution of the Union of South Africa, the Constitution of Ireland since 1937, and even the new Constitution of the Republic of India in the few years since it came into force, suggests that judicial interpretation will continue in the future to be the most significant factor in constitutional growth and decay in the various Commonwealth countries outside the United Kingdom.

In treating of the role of judicial interpretation as an agency of constitutional change, I propose to distinguish at the outset between two modes of judicial action in relation to constitutional law. The first is where a court, as a formal matter, has or exerts the power to annul or override enactments of the legislature on the ground that they are "unconstitutional"; this we will refer to as direct judicial review, and it has, as a concomitant, the presence of a rigid constitution, changeable only by some extraordinary process, for otherwise the legislature could simply "correct" the judicial declaration of "unconstitutionality" by proceeding immediately to pass fresh legislation. The second is where a court, either not having the power to annul or override enactments of the legislature as "unconstitutional" or else simply choosing not to exert that power in the instant case, says, in effect, in the process of interpretation of a statute, that the legislature may or may not have the claimed legislative power, but it has not, in the language it has used in the enactment now in question, employed that power. This latter type of judicial action, a form of indirect judicial review frequently referred to as "judicial braking," though it will be significant principally in the case of countries with flexible, uncontrolled constitutions like the United Kingdom, may also be observed in action from time to time in those countries, like the United States, Canada, Australia, and the Republic of India, having direct judicial review as an accepted part of the machinery of government.

The historical origins of direct judicial review in the Commonwealth countries seem to reduce to the fact that the Privy Council originally exercised that power in relation to the overseas Empire, just as it did in relation to the thirteen American colonies before 1776. The essential premise on which the Privy Council proceeded was that colonial legislatures were subordinate legislative bodies vis-à-vis the United Kingdom

Parliament, and that their enactments were therefore subject to review by the courts on the same basis as, for example, regulations passed by local government bodies within the United Kingdom. It is to be noted, however, that the Privy Council continued to exercise that power long after many of the colonies had ripened into self-governing Dominions and therefore long after their legal subordination to the United Kingdom Parliament had effectively disappeared. Even after the abolition of the appeal to the Privy Council, the Canadian Supreme Court, for example, continues to exercise the power of direct judicial review in relation to legislation passed by the Canadian Parliament and the provincial legislatures; and right from the outset of the Australian Constitution the High Court of Australia assumed the power to invalidate, on the grounds of unconstitutionality, legislation concerning the powers *inter se* of the national and the state governments of Australia, a category of matters in which the Australian Constitution expressly provides that an appeal does not lie as of right to the Privy Council.

In respect to federal states like Canada, Australia, India, and Pakistan, there is no doubt a certain logic in the courts' assuming the power of judicial review, as umpires, as it were, of the federal system. Yet in no one of these cases can it be said that direct judicial review, when exercised, has been confined wholly to federal (that is, division of legislative powers) questions; while in at least one case, that of Australia, it must be stated that federal questions have comprised only a minor portion of the court's work. Since none of the constitutions of the Commonwealth contains express provision for direct judicial review, the carry-over of the practice by both the Privy Council and local appellate tribunals, long after these parliaments have ceased to be subordinate legislative bodies vis-à-vis the United Kingdom Parliament, would seem primarily due to the fact that the practice has become ingrained over the years and its historical roots and justification have been forgotten, an example perhaps of long-time user and practice ripening into a binding "convention" of constitutional law.[23]

Of course, once the power of direct judicial review has been successfully asserted under a given constitution, its continued existence may quite readily be justified on pragmatic grounds. The constitutional lawyer in the

---

[23]It is to be noted in passing that the Privy Council has itself been baffled at times as to the exact nature of the function it has been performing. See the doubts expressed by the Lord Chancellor, Lord Halsbury, in *Webb* v. *Outrim*, [1907] A.C. 81 (P.C.), as to whether there could be such a thing as an "unconstitutional" act of a Dominion or colonial legislature, once assented to by the Crown; and note the criticism of this judicial dictum by Latham, in W. K. Hancock, ed., *Survey of British Commonwealth Affairs* (1937), 566.

Commonwealth countries, especially if he remembers Dicey's strictures upon the utility of fundamental guarantees and affirmations in the written constitutions of Continental Europe, may well conclude that the power of direct judicial review is necessary to the effectiveness of any written constitutional instrument. It does seem clear that considerations of utility of this nature bulked large in the decision by the Supreme Court of South Africa, during the recent constitutional crisis, to assert what amounts to a power of direct judicial review in relation to the "entrenched clauses" of the South Africa Act; it had been widely assumed up to that time that the Parliament of the Union of South Africa possessed sovereign, unlimited law-making power, even in relation to the "entrenched clauses," in the same way as the United Kingdom Parliament. Considerations such as these are, of course, strictly irrelevant to the question of whether the power of direct judicial review actually exists under a given constitutional instrument. But the obscurity surrounding the origins of direct judicial review in the Commonwealth countries, and the consequent difficulties in affirmatively justifying its continuance at the present day on any other than broad, pragmatic grounds, are no doubt important contributing factors to the difficulties of positivist-minded judges in the Commonwealth countries in facing up to the full implications and also the responsibilities of the exercise of direct judicial review under a written and rigid constitution.

It would, of course, be an error to write off altogether the opportunities possessed by judges in the United Kingdom, in the face of a "sovereign" Parliament, of delaying and frustrating legislative majorities through indirect judicial review—the process of "interpretation" of statute law.[24] Yet the position of a supreme court exercising direct judicial review under a written and rigid constitution, as in the Commonwealth countries, clearly differs very greatly from that of the House of Lords in the United Kingdom, sitting as the highest tribunal in a jurisdiction that is mainly concerned with private law matters. The experience of the judges of the House of

---

[24]The success of indirect judicial review is clearly an example of "victory by attrition": although Parliament may always in theory correct the worst rigours of harsh judicial construction of statute law by further legislation, at best this is likely to involve time-consuming delays, and at worst the "corrective" legislation may bog down completely. See C. K. Allen, *Law in the Making* (5th ed., 1951), 472–3, and instances there cited. We have referred to the controversy over whether direct judicial review exists in relation to the "entrenched clauses" only of the South Africa Act: in respect to all other areas of the South African Constitution, direct judicial review clearly does not exist. The degree of success the South African judges have had, nevertheless, in arresting the Malan Government's apartheid programme in these other areas, has, it will be noted, been achieved perforce by indirect judicial review—harsh judicial construction of statute law, forcing the South African Parliament each time to enact fresh legislation.

Lords, when sitting as members of the Privy Council and exercising the historical role of direct judicial review of constitutional law cases stemming from the old British Commonwealth, is an illustration of this. The story is one of a cramped, fettering approach on the part of judges who have devoted most of their professional lives to the fine determination of private law cases and are suddenly confronted for the first time with the broad policy problem inherent in the adjudication of constitutional law. Their approach has been to treat the constitutions in question as ordinary statutes only, and to subject them to the same restrictive canons of construction normally applied by the common law judges to the interpretation of statute law.

There seems, however, little to choose between the approach of the Privy Council to the task of constitutional adjudication and that of appellate courts within the various countries of the Commonwealth. Their attitude has been uniformly (in stated design anyway) baldly positivist. This has meant a drastic self-imposed limitation on the part of the judges as to the materials available to them in reaching their decisions—a deliberate refusal, for example, after the fashion of the English judges, to consider the parliamentary history or the speeches in debates in the House (the so-called *travaux préparatoires)* as a guide to the meaning of contested legislation.[25] It has meant a tart refusal to allow counsel to refer to legal periodicals as authorities in their argument of cases;[26] a refusal also to consider these social and economic materials

[25]See generally, D. G. Kilgour, "The Rule against the Use of Legislative History: 'Canon of Construction or Counsel of Caution?'" (1952) 30 *Can. B. Rev.* 769. The first bench of the High Court of Australia was quite prepared to allow reference to draft constitution bills submitted to federal conventions held in 1891 and in 1897–8 as a guide to the meaning of the Constitution; but Griffith C.J. justified this as a "matter of history of legislation" to accord with the traditional English common law view that *travaux préparatoires* and the opinions of members of the legislature cannot be referred to as a guide to the meaning of statutes. *Tasmania* v. *Commonwealth*, (1904) 1 C.L.R. 329.

[26]"During the recent hearing of the Rentals Reference before the Supreme Court of Canada the Chief Justice refused to allow counsel to refer to an article in the Canadian Bar Review. He remarked that 'the Canadian Bar Review is not an authority in this Court' and followed with some variously-reported comments on legal periodicals in general. Possibly the Chief Justice's refusal did not represent the considered opinion of the Court as a whole; even in his own case it may have been little more than a sign of impatience with the length or line of argument. . . . Its implications require examination, particularly now that the Supreme Court is in all matters Canada's final court of appeal." G. V. V. Nicholls, "Legal Periodicals and the Supreme Court of Canada," (1950) 28 *Can. B. Rev.* 482.

In contrast to this attitude, however, note the marked degree of respect accorded by the Supreme Court of South Africa to the views of the text-writers. See, for example, Chief Justice Centlivres' recent decision in *Harris* v. *Minister of the Interior*, [1952] 2 S.A.L.R. 428. No doubt the attention given to the text-writers

with which the United States Supreme Court has become familiar since the Brandeis Brief was first employed and from which alone constitutional formulae, however broadly worded, can derive full meaning. Thus in the recent Australian *Bank Nationalization Case*,[27] where the question at issue was the constitutionality of legislation passed by the Labour Government of Australia nationalizing the private trading banks, the High Court of Australia, and after it the Privy Council on appeal, ignored altogether the economic materials submitted by the parties to the case and, in judgments running into hundreds of pages apiece, purported to derive the actual decision from the past cases alone, unassisted by the economic evidence.

The positivist approach has meant also a characteristically mechanical attitude to the question of *stare decisis* and the binding force of precedents. The English judicial attitude to prior decisions, of course, as laid down in the *London Tramways Case*,[28] is that the House of Lords is bound by its own decisions; but the House of Lords[29] itself has developed to such a fine art the practice of "distinguishing," as distinct from overruling, prior decisions, as to make the limits of this rule rather amorphous in practice. The attitudes and practices of the final appellate courts in each of the Commonwealth countries in this regard are curiously similar. Thus the High Court of Australia has said that it will follow the English practice and only review a previous decision when it regards that decision as *manifestly* wrong.[30] On one notable occasion,[31] indeed, the High Court of Australia, in deference to this rule, felt bound to follow a decision it had given in an earlier, more experimental period of its history, even

---

in South Africa, in comparison with the United Kingdom and the other Commonwealth countries, stems from the presence in South Africa of the Roman-Dutch civil law tradition side by side with the English common law tradition: yet since this condition pertains also in Canada, where the province of Quebec has a civil law tradition, the attitude of the then Chief Justice of Canada in adhering so immovably to the English attitude in this regard is rather surprising.

[27]*Bank of New South Wales* v. *Commonwealth*, (1948) 76 C.L.R. 1; *Commonwealth* v. *Bank of New South Wales*, (1949) 79 C.L.R. 497 (P.C.).

[28]*London Street Tramways* v. *London County Council*, [1898] A.C. 375.

[29]In strict theory, the Privy Council, as a result of the anomaly that it merely "advises" the Crown, is not bound by its own prior decisions. In practice, however, and possibly as a result of the fact that the changing personnel of the Privy Council have normally sat also in the House of Lords, the Privy Council has tended to hew somewhat closely to the House of Lords' conception of *stare decisis*.

[30]*R.* v. *Commonwealth Court of Conciliation and Arbitration and Australian Tramway Employees' Association*, (1914) 18 C.L.R. 54; reaffirmed, *Attorney-General for New South Wales* v. *Perpetual Trustee*, (1952) 85 C.L.R. 189. But when are decisions manifestly wrong?

[31]*James* v. *Commonwealth*, (1935) 52 C.L.R. 570.

though the individual High Court judges felt that that decision was wrong; at the same time, however, the High Court judges expressed the hope that the Privy Council would overrule the earlier decision when the present case went to it on appeal, and this in fact the Privy Council obligingly did.[32] Likewise, the Supreme Court of South Africa has laid down the general rule that it is bound to follow its own decisions, but that it may depart from this rule when it is "clear that the decision is wrong" or arrived at "on some manifest oversight or misunderstanding," or where there had been "something in the nature of a palpable mistake" or "where a court was satisfied that its previous decision was wrong" or "more particularly where the point was not argued."[33] All the dicta quoted by the Supreme Court of South Africa as to the application of the rule of *stare decisis* in South Africa, and in fact also the principle on which the High Court of Australia proceeds, have this in common: though establishing that the Court will, in certain circumstances, depart from previous decisions, they do not further enlighten us on what those circumstances are, or provide us with any definite criteria for determining the existence of such circumstances in future cases. In the final result these tests are essentially circular, and therefore of no use in predicting *when* the Court will overrule a previous decision.[34]

Rather more rigid is the attitude in Canada towards the binding force of past judicial decisions, and in particular the attitude towards decisions of the Privy Council. Some Canadian authorities, indeed, have seemed in the past to fear that the weight of the Privy Council decisions may be so heavy upon the Canadian judges as to leave them no freedom of action for the future, and that the only way of getting around the past may be by direct constitutional amendment.[35]

THE IMPACT OF JUDICIAL REVIEW ON CONSTITUTIONAL LAW

In the light of the experience of the United Kingdom and the various Commonwealth countries, certain basic points can be made as to the

[32]*James* v. *Commonwealth*, [1936] A.C. 578 (P.C.).

[33]*Harris* v. *Minister of the Interior*, [1952] 2 S.A.L.R. 428, the "coloured voters" case (*supra*).

[34]See generally Julius Stone, *The Province and Function of Law* (1946), "Fallacies of the Logical Form in Legal Reasoning," especially 166 *et seq.*

[35]W. P. M. Kennedy, "The British North America Act: Past and Future," (1937) 15 *Can. B. Rev.* 393, 399; V. C. MacDonald, "The Constitution in a Changing World," (1948) 26 *Can. B. Rev.* 21, 45; MacDonald, "The Canadian Constitution Seventy Years After," (1937) 15 *Can. B. Rev.* 401, 425. The Canadian Supreme Court, since the abolition by Canada of the appeal to the Privy Council, has reaffirmed the strict principle of *stare decisis*: *Woods Manufacturing Co.* v. *The King*, [1951] 2 D.L.R. 465.

record of judicial review. First, it may not always, in terms of end result, matter too much whether or not a power of direct judicial review exists under a given constitution, so long, at any rate, as the courts are conscious of the possibilities of requiring legislative majorities to give second thoughts to legislation by harsh judicial construction in the processes of statutory interpretation. Apart from the record of the courts in England in this regard, it seems clear that the courts in South Africa have been able to check and delay the more overt features of Prime Minister Malan's apartheid programme quite as effectively through simple statutory interpretation as they have by direct judicial review in those areas of the constitution (the "entrenched clauses") where alone they have been able to assert this power.

Again, and considering especially the role of the constitutional text, it does seem at times that the actual words of a constitutional instrument may play a rather secondary role in its day-by-day working operation. This implies, of course, that the lengthy, exhaustive constitutional instrument is likely to be something of a vain exercise in legal draftsmanship, with its very prolixity an encouragement to judges to prune away its excess detail by selective interpretation, that is, by the regular judicial use of only a handful of provisions in key areas of the constitution. This process can be observed even in the case of tidier, less sprawling, documents than the new Indian Constitution—note the recurrence by the High Court of Australia, time and again, to section 92 of the Constitution; for that matter observe also the multitude of cases spawned by the "due process" clauses of the Fifth and Fourteenth amendments to the United States Constitution, which seem to have been selected almost casually by the United States Supreme Court as the reigning constitutional formulae in the area of economic regulation, in preference to formulae like the "equal protection" clause and the "privileges and immunities" clause.

The texts of constitutional instruments, in this respect, seem merely to be the servants of ultimate judicial policies. Thus the Canadian and Australian constitutions, like the United States Constitution, have assisted materially in the maintenance of economic laissez-faire—the insulation of business and commercial activity generally against the rising tide of collectivist legislation. Lacking anything corresponding to the American due process clauses, the courts in the case of Australia turned to section 92 of the Australian Constitution, a relatively innocent provision as it was originally drafted, designed to protect the new Australian federation against the "barbarism of borderism," the problem of border tariffs which had so plagued the six pre-federation Australian colonies. Section 92 has, however, been turned by the judges into a sort of natural-law guarantee of freedom from social and economic planning by the national or state governments. At the same time, and independently of the Australian experience, social and economic planning legislation was also being out-lawed in Canada as unconstitutional. Since the Canadian Constitution had nothing remotely corresponding to the American due process clauses, or even to section 92 of the Australian Constitution, this end result had perforce to be achieved, and was in fact achieved, by harsh judicial con-struction of those sections of the Canadian Constitution allocating heads of legislative power to the national government, as distinct from the provincial governments, the national government being the government primarily interested in sponsoring such legislation in Canada. The courts simply treated the Canadian Constitution as an "ordinary" statute (as distinct from a constitution), and therefore as subject to the normal common-law rules of statutory construction, and so arrived inevitably at a cramped, fettering ruling as to the ambit of national legislative powers.

This same proposition as to the secondary role of the actual words of the constitutional text holds good also, it is suggested, when we turn to the area of political and civil rights. Only the post–1931 constitutions of the Commonwealth have any formal bills of rights, or for that matter any other systematized provisions of this nature. The actual record of judicial utilization of the Bill of Rights in the Irish Constitution of 1937 has nevertheless, it is suggested, been rather narrow in the light of the comprehensiveness of the written provisions of that Constitution. In fact, the most striking judicial action in protection of political, social, and economic rights has occurred in the Union of South Africa, whose con-stitutional instrument indeed, outside of the protection of the voting rights of "coloured" voters in the Cape Province (through the "entrenched clauses"), offers no assistance at all to the judges in this regard. Tense issues in the area of political and civil rights have understandably been much less frequent in Canada and Australia than in South Africa, and the courts have therefore had very few occasions for passing on such problems. Nevertheless, the protection of civil liberties as an end result—actually claims of free speech and association—was in fact reached by the High Court of Australia in the *Communist Party Case*[36] through harsh con-struction of the national government's legislative power over defence. And individual members of the Supreme Court of Canada, in spite of the absence of a formal bill of rights in the constitutional instrument, have before this gone on record in support of a "right of free public discussion

[36]*Australian Communist Party* v. *Commonwealth*, (1951) 83 C.L.R. 1.

of public affairs";[37] while Mr. Justice Rand of the present bench of that Court seems to be bending his energies towards the judicial creation of certain "inherent rights of the Canadian citizen,"[38] which will be immune from abridgment by the provinces of Canada,[39] and which will include "freedom of speech, religion and the inviolability of the person."[40]

What we may be seeing in operation in all these instances are the beginnings of a dramatically new and different approach (from the viewpoint of the Commonwealth, that is) to the task of constitutional adjudi-

[37]*Re Alberta Statutes*, [1938] 2 D.L.R. 81. The Supreme Court of Canada there invalidated the Alberta Press Bill which had been enacted by the newly-elected Social Credit Government of Alberta as a measure to prevent adverse criticism in the press of its novel and unorthodox financial theories and programme. The strict *ratio* of the Supreme Court of Canada's decision in this case was simply that the Bill in question, being part of and dependent upon a general scheme of Alberta Social Credit legislation already invalidated on other constitutional grcunds by the Court, fell with that other legislation. But see the dicta by Duff C.J. at 107–8: "The Preamble of the [B.N.A. Act], moreover, shows plainly enough that the constitution of the Dominion is to be similar in principle to that of the United Kingdom. The statute contemplates a Parliament working under the influence of public opinion and public discussion. There can be no controversy that such institutions derive their efficacy from the free public discussion of affairs, from criticism and answer and counter-criticism, from attack upon policy administration and defence and counter-attack; from the freest and fullest analysis and examination from every point of view of political proposals." And see also *per* Canon J. at 119: "Under the British system, which is ours, no political party can erect a prohibitory barrier to prevent the electors from getting information concerning the policy of the Government. . . . There must be an untrammelled publication of the news and political opinions of the political parties contending for ascendancy."

[38]The beginnings of Rand J.'s approach in this regard are perhaps to be seen in his concurring opinion in the *Reference re Exemption of U.S. Forces from Canadian Criminal Law*, (1943) 80 Can. C. C. 161, 204–5, where he postulated the principle of "equality before the law" as a "Canadian civil liberty."

[39]See his concurring opinion in *Winner v. S.M.T. (Eastern) Ltd. and Attorney-General of New Brunswick*, [1951] 4 D.L.R. 529, in which he postulated a "right or capacity to remain and to engage in work in the province." In the *Winner Case* the Supreme Court held that, though the Canadian provinces have constitutional power to control purely intraprovincial bus traffic, it was *ultra vires* a provincial legislature to prohibit a bus line, organized under the laws of the State of Maine (U.S.A.) and operating from there, from bringing passengers into the province from a point outside, or from carrying passengers from a point within the province to a point outside, or from carrying passengers to whom stopover privileges had been extended as incident to a contract of through carriage between points within the province. In enunciating his new "rights of the Canadian citizen" concept, Rand J. was prepared in his concurring opinion to rule that the Maine bus operator, as a "subject of a friendly foreign country," for practical purposes in Canada enjoyed all the rights of a Canadian citizen.

[40]See his concurring opinion in *Saumur v. City of Quebec and Attorney-General of Quebec*, [1953] 4 D.L.R. 641, 670: "Strictly speaking, civil rights arise from positive law; but freedom of speech, religion and the inviolability of

cation. Instead of the old attitude of statutory construction—the search for legislative "intent" in the words of the constitution, and the concomitant notion that the words themselves have an absolute meaning that can be found, with the aid, perhaps, of the dictionary, if enough diligence is used —we have judges beginning to accept the fact that this is at best a rather barren exercise and turning instead to a search for the fundamental principles on which a free society must be based and which, after all, a constitutional instrument ultimately is designed to serve. This attitude exists most strikingly, and certainly most consciously and creatively, in the opinions of Mr. Justice Rand already referred to: in the other cases mentioned, it is suggested that the judicial policy-making that has taken place has been somewhat veiled and has tended to depend therefore on "inarticulate major premises."

What are the fundamental principles to which the judges should look in the decision of constitutional cases? Are there, in fact, any basic principles of constitutional law that the Commonwealth countries share in common in spite of manifest differences of race, religion, and social and

---

the person, are original freedoms which are at once the necessary attributes and modes of self-expression of human beings and the primary conditions of their community life within a legal order."

The *Saumur Case* concerned the constitutional validity of a by-law of the City of Quebec forbidding the distribution in the city streets of any book, pamphlet, booklet, circular, or tract, without the prior written permission of the chief of police. The Supreme Court, by a five-to-four vote, held that the by-law did not apply to prevent defendant, as a member of Jehovah's Witnesses, from distributing the tracts and material of that group in Quebec City streets without permission, the final decision in favour of the defendant in fact being determined by a single judge (Kerwin J.) who ruled that the effect of existing Quebec provincial law and also pre-Confederation law was to make the by-law inapplicable, as a matter of construction in view of the generality of its terms, to members of Jehovah's Witnesses. The other four justices making up the Supreme Court majority (including of course Rand J.) go considerably beyond Kerwin J.'s narrow holding, and would seek, on a number of different grounds, to deny the power of the province to authorize the by-law in question in the instant case. See generally B. Laskin, "Our Civil Liberties—The Rôle of the Supreme Court," (1955) 41 *Queen's Quarterly* 455.

Rand J.'s opinion in the *Saumur Case*, so far as it relates to "freedom of religion," was reaffirmed by him in his specially concurring opinion in the *Birks Case, Henry Birks and Sons (Montreal) Ltd.* v. *Montreal and Attorney-General of Quebec*, [1955] 5 D.L.R. 321, at 324–5. The *Birks Case* concerned the constitutionality of a by-law, adopted by the city of Montreal pursuant to authority granted it by an enabling Act passed by the province of Quebec, directing the closing of all shops and department stores in the municipality on six "holy days" prescribed by the religious (canon) law of the Roman Catholic Church. The Canadian Supreme Court, in a unanimous decision, held the by-law and the enabling Act to be *ultra vires* provincial legislative authority, primarily on the score that the nature and character of the law had to do with the moral and religious order and so was "criminal law," with the further consequence that the law fell within national legislative power but outside provincial powers.

economic beliefs and the polar extremes of constitution? To answer this question in a finite way would necessarily require a detailed and comprehensive examination of the key concepts of society in each of the countries of the Commonwealth, taken seriatim; nevertheless it does seem possible, without too much difficulty, to discern certain minimum principles common to all of the Commonwealth countries.

Recently Professor Goodhart, in seeking an explanation for the maintenance of civil liberties in England under the stress of the Cold War crisis, notwithstanding the fact that the Government of the day, as a matter of the positive law of the constitution, has no limits to its legislative powers, has attempted to find it in what he defines as a "moral law":

. . . under the unwritten Constitution there are certain established principles which limit the scope of Parliament. It is true that the courts cannot enforce these principles as they can under the Federal system in the United States, but this does not mean that these principles are any the less binding and effective. For that matter some of them receive greater protection today in England than they do in the United States.[41]

This is reminiscent to a considerable extent of Dicey's teachings as to the nature of the English Constitution, but Professor Goodhart's thesis appears to go beyond Dicey in this important respect. Dicey's constitutional liberties of Englishmen were common law liberties, that is, the consequences of the ordinary decisions of the ordinary law courts and therefore subject to potential abridgment by parliamentary action: Goodhart, on the other hand, seems almost to regard his principles as normative and binding in relation to Parliament itself: ". . . Those who exercise power in the name of the State are bound by the law, and there are certain definite principles which limit the exercise of that power."[42] Goodhart has identified four major principles of the English "moral law":[43] first and most fundamental, that no man is above the law; that those who govern Great Britain do so in a representative capacity and are subject to change—the elections that are held are not a meaningless ritual; that the so-called freedoms of speech, of thought, and of assembly are an essential part of any constitution which provides that the people shall be free to govern themselves, because without them self-government becomes impossible; and finally that the judiciary must be independent. In a similar vein, Lord Justice Denning of the English Court of Appeal, one of the most creative, intellectually, of the present-day judges of the Commonwealth, has recently suggested, in searching for the spirit of the British Constitution,[44] that it rests upon three main "instincts": the instinct

[41]A. L. Goodhart, *English Law and the Moral Law* (1953), 54 *et seq.*
[42]*Ibid.*, 61.   [43]*Ibid.*, 56–60.
[44]Denning, *The Changing Law* (1953).

for justice, which he associates particularly with independence of the judges and certainty of the law; the instinct for liberty, which involves freedom of discussion (including freedom of the press) and also freedom of association (including the right to form political parties); finally, a practical instinct which leads to a balancing of "rights with duties, and powers with safeguards, so that neither rights nor powers shall be exceeded or abused. Throughout all this runs the Christian instinct and with it a sense of the supreme importance of the individual and a refusal to allow his personality to be submerged in an omnipotent State."[45]

This last "instinct" cited by Lord Justice Denning, the "practical" instinct, is particularly important, for it recognizes that the problem for the decision-maker, executive and legislative as well as judicial, may frequently be the reconciliation of a number of mutually conflicting interests. Thus, though the interest in free speech rates very high, it may have to be balanced against countervailing interests in national security. The judicial decision-maker should at least be aware that such a conflict is involved. I think the principal criticism to be advanced of the Australian High Court's decision in the *Communist Party Case* is that in reaching their decision favouring the interest in free speech and association the judges, because of their rigorously positivist approach, did not seem to be aware that a conflict between the interest in free speech and association and a countervailing interest in national security (especially dominant during the Cold War crisis) was what was involved. Likewise, the decisions upon both the Canadian and the Australian constitutions, which so effectively assisted in maintaining economic laissez-faire against governmental planning legislation, may validly be censured, not for their end results favouring claims of private property, even though at times these may have seemed to require considerable judicial ingenuity in the handling of legal doctrine, but because the judges did not (and perhaps could not) understand that such claims may sometimes have to be adjusted against conflicting claims of community welfare.

In the cases we have looked at, it is very frequently possible to see Lord Justice Denning's instinct for liberty—freedom of discussion, the press, and association (acknowledged also by Professor Goodhart)— fully operating on the judicial choice, notwithstanding the absence of express positive law support in the form of a bill of rights or similar formalized guarantees in the constitutional instrument. These freedoms may thus be said to exist in effect in the Commonwealth countries as "living law" postulates of democratic government,[46] guiding the decision-maker,

[45]*Ibid.*, 3.

[46]Cf. Jerome Hall, *Living Law of Democratic Society* (1949); F. S. C. Northrop, *The Meeting of the East and West* (1950), chaps. III, IV.

legislative, executive, or judicial, in exercising a policy choice. To supplement the quota of political freedoms, we might add also a postulate of political democracy—the full realization of the Benthamite principle of every man to count for one—recognized by Professor Goodhart in his emphasis on the representative character of government. Political democracy was attained effectively in England with the Reform Acts of the nineteenth century and the extension of women's suffrage and the related changes of more recent years, and this record was duplicated, or even anticipated, in most of the other countries now making up the Commonwealth. In the area of voting rights, the courts in South Africa have been tending towards bringing their country into line ultimately with such a principle, in the face of a most complex racial situation hardly paralleled elsewhere in the Commonwealth, except perhaps to some extent in its more recent Asian members.

In economic and property matters, Lord Justice Denning and Professor Goodhart do not try to offer any guides. The general political principles that they have already enunciated, of course, stem ultimately from the classic concepts of political liberty of nineteenth-century English liberalism. It will be noted that in the case of both Canada and Australia the judges have arrived, through the processes of direct judicial review, at a working constitution reflecting that other aspect of nineteenth-century English liberalism, economic laissez-faire. It would be easy, remembering the parallel invalidation of social and economic planning legislation by the United States Supreme Court in the period after the Civil War right up to 1937, to essay a partisan political interpretation of the value preferences and attitudes of the Commonwealth judges (both Privy Council and local appellate judges) as revealed in economic cases, just as the American critics of the Old Court tended to do in the early New Deal era. This would, I suggest, be not merely an over-simplification[47] but also a misreading of the extent to which the courts have stood in the way of dominant popular opinion. From 1896 onwards, when Lord Watson, Lord Haldane, and their successors restricted Dominion powers in the name of provincial rights, the Liberal party was dominant in Canada, and it rested for its parliamentary majority (as the Conservative party never did) upon the French as well as the English voting population. While, therefore, one may suspect at time that states' rights are being raised in the United States merely as a protective umbrella under which economic special interests may shelter,[48] by comparison this plea may frequently spring in

[47]Cf. B. Laskin, " 'Peace, Order, and Good Government' Re-examined," (1947) *Can. B. Rev.* 1054, 1055.

[48]Thus, Mr. Justice Jackson, in *The Struggle for Judicial Supremacy* (1941), 21, comments on *Carter* v. *Carter Coal Co.,* (1936) 298 U.S. 238: "Seven states

Canada from some more deeply rooted claim for the treatment of a problem at the local level, pointing towards something of a pluralist approach to government with a large degree of policy-making conducted at the local level rather than at the centre.[49]

In the case of Australia, also, one might tend too easily to exaggerate the extent to which the courts have stood in the way of popular opinion. The Privy Council decision in *James v. Commonwealth* in 1936 declaring section 92 of the Australian Constitution henceforth to apply to the Commonwealth as well as to the states, which had the effect immediately of striking down Commonwealth marketing control legislation, was given at a time when the worst effects of the economic depression were diminishing and when the immediate pressures for such centralized economic controls had therefore abated somewhat. And the Privy Council decision of 1936 may perhaps be regarded as having received some sort of popular ratification from the fact of the rejection soon afterwards by the Australian voters, at a public referendum held in 1937, of a proposal to confer centralized marketing powers of this nature on the Commonwealth government by way of a constitutional amendment.[50] Likewise the rejection by the courts after World War II, in terms of section 92 once again, of the Labour Government's legislation nationalizing the private trading banks was followed by the defeat of the Labour Government at an election fought primarily on the issue of nationalization.

It is to be noted, of course, that the record of judicial review that we have surveyed has been sometimes the work of the Privy Council and sometimes the work of local appellate tribunals. In spite of the understandable tendency to heap full blame on the Privy Council for the diffi-

---

appeared and joined with the Federal Government in support of the Act—no state appeared against it. Nevertheless the Court spoke of the danger of the states' being 'despoiled of their powers' and being reduced to 'little more than geographical sub-divisions of the national domain.' "

[49]Note recent French-Canadian argument in favour of "provincial autonomy": L.-P. Pigéon, "The Meaning of Provincial Autonomy," (1951) 29 *Can. B. Rev.* 1126, 1134. Contrast with this, F. R. Scott, "Centralization and Decentralization in Canadian Federalism," (1951) 29 *Can. B. Rev.* 1095; and see also F. R. Scott, "The Constitutional Background of Taxation Agreements," (1955) 2 *McGill L.J.* 1, 10.

[50]Under s. 128 of the Australian Constitution Act, as noted, proposals for alteration of the Constitution must be passed by both Houses of the national Parliament and then submitted to a popular referendum for approval; the proposal for the amendment then becomes effective as an amendment to the Constitution if it is approved at the referendum by a majority of the voters throughout the nation, and also by a majority of the voters in a majority of the states. It must be stated, however, that in practice this machinery, like the procedures for amendment under article V of the United States Constitution, has been generally unproductive of constitutional changes.

culties flowing from constitutional decisions, particularly decisions given during the Depression era,[51] it is submitted that there is no very significant line of demarcation between the decisions of the Privy Council and those of the local courts. It might be possible in theory, of course, to absolve the local courts from responsibility altogether, on the score that as inferior tribunals they are bound by the doctrine of precedent to accept the decisions of a superior court, in this case the past decisions of the Privy Council.[52] But, as a leading critic of the Privy Council, himself a Canadian, concedes, the decisions of the Canadian Supreme Court, and especially of Sir Lyman Duff, its Chief Justice during the time of the crucial decisions of the 1930's, result as much from personal choice as from the dictates of *stare decisis*.[53] Likewise, the decisions given by the High Court of Australia, in respect of those matters (concerning the powers *inter se* of the nation and of the states) in which it is final appellate tribunal, do not, it is submitted, differ in substance or form from the decisions given by the Privy Council as final appellate tribunal in respect to all the other matters arising under the Australian Constitution.[54]

What all this points to is to the pervasive, if subtle, influence of a common legal education and training, and a common system of professional organization throughout the Commonwealth countries, the more striking because, in the case of Ireland at least and perhaps of India too, it was recognized by local leaders who made a consequent endeavour to break away from it for the future. On its negative side, this influence is to be observed in the uniformly positivist judicial attitudes to constitutional adjudication: the "strict statutory construction" approach to the consti-

[51]Cf. F. R. Scott, "The Consequences of the Privy Council Decisions," (1937) 15 *Can. B. Rev.* 485, 494: "To imagine that we shall ever get consistent and reasonable judgments from such a casually selected and untrained court [as the Privy Council] is merely silly."

[52]Cf. Kennedy, *The Constitution of Canada*, 550.

[53]Laskin, " 'Peace, Order and Good Government' Re-examined," (1947) 25 *Can. B. Rev.* 1054, 1056; and see also Laskin, "The Supreme Court of Canada: A Final Court of and for Canadians," (1951) 29 *Can. B. Rev.* 1038, 1057 *et seq.*

[54]It is, of course, strictly a *non sequitur* to assume that because a tribunal like the Privy Council is an alien (in the sense of non-local) body, it must necessarily be insensitive to and ignorant of local conditions and needs; though the very turgidness of style and complexity of detail of some of the Privy Council's major opinions have no doubt contributed to the development of this notion among some of the more vigorous of the Privy Council's overseas critics. It is, however, clearly preferable that if judicial "mistakes" are to be made, they should be made, and political responsibility for them assumed, by local tribunals; and the Privy Council's voluntary paving of the way for the various Commonwealth countries to abolish its appellate jurisdiction in relation to their courts (*Attorney-General for Ontario* v. *Attorney-General for Canada*, [1947] A.C. 127 (P.C.)), undoubtedly represents judicial statesmanship of a high order.

tutional instrument; the insistence upon a full and complete divorcement between law and politics, sociology, and economics,[55] and consequent refusal to consider materials drawn from these other social sciences which might give the dry provisions of the constitutional text an ampler meaning; the adherence to *stare decisis* and the doctrine of precedent in its most mechanical form. This means that in the past there has been something of an equation of the responsibilities of a final appellate tribunal in the constitutional law field with those of the normal private law courts deciding private litigation between private parties: such an equation is perhaps inevitable in view of the rigorous professional criteria employed in the recruitment of the judges who ultimately sit on constitutional law cases in the Commonwealth countries. It should occasion no surprise that a tribunal like the Privy Council, or for that matter the Supreme Court of Canada, or the High Court of Australia, should approach the adjudication of constitutional law with a predisposition towards cabining and confining the governmental powers set out in the constitutional instrument, if their personnel are essentially composed of men drawn from the property and equity bar, habituated by their training to regard any form of legislator's law (whether constitution or simple statute) as something of an alien intruder on the traditional common law and to be resisted as such.[56] In the United States, on the other hand, strict professional expertise plays a comparatively minor part in the selection of personnel for appointment to the

[55]Cf., *per* Latham C.J., *South Australia* v. *Commonwealth*, (1942) 65 C.L.R. 373, 409: "Thus the controversy before the Court is a legal controversy, not a political controversy. It is not for this or any court to prescribe policy or to seek to give effect to any views or opinions upon policy. We have nothing to do with the wisdom or expediency of legislation. Such questions are for Parliament and the people."

Per Kania C.J., *Gopalan* v. *State of Madras*, (1950) 13 Supreme Court Journal 174, 191: ". . . The Courts are not at liberty to declare an Act void because in their opinion it is opposed to a spirit supposed to pervade the Constitution but not expressed in words. Where the fundamental law has not limited either in terms or by necessary implication, the general powers conferred upon the legislature we cannot declare a limitation under the notion of having discovered something in the Constitution which is not even mentioned in the instrument."

Per Hanna J., *Pigs Marketing Board* v. *Donnelly (Dublin) Ltd.*, [1939] I.R. 413, 418: "In a Court of Law [social justice] seems to me to be a nebulous phrase involving no question of law for the Court, but questions of ethics, morals, economics, and sociology, which are, in my opinion, beyond the determination of a Court of law, but which may be, in their various aspects, within the consideration of the Oireachtas, as representing the people."

[56]Compare the strictures of Professor Dicey: "Parliamentary legislation, in short, if it is sometimes rapid and thorough-going, exhibits characteristic faults. It is the work of legislators who are much influenced by the immediate opinion of the moment, who make laws with little regard either to general principles or logical consistency, and who are deficient in the skill and knowledge of experts." A. V. Dicey, *Law and Opinion in England* (1905).

Supreme Court, and broad intellectual qualities, as manifested in distinguished service in public life or in the executive branch of government (for example, as Attorney-General or Solicitor-General), or as manifested in academic achievement in the universities and law schools, receive prime attention. And it seems clear that this wide basis of selection of judges has done much to mould the broadly pragmatic, policy-making approach that characterizes constitutional decision-making in the United States today, even though the forms and practices of private law adjudication are still conventionally adhered to by the Court.[57]

On the affirmative side, it is suggested, the common system of legal training and professional organization throughout the Commonwealth countries is a prime contributor to that distinct bias towards civil liberties that we have observed in the judicial opinions in the cases discussed earlier: whatever the formal theory, English legal positivism, resting as it does on the traditions and ethics of the ancient universities and the Inns of Court, has always meant something more, in action, than strict and literal interpretation. If this be so, then Lord Justice Denning's "spirit of the English Constitution" and Professor Goodhart's English "moral law" have been carried to the Commonwealth countries overseas, not so much in the assorted words and formulae of their constitutional texts as in the minds and attitudes of the judges passing on them and the lawyers arguing the cases before the courts. In an age when the old positive law bonds of Empire and Commonwealth have largely been sundered, this heritage of ideas is, I believe, of lasting importance and significance.

The major vice of all the decisions of the Privy Council and of the local courts in constitutional matters remains, however, their incurable positivism, which has obscured the process of analysis of the conflicting interests involved in the cases before the courts and thereby prevented any very conscious, intelligent balancing of those interests to arrive at the end decision. Though policy considerations have (as I have suggested throughout) very clearly intruded into the courts' decision-making, they have all too frequently entered by the back door to operate as "inarticulate major premises" only for the courts' ultimate holdings. The essential weakness of the pure positivist position in this respect has been the failure to recognize that it is not a choice between judicial policy-making and absence of

[57]The fact that the business of the United States Supreme Court is now effectively confined to public law cases, of course, enormously simplifies the problem of judicial recruitment at the Supreme Court level. Aliter in the case of final appellate tribunals in the various Commonwealth countries: these courts invariably have substantial private law as well as public law responsiblities, and indeed, and especially in the non-federal countries, private law cases will normally comprise the overwhelming majority of matters on the docket before the court.

judicial policy-making; but between policy-making based on a full and open canvassing of alternative lines of action and policy-making in the dark. If the constitutions of the various Commonwealth countries, in their future development, are to continue to retain the best "instincts," as Lord Justice Denning has defined them, of English constitutionalism—the principles, also, of Professor Goodhart's "moral law"—a more consciously creative and informed approach to adjudication on the part of the judges will manifestly be required in the future.

2

PARLIAMENTARY SOVEREIGNTY
AND THE RULE OF LAW
IN THE UNITED KINGDOM

Professor Dicey, the doyen of English constitutional lawyers, saw the general principles of the British Constitution as the result of the ordinary law of the land, the outcome of the judicial decisions determining the rights of private persons in particular cases brought before the courts.[1] This opinion was rejected by Sir Ivor Jennings, Dicey's most authoritative latter-day interpreter, as a very inadequate view of the facts.[2] But most authorities would agree with Dicey that English constitutional law includes two elements—rules of law (whether judge-made law or statute law), and conventions of the Constitution.[3] The disagreements are over the choice of those rules of law and conventions which shall be classified, for purposes of convenience, as the law of the Constitution. A contemporary writer lists, as examples of fundamental rules of statute law, Magna Carta, the Bill of Rights, the Settlement Act, the Abdication Act, the Royal Marriages Act, the Civil List Acts, and certain acts affecting the conduct of elections and the organization of the civil service.[4] We would certainly have to include today the Statute of Westminster and other arrangements defining the United Kingdom's relations with the former British Dominions.

The point is, of course, that since the laws of the Constitution do not differ from other laws, either in form or in source, the English Constitution may be amended or repealed by means of an ordinary act of Parliament, that is to say, a bill passed by both Houses and formally approved by the King. Parliament is thus both a legislative body and a constituent assembly,[5] and major political changes or even popular revolutions can be effected in the guise of constitutional reforms. The great Reform Bill

[1]A. V. Dicey, *Law of the Constitution* (9th ed., 1939), 195.
[2]Sir Ivor Jennings, *The Law and the Constitution* (3rd ed., 1943), 38.
[3]Dicey, *Law of the Constitution*, 23.
[4]H. R. G. Greaves, *The British Constitution* (1938), 21.   [5]*Ibid.*

of 1832, for example, while making extensive reforms in the parliamentary franchise, meant also the transfer of the substance of political power
in England from the old landed gentry and aristocracy to the new manufacturing middle class, which had sprung up following the Industrial
Revolution; though sometimes, it is true, a political change may be trans-
lated into law only after the transfer of power has occurred—the Restoration and the Revolution of 1688 were in effect validated *ex post facto* by
retrospective acts of Parliament passed to that effect.[6]

That "flexibility" is the general rule of the British Constitution, however, has been denied in recent years, with the assertion that changes in
the Constitution depend on the power and tenacity of those who wish to
change or retain it; that in particular

> if a reform conflicts with the views of the House of Lords or even of the King,
> it is subject to delays and special obstacles. If it conflicts with the interests of
> that section of the community which . . . so largely controls the Press, the
> Church, and other organs of opinion, which has special privileges in the
> electoral process, and which so generally officers the administrative services
> and the armed forces, it is far from likely to be easy.[7]

Certainly the great constitutional changes of the last few generations have
come slowly at times and have normally been preceded by long years
of consideration and party manœuvres. Thus the House of Lords resisted
to the utmost any reduction in its hereditary powers, insisting throughout
that it was the only existing defence against the interference of a chance
majority in the Commons with fundamental institutions; though it seems
clear that the only fundamental institutions which the overwhelmingly
Conservative House of Lords safeguarded were those opposed by the
Liberal majorities in the Commons.[8]

The notion of the complete flexibility of the English Constitution, of
course, stems from the juridical concept of the sovereignty of Parliament,
itself a product of the successful assertion of the political supremacy of
the legislative arm of English government in the great constitutional strug-
gles of the seventeenth century. The sovereignty of Parliament involved,
in the view of Professor Dicey writing at the end of the nineteenth century,
the idea of unlimited law-making power in Parliament, and in particular
(and by contrast with the case of non-sovereign law-making bodies) three
central propositions:

> *First,* there is no law which Parliament cannot change . . . acting in its
> ordinary legislative character. A Bill for reforming the House of Commons,

[6]F. W. Maitland, *The Constitutional History of England* (1st ed., 1908), 282
et seq.

[7]Greaves, *The British Constitution*, 20.

[8]H. Finer, *Theory and Practice of Modern Government* (rev. ed., 1950), 138.

a Bill for abolishing the House of Lords, a Bill to give London a municipality, a Bill to make valid marriages celebrated by a pretended clergyman, who is found after their celebration not to be in orders, are each equally within the competence of Parliament, they each may be passed in substantially the same manner, they none of them when passed will be, legally speaking, a whit more sacred or immutable than the others. . . .

Secondly, there is under the English Constitution no . . . distinction between laws which are not fundamental or constitutional and those laws which are fundamental or constitutional.

Thirdly, there does not exist . . . any person or body of persons, executive, legislative, or judicial, which can pronounce void any enactment passed by the British Parliament on the ground of such enactment being opposed to the constitution, or on any ground whatever, except, of course, its being repealed by Parliament.[9]

In laying down these propositions Professor Dicey meant by Parliament the King-in-Parliament, that is to say, the King, the House of Lords, and the House of Commons acting together.[10] Dicey himself specifically excluded from the scope of his definition the actions of any one of these three constituent elements acting alone, thus expressly denying the force of law to royal proclamations[11] or to resolutions of a single House of Parliament;[12] though at the same time allowing that each House of Parliament has complete control over its own proceedings including the right to commit for contempt.[13] Lest it should be thought that *Stockdale* v. *Hansard* might allow the courts to assume a power of scrutinizing the carrying out of the legislative mechanics, it must be noted that the "enrolled bill rule" stemming from the decision in *Pylkington's Case* in the fifteenth century established clearly that an act approved by King, Lords, and Commons, and duly enrolled, is conclusive upon the courts. Professor Dicey himself did not refer to *Pylkington's Case* or to the "enrolled bill rule" as such, preferring to approach the question of the role of the judiciary vis-à-vis Parliament much more broadly. As he noted: "English judges do not claim or exercise any power to repeal a Statute, whilst Acts of Parliament may over-ride and constantly do over-ride the law of the judges. Judicial legislation is, in short, subordinate legislation, carried on with the assent and subject to the supervision of Parliament."[14] It must be noted too that Dicey himself, in discussing the sovereignty of Parliament, seemed to desire to treat it as a purely legal concept, and in par-

[9]Dicey, *Law of the Constitution,* 88–91.
[10]*Ibid.,* 39.
[11]*Case of Proclamations,* (1610), 12 Co. Rep. 74.
[12]*Stockdale* v. *Hansard,* (1839) 9 A. & E. 1.
[13]*Case of the Sheriff of Middlesex,* (1840) 11 A. & E. 273; Dicey, *Law of the Constitution,* 50–61.
[14]Dicey, *Law of the Constitution,* 60–1.

ticular to make a distinction between legal sovereignty and political sovereignty.

The former [he noted], in the sense in which Austin sometimes uses it, is a merely legal conception, and means simply the power of law-making unrestricted by any legal limit. If the term "sovereignty" be thus used, the sovereign power under the English constitution, is clearly "Parliament". But the word "sovereignty" is sometimes employed in a political rather than a strictly legal sense. That body is "politically" sovereign or supreme in a state the will of which is ultimately obeyed by the citizens of the state. In this sense of the word the electors of Great Britain may be said to be, together with the Crown and the Lords, or perhaps, in strict accuracy, independently of the King and the Peers, the body in which sovereign power is vested.[15]

ASSIMILATION OF THE LEGAL AND THE POLITICAL SOVEREIGNS

Though by Parliament, Dicey meant the King-in-Parliament, even in Dicey's day the powers of the Crown in relation to legislation were purely formal. The prerogative power of refusing assent to a Bill has not in fact been exercised by any monarch after Queen Anne at the beginning of the eighteenth century, and it is a recognized convention that the royal assent must be given.[16] So far as the House of Lords is concerned, though in strict theory its powers were, for legislative purposes, co-ordinate with the House of Commons, it had conceded as early as 1614 the exclusive right of the House of Commons to initiate money bills; while in 1671 the Commons had successfully challenged and denied the right of the Lords to reduce taxes. In practice too, as a result of the shift of the centre of political gravity to a cabinet based upon the House of Commons, and the consequent centring of the time-table of government business in the House of Commons, it had come to pass that by the end of the nineteenth century very few bills were actually introduced in the House of Lords;[17] though the House of Lords was still prepared, in the Duke of Wellington's phrase, to "save the country" by a very vigorous use of its powers of rejecting ordinary legislation.

Almost every Liberal measure was amended or rejected, while Conservative measures which most accorded with its interest-begotten prejudices received usually a safe passage, until even Gladstone was moved to become the herald of the ultimate storm against the profession of the House of Lords that it represented the permanent opinion of the country. The landlords' position in regard to tenants' improvements was defended; religious and political equality was denied, the universities were kept closed to Dissenters; army privileges were maintained; counsel for poor prisoners refused. Ireland maltreated, municipal improvement thwarted: parliamentary reform (bribery and ballot

15*Ibid.*, 72–3.
16Jennings, *The Law and the Constitution*, 134.
17Finer, *Theory and Practice of Modern Government*, 408.

laws) rejected or mutilated; humane measures (like the Deceased Wife's Sister Bill) held up for years; the first Employer's Liability Bill decisively rejected. The House of Lords bolstered the Church of England at the expense of Nonconformist rate-payers, and then, in the Liberal era of 1906 to 1914, they well-nigh stultified its great majority by defeating the Education Bill, the Licensing Bill, the Scottish Land Bill and Plural Voting Bill of 1912. The methods adopted were ingenious: principles were destroyed obliquely, without the enunciation of the true motives which caused their destruction; it was pretended that bills had come up to the Lords too late in the session for due deliberation; so many impossible amendments were added that the purpose and efficacy of legislation were frustrated (forcing a compromise).[18]

This situation, in which the almost consistently Liberal majorities in the "reformed" House of Commons after the first Reform Bill of 1832 were held up by the Conservative forces in the hereditary House of Lords, could obviously not continue indefinitely. The show-down came when the House of Lords in 1909 voted to reject the Finance Bill of that year. It is true that the budget proposals of 1909 were an intimate part of the over-all social reform programme of the Liberal Government of the day, and Mr. Lloyd George, as Chancellor of the Exchequer, had provided in his budget for steeply progressive income tax and death duties, and for land-values duties and taxes upon mine royalties. Yet it is clear that in voting to reject the budget the House of Lords departed from a practice which it had followed since the modern budget system had been developed, and the Liberal party leaders were quick to label the Lords' action as a usurpation of the rights of the Commons and necessarily a breach of the Constitution. The Prime Minister, Mr. Asquith, promptly appealed to the electors, by way of a dissolution and a general election, and, on being returned to office, reintroduced the Finance Bill; the House of Lords then gave way and passed it.

Mr. Asquith, however, now proceeded to the task of curtailing the veto powers of the House of Lords. Since the Liberal party did not have an absolute majority in the new House of Commons, he entered into a bargain with the Irish Nationalist members (84 in number) to introduce Home Rule for Ireland in return for their support against the House of Lords. The proposals which were subsequently to become law as the Parliament Act of 1911 provided that if the Lords withheld for more than one month their assent to a money bill, it might be presented to the King, and on his assent become law; that Mr. Speaker should certify whether a bill was or was not a money bill; that in reference to ordinary legislation the power of the House of Lords should henceforth be limited to a suspensive veto of two years: and that the term of Parliaments should be reduced from seven to five years. The Parliament Act was finally approved by the

[18]*Ibid.*, 409–10.

Lords in the terms in which it was passed by the Commons, but only after a further dissolution of Parliament had resulted once more in the return of the Liberal Government, and after the King had agreed, in view of this clear electoral endorsement of the Liberal Government's policy (though not, it seems clear, without extreme personal reluctance), to create a sufficient number of new peers to swamp the Conservative forces in the Lords. In the face of this damaging threat to its prestige the Lords gave way and passed the measure.

Since the passage of the Parliament Act in 1911 it is largely true to say that the powers of the Lords have dwindled away almost to the vanishing point. The absolute power of the Commons to pass money bills without the consent of the House of Lords is of substantial importance in view of the fact that most modern legislation involves substantial financial changes, even though "money bill" has been very strictly defined and very strictly interpreted and many finance bills have not been certified by Mr. Speaker.[19] And the two-year suspensive veto of ordinary legislation has not proved unduly onerous for the Commons, as up to the Parliament Act of 1949 only two measures, the Government of Ireland Act of 1914 and the Welsh Church Act of 1914, appear to have been passed under the machinery of the Parliament Act of 1911 without the consent of the House of Lords. Yet this is partly accounted for by the fact that, from 1911 right up until Mr. Attlee's Labour Government of 1945, the governments having majorities in the Commons have generally been Conservative or Coalition governments and therefore in accord with the Lords. Mr. Asquith's Liberal Government could rely on the support of the Irish Nationalists in the House of Commons and could therefore afford to wait the two-year period to enact measures opposed by the Lords. Mr. Ramsay MacDonald's two Labour ministries were minority governments with only shaky control of the Commons, and when the Lords in 1930 killed a bill against plural voting and controlling election practices, and in 1931 the Education Bill raising the age of free education, there was nothing the Prime Minister could do.

When Mr. Attlee came to office in 1945 there were immediate demands in the Labour party for abolition of the House of Lords, but the Government seems to have preferred to concentrate its immediate energies in carrying out its socialization programme. The House of Lords in fact made a number of amendments to the Coal Mines Nationalisation Bill of 1946 and to the Transport Bill of 1947, which were accepted by the Government in preference to relying on the machinery provided in the Parliament Act, 1911, and waiting the two-year period so that those bills might

[19]Jennings, *The Law and the Constitution*, 133–4.

become law in their unamended form. In 1947, however, the Attlee Government introduced a further Parliament Bill, cutting down the duration of the suspensive veto of the Lords from two years to one year, and since this measure met with vigorous opposition from the Conservative party the Government thereupon set about passing it, if necessary, without the concurrence of the Lords, under the machinery of the Parliament Act of 1911. In anticipation of a probable rejection by the House of Lords, the Bill was introduced in the 1947-8 session of Parliament in order that it might if necessary become law, without the consent of the House of Lords, within the life of the Parliament which was dissolved on February 3, 1950; and after three rejections by the House of Lords the Bill became an Act (as the Parliament Act, 1949) without the Lords' consent, in accordance with the terms of the Parliament Act, 1911.

The trend has therefore very clearly been to concentrate effective law-making power in the popularly elected organ, the House of Commons, and to render the part played by the Crown and by the Lords at the present day largely formal in nature. Legal sovereignty today is effectively exercised by the House of Commons.

And by the same token, if the political sovereign was, in Dicey's view, the electorate at large, the trend to the present day has been more and more to make the House of Commons a reflection of voting patterns in the electorate. The movement triumphantly begun with the first great Reform Bill of 1832 and continued with the Reform Bills of 1867 and 1884, for the extension of the franchise and the sweeping away of electoral abuses of which the "pocket" and "rotten" boroughs were merely the most notorious, reached a logical culmination in the Representation of the People Act of 1918, which revolutionized the basis on which the House of Commons rests. Under the Act, the qualification of electors was greatly simplified. The property qualification was abolished and no person could henceforth vote in more than two constituencies—first, on a residential qualification, and second, for business premises or for a university. In addition to certain temporary provisions for soldiers and sailors who were serving or had served in the war and for the disqualification of conscientious objectors, the Act provided that all men of twenty-one years of age who were qualified by six months' residence or by the occupation of business premises, and all women of thirty years of age who were local government electors or wives of such electors, should have a parliamentary vote. The principle of single-member constituencies of approximately equal size was as far as possible preserved, and the total membership of the House (including 105 Irish members) now became 707 members. In comparison with the Act of 1918, previous Reform Acts seemed almost insignificant. The Act of 1832 added about 450,000 electors to the register: that of 1918 added nearly 13,000,000 of whom 9,000,000 were women, and the total electorate, even excluding southern Ireland, was thus increased to about 21,000,000.[20] A still further extension of the electorate occurred with the Equal Franchise Act of 1928 when women were placed in the same position as men as regards parliamentary elections, and universal adult suffrage thus became the general rule.

In the same vein, too, measures have recently been taken to remove undue pressures upon public opinion at election time, and to ensure that with the granting of universal suffrage the elector will have a free and an informed choice in exercising his vote. The Representation of the People Act, 1949, is in reality an extensive code (much of it in fact being a reproduction of earlier legislation in the same field) governing electoral conduct and practices. It places drastic restrictions upon campaign expenditures accompanied by detailed provisions for reporting of expenses incurred so as to ensure that these requirements are not evaded; while the form and methods of electoral propaganda are also severely restricted. It is of course true that these measures for more accurately translating the popular will into voting strengths in the House of Commons may be offset by the corresponding shift of the locus of legislative decision-making from the legislative chamber to the cabinet room, a trend that seems in fact to have begun in the early nineteenth century and that has become more and more marked as the party system has become rigid. Yet the essence of the parliamentary-executive type of government is that a cabinet can only exist so long as it can command a majority in the House of Commons, and measures that broaden the basis of representation in the Commons therefore help to produce more representative cabinets.

LIMITATIONS ON THE SOVEREIGNTY OF PARLIAMENT TODAY

Conventional Limitations

We are here referring to customarily observed limitations on the user of the powers of parliamentary majorities. Professor Dicey was somewhat concerned to point out that, though the conventions of the Constitution could not be directly enforced by courts of law, they were nevertheless obeyed. He came to the conclusion that the conventions were obeyed because otherwise a breach of the law would ultimately result:

The Army (Annual) Act would in the first place expire. Hence the Army Act, on which the discipline of the army depends, would cease to be in force. But thereupon all means of controlling the army without a breach of law would

[20]See generally, Sir John Marriott, *English Political Institutions* (4th ed. repr., 1948), xxxii.

cease to exist. Either the army must be discharged, in which case the means of maintaining law and order would come to an end, or the army must be kept up and discipline must be maintained without legal authority for its maintenance. If this alternative were adopted, every person, from the Commander-in-Chief downwards, who took part in the control of the army, and indeed every soldier who carried out the commands of his superiors, would find that not a day passed without his committing or sanctioning acts which would render him liable to stand as a criminal in the dock. Then, again, though most of the taxes would still come into the Exchequer, large portions of the revenue would cease to be legally due and could not be legally collected, whilst every official, who acted as collector, would expose himself to actions or prosecutions. The part, moreover, of the revenue which came in, could not be legally applied to the purposes of the government. If the Ministry laid hold of the revenue they would find it difficult to avoid breaches of definite laws which would compel them to appear before the courts. . . . The rule, therefore, that Parliament must meet once a year, though in strictness a constitutional convention which is not a law and will not be enforced by the courts, turns out nevertheless to be an understanding which cannot be neglected without involving hundreds of persons, many of whom are by no means specially amenable to government influence, in distinct acts of illegality cognisable by the tribunals of the courts. This convention therefore of the constitution is in reality based upon, and secured by, the law of the land.[21]

Yet Dicey's explanation for the obedience accorded to the conventions of the Constitution is rejected by Jennings. Jennings points out that there are in fact many conventions that are quite unsupported by law, the failure to obey which would clearly not be followed by actual breaches of law.[22] As Jennings also points out, it is clear that Government would be possible without the co-operation of the Opposition.

The Government majority would march through the lobbies, voting for the Government, with monotonous regularity. The Government would get its legislation and its financial resources: The Parliamentary sessions would be shorter and ministers would be in the unusual position of having plenty of time for controlling their departments. It would, no doubt, be the end of Parliament as a living institution just as the absence of debate has made the Privy Council into a formal instrument of no importance. Nevertheless it would be possible, and only the conventions provide for the continuance of the present system.[23]

That none of the possibilities that Jennings adverts to has so far occurred seems due simply to the fact that parliamentary majorities have always felt morally constrained to use their powers with due regard to the rights of the minorities in the legislature. This itself no doubt stems from the fact that there has always been, to date, a certain minimum of agreement as to fundamentals on the part of both Government and Opposition in the House of Commons. Although one might hesitate completely to approve

---

[21]Dicey, *Law of the Constitution*, 445 et seq.
[22]Jennings, *The Law and the Constitution*, 124.   [23]*Ibid.*, 90–1.

as a description applicable to present-day England the Abbé Sieyès criticism of English parliamentary government at the time of the Revolution as "le pseudo parlementarisme des deux faux partis, des deux 'blocs' d'intérêts, séparés seulement par le désir d'accaparer le pouvoir," there has been a willingness for the rival parties at least to agree on the "rules of the game."

The Limitation of the Electoral "Mandate"

The "mandate" concept, insofar as it can be said to exist as a principle of the English Constitution, is a special instance of a convention of the Constitution. Just when it originated is by no means certain. Jennings seems to trace its origin to the aftermath of the general election of 1852 when the Conservative party decided, in view of the result of the election, to renounce its policy of protection for agriculture.[24] Yet there seem to have been some precursors for the "mandate" concept in the events preceding the passage of the first Reform Bill in 1832. The question of reform of the system of parliamentary representation had been a main issue in the general election held late in 1830, when the Whig Government took office. A Reform Bill was promptly introduced early in 1831 and passed at its second reading, though the Government was defeated in the Commons shortly afterwards. The Whig Government, however, secured a dissolution of Parliament, and at the ensuing general elections was returned once again with a very big majority, whereupon it proceeded with the Reform Bill once more and immediately struck opposition from the Lords. The decision that was then made very reluctantly by the King to create sufficient additional members of the House of Lords to give a majority in the Lords for the passage of the Reform Bill was formed against a background of the success of the Whig Government in the election of 1830 and again in the election of 1831.

The actual term "mandate" seems first to have been used in the United Kingdom by Lord Hartington in opposing the Home Rule Bill in 1886:

Although no principle of a "mandate" may exist, there are certain limits which Parliament is morally bound to observe, and beyond which Parliament has, morally, not the right to go in its relations with the constituents. The constituencies of Great Britain are the source of the power at all events of this branch of Parliament, and I maintain that, in the absence of an emergency that could not be foreseen, the House of Commons has no right to initiate legislation, especially immediately upon its first meeting, of which the constituencies were not informed, and of which the constituencies might have been informed, and of which if they had been informed, there is, at all events, the very greatest doubt as to what their decision might be.[25]

[24]Jennings, *The Law and the Constitution*, 158.
[25]Sir Ivor Jennings, *Cabinet Government* (1936), 388–9.

The "mandate" concept in England obviously owes much to the imperative mandate (or *mandat contractuel,* as Victor Hugo called it) of Continental constitutional jurisprudence with its notion of an absolute identity of aim between the member and the geographical constituency by which he has been elected, a notion, however, which was bitterly contested by Esmein in favour of the theory of "representation," that is, that the member is responsible to the nation as a whole. The French Constitution of 1875 in fact expressly rejected the idea of an imperative mandate in declaring: "All imperative mandates are null and void." The important distinction between the imperative mandate of the Continent and the English mandate concept, however, lies in the fact that the imperative mandate on the Continent proceeds in terms of a responsibility of an individual member to his own particular constituency; while in England, in view perhaps of the strong party system, the mandate is conceived solely in terms of the responsibility of a government party vis-à-vis the electorate at large.

The main difficulties with the notion of the party mandate in England are with the uncertainty of its boundaries. A mandate for what? Does the mandate extend to the whole of a party's legislative programme or only to the high-lights? Must a mandate be secured in advance for the specific details of legislation or is it only necessary to secure electoral approval for general principles? How long does a mandate last—does it run throughout the whole of a party's term of office, or does it, for example, come to an end when a run of losses in parliamentary by-elections points to an impending defeat of the Government at the next general elections? Mr. Balfour in 1905 interpreted these latter signs as meaning that his Conservative Government's mandate had run out; though Professor Laski has pointed out that Prime Minister Baldwin proceeded to introduce the controversial Trade Union Law Amendment Act in 1927, though he had no prior electoral approval for this measure, and though the results of the by-elections were already presaging the defeat of the Conservative Government at the next general elections.[26]

Some indication of the confusion resulting in the argument as to just what a mandate consists of may be seen in connection with the vexed question of Home Rule for Ireland. Lord Salisbury, the Conservative leader, announced before the election of 1892 that the Opposition had put so many matters before the electors that he would not regard a Liberal majority as giving a mandate for Home Rule. Lord Hartington moved the rejection of the Home Rule Bill in the following year on the ground that in a case so serious not only the principle but the form of the measure

[26]Harold Laski, *Parliamentary Government in England* (1947), 83.

should be presented to the country prior to the election, before a mandate could be said to have been given to the victorious Liberal party. Other opponents of Home Rule argued that if the electors or Ireland were not counted, the Government had not a mandate at all. It was again contended in 1913 by such distinguished constitutional authorities as Professor Dicey and Sir William Anson that the Liberal Government of the day should go to the country on the Home Rule question, though that Government had fought two special general elections in 1910 on certain other aspects of its legislative programme. This problem, however, lapsed with the outbreak of the World War.

On the positive side, however, the need for a "mandate" seems definitely to have been recognized, albeit under duress, in the crisis of 1910 when the Liberal Government of the day twice went to the country to secure popular approval for a programme held up by Conservative majorities in the House of Lords: in the first instance, the controversial Finance Bill of 1909 was considered to have secured popular approval at the ensuing election and the Lords gave way; in the second instance, the measure involved was the law that was to become the Parliament Act of 1911, and with the return of the Liberal Government once more, the House of Lords was persuaded finally (with the threat of the creation of additional peers lingering in the background) to agree to the drastic limitation, almost to the vanishing point, of its own powers. In the same light, too, Mr. Baldwin dissolved Parliament in 1923 because he wanted a mandate for tariff reform: he did not introduce a general tariff between 1924 and 1929, because, as he admitted, he had no mandate for it. However, the "national" Government that was formed in 1931, mainly with Conservative party support, felt able to introduce tariff reform the following year, because it had, it was insisted, secured a "doctor's mandate" to do what seemed best to redress the "adverse balance of trade."[27]

Professor Jennings has described the mandate concept in England as "a stick to beat the Government . . . its plausibility is obvious. It is a useful argument that the Government has used its majority to effect changes to which the electorate has not been asked to consent."[28] It seems clear, too, that in its historical development the concept has been a means whereby the overwhelmingly Conservative majorities in the Lords have rationalized their holding up of the legislative programmes of Liberal or Labour majorities in the popular elected House of Commons. Except insofar as the House of Lords has been able, by rejecting a government's legislative programme, to force a general election, it is clear that the "man-

[27]Jennings, *Cabinet Government*, 390.   [28]*Ibid.*, 390.

date" concept has had no more efficacy than any other convention of the Constitution. Now that the House of Lords' powers have effectively been taken away by the Parliament Acts of 1911 and 1949, whatever binding force the "mandate" concept has must be derived from constitutional convention alone.

The conflicting constitutional practice in the past would seem to point to the fact that the "mandate" concept today is probably no stronger than the awareness by legislative majorities of the socio-ethical limits to the effectiveness of any legal action, the necessity for having a sufficient consensus of public opinion behind one before proceeding to put a controversial legislative programme into action—evidenced perhaps in the noticeable "marking-time" in its nationalization programme on the part of the Attlee Government after its re-election in 1950 with, however, only a hair-line majority in the House of Commons.

PARLIAMENTARY SOVEREIGNTY AND THE ROLE OF THE JUDICIARY

The Supposed Rivalry between the Common Law and Statute Law

"I think it is true to say that in England . . . when a judge or counsel finds himself faced by a statute . . . he makes an appropriate and specific adjustment of his mind, very much as a common lawyer does when he finds that he has strayed into the domain of equity."[29] This mental adjustment no doubt derives to a large extent from the autonomous training and tradition of the legal profession in England with its widespread emphasis on case law.[30] The setting up of the common law as a form of concreted reason, in opposition to a statute law that was regarded as a crude and alien intruder, is perhaps a logical outcome of the strong professional *esprit de corps* of the Inns of Court. For, as Professor Dicey, observed: "Parliamentary legislation in short, if it is sometimes rapid and thoroughgoing, exhibits characteristic faults. It is the work of legislators who are much influenced by the immediate opinion of the moment, who make laws with little regard either to general principles or to logical consistency, and who are deficient in the skill and knowledge of experts."[31]

The problem of the role of the judiciary in relation to the legislature in England reduces to the question of the psychological approach of judges disciplined, both by training and by professional practice in the mental patterns of the common law, to statutory encroachments upon the common law, particularly where the statutes in question are public law in character.

[29]Sir Maurice Amos, "The Interpretation of Statutes," (1934) *5 Camb. L.J.* 163–73.
[30]W. Friedmann, *Legal Theory* (1st ed., rev., 1947), 295.
[31]A. V. Dicey, *Law and Opinion in England* (1905), 395–6.

Ultimately, of course, Parliament in England can override the judiciary at will, for a simple legislative enactment can render nugatory a judicial decision that is considered out of accord with predominant opinions in the legislature. The most that can be done by the judiciary in the United Kingdom is to delay and irritate a parliamentary majority by "holding-in" of statutes. In the end, notwithstanding judicial tenacity, Parliament can prevail, provided it has the necessary interest and patience to do so. It must be conceded, however, that there is an inevitable time-lag in this process of legislative correction of judicial decisions. To take the politically innocuous example of the Married Women's Property legislation, it was held[32] that though the Act of 1882 gave a married woman power to dispose as a feme sole of real estate, being separate property, of which she was legal owner, this did not apply to enable her to alienate lands of which she was active trustee without the consent of her spouse; it took eleven years before the result of this judicial construction could be remedied by the Act of 1907. In the same way, the Act of 1907, stating that a husband *need* not be joined in an action of tort against the wife, was held by the House of Lords[33] to be merely permissive, so that though a husband was not liable for his wife's contracts, he could still be liable for her torts: this was not corrected until the Law Reform (Married Women and Tortfeasors) Act, 1935. So far as the earlier Married Women's Property legislation is concerned, a rationale in justification of the judges' hostile attitude to that legislation was provided by Professor Dicey: "The plain truth is that Parliament tried, whether wisely or not, to reform the law in accordance with ideas borrowed from equity, and some even of the lawyers by whom Parliament was guided did not fully understand the principles of equity which they meant to follow. Hence recurring blunders which one may hope, though without any great confidence, have been at last corrected."[34]

In fact, it is difficult to explain a good deal of judicial interpretation of legislation in the field of public law, except upon the assumption that the judges did not like what Parliament was doing, and sought to confine Parliament's activity to the narrowest possible area. Without entering into a detailed survey of the scope and effects of judicial interpretation of statute law in England, one may perhaps consider judicial attitudes to statute law, and measures taken by Parliament subsequently to correct those judicial attitudes, in one particular area of subject-matter, economic

[32]*Re Harkness and Allsopp's Contract*, [1896] 2 Ch. D. 358.
[33]*Edwards* v. *Porter*, [1925] A.C. 1.
[34]Dicey, *Law and Opinion in England*, 367. As to the subject of Married Women's Property legislation generally, see also C. K. Allen, *Law in the Making* (5th ed., 1951), 472–3.

interests,[35] taking especially the famous example of the House of Lords' decision in the *Osborne Case*.[36]

This case arose following on the highly successful trade union support of Labour candidates at the general elections of 1906. The plaintiff Osborne, a member of the trade union in question, sought a declaration of the invalidity of a union rule providing for the levy of contributions for payment of salaries or maintenance allowances to members of Parliament pledged to observe the conditions imposed by the constitution of the Labour party. A majority of the House of Lords held that such a rule was beyond the powers given to trade unions by the Trade Union Act of 1871 and the Trade Union Amendment Act of 1876, Lord Shaw and Lord James of Hereford concurring specially on the ground that certain conditions imposed upon members of Parliament by the constitution of the Labour party were contrary to public policy. Of this decision, Professor Laski has commented, "it is hardly possible to say other of the famous Osborne decision than that it represented the views of men at once ignorant of and prejudiced against the methods of trade unionism in the modern state."[37] The decision was the more serious a blow to the incipient Labour political movement in England in that members of Parliament were still unpaid at the time the decision was handed down. Ultimately Mr. Asquith's Liberal Government reversed the *Osborne Case*

[35]"Anyone who considers the history of the statutes dealing with workmen's compensation would, I conceive, find it difficult to avoid the conclusion that some of the judges, at least, misled by their no doubt unconscious dislike of limitations upon freedom of contract imposed by these statutes, minimised much of their force by interpreting away their safeguards. It is, I think, also clear that in the history of trade union legislation principles of the Common Law, previously unknown, were invoked to narrow their purposes in a way which defeated the clear intention of those statutes;—the Taff Vale case, [1901] A.C. 426, and the contrast between the decision in the Mogul Steamship case, [1892] A.C. 25, on the one hand, and the line of judgments beginning with Lumley v. Gye, 2 E. & B. 224, and ending with Quinn v. Leathem, [1901] A.C. 495, will sufficiently illustrate this thesis. When the Divisional Court held that attendance by school children at performances of Shakespeare's plays could not be regarded as an object of 'educational' expenditure, R. v. Lyon, 38 T.L.R. 62; or when it is held by the House of Lords that a power in Local Authorities to pay 'such salaries and wages as they . . . may think fit' means, in fact, such salaries and wages as the House of Lords may consider 'reasonable', R. v. Roberts [1925] A.C. 578, it seems to me clear that there is a discretion beyond the mere compulsion of words in the judicial interpretation of statutes. And this discretion, as I think, enables the judge to substitute his private notions of legislative intention for those which the authors of the statute sought to fill." Committee on Ministers' Powers, *Report* (1932), 135, Annex V (note by Professor Laski).

[36]*Amalgamated Society of Railway Servants* v. *Osborne*, [1910] A.C. 87.

[37]Harold Laski, *Studies in Law and Politics* (1932), 203–4. See also the pungent comments in Julius Stone, *The Province and Function of Law* (1946), 630–1; and in G. B. J. Hughes, *Jurisprudence* (1955), 508–11.

rule by passing through Parliament the Trade Union Act of 1913 which allowed the expenditure of trade union funds for political purposes, subject to certain safeguards; though this new right was itself somewhat curtailed by the Conservative Government's Trade Disputes and Trade Union Act of 1927.[38]

The explanation for what clearly seems to be obstructive or delaying tactics on the part of the English judiciary in the guise of "interpretation" of statute law has been suggested by Professor Laski in rather naked "economic" terms:

> The point I am concerned to make is the simple one that the tendencies of the modern state run counter to the main principles upon which the Common Law has been built. The result is an effort upon the part of the judiciary to minimise the consequences of those tendencies in a way which consciously hampers the purpose of the administration. The judges spare no pains in attacking parliamentary decisions it is not their function to criticise. They are occupied in the construction of what is hardly less than a fundamental law which they use to confine the ambit of statutes within the limit of policies they happen to approve. . . . They interpret the "rule of law" as though they are themselves the masters of a "higher law" than that of a sovereign legislature the content of which they themselves determine and the particular relevance of which they themselves decide. It is at least not excessive to say that they bring to the interpretation of the modern state and its processes habits of interpretation which, at least by implication deny the validity of many of the ends to which its power is devoted.[39]

The Rule of Law during an Emergency—A Change of Heart?

Our survey of the operation of judicial interpretation of statute law in England would not, however, be complete without noticing an antithetical trend in the patterns of interpretation which seems to run counter to Professor Dicey's rule of law concept, at least in the sense in which

---

[38]Parallel to the judicial attitudes to trade unions manifested in the *Osborne Case* decision, though not in fact a judicial interpretation based on statute law, was the decision in the *Taff Vale Case (Taff Vale Railway v. Amalgamated Society of Railway Servants*, [1901] A.C. 426) that union funds were liable for torts committed by union members in the course of disputes. This decision was over-ridden by the new Liberal Government that came to office in 1905—the Trades Disputes Act of 1906 forbade civil actions against trade unions for tortious acts alleged to have been committed by them or on their behalf. The Act also declared lawful, ordinary peaceful picketing, thereby overcoming the decision in *R. v. Hilbert*, (1872) 15 Cox C.C. 82; and it contained provisions designed to relieve trade unions from liability for the common law tort of conspiracy, thus circumventing the decision in *Quinn v. Leatham*, [1901] A.C. 495.

For further interesting discussions in this area, see generally Stone, *The Province and Function of Law*, chap. xxiii, 607 *et seq.*; Hughes, *Jurisprudence*, chaps. xix, xx, 481 *et seq.*

[39]Laski, *Parliamentary Government in England*, 309–10.

Dicey contrasted the English legal system to "every system of government based on the exercise by persons in authority of wide, arbitrary, or discretionary powers of constraint."[40] The much-discussed decision in *Liversidge* v. *Anderson*[41] upon the English Defence (General) Regulations, 1939, which in its end result screened from judicial scrutiny the reasonableness of the user of the Home Secretary's powers of preventive detention during a war emergency, continues and develops a judicial attitude manifested in *R.* v. *Halliday*[42] during the First World War. This judicial attitude, based apparently on the idea of not embarrassing the executive in time of war, necessarily involves a most beneficial judicial construction of the emergency powers conferred on the administration by statute law.

In *Liversidge* v. *Anderson,* the legislative enactment drawn in question was Regulation 18(B) of the Defence (General) Regulations, 1939, which provided:

> If the Secretary of State has reasonable cause to believe any person to be of hostile origin or associations or to have been recently concerned in acts prejudicial to the public safety or the defence of the realm or in the preparation or instigation of such acts and that by reason thereof it is necessary to exercise control over him, he may make an order against that person directing that he be detained.

The question which the Court faced was whether the judges could examine the "cause" of the Secretary of State's "belief" and pass upon its "reasonableness." In their decision, the majority judges in the House of Lords chose to regard the phrase "reasonable cause to believe" as ambiguous, since in their view it might equally mean either that the Secretary of State must in fact have reasonable cause, or alternatively merely that the Secretary of State must in good faith think he has reasonable cause. The question as to whether the "reasonableness" of the Secretary of State's belief should be tested by objective standards, or alternatively, subjectively in terms of the Secretary of State's own mental processes, was resolved by the Court in the context and in the light of the policy of the Regulation, the majority judges holding that the good faith of the Minister being admitted, the court could not enquire into the reasonableness of his belief. On the other hand, Lord Atkin, in dissenting from the majority opinion, refused to agree that the phrase "reasonable cause to

[40]Dicey, *Law of the Constitution*, 188.

[41][1942] A.C. 206. See, for example, the interesting discussions by Holdsworth, (1942) 58 *Law Q. Rev.* 1; A. L. Goodhart, (1942) 58 *Law Q. Rev.* 3; C. K. Allen, "Regulation 18B and Reasonable Cause," (1942) 58 *Law Q. Rev.* 232; Stone, *The Province and Function of Law*, 193–4.

[42][1917] A.C. 260.

believe" was ambiguous, and in his opinion stressed the dangerous effects upon individual liberty if, in the many statutes in which a similar formula was employed, judicial enquiry was barred.

It is clear that the majority's finding of ambiguity was aided by the background of the times and England's critical military situation: without a finding of ambiguity, of course, the majority judges could not have looked to policy considerations to determine their final interpretation, since according to the traditional principles for the interpretation of statute law in England policy of any kind may not be referred to by the judges if the provision in question is clear and unambiguous in its ordinary meaning. In fact, both the majority and the minority justices in *Liversidge* v. *Anderson* seem to have resorted to policy factors right from the outset in order to determine that the provision there in question was ambiguous—in the case of the majority, the policy of according the widest possible latitude of discretion to the executive at the height of a great war; in the case of the minority, the policy bound up in Dicey's rule of law concept of resisting to the utmost executive encroachments upon individual liberties. The minority view in *Liversidge* v. *Anderson,* of course, represents the old common law attitude of hostility to statute law, especially where the statute in question involves an encroachment or trenching upon branches of law formerly covered by actual decisions of the common law judges. The majority view, by contrast, involves a direct counter to Dicey's fundamental postulates of the English Constitution, and, to borrow an analogy from the constitutional law of the United States, may well indicate that, in times of crisis at least, the English judges are prepared to apply something of a "presumption of constitutionality" to legislation passed by Parliament, and not to delay the executive by the "holding-in" of statutes so as to conform to notions carried over from the old common law.

3

THE PRIVY COUNCIL
AS FINAL APPELLATE TRIBUNAL
FOR THE OVERSEAS EMPIRE

One of the most important links of the old British Empire was formed by the Judicial Committee of the Privy Council.[1] The somewhat anomalous nature of its appellate jurisdiction was discussed, by the Privy Council itself, in *British Coal Corporation* v. *The King:*

The Judicial Committee is a statutory body established in 1833 by an Act of 3 & 4 Will. IV, c.41, entitled an Act for the better Administration of Justice in His Majesty's Privy Council. . . . The Act . . . provides for the formation of a Committee of His Majesty's Privy Council, and enacts that "all appeals or complaints in the nature of appeals whatever, which either by virtue of this Act or of any law, statute or custom may be brought before His Majesty in Council" from the order of any Court or judge should thereafter be referred by His Majesty to, and heard by, the Judicial Committee, as established by the Act, who should make a report or recommendation to His Majesty in Council for his decision thereon, the nature of such report or recommendation being always stated in open Court. . . . It is clear that the Committee is regarded in the Act as a judicial body or Court, though all it can do is to report or recommend to His Majesty in Council, by whom alone the Order in Council which is made to give effect to the report of the Committee is made.

But according to constitutional convention it is unknown and unthinkable that His Majesty in Council should not give effect to the report of the Judicial Committee, who are thus in truth an appellate Court of law, to which by the Statute of 1833 all appeals within their purview are referred. . . .[2]

[1]The Long Parliament in 1641, by abolishing the Court of the Star Chamber, had deprived the Privy Council of all jurisdiction in England; but the Privy Council still remained the supreme Court of Appeal for admiralty cases and for all the King's overseas dominions; though its jurisdiction in this regard extended at that time (1641) only to the Channel Islands, the Isle of Man, and the American "plantations." The jurisdiction of the Privy Council was made statutory in 1833 by the Judicial Committee Act of that year.

[2][1935] A.C. 500, at p. 510. And see generally V. C. MacDonald, "The Privy Council and the Canadian Constitution," (1951) 29 *Can. B. Rev.* 1021, and address of the Right Hon. Lord Morton of Henryton, P.C., M.C., (1949) 32 *Proceedings of the Canadian Bar Association* 107.

Down to 1833 the judicial work of the Privy Council was performed by such members of the Privy Council as had held high judicial office: by the Act of 1833, however, its judicial work was transferred to the special judicial committee created by the Act, this committee consisting of the Lord President, the Lord Chancellor, and such other members of the council as had held high judicial office. In 1871 four paid members were appointed, but their places have now been taken by the Lords of Appeal in Ordinary, the law lords designated by the Act of 1876 for the judicial work of the House of Lords. In 1887 Scottish and Irish judges, in 1895 certain Dominion judges, and in 1908 certain Indian judges were made eligible to sit in appeals heard by the Judicial Committee. Normally, for the adjudication of cases, the boards of the Judicial Committee have consisted of five members, the actual personnel of the board for each occasion being selected by the Lord Chancellor of the day from the large pool of eligibles.[3]

Certain general points can be made about the work of the Privy Council when sitting as a final appellate tribunal for cases from the old Dominions. First, in spite of the express provisions allowing representation of Dominion judges on the various boards of the Privy Council (which provisions might reasonably have been taken as envisaging the active employment of Dominion judges, at least in Dominion appeals), cases before the Privy Council have been heard almost exclusively by English or Scottish law lords.[4] Again, the Judicial Committee, when sitting as a final appellate

---

[3]See, generally, E. C. S. Wade and G. Godfrey Phillips, *Constitutional Law* (2nd ed., 1935), 462 *et seq.*; Hood Phillips, *The Constitutional Law of Great Britain and the Commonwealth* (1952), 221 *et seq.*; and Lord Morton, (1949) 32 *Proc. Can. B. Assn.* 107, 114. "There are nine Lords of Appeal and, of the present nine, six had their legal training in England, two in Scotland and one in Northern Ireland. Southern Ireland is of course not represented, having cut herself entirely away from the Privy Council. The nine of us divide our time between sitting in the House of Lords, hearing appeals from England, Scotland, Wales, and Northern Ireland, and sitting in the Judicial Committee. Lords of Appeal who are members of the English Bar have usually, though not invariably, gone through the following stages: first, appointment as King's Counsel; second, selection to be a judge of the High Court; third, selection from all the judges of the High Court to be a member of the Court of Appeal; and lastly, promotion from the Court of Appeal to the House of Lords. I am glad to say that at the present time no consideration of politics enters into the selection at any of those stages, nor does selection at any stage go by seniority. If it did, I think we should all rival Methuselah in age."
[4]For a somewhat idealized picture of the Privy Council at work, see Lord Haldane in *Hull v. McKenna and Others*, [1926] I.R. 402: "The Judicial Committee of the Privy Council is not an English body in any exclusive sense. It is no more an English body, than it is an Indian body, or a Canadian body, or a South African body, or, for the future, an Irish Free State body. There sit among our numbers Privy Councillors who may be learned judges of Canada—there was one sitting with us last week—or from India, or we may have the Chief Justice, and

tribunal in cases from the Dominions, has been a court of frequently changing personnel, a factor tending to produce (and most notably in constitutional cases) a board the bulk of whose members have been unfamiliar with the Dominion constitutional law they have been called on to handle.[5] Two important consequences flow from this that are somewhat antithetical in nature. On the one hand, those members of the board who have managed to sit on Dominion constitutional cases with some regularity have attained a position of intellectual dominance over their more transient colleagues—Lord Watson, and his disciple Lord Haldane after him, were for this reason able to give a bias to the interpretation of the Canadian Constitution that was strongly personalized in nature.[6] On the other hand, rapidly changing personnel, coupled with the pre-eminence over successive periods of different judicial personalities, has meant the development of alternative "lines" in interpretation: the Watson-Haldane ("provincial-rights") approach to the Canadian Constitution[7] is balanced by Lord Sankey's broad, beneficial construction of Dominion powers in the depression era,[8] just as the arboreal metaphor developed by Lord

very often have had others, from the other Dominions, Australia, and South Africa. I mention that for the purpose of bringing out the fact that the Judicial Committee of the Privy Council is not a body, strictly speaking, with any location."

And see Lord Morton, (1949) 32 *Proc. Can. B. Assn.* 107, 108: "Only about a month ago I was sitting in the Judicial Committee with the Chief Justice of Canada. We all welcomed his presence and help. He is a learned and charming representative of that grand French stock which has given Canada her present Prime Minister." At p. 113, Lord Morton continued: "There is one thing which should never be forgotten. The Judicial Committee is not an English or a British Court considering, and sometimes overruling, decisions of the Canadian Courts. It consists of all members of the Privy Council who have held certain high judicial offices, one of which is, of course, the Chief Justice of Canada. It is true that, because the Judicial Committee sits in London, the five or seven men who hear the appeals from Canada are usually British Lords of Appeal, but Canadian members are always welcome. I have already mentioned the recent visit of Chief Justice Rinfret and, as you all know, the Board has often been assisted by the presence of his predecessor, that great judge, Sir Lyman Duff, whom I had the privilege of meeting, in excellent health, last week in Montreal."

[5]Cf. F. R. Scott, "The Consequences of the Privy Council Decisions," (1937) 15 *Can. B. Rev.* 485, 494: "To imagine that we shall ever get consistent and reasonable judgments from such a casually selected and untrained court [as the Privy Council] is merely silly."

[6]See Lord Haldane's tribute to his mentor, "The Judicial Committee of the Privy Council," (1923) 1 *Camb. L.J.* 143, 150.

[7]See, for example, Lord Watson's opinion in *Attorney-General for Ontario* v. *Attorney-General for Canada*, [1896] A.C. 348, and also in *Tennant* v. *Union Bank*, [1894] A.C. 31. These opinions are paralleled and extended by Lord Haldane's opinions in *In re Board of Commerce Act*, [1922] 1 A.C. 191, and *Toronto Electric Commissioners* v. *Snider*, [1925] A.C. 396.

[8]See, for example, *Edwards* v. *Attorney General for Canada*, [1930] A.C. 124.

Sankey to achieve his end[9] finds its counterpart, in its turn, in Lord Atkin's marine metaphor[10] which would restrict Dominion legislative powers and correspondingly enlarge those of the provinces.

The vagaries of judicial interpretation of the Canadian Constitution are indeed an excellent index to the uncertainty of tenure of the personnel of the Privy Council. The formation of Mr. Ramsay MacDonald's second Labour Government in 1929 brought with it the appointment of Lord Sankey as Lord Chancellor, and Lord Sankey personally inaugurated a dramatically new approach to the Canadian Constitution that contrasted strangely with the preceding Watson-Haldane era. Lord Sankey survived as Lord Chancellor the transition in 1931 from the MacDonald Labour Government to the MacDonald All-Party "National" Government, dominated as that was by Mr. Baldwin's Conservative party. However, when Mr. Baldwin finally took over the reins of office from Mr. MacDonald, Lord Sankey was soon dropped, being displaced by Lord Hailsham in a horse-trading deal after the general elections of 1935: with Lord Sankey's departure, there promptly ended also his broad approach to the construction of Dominion legislative powers. As Sir Ivor Jennings comments: "It is possible, though it cannot be proved, that the desire of Mr. Ramsay MacDonald in 1935 to safeguard his son's political career, and the anxiety of Lord Hailsham to leave the War Office for the more exalted and better paid position on the Woolsack—circumstances which sent Lord Sankey into retirement on a change of government—invalidated a large part of the Canadian New Deal."[11]

In theory, since the Judicial Committee, as they themselves noted, only "advise" the Crown, they must present united counsel to the Crown. The Judicial Committee's judgments, therefore, unlike those of the House of Lords, are always unanimous, though the seeming agreement may well cover basic differences of opinion among the personnel of the various boards. I must confess that, whatever the merits of the notion of "advice" to the Crown as an historical basis for the origin of the single-opinion practice, it does not seem an entirely satisfactory explanation for the continuance of that practice in modern times. It is possible to speculate that what was originally a matter only of history was reinforced by policy considerations in the course of the nineteenth century. This was, after all,

[9]*Ibid.* at 136: "The [B.N.A.] Act planted in Canada a living tree capable of growth and expansion within its natural limits. . . ."

[10]In *Attorney-General for Canada* v. *Attorney-General for Ontario*, [1937] A.C. 326, 354: "While the ship of state now sails on larger ventures and into foreign waters she still retains the water-tight compartments which are an essential part of her original structure."

[11]Sir Ivor Jennings, "Constitutional Interpretation—the Experience of Canada," (1937) 51 *Harv. L. Rev.* 1, 36.

the hey-day of the British colonial empire and the period of the political dominance in the United Kingdom (after the first Reform Bill of 1832) of the manufacturing middle class: the teachings of Austin and the positivist school reinforced the demands of the merchant class, at the height of laissez-faire, for clarity and certainty in law. The House of Lords, though not limiting itself to any single-opinion practice, hemmed itself in by an overly strict conception of the binding force of *stare decisis*[12] and by an equally uncompromising insistence that the judicial function was simply "law-finding" (as distinct from "law-making") so that there was no area of discretion left to the judges. In the same way, no doubt, the continuance only by the Privy Council of the practice of a single opinion might be justified, on policy grounds, by the seemingly universal and all-embracing character of a single opinion, as compared with multiple opinions, and also by the argument that a single opinion offered clarity and certainty to inferior tribunals within the rapidly proliferating colonial empire.

We know little about the internal workings of the Judicial Committee of the Privy Council over the years. Is a simple vote taken and the matter then left to the unfettered discretion of an individual judge appointed by the Lord Chancellor to write the opinion? The more notable Watson-Haldane opinions, for example, bear all the hallmarks of such a procedure. Alternatively, is there anything in the nature of a formal judicial conference, corresponding to the United States Supreme Court's procedure, involving a regularized interchange of ideas among the members of the panel with a view to thrashing out the policy alternatives, followed by circulation of the draft opinion of the court for comment and, if necessary, alteration? Lord Morton's remarks[13] upon the practice of the Privy Council in decision-making and opinion-writing during the period of his own membership of that body would suggest that, at least in recent years, the latter type of approach has been followed:

In the Judicial Committee, as you know, one judgment goes out as a judgment of the Board. Now how is that achieved?

Of course, as you can well imagine, we have many discussions as to the arguments each day when we adjourn at four o'clock, but nobody makes up his mind finally until the argument is over. Then, when the direction "Counsel and parties will withdraw" is given, and we are left alone, a very full discussion takes place and we all state our personal views. I do not think that it is a breach of confidence to say that the junior member of the Board is invited to state his views first. The discussion may be prolonged. If it turns out

[12]The House of Lords' holding that it is bound by its own decisions was actually delivered at the close of the nineteenth century: *London Street Tramways* v. *London County Council*, [1898] A.C. 375.

[13](1949) 32 *Proc. Can. B. Assn.* 107. The quotations that follow are from pp. 115–16 and 113, respectively.

that we are unanimous, we go on to decide who shall draft the judgment and what form it shall take. If, however, for the moment, we are three to two or four to one, further discussions follow either then or at a later stage, at which our various views are fully discussed. It may be that unanimity is thus achieved. If it is not, at least the points of divergence emerge clearly. If we are still divided in opinion, a member of the majority drafts the judgment, but our task is by no means finished at that stage, as you can well appreciate. When the draft judgment has been prepared it is fully considered and freely criticized by the other four members of the Board. That accounts, I think, for what may sometimes seem a long delay before the judgment is finally issued. We are most anxious to ensure, if possible, that no words are used which may be misunderstood. The responsibility is great, and infallibility is always rather a burden, since no one is entitled to say, no matter what he may think, that the ultimate decision is wrong. As we are human, I cannot feel that we are never mistaken, but I feel that if five or seven trained minds all concentrate on trying to produce a judgment that is right, they should have a reasonable chance of succeeding.

What happens to those members who cannot agree with the conclusions of the majority in an instant case? As Lord Morton observes: "The judgment of the Board takes the form of advice to His Majesty and no dissenting judgments are written. I feel sure on the whole that it is a good plan, although it may sometimes cause mild irritation on the part of members of the Board in a minority, in any case where there is a difference of opinion."[14] It may be, in this connection, that obscurities in the reasons of occasional opinions of the Privy Council merely cover the fact that the judges have not been as one in their approach and that the opinion has been modified to take account of their differences.

In theory, since the Judicial Committee is not strictly a court of law, it

[14]A dramatic illustration of the "mild irritation" of minority members of the Privy Council who are thus bound in anonymous silence to the majority opinion in any case is furnished by Lord Wright in the course of a recent tribute to Sir Lyman Duff, (1955) 33 *Can. B. Rev.* 1123. Lord Wright there goes far towards suggesting that in the landmark case of Canadian constitutional law, *Attorney-General for Canada* v. *Attorney-General for Ontario*, [1937] A.C. 326 (P.C.), his own was a dissenting voice that was stifled by the Privy Council's practice of issuing only a single *per curiam* opinion. See generally the comments, "Labour Conventions Case: Lord Wright's Undisclosed Dissent?" by F. R. Scott, (1956) 34 *Can. B. Rev.* 114; B. J. MacKinnon, *ibid.* 115; E. McWhinney, *ibid.* 243. Mr. MacKinnon in fact speculates that the deciding vote in the Privy Council in the *Labour Conventions Case* was cast by Sir Sidney Rowlatt, "a 'taxation judge' who . . . sat throughout the 1937 hearings in his overcoat making neither note nor comment." *Ibid.*, 117.

For a somewhat parallel instance of the *ex post facto* expression by Lord Wright of doubts concerning a major Privy Council decision in which he himself participated, see his courageous statements concerning *James* v. *Commonwealth*, [1936] A.C. 578 (P.C.), a leading case on the Australian Constitution: "Section 92—A Problem Piece," (1954) 1 *Sydney L. Rev.* 145. Lord Wright actually wrote the opinion of the Privy Council in *James* v. *Commonwealth*.

is not bound by its own previous decisions. In practice, however, and possibly as a result of the fact that the changing personnel of the various boards of the Judicial Committee have normally sat in the House of Lords, the Judicial Committee has tended to follow somewhat closely the House of Lords' concept of *stare decisis* in all its rigidity; so that we will frequently find, in examining the Judicial Committee's work, the same tenuous attempts to "distinguish" unwanted prior decisions, rather than directly overrule them. As a purely abstract question, of course, it is true that the presence of more than one opinion in a case increases the possibility of a "distinguishing" of the instant case in the future, insofar as the *ratio decidendi* of the case must be limited so as to fit the sum of all the facts held material by the various judges writing individual opinions:[15] and likewise the fact that there is more than one majority opinion necessarily multiplies the number of propositions from which alternative major premises may be derived for future cases. To that extent a strict approach to *stare decisis,* as for example the approach of the House of Lords, is fairly readily tolerable where the members of the Court indulge in the writing of individual opinions, in view of the greater ease with which unwanted precedents may thereby be "distinguished" in the future.[16] Correspondingly the strains on *stare decisis* are likely to be severest when the Court permits itself only a single opinion—it is perhaps not by accident that the Privy Council does not (formally at least) regard itself as bound by its own decisions.[17]

The appellate jurisdiction of the Judicial Committee of the Privy

[15]A. L. Goodhart, *Essays in Jurisprudence and the Common Law* (1931), 26.

[16]There is reason for believing that Dr. Goodhart, in his brilliant essay on determining the *ratio decidendi* of a case (*Essays in Jurisprudence and the Common Law*), was seeking in his own way to assist the process of sterilizing obnoxious and unwanted rules in English courts. Dr. Goodhart's rules for ascertaining the "principle" of a decision, insofar as when applied they must limit and narrow the grounds of decision of any case, are peculiarly attuned to the operational needs of the device of "distinguishing" cases in effect forced on the English judges by the extreme strictness of the doctrine of *stare decisis* as officially followed in England since 1898. In spite of Judge Frank's pungent criticisms, in *Courts on Trial* (1949), 63 (and cf. Goodhart's reply, (1951) 67 *Law Q. Rev.* 535), Dr. Goodhart seems to have a more flexible, instrumental approach to past judicial decisions than most of his English colleagues. See his recent plea for a relaxation of the strictness of *stare decisis,* in (1955) 220 *Law Times* 1.

[17]Cf. G. W. Paton, *Jurisprudence* (1st ed., 1946), 164; also P. A. Freund, "A Supreme Court in a Federation: Some Lessons from Legal History," (1953) 53 *Col. L. Rev.* 597, 614. Of course the Legal Realists, in accord with their thesis that the binding force of precedent is only an illusion anyway (cf. Frank, *Courts on Trial,* 278 *et seq.*) would, I think, necessarily maintain that it matters little whether the *ratio* of a case is derived from a single or from several opinions.

And see generally, Julius Stone, *The Province and Function of Law* (1946), 166 *et seq.*

Council in relation to the overseas Dominions and colonies extended to both private law and public law matters. Our concern here is solely with the role played by the Judicial Committee in exercising judicial review of the constitutions of the self-governing members of the Commonwealth. With several exceptions only, that role today is purely of historical significance. The jurisdiction of the Privy Council in relation to appeals of any kind from the courts of member countries of the Commonwealth has generally been swept away by statutes passed by the legislatures of those countries individually in the period since World War II.[18] The power of the member countries themselves to act to abolish the appeal to the Privy Council was in effect fully established by the United Kingdom Parliament with the passage of the Statute of Westminster in 1931; and if there were any doubts on this score they were put at rest by the Privy Council's own holding that such a power existed.[19] But even apart from the question of formal abolition of the appeal, the Privy Council itself had chosen in the past to place some working limits on its jurisdiction. As Lord Haldane observed in *Hull* v. *McKenna and Others:*

. . . It is obviously proper that the Dominions should more and more dispose of their own cases, and in criminal cases it has been laid down so strictly that it is only in most exceptional cases that the Sovereign is advised to intervene. In other cases the practice which has grown up, or the unwritten usage which has grown up, is that the Judicial Committee is to look closely into the nature of the case, and, if, in their Lordships' opinion, the question is one that can best be determined on the spot, then the Sovereign is not, as a rule, advised to intervene, nor is he advised to intervene normally—I am not laying down precise rules now, but I am laying down the general principles—unless the case is one involving some great principle or is of some very wide public interest. It is also necessary to keep a certain discretion, because when you are dealing with the Dominions you find that they differ very much. For instance, in States that are not unitary States—that is to say, States within themselves —questions may arise between the Central Government and the State, which, when an appeal is admitted, give rise very readily to questions which are apparently very small but which may involve serious considerations, and there leave to appeal is given rather freely. In Canada, there are a number of cases in which leave to appeal is granted because Canada is not a unitary State, and because it is the desire of Canada itself that the Sovereign should retain the power of exercising his Prerogative; but that does not apply to internal disputes not concerned with constitutional questions, but relating to matters of fact. There the rule against giving leave to appeal from the Supreme Court

18See, for example, Canada, The Supreme Court Act, 1949 (13 Geo. VI, c. 37); South Africa, The Privy Council Appeals Act, 1950 (No. 16 of 1950); India, The Abolition of Privy Council Jurisdiction Act, 1949 (Constituent Assembly Act No. V of 1949).

19*Attorney-General for Ontario* v. *Attorney-General for Canada*, [1947] A.C. 127 (P.C.).

of Canada is strictly observed where no great constitutional question, or question of law, emerges. In the case of South Africa, which is a unitary State, counsel will observe that the practice has become very strict. We are not at all disposed to advise the Sovereign, unless there is some exceptional question, such as the magnitude of the question of law involved, or it is a question of public interest in the Dominion to give leave to appeal. . . . In South Africa, we take the general sense of that Dominion into account, and restrict the cases in which we advise His Majesty to give leave to appeal.[20]

The Privy Council's most active work has been in relation to the federal states within the Commonwealth. Lord Haldane's distinction between the Privy Council's approach to unitary states and its approach to federal states is a real one in this sense, that the Privy Council has taken very few constitutional law cases arising within unitary states such as New Zealand and South Africa. The Privy Council's practice in relation to South Africa, for example, was to grant leave to appeal to itself only in cases raising "serious" constitutional issues, a requirement which it interpreted most strictly;[21] but by contrast the Privy Council showed itself very ready to take constitutional cases arising from the two federal states within the Commonwealth, Canada and Australia. In fact, the most important constitutional holdings in these countries are Privy Council decisions, this notwithstanding the fact that under the Australian Constitution the categories of constitutional matters which may be taken on appeal to the Privy Council from Australian courts are severely limited. Under section 74 of the Australian Constitution, no appeal lies to the Privy Council from the High Court of Australia upon any question, however arising, as to the limits *inter se* of the constitutional powers of the Commonwealth and of the states, without leave of the High Court of Australia. The restrictive operation of section 74 is accentuated by the decision of the High Court of Australia[22] that the High Court (and not the Privy Council) is the sole arbiter of what constitutes an *inter se* question for purposes of section 74.

It should be stressed that, in the exercise of what amounts to a power of judicial review in relation to the constitutions of the members of the Commonwealth, and the concomitant power to strike down as invalid laws passed by the parliaments of those countries, the premise upon which the Privy Council has proceeded is essentially the principle stemming from the old colonial days that all colonial legislatures are subordinate to the Imperial (i.e., the United Kingdom) Parliament. This was in fact the principle applied by the Privy Council in relation to the legislation of certain of the American colonies prior to 1776. As Todd observed:

[20][1926] I.R. 402.
[21]*Whittaker* v. *Durban Corporation*, (1921) 90 L.J.P.C. 119; *Beier* v. *Minister of Interior*, [1948] 3 S.A.L.R. 430 (A.D.).
[22]*Baxter* v. *Commissioner of Taxes*, (1907) 4 C.L.R. 1087.

It is the general condition of all legislation by subordinate and provincial assemblies, throughout the British Empire, that the same "shall not be repugnant to the law of England". This condition is enforced . . . by the decision of the local judiciary in the colony, in the first instance, and ultimately of her Majesty's imperial privy council, upon an action or suit at law, duly brought before such a tribunal, to declare and adjudge a colonial, dominion, or provincial statute, either in whole or in part, to be ultra vires and void, as being in excess of the jurisdiction conferred upon the legislature by which the same was enacted, or at variance with some imperial law in force in the colony; or otherwise, by a similar decision, to confirm and approve of the legality of the act the validity of which had been impugned.

The power of interpreting colonial statutes, and of deciding upon their constitutional effect and validity, is a common and inherent right, appertaining to all her Majesty's courts of law before which a question arising out of the same could be properly submitted for adjudication. . . . By this process, a final and authoritative decision can be obtained, in respect to the legality of any provincial enactment, from the highest level tribunal in the empire. And if the decision should be adverse, the statute in question would become void and of no effect.[23]

Although in strict theory the Privy Council originally exercised the power of judicial review on the premise that the colonial legislatures were subordinate legislative bodies vis-à-vis the United Kingdom Parliament, it continued to exercise that power long after many of the colonies had ripened into self-governing Dominions and indeed long after the Imperial Conference of 1926 had declared, on the question of the status of the United Kingdom and the Dominions, that the Dominions were "autonomous communities . . . equal in status, in no way subordinate one to another in any aspect of their domestic or external affairs." It is true that the Statute of Westminster, 1931, to which the Imperial Conference of 1926 gave rise, allowed a logical solution for the anomaly—that while the legal subordination of the Dominion legislatures no longer existed the jurisdiction of the Privy Council over them still remained—by permitting the parliaments of the various Dominions to abolish the appeal to the Privy Council, a step which (as we have already noted) has been taken in the last few years by all of the old Dominions except Australia and New Zealand.

Yet even after the abolition of the appeal to the Privy Council, the Canadian Supreme Court, for example, continues to exercise the power of judicial review in relation to legislation passed by the Canadian Parliament. And right from the outset, the High Court of Australia assumed the power to invalidate, on the grounds of unconstitutionality, legislation passed by the Australian Parliament on matters coming within section 74 of the Australian Constitution, and in respect to which, therefore, any

[23]*Parliamentary Government in the British Colonies* (1880).

appeal to the Privy Council was prohibited by the Constitution. Neither the Canadian nor the Australian Constitution makes any mention of or provision for judicial review. The Canadian and Australian constitutions are of course both patterned to a considerable extent on the Constitution of the United States, and there would clearly be a strong temptation for appellate judges in both Canada and Australia unconsciously to adopt the American practice of judicial review without adverting to its rather different historical origins. Yet the carry-over of the practice of judicial review in relation to the Canadian and the Australian constitutions, both by the Privy Council and by local appellate tribunals, seems primarily due to the fact that the practice had long since become ingrained and its historical roots and justification forgotten.[24]

More striking even than the direct impact of the Privy Council on the constitutional law of the Commonwealth countries, in terms of jurisdiction actively exercised as a final appellate tribunal for the Commonwealth, is the influence of English judicial techniques and practices and of the traditions of English legal thought. The training and organization of the legal profession in the countries of the Commonwealth is largely patterned on that of the United Kingdom, and the judicial decision-makers in the Commonwealth to a quite considerable extent have actually been trained in the United Kingdom itself. The effect has been to produce a group of legal decision-makers, trained in the strict disciplines of the ancient universities and of the Inns of Court, and equipped thereby with a highly specialized professional skill and expertise, but nevertheless completely untainted by acquaintance with other sciences than law. It is to be noted, however, that none of the final appellate tribunals of the Commonwealth has seen fit to follow the Privy Council in its practice of issuing only a single *per curiam* opinion in the deciding of cases; but the multiple opinion-writing of the House of Lords is, historically anyway, quite as good a precedent to follow as the example of the Privy Council, and the advantages in flexibility and individuality afforded by the House of Lords'

[24]Thus Lord Halsbury L.C., in *Webb* v. *Outrim*, [1907] A.C. 81, seemed disposed to challenge the notion that there could be such a thing as an "unconstitutional" act of a Dominion or colonial legislature, once that act had been assented to by the Crown. During the argument in *Webb* v. *Outrim*, Lord Halsbury, in reply to counsel's contention that a law was *ultra vires*, observed: "That is a novelty to me. I thought an Act of Parliament was an Act of Parliament and you cannot go beyond it. . . . I do not know what an unconstitutional act means." Quoted in M. Ollivier, *Le Canada, pays souverain?* (1935), 223. R. T. E. Latham, "The Law and the Commonwealth," in W. K. Hancock, ed., *Survey of British Commonwealth Affairs* (1937), 566, describes Lord Halsbury's contribution as a "major blunder." The justification for the exercise of judicial review in these countries today can no doubt be rested upon long-time user and practice ripening into a convention of constitutional law.

practice are obvious enough to commend it in preference to the Privy Council's practice.[25]

If the Privy Council has tended to treat the constitutions of the Commonwealth countries no differently than ordinary pieces of statute law and if it has in consequence applied to those constitutions the same fettering, restrictive rules of interpretation that it would apply to the ordinances of municipal councils or any other subordinate law-making bodies, it is submitted that the appellate tribunals within the Commonwealth Countries themselves have not reacted very differently to the task of constitutional adjudication. If it is desired to produce a change in the basic course of judicial interpretation of the constitutions of the Commonwealth countries, therefore, it may be more than a matter of abolishing the appeal to the Privy Council and so obtaining juridical independence from the United Kingdom, if the local judges are to continue to retain strong affinities with the attitudes and the practices of the English judiciary. There does seem, for example, basis for saying that the Canadian Supreme Court and other Commonwealth appellate tribunals have hewed rather more enthusiastically to the lines of interpretation marked out by the Privy Council than *stare decisis* and the deference due to a superior appellate tribunal alone would require.[26]

[25]See generally, E. McWhinney, "Judicial Concurrences and Dissents: A Comparative View of Opinion-Writing in Final Appellate Tribunals," (1953) 31 *Can. B. Rev.* 595.

[26]See, for example, B. Laskin, " 'Peace, Order and Good Government' Reexamined," (1947) 25 *Can. B. Rev.* 1054, 1086.

4

THE CANADIAN CONSTITUTION UNDER THE
IMPACT OF JUDICIAL REVIEW

In its preamble, the Constitution of Canada speaks of the desire of the provinces of Canada to be "federally united into one Dominion under the Crown of the United Kingdom of Great Britain and Ireland, with a Constitution similar in principle to that of the United Kingdom." Historically, then, the Constitution of Canada, like the Constitution of the United States, stems from a compact between a number of different territorial units: the provinces of Lower Canada (Quebec), Upper Canada (Ontario), and the two Maritime Provinces of Nova Scotia and New Brunswick, joined together in 1867 to form the new Dominion of Canada, a number of other provinces having been admitted to the union since that time. Juridically speaking, however, the origins are rather different. The fundamental instrument in which the Canadian Constitution is embodied, the British North America Act of 1867,[1] is a statute of the United Kingdom Parliament, and thus, though Canada in 1867 became a self-governing Dominion within the then British Empire by virtue of the Act, her status for many purposes internationally was still something less than a full sovereign state. By 1931, although the highly developed conventions governing the relationship of the United Kingdom to the self-governing Dominions had crystallized into the positive law rules of the Statute of Westminster, some vestiges of Canada's former subordinate position still remained.

First, since the B.N.A. Act contains no provision as to its own amendment, constitutional change in Canada had perforce to be achieved by recourse to the original source of the Canadian Constitution, the United Kingdom Parliament. The considerable number of amendments that have been effected since 1867 have been in the form of acts of the United Kingdom Parliament. Even today, when all political parties are satisfied as to the desirability of some amending procedure that can be operated

[1] 30 & 31 Vict., c. 3 (1867).

by the Canadian people themselves, it is agreed that the exact formula for amendment, a matter of some considerable controversy as yet, must finally be embodied in an act of the United Kingdom Parliament in order to become effective.[2] This is indeed a full concession to the formalism of Austinian jurisprudence.

A second important feature was that until 1949[3] an appeal existed from the Canadian Supreme Court to the Privy Council, the highest appellate tribunal of the British Empire, and of the British Commonwealth which succeeded the British Empire. The role that the Privy Council actually played in exercising ultimate judicial review of the Canadian Constitution is perhaps the most controversial aspect of Canadian constitutional history after the passage of the B.N.A. Act in 1867.[4]

The system of government as finally provided for Canada under the B.N.A. Act was a composite as opposed to a unitary system. The special interests of the French inhabitants of Lower Canada and in particular of the Roman Catholic Church had been recognized by the British government soon after the abandonment of France's colonial interests in North America to the British, with the passage by the British Parliament of the Quebec Act of 1774 with the guarantees for those interests that it contained. It was clear in 1867 that a large degree of local autonomy was necessary if the interests of the French settlers and, for that matter, too, the special economic position of the British settlers in the Maritime communities were to be protected. On the other hand, the recent experience of the American Civil War was widely considered in 1867 to point to the need for a strong government at the centre and to the dangers of allowing too much power to be exercised at the periphery.

It seems clear that the intentions of the drafters of the Canadian Constitution were that the Dominion Parliament's legislative powers should be of paramount importance; that insofar as the system of government under the B.N.A. Act was a federal system it should be a centralized federalism.[5] The B.N.A. Act, as finally passed by the United Kingdom

[2]W. H. Livingston, "The Amending Power of the Canadian Parliament," (1951) 45 *Am. Pol. Sci. Rev.* 437; P. Gérin-Lajoie, "Du pouvoir d'amendement constitutionnel au Canada," (1951) 29 *Can. B. Rev.* 1136.

[3]Supreme Court Act, 1949, 13 Geo. 6, c. 37, s. 3, an Act of the Canadian Parliament. The right of Canada so to abolish the appeal to the Privy Council had already been upheld by the Privy Council, *Attorney-General for Ontario* v. *Attorney-General for Canada*, [1947] A.C. 127 (P.C.).

[4]See, e.g., a symposium on "Nationhood and the Constitution," in (1951) 29 *Can. B. Rev.* 1019–97.

[5]V. C. MacDonald, "The Constitution in a Changing World," (1948) 26 *Can. B. Rev.* 21.

Parliament, establishes a distribution of legislative authority between the Dominion (or federal) government and the provincial governments, the purpose being to allocate all powers of government between the two types of governing authority. Unlike the United States Constitution, therefore, there are no legislative powers which are denied to both federal and provincial governments—there is no Canadian bill of rights. As the Lord Chancellor, Lord Loreburn, said, "there can be no doubt that under this organic instrument the powers distributed between the Dominion on the one hand and the provinces on the other hand cover the whole area of self-government within . . . Canada. It would be subversive of the entire scheme and policy of the Act to assume that any point of internal self-government was withheld from Canada."[6]

Under section 91 of the B.N.A. Act, the Dominion government is given a general power to make laws for the "Peace, Order, and good Government of Canada, in relation to all Matters not coming within the Classes of Subjects by this Act assigned exclusively to the Legislatures of the Provinces." Section 91 goes on to declare that "for greater Certainty, but not so as to restrict the Generality of the foregoing Terms," the legislative authority of the Dominion Parliament shall extend to all matters coming within a list of 29 enumerated subjects. Under section 92, on the other hand, the provincial legislatures are given exclusive legislative authority over a list of sixteen subjects, of which perhaps the two most interesting from the constitutional viewpoint have been section 92(13), "Property and Civil Rights in the Province," and section 92(16), "Generally all Matters of a merely local or private Nature in the Province."

It seems clear that the general power conferred on the Dominion Parliament under section 91 to make laws for the "Peace, Order, and good Government of Canada" was intended to be the major source of Dominion legislative power, with the 29 specific heads of federal legislative power, enumerated in section 91, being merely illustrations of the general power. As Dean Kennedy said:

The federal powers are wholly residuary for the simple reason that the provincial powers are exclusive; and the twenty-nine "enumerations" in Section 91 cannot add to the residue; they cannot take away from it. . . . They have no meaning except as examples of the residuary power, which must be as exclusive as is the grant of legislative powers to the provinces. The enumerated examples of the residuary power cannot occupy any special place; they cannot be exalted at the expense of the residuary power, for that would "restrict the generality" of that power. It all looks reasonably simple, and

[6]*Attorney-General for Ontario* v. *Attorney-General for Canada*, [1912] A.C. 571, 581 (P.C.).

Sir John A. MacDonald was perhaps justified as he looked at the scheme in hoping that "all conflict of jurisdiction" had been avoided.[7]

Certainly, by comparison with the United States Constitution it might have been expected that Canada, both by reason of the very precise delineation of the respective powers of the Dominion and the provincial governments and also of the absence of any formal bill of rights, would have been spared the storms and battles that centred around the United States Constitution in the period from the Civil War up to the Court Revolution of 1937. Instead we find a surprisingly parallel development, though in place of the due process clauses of the Fifth and Fourteenth amendments the conflict revolves around an apparently simple choice in modes of judicial interpretation—whether the Constitution is to be regarded as an ordinary statute to be interpreted according to the ordinary rules of statutory construction, or whether it is something more—a "constitutional statute"—and therefore deserving of more "beneficial" interpretation than the normal rules of statutory construction might allow. The judicial approach to the interpretation of the Canadian Constitution has fluctuated widely between these two alternative approaches, and the fluctuations tend to accord with two and possibly three basic periods.

In the first period, from the passing of the B.N.A. Act in 1867 until the middle 1890's, the Privy Council, as final appellate court in Canadian constitutional cases, was disposed to construe the legislative powers of the Dominion Parliament broadly, and in particular to concede full value to the Dominion government's general power under section 91 to legislate for the "Peace, Order, and good Government of Canada."[8]

The second period, beginning about 1896 and lasting generally right up to the present day, is notable for the contraction of Dominion legislative powers, and the concomitant assertion of provincial rights. Under Lord Watson, and also under Lord Haldane, his spiritual successor, the Dominion's general legislative power under section 91 is cut down by deference to the heads of provincial power enumerated in section 92—the Dominion cannot legislate under the general power in section 91 where the effect is to "trench" upon the provincial classes of subjects.[9] Lord

---

[7]W. P. M. Kennedy, "The Interpretation of the British North America Act," (1942) 8 *Camb. L.J.* 146, 150.

[8]*Russell* v. *The Queen*, (1882) 7 App. Cas. 829, 839, *per* Sir Montague E. Smith: "Few, if any, laws could be made by Parliament for the peace, order, and good government of Canada which did not in some incidental way affect property and civil rights; and it could not have been intended, when assuring to the provinces exclusive legislative authority on the subjects of property and civil rights, to exclude the Parliament from the exercise of this general power whenever any such incidental interference would result from it."

[9]*Attorney-General for Ontario* v. *Attorney-General for Canada*, [1896] A.C.

Haldane, indeed, went even further than Lord Watson and enunciated the so-called "emergency" doctrine under which the Dominion's legislative power under section 91 was confined to use in periods of national emergency, such as war, famine, or pestilence.[10]

Further, the Dominion's power under section 132 to legislate to implement the obligations of Canada or any province "as part of the British Empire . . . arising under Treaties between the Empire and such Foreign Countries" was held not to cover obligations entered into by Canada herself in her new status as an international person,[11] this notwithstanding that the Privy Council expressly took notice of the constitutional developments in Dominion status since the enactment of the B.N.A. Act.[12]

Even the Dominion government's head of power over the "regulation of trade and commerce,"[13] a power which has proved so fertile a source of federal legislative authority in the United States, was deprived of any real significance. Lord Haldane went so far as to rule in the *Board of Commerce Case* [14] that the trade and commerce power was available only to "aid" the Dominion in an exceptional situation to exercise the powers conferred by the general language of section 91; that where no power was possessed by the Dominion Parliament independently of the trade and commerce section, the trade and commerce section could not operate. So low indeed did the trade and commerce power fall that Chief Justice Anglin of the Canadian Supreme Court was moved to protest that it had

---

348 (P.C.), *per* Lord Watson. See also Lord Watson's decision in *Tennant* v. *Union Bank*, [1894] A.C. 31 (P.C.).

[10]*In re Board of Commerce Act*, [1922] 1 A.C. 191 (P.C.); *Toronto Electric Commissioners* v. *Snider*, [1925] A.C. 396 (P.C.).

[11]*Attorney-General for Canada* v. *Attorney-General for Ontario*, [1937] A.C. 326 (P.C.).

[12]"While it is true . . . that it was not contemplated in 1867 that the Dominion would possess treaty-making powers, it is impossible to strain the section so as to cover the uncontemplated event." *Per* Lord Atkin, in *Attorney-General for Canada* v. *Attorney-General for Ontario*, [1937] A.C. 326, 350 (P.C.). See also *In re Regulation and Control of Radio Communication*, [1932] A.C. 304 (P.C.). However, the authority of the Privy Council's last and major decision on the Canadian treaty-making power, *Attorney-General for Canada* v. *Attorney-General for Ontario*, [1937] A.C. 326 (P.C.), must be regarded as severely challenged by the recent frank and courageous revelation by Lord Wright: see (1955) 33 *Can. B. Rev.* 1123; and see the ensuing comments, "Labour Conventions Case: Lord Wright's Undisclosed Dissent?" by F. R. Scott, (1956) 34 *Can. B. Rev.* 114; B. J. MacKinnon, *ibid.* 115; E. McWhinney, *ibid.* 243. See also Lord Wright's similar disclosures regarding the Privy Council decision in *James* v. *Commonwealth*, [1936] A.C. 578 (P.C.), the leading case under the Australian Constitution: Wright, "Section 92—A Problem Piece," (1954) 1 *Sydney L. Rev.* 145.

[13]Section 91(2).

[14]*In re Board of Commerce Act*, [1922] 1 A.C. 191 (P.C.).

been "denied all efficacy as an independent enumerative head of Dominion legislative jurisdiction."[15]

Although this second period cannot yet be regarded as having come to an end, there is a trend of decisions from the 1930's onwards which may represent something more than the mere working out of the dialectic. Thus Lord Sankey declared in the *Persons Case* in 1930: "The [B.N.A.] Act planted .in Canada a living tree capable of growth and expansion within its natural limits. The object of the Act was to grant a Constitution to Canada. . . . Their Lordships do not conceive it to be the duty of this Board—it is certainly not their desire—to cut down the provisions of the Act by a narrow and technical construction, but rather to give it a large and liberal interpretation. . . ."[16] It is true that Lord Sankey rather cut down the sweep of his comments by going on to add that in making his remarks he was not considering the question of the respective legislative competence of the Dominion and of the provinces under sections 91 and 92 of the Act. But in *British Coal Corporation* v. *The King*,[17] Lord Sankey, in upholding the right of the Dominion Parliament to abolish appeals from Canadian courts to the Privy Council in criminal cases, quoted his own remarks in the *Persons Case* but without the caveat as to sections 91 and 92, and expressly recognized that "in interpreting a constituent or organic statute such as the [B.N.A.] Act, that construction most beneficial to the widest possible amplitude of its powers must be adopted."[18] It was in the tradition laid down by Lord Sankey in these two cases that the Privy Council in 1947 approached the question of the legislative competence of the Dominion Parliament to abolish altogether appeals from Canadian courts to the Privy Council, in all classes of cases. Although the case did not directly concern sections 91 and 92 of the B.N.A. Act, but principally section 101 of the Act, the Privy Council approached most boldly the task of signing its own death warrant so far as Canadian appellate jurisdiction was concerned. "It is . . . irrelevant that the question is one that might have seemed unreal at the date of the [B.N.A.] Act. To such an organic statute the flexible interpretation must be given which changing circumstances require. . . ."[19]

It might be unwise to make too much of these few decisions. Thus, even while Lord Jowitt was giving the *Privy Council Appeals Case* decision, Lord Wright in the *Japanese Canadians Case*[20] was apparently

[15]*The King* v. *Eastern Terminal Elevator Co.*, [1925] S.C.R. 434, 442.
[16]*Edwards* v. *Attorney-General for Canada*, [1930] A.C. 124, 136 (P.C.).
[17][1935] A.C. 500 (P.C.).   [18]*Ibid.* at 518.
[19]*Per* Jowitt, L.C., *Attorney-General for Ontario* v. *Attorney-General for Canada*, [1947] A.C. 127, 154 (P.C.), (*Reference re Privy Council Appeals*).
[20]*Co-operative Committee on Japanese Canadians* v. *Attorney-General for Canada*, [1947] A.C. 87 (P.C.).

reaffirming Lord Haldane's "emergency" theory[21] of the Dominion's general legislative power under section 91, even though only the previous year Lord Simon had thrown cold water on the emergency doctrine.[22] Still, if the Canadian Supreme Court, in its capacity of final arbiter of the interpretation of the B.N.A. Act now that the appeal to the Privy Council has been finally abolished, wishes to chart out a liberal course of interpretation of Dominion legislative powers, Lord Sankey's "living tree" metaphor is available as a doctrinal justification.[23]

Necessarily, most of the controversy as to the role played by the Privy Council centres around the period from 1896 onwards, and the judicial personalities of Lord Watson and Lord Haldane.[24] In treating the B.N.A. Act as an ordinary statute without regard to the intentions of the "fathers" of the Constitution, the Privy Council after 1896 reached a "result which the historian knows to be untrue,"[25] and a Constitution which "(rightly or wrongly) embodied a Centralized Federalism in which Dominion legislative power was of paramount importance . . . has yielded a Decentralized Federalism in terms of legislative power; and one, moreover, that is ill-adapted to present needs."[26]

Vincent MacDonald has collected an impressive list of Dominion social and economic legislation held invalid as encroaching upon provincial powers under sections 92(13) and 92(16) or otherwise beyond the powers of the Dominion Parliament.[27] It does not, it seems, require a

---

[21]As enunciated in *Toronto Electric Commissioners* v. *Snider*, [1925] A.C. 193 (P.C.).

[22]*Attorney-General for Ontario* v. *Canada Temperance Federation*, [1946] A.C. 193 (P.C.).

[23]As the antithesis to Lord Sankey's "living tree," we have Lord Atkin's "ship of state." "While the ship of state now sails on larger ventures and into foreign waters she still retains the watertight compartments which are an essential part of her original structure." *Per* Lord Atkin in *Attorney-General for Canada* v. *Attorney-General for Ontario*, [1937] A.C. 326, 354 (P.C.).

[24]"Since . . . the privy council has treated the B.N.A. Act as an ordinary statute and not as a constitutional document, it has given no consideration to the intention of the 'fathers,' but has adhered to the view that the 'intention of parliament' must be interpreted as laid down in the act itself, in the words and context of which alone its meaning must be discovered. . . . The use of extraneous evidence has been eschewed, and the board has sought the meaning of the act in the text, 'aided only by the flickering illumination afforded by rules of textual construction evolved with respect to ordinary statutes.'" R. Tuck, "Canada and the Judicial Committee of the Privy Council," (1941) 4 *U. of Toronto L.J.* 33, 40.

[25]H. A. Smith, (1927) 9 *J. Comp. Leg. & Int'l L.* 160, quoted in *ibid.*, 40–1.

[26]MacDonald, "The Constitution in a Changing World," (1948) 26 *Can. B. Rev.* 21, 44.

[27]*Ibid.* The list includes the following: legislation for the abolition of the liquor traffic, *Attorney-General for Ontario* v. *Attorney-General for Dominion*, [1896] A.C. 348 (P.C.); for the regulation of "through traffic" over provincial and Dominion railways, *Montreal* v. *Montreal Street Ry.*, [1912] A.C. 333

bill of rights or a due process clause for natural law concepts as to the proper sphere of governmental activity to operate in the field of constitutional law.

Granted the premise that the B.N.A. Act is to be treated as an ordinary statute, and not as "constitutional" statute, do the Privy Council decisions flow inevitably from the words of the B.N.A. Act? Dean Kennedy seems convinced that any hope that effect would be given to the intentions of the framers of the Act was doomed to disappointment. The study of those intentions may be interesting, but it is of no value except in showing the futility of the hope that the intentions and statute will accord. The Privy Council's approach is in accord with the "rules of the legal game."[28]

> After a careful examination of every case, in every jurisdiction, dealing with the interpretation of the Act, I venture to submit that in not one of them has the ratio decidendi depended on reasons external to the Act. . . . So generally uniform has been the approach of the judicial committee that, on the basis of it, I anticipated almost all these judgments except that on unemployment insurance, before their subject-matters were referred to the Supreme Court, and thence to London.[29]

But other commentators are not so certain as to the inevitability of the course of the Privy Council's decisions. Indeed, Professor Laskin goes so far as not merely to repudiate any idea of inevitability, but to

---

(P.C.); prohibiting trade combinations and hoarding and regulating the sale and fixation of prices of commodities, *In re Board of Commerce Act*, [1922] A.C. 191 (P.C.); for the regulation of the grain trade of Canada and of the business of those who deal in grain as warehousemen, etc., *Eastern Terminal Elevator Co.* v. *The King*, [1925] S.C.R. 434; regulating sales and deliveries of eggs within a province, *R.* v. *Zaslavsky*, [1935] 2 W.W.R. 34, [1935] 2 D.L.R. 788, 64 C.C.C. 706 (Sask.); *R.* v. *Thorsby Traders Ltd.*, [1935] 3 W.W.R. 475, 65 C.C.C. 109 (Alta); *R.* v. *Brodsky*, 43 Man. R. 522, [1936] 1 W.W.R. 177, [1936] 1 D.L.R. 578, 65 C.C.C. 4; for the regulation of individual forms of trade within a province such as marketing transactions in natural products having no connection with interprovincial or external trade, *Attorney-General for British Columbia* v. *Attorney-General for Canada*, [1937] A.C. 377; for the validation of agreements between persons in an industry as to competition in a trade within a province, *In re Trade and Industry Act*, [1936] S.C.R. 379; cf. *Attorney-General for Ontario* v. *Attorney-General for Canada*, [1937] A.C. 405; regulating the licensing of fish canneries and the trade processing of fish, *Attorney-General for Canada* v. *Attorney-General for British Columbia*, [1930] A.C. 111; for regulation of business of non-Dominion insurance companies, see V. C. MacDonald, "The Regulation of Insurance in Canada," (1946) 24 *Can. B. Rev.* 257; for the prevention of strikes and lock-outs and the settlement of industrial disputes between employers and employees, *Toronto Electric Commissioners* v. *Snider*, [1925] A.C. 396; relating to weekly rest, minimum wages, and limitation of hours of labour, *Attorney-General for Canada* v. *Attorney-General for Ontario*, [1937] A.C. 326.

[28]W. P. M. Kennedy, "The Constitution of Canada," (1937) 2 *Politica* 356.

[29]W. P. M. Kennedy, *The Constitution of Canada* (2nd ed., 1938), 550.

assert, "if anything, [the course of decisions] indicates conscious and deliberate choice of a policy which required, for its advancement, manipulations which can only with difficulty be represented as ordinary judicial techniques."[30]

Ultimately, to appraise the Privy Council's work, we must face up squarely to the question of whether judges legislate, in the sense of making conscious choices between conflicting policy alternatives. Although since the Court Revolution of 1937, few in the United States would hesitate to answer this question in the affirmative, the theory of the judicial slot-machine is still powerful in a country whose jurisprudence is dominated, as Canada's is, by the worst rigours of Austinian formalism.[31] It is not without significance that the controversy over the Privy Council's interpretation of the B.N.A. Act should all too frequently proceed in the form of a dispute over alternative rules of statutory construction, rather than in terms of the actual consequences to Canadian national life flowing from the individual decisions.

The need for a critical examination of the values employed by judges in making their decisions has been obscured all too frequently by much unproductive wrangling over the formulae in which the judges subsequently embody those values, although the varied members of the Privy Council have occasionally adverted directly to the consequences of their decisions. Thus Lord Haldane, in summing up in 1923 the work of his predecessor and mentor Lord Watson, paid eloquent tribute: "As a result of a long series of decisions, Lord Watson put clothing upon the bones of the Constitution, and so covered them over with living flesh that the Constitution of Canada took a new form. The Provinces were recognized as of equal authority co-ordinate with the Dominion, and a long series of decisions were given by him which solved many problems, and produced a new contentment in Canada with the Constitution they had got in 1867. It is difficult to say what the extent of the debt was that Canada owes to Lord Watson."[32]

It may be, indeed, that seen against a background of developing Cana-

[30]B. Laskin, " 'Peace, Order and Good Government' Re-examined," (1947) 25 *Can. B. Rev.* 1054, 1086.

[31]See, e.g., the controversy over the *Canadian Wheat Board Case*, Notes, (1951), 29 *Can. B. Rev.* 296; *ibid.* 572.

[32]"The Judicial Committee of the Privy Council," (1923) 1 *Camb. L.J.* 143, 150. This concern for provincial autonomy runs through Lord Watson's seminal opinion upon the Dominion government's general legislative power under s. 91, *Attorney-General for Ontario* v. *Attorney-General for Canada*, [1896] A.C. 348 (P.C.), especially at 360; and we find it expressed again as late as 1937 in Lord Atkin's judgment on Canada's treaty-implementing power under s. 132, *Attorney-General for Canada* v. *Attorney-General for Ontario*, [1937] A.C. 326 (P.C.) (*Hours of Labour Case*).

dian nationhood, the Privy Council's work is not entirely deserving of censure. The period from the passing of the B.N.A. Act in 1867 until 1896, represented in the judicial arena by the Privy Council decision in *Russell* v. *The Queen*[33] favouring a broad interpretation of Dominion powers even at the expense of the provinces, coincides with the dominance in the legislative arena of Sir John A. Macdonald and the Conservative party. This was the era of the "moving frontiers," when the settlers advanced ever westward and into the north, when the railway was pushed across the continent, and new provinces were progressively admitted to the Canadian confederation as the settlers' frontiers extended. It was a period when a strong centralized administration could aid and foster this expansion.

The period from 1896 onwards, however, when first of all Lord Watson, and then Lord Haldane and his successors, restricted Dominion powers in favour of provincial rights, was the period of the substantial political dominance of the Liberal party of Laurier and Mackenzie King, which depended on the French for its parliamentary majority far more than the Conservative party had ever done. It was a period introduced, appropriately enough, by the Manitoba education crisis when Laurier (a French Catholic himself) sacrificed short-range French Catholic interests in separate schools for the French Catholic minority in the province of Manitoba for the long-range safeguard to French Catholic Quebec of the autonomy of provincial administrations as against interference by the Dominion government. This is what Dean Kennedy, appropriately enough, has hailed as an "experiment in sovereignty . . . a serious contribution to the destruction of the Austinian idea. Every province is from one point of view at least—in relation to the federal government—an example of a group with a life and purpose of its own."[34]

Thus, the provincial rights plea may frequently spring in Canada from deeply rooted claims for the treatment of problems at the local level. The existence in Canada of two distinct racial groups differing radically in language, religion, and social customs points to the existence of two distinct "living laws" within the Canadian nation, perhaps requiring a more pluralist organization of national life with a large degree of policy-making located at the periphery rather than at the centre.[35] Nor has the interdiction of the Dominion government's social and economic planning legislation necessarily created a complete legislative no-man's land in these matters—for example, although the field of labour law seems effec-

[33](1882) 7 App. Cas. 829.   [34]Kennedy, *The Constitution of Canada*, 431.
[35]See the recent plea for "provincial autonomy" raised by a French-Canadian jurist, L.-P. Pigéon, "The Meaning of Provincial Autonomy," (1951) 29 *Can. B. Rev.* 1126, 1134: "[I]t is wrong to assume that the same laws are suitable for

tively barred to the Dominion government,[36] most of the provinces have in fact legislated in this field.[37] And there is also considerable scope for legislative co-operation between the Dominion government and the provinces, though the difficulties here should not be underestimated.[38] The special position of the French Canadians and the Catholic Church was recognized by the United Kingdom government as early as 1774 with the passage of the Quebec Act. The denominational schools in the provinces were given special protection under section 93 of the B.N.A. Act.[39] Even the invalidation by the Privy Council of the Canadian "New Deal" legislation introduced by the Conservative Government of Mr. R. B. Bennett (which seems to have aroused more ire among the critics than anything else)[40] was largely an academic question at the time when the decisions were given. The Conservative Government had been defeated at the general elections, and it was Mr. Mackenzie King's Liberal Government which had referred its predecessor's legislation to the courts for an opinion.

It may be that the beginning of a new favouring of Dominion legislative powers, as evidenced in Lord Sankey's "living tree" doctrine and the

all peoples. On the contrary, laws have a cultural aspect; hence due consideration should be given in framing them to the character, condition and beliefs of those for whom they are made. Autonomy is designed for the very purpose of meeting this requirement. The French-speaking population of the province of Quebec is obviously the group of Canadian citizens specially interested in it. For them autonomy is linked up with the preservation of their way of life."

For a contrary viewpoint, see F. R. Scott, "Centralisation and Decentralisation in Canadian Federalism," (1951) 29 *Can. B. Rev.* 1095. Professor Scott has recently stated the position, as he sees it, of official spokesmen of the province of Quebec, in the following terms: "Canada is seen not just as one central government and ten provincial governments, Quebec being merely one of the ten: rather is it looked upon as composed of two races, equal in status, one of which speaks through the government of Quebec and the other through Ottawa. Hence Quebec on this view is one of two governments. The notion of Canada as a dyarchy, or a dual monarchy, is implicit in much of the contemporary discussion on federal-provincial relations." Scott, "The Constitutional Background of Taxation Agreements," (1955) 2 *McGill L.J.* 1, 10.

[36]*Toronto Electric Commissioners* v. *Snider*, [1925] A.C. 396 (P.C.).
[37]See MacDonald, "The Constitution in a Changing World," (1948) 26 *Can. B. Rev.* 21, 44, and further examples there listed.
[38]*Ibid.* at 39–40.
[39]British North America Act, 1867, s. 93: "In and for each Province the Legislature may exclusively make Laws in relation to Education, subject and according to the following Provisions:—
"(1) Nothing in any such law shall prejudicially affect any Right or Privilege with respect to Denominational Schools which any Class of Persons have by Law in the Province at the Union."
[40]See especially Kennedy, "The Interpretation of the British North America Act," (1943) 8 *Camb. L.J.* 154; Kennedy, "The British North American Act: Past and Future," (1937) 15 *Can. B. Rev.* 393; V. C. MacDonald, "The Canadian Constitution Seventy Years After," (1937) 15 *Can. B. Rev.* 401; Tuck, *supra*, note 24.

cases which followed it, presages a new trend to centralization in a world rapidly shrinking under pressure of external events. But again, the situation can be overstated. If Lord Watson and Lord Haldane were consciously and overtly influenced in their approach to the interpretation of the B.N.A. Act by a bias in favour of provincial powers, their approach seems nevertheless to have been a vague, impressionistic one, without the benefit of a detailed analysis and weighing of the policy alternatives involved in each case.[41] And with these two exceptions, the composition of the Privy Council boards sitting on Canadian constitutional cases has been so varied and so changing as to make, even with the best of intentions, for only a piecemeal or erratic exertion of legislative power on the part of the judges.[42] In any case, where the history of judicial review in the United States from the Civil War onwards indicates how readily conservative-minded judges could accommodate a Constitution to the demands of corporate enterprise to be free from governmental regulation, the history of the Privy Council's interpretation of the constitutions of Dominions other than Canada is also evidence that the traditional common law hostility to statute law[43] can lend itself easily to the maintenance of political laissez-faire.[44]

[41]Laskin suggests, indeed, that Lord Haldane's views on the B.N.A. Act may have been influenced by his long apprenticeship at the Bar as counsel for the provinces of Canada in at least ten Privy Council cases. He is careful to add that Lord Haldane also made several appearances for the Dominion government. Laskin, " 'Peace, Order and Good Government' Re-examined," (1947) 25 *Can. B. Rev.* 1054, 1055.

[42]See F. R. Scott, "The Consequences of the Privy Council Decisions," (1937) 15 *Can. B. Rev.* 485, 493; MacDonald, "The Canadian Constitution Seventy Years After," (1937) 15 *Can. B. Rev.* 401, 427.

[43]Thus Amos, "The Interpretation of Statutes," (1937) 5 *Camb. L.J.* 163, 173, speaks of the "appropriate and specific adjustment of his mind" which the English judge makes when he finds himself confronted by a statute. See also W. Friedmann, *Legal Theory* (1st ed., 1944), 295.

[44]Incidentally, Kennedy, *The Constitution of Canada*, is in error in maintaining at 405–6, "The Australian High Court maintains that the Australian Constitution cannot be subject to the ordinary rules governing a British statute, which must be modified by the conception of the Constitution in the minds of the founders of the Commonwealth." This was substantially the position up to 1920, but the decision by the High Court of Australia in the *Engineers' Case* in that year (*Amalgamated Society of Engineers* v. *Adelaide Steamship Co. Ltd.*, (1920) 28 C.L.R. 109) established the pattern of interpretation for the Commonwealth Constitution that the High Court and Privy Council have followed since that time, that the Constitution is a British statute to be interpreted according to normal (restrictive) rules of statutory construction. Professor Laskin, also, seems somewhat to have overemphasized the influence of American precedents in Australian constitutional jurisprudence. Thus Laskin, "The Supreme Court of Canada: A Final Court of and for Canadians," (1951) 29 *Can. B. Rev.* 1038, 1045: "It is a paradox that Australia, which is more 'English' than Canada and less 'American', has been influenced more by 'American' decisions and less by 'English' decisions." And

What of the future? With the final abolition of the appeal from Canadian courts to the Privy Council, the Canadian Supreme Court is left as final arbiter as to the meaning of the B.N.A. Act. What will the Canadian judges do? The decisions of the Privy Council on the B.N.A. Act, coming to the Privy Council as they did on appeal from the Canadian Supreme Court, do not differ very substantially from decisions of the Canadian Supreme Court in the first instance.[45] Dean Kennedy is at some pains to absolve the Canadian Supreme Court judges from any share of responsibility for the Privy Council's decisions. "The Supreme Court is bound by the judgments of the Privy Council, and it must profess to follow them to the best of its ability. The generality of judicial methods observed by the judicial committee almost made the decisions of the supreme court inevitable."[46] This view is, however, strongly challenged by Professor Laskin. Although it is true that Chief Justice Anglin indicated opposition to the Watson-Haldane viewpoint,[47] the views of Chief Justice Sir Lyman Duff[48] are "not solely the result of the compulsion of Privy Council decisions. The 'locus classicus' accolade bestowed by the Privy Council [in 1937] on [Duff's] judgment in the *Natural Products Marketing Act* reference[49] may, in part, have been merely a self-serving tribute to a skilful and faithful exposition of its own course of decision but Sir Lyman showed, as early as the *Board of Commerce* case [in 1920],[50] that he had embarked on that course as much by his own choice as by the dictate of *stare decisis.*"[51] Even in Australia where the categories of constitutional matters that may be appealed to the Privy Council are limited by the Constitution[52] and the final appellate jurisdiction of the High Court has therefore always been considerable, it may be questioned

again, Laskin refers somewhat wistfully to the "absence in Canada of independent judicial tradition like that in Australia."

[45]But F. R. Scott, "The Privy Council and Minority Rights," (1930) 37 *Queen's Quarterly* 668, assails the "myth" that the Privy Council has been more impartial than the Canadian Supreme Court on matters of minority rights. And as to this point, see also V. C. MacDonald, "The Privy Council and the Canadian Constitution," (1951) 29 *Can. B. Rev.* 1021, 1031: "It is history that, contrary to Lord Carnarvon's hopes, the Privy Council has not been a protector of minorities so much as it has been a protector of the provinces. . . ."

[46]Kennedy, *The Constitution of Canada,* 550.

[47]See especially *In re Board of Commerce Act,* (1920) 60 S.C.R. 456; *The King v. Eastern Terminal Elevator Co.,* [1925] S.C.R. 434.

[48]See *Attorney-General for Canada* v. *Attorney-General for Ontario,* [1937] A.C. 326 (P.C.).

[49]*In re Natural Products Marketing Act,* [1936] S.C.R. 398.

[50]*In re Board of Commerce Act,* (1920) 60 S.C.R. 456.

[51]Laskin, " 'Peace, Order and Good Government' Re-examined," (1947) 25 *Can. B. Rev.* 1054, 1056; see also Laskin, "The Supreme Court of Canada: A Final Court of and for Canadians," (1951) 29 *Can. B. Rev.* 1038, 1057 *et seq.*

[52]Commonwealth of Australia Constitution, s. 74.

whether any marked pattern of divergence has appeared between the type of decisions given by the High Court on the one hand and the Privy Council on the other.

Some Canadian authorities fear that the weight of Privy Council decisions may be so heavy upon the Canadian judges as to leave them no freedom of action for the future, even now that the appeal to the Privy Council has been finally abolished; that the only way of getting around the past may be direct constitutional amendment.[53] But such a proposal ignores the fact that the Constitution, even when amended, will still be subject to judicial interpretation. If, as Professor Laskin has suggested,[54] there was nothing that was inevitable in the interpretations that were in fact made of the B.N.A. Act, it may be that no amount of amendments will avail if the judges do not want it so. Similarly I think Laskin's suggestion that members of the Canadian Supreme Court should, in the future, exercise to the full their privilege of writing separate opinions in constitutional cases[55] grasps at the form rather than at the substance. Even if they do not care to overrule a previous decision, common law judges have developed a real facility in "distinguishing" unwanted precedents; and the decisions of the Privy Council upon the B.N.A. Act make even the use of a device such as this unnecessary. For a strict holding as to Dominion legislative powers and a corresponding enlargement of the sphere of provincial powers, to which, certainly, the bulk of the decisions point, Lord Atkin's marine metaphor[56] is available for invocation; for a broad construction of Dominion powers, Lord Sankey's arboreal metaphor[57] is the magic formula.[58]

It may, in fact, be a matter of changing the judges rather than of changing the Constitution. Whatever the excellence of the decisions of

[53]Kennedy, *The Constitution of Canada*, 550–1; Kennedy, "The British North America Act: Past and Future," (1937); 15 *Can. B. Rev.* 393, 399; MacDonald, "The Constitution in a Changing World," (1948) 26 *Can. B. Rev.* 21, 45; MacDonald, "The Canadian Constitution Seventy Years After," (1937) 15 *Can. B. Rev.* 401, 425.

[54]Laskin, " 'Peace, Order and Good Government' Re-examined," (1947) 25 *Can. B. Rev.* 1054, 1086.

[55]*Ibid.* It must be noted that Laskin seems now more hopeful that the Canadian Supreme Court, as the final Canadian appellate court, might be persuaded to reverse itself: Laskin, "The Supreme Court of Canada: A Final Court of and for Canadians," (1951) 29 *Can. B. Rev.* 1038, 1069 *et seq.*

[56]*Per* Lord Atkin, *Attorney-General for Canada* v. *Attorney-General for Ontario*, [1937] A.C. 326 (P.C.).

[57]*Per* Lord Sankey, in the *Persons Case, Edwards* v. *Attorney-General for Canada*, [1930], A.C. 124, 136 (P.C.).

[58]The situations where two lines of conflicting decisions, each line yielding a different result in the instant case, are available to the judges have been classed as legal categories of competing reference, fallacies of the logical form. Julius Stone, *The Province and Function of Law* (1946), 176.

the judges of the Privy Council in the field of private law, there has been, perhaps, a certain rigidity and inflexibility in the approach of those same judges to public law questions—a product no doubt of the autonomous training and traditions of the legal profession in England and the Commonwealth, with the widespread emphasis on case law.[59] It will be interesting to see how the present judges of the Canadian Supreme Court, recruited as they were for a jurisdiction that was substantially private law at the time of their appointment, will adjust themselves to their new and extra public law responsibilities, now that the Canadian Supreme Court is the final appellate court in constitutional matters. The frank acceptance of the essentially policy-making role of a Supreme Court exercising judicial review under a written and rigid Constitution has led in the United States, especially since 1937, to a very broad basis of selection for Supreme Court justices, in which considerations of competence in purely technical legal questions play a lesser (one might almost say a minor) role; and in which the opportunity may be taken, through the working of the constitutional requirement of Senate confirmation of nominees to judicial office, to scrutinize very closely the background and the value preferences of the candidates for judicial appointment. Canadian governments have, right from the outset, recognized the importance of regional and sectional factors in making appointments to the Canadian Supreme Court,[60] and it remains to be seen whether Canada will also follow the United States pattern in looking beyond the closed ranks of the leaders of the Bar for future Supreme Court material. In that case we may yet see a law professor or two gracing the Canadian Supreme Court Bench.

The main task for the future, however, will be to develop in Canada an informed body of opinion capable of appraising and criticizing the decisions of the judges as they are handed down. There is, as yet, a real shortage of high-calibre law journals capable of undertaking such a role —this, indeed, is a condition unfortunately common to all of the common law countries except the United States. Yet legal education in Canada is at last breaking away from the fetters of professional control,[61] and far-reaching changes, therefore, may not be long in coming.

[59]Friedmann, *Legal Theory*, 295.

[60]For example, the Supreme Court Act, 1875, s. 4, provided that two judges out of a Bench of six should come from Quebec. The Supreme Court Act of 1949, in addition to its main task of abolishing the appeal to the Privy Council, increased the membership to nine judges, and at the same time provided that one-third of these judges shall come from Quebec. See generally Laskin, "The Supreme Court of Canada: A Final Court of and for Canadians," (1951) 29 *Can. B. Rev.* 1038, 1041.

[61]See C. A. Wright, "Should the Profession Control Legal Education?" (1950) 3 *J. Legal Educ.* 1.

5

LEGAL POSITIVISM AND JUDICIAL REVIEW
IN AUSTRALIA

In a speech delivered late in 1951, the then Lord Chancellor of the United Kingdom, Lord Jowitt, took the opportunity of restating, in unusually emphatic form, the positivist conception of the nature and scope of the judge's task.

> You know [said the Lord Chancellor], there was a time when the earth was void and without form, but after these hundreds of years the law of England, the common law, has at any rate got some measure of form in it. . . . The problem is not to consider what social and political conditions of to-day require; that is to confuse the task of the lawyer with the task of the legislator. It is quite possible that the law has produced a result which does not accord with the requirements of to-day. If so, put it right by legislation, but do not expect every lawyer, in addition to all his other problems, to act as Lord Mansfield did and decide what the law ought to be. He is far better employed if he puts himself to the much simpler task of deciding what the law is. . . . If this case does come to the House of Lords, if we examine it and discover that there is a case which is precisely in point, then whether we think it accords with modern requirements and conditions or whether we think it does not, we shall follow loyally the decision which has already been come to. In that way and that way only can we introduce some certainty into the law.[1]

One may, of course, have some doubts on the wisdom of pursuing as the ultimate judicial goal any single aim of introducing certainty into the law, especially where the judge concerned is sitting (as the Lord Chancellor is) as a member (and in this case the senior member) of a final appellate tribunal; it may be that on occasion "certainty" could with advantage yield to "modern requirements and conditions" where the two are in conflict. But by and large, of course, Lord Jowitt has succumbed too easily to what Judge Frank has called the "legal-certainty myth"—the illusion that law is, or can be made, unwavering, fixed, and settled, and which Judge Frank has likened to the infant's craving for the infallible

[1]Address by Viscount Jowitt to the Seventh Annual Convention of the Law Council of Australia, (1951) 25 *Aust. L.J.* 296.

authority of its father.[2] For it is precisely in deciding "what the law is" and whether or not a case actually is "precisely in point" that subjective considerations operate so strongly on the judicial choice and the way is opened for the entry of the "inarticulate major premise". In this regard, the House of Lords' habit of "distinguishing" (as distinct from overruling) unwanted precedents makes the rule of the binding force of precedents as laid down in the *London Tramways Case*[3] substantially inoperative in practice. The essential weakness of the pure positivist position in this respect, of course, is its failure to recognize that a choice is to be made, not between judicial policy-making and absence of judicial policy-making, but between policy-making based on a full investigation of the alternatives and policy-making in the dark. Nor can the Lord Chancellor's advice to "put it right by legislation" be accorded any undue weight at the present day. The history of the attempts by the British Parliament to bring the common law into line with "social and political conditions of to-day" is one of tenacious judicial opposition and time-consuming delays before Parliament could offset by further legislation the worst rigours of harsh judicial interpretation of the original statutory corrections of the common law.[4] It is unreasonable, to say the least, to expect the British Parliament today, weighted down as it is by the pressures of ordinary business of the "complex-economically-organized society"[5] that is present-day Britain, to assume the additional function of surveillance of the common law so as to make it "accord with the requirements of to-day." Lord Jowitt, whose term as Lord Chancellor began with his appointment by the postwar Labour Government and ended with its defeat, should at least be aware of that.

I

Significant as is the part played by the judges in relation to statute law in a country like the United Kingdom which has no written constitution and whose legislature is recognized to be omnipotent, it obviously still differs *toto caelo* from that of judges who are exercising judicial review under a written and rigid federal constitution, involving a division of powers between a central government and member states—as is the case, for example, with the United States and several of the countries of the Commonwealth.

The scheme of division of legislative powers made under the Australian

[2]Frank, *Law and the Modern Mind* (1930), 20.
[3]*London Street Tramways Company* v. *London County Council*, [1898] A.C. 375.
[4]C. K. Allen, *Law in the Making* (5th ed., 1951), 472-3.
[5]The term used in S. P. Simpson and Julius Stone, *Law and Society* (1950).

Constitution Act resembles the American model somewhat more closely than does that of the Canadian Constitution. Section 51 of the Australian Constitution confers on the Commonwealth (that is, national) Parliament power to legislate "for the peace, order, and good government of the Commonwealth" with respect to a list of 40 classes of subjects. The Constitution does not specifically and in terms provide for the allocation of the residue of legislative powers, but it has been assumed right from the outset that these remain with the states. Under section 109, Commonwealth laws prevail over inconsistent state laws and the latter are, to the extent of the inconsistency, invalid. There is no formal bill of rights written into the Constitution.

So far as more strictly federal matters are concerned, that is to say matters involving the division of legislative powers between the Commonwealth and the states, the Australian courts showed some disposition, early, to flirt with the American doctrine of the immunity of instrumentalities, with its implied prohibition upon either state or federal governments' legislating against the other.[6] This doctrine, however, was soon perceived by the courts to be unnecessarily fettering and restrictive in its operation on both Commonwealth and states, and was soon abandoned.[7]

The most significant developments affecting the constitutional distribution of legislative powers between Commonwealth and states have occurred during time of war. During these periods there has been a sustained and marked expansion of the area and extent of Commonwealth legislative powers, always at the expense of the states. In time of war, as Mr. Justice (later Chief Justice) Isaacs noted during the course of World War I, the Commonwealth defence power becomes the "pivot of the Constitution, because it is the bulwark of the State," having a kind of overriding force in relation to the rest of the Constitution.[8] The apogee of beneficial judicial construction of Commonwealth legislative powers was the *Uniform Taxation* decision during World War II[9] when the courts held that the Commonwealth could validly move so as to exclude the states altogether from the field of income taxation, the decision being rested by the judges not merely on the Commonwealth's legislative power over defence, but also upon the Commonwealth's general taxation powers allied with the provision in section 109 of the Constitution for the supremacy of Commonwealth laws over inconsistent state

---

[6]See, for example, *D'Emden* v. *Pedder*, (1904) 1 C.L.R. 91, applying *McCulloch* v. *Maryland*, (1819) 4 Wheat. 316 and *Collector* v. *Day*, (1870) 11 Wall. 113.

[7]*Amalgamated Society of Engineers* v. *Adelaide Steamship Co.* (*The Engineers' Case*), (1920) 28 C.L.R. 129. For attempt at a qualified revival of the doctrine, somewhat in accord with the principle of *New York* v. *U.S.*, (1946) 326 U.S. 572, see *Melbourne Corporation* v. *Commonwealth*, (1947) 74 C.L.R. 31.

[8]*Farey* v. *Burvett*, (1916) 21 C.L.R. 433, 453.

[9]*South Australia* v. *Commonwealth*, (1942) 65 C.L.R. 373.

laws; with the necessary consequence that the Commonwealth power in this regard availed in peacetime as well as in war.

Now it might, perhaps, have been expected that, in those Commonwealth countries (Canada and Australia) whose constitutional systems are patterned to a substantial extent on that of the United States, the judges in the highest appellate tribunals at least might have come round to an approach somewhat similar to that now followed by the United States Supreme Court with the direct and open canvassing of the merits of the alternative lines of action in any decision. Yet this has not proved to be the case. The Canadian Constitution, as interpreted by the Privy Council and by the Canadian Supreme Court, has been treated as an ordinary statute as distinct from a constitution, and to be construed according to the ordinary (restrictive) canons of statutory construction. The Australian Constitution, likewise, notwithstanding the short-lived judicial disposition to invoke the American doctrine of the immunity of instrumentalities, has been ruled to be a British statute and to be interpreted as such, without regard to American constitutional experience.[10] Not merely is there no recognition of the essentially creative, legislative role of a judge exercising the power of judicial review of a written constitutional instrument, but we even find judges like Mr. Justice Dixon of the High Court of Australia, who has, indeed, only recently been promoted as Chief Justice in succession to Sir John Latham, laying down their own philosophies of action in terms as baldly positivist as Lord Jowitt's conception of his own office. Sir Owen Dixon, indeed, is not without some acquaintance with the United States Supreme Court's work, having spent the wartime years in Washington as ambassador to the United States while on leave from the Australian High Court bench. Yet he made the ceremony at which he was sworn in as Chief Justice, following his recent promotion to that office, the occasion for a stern rebuke to those who had criticized the High Court of Australia as being excessively "legalistic." As the Chief Justice asserted:

It is not sufficiently recognised that the Court's sole function is to interpret a constitutional description of power or restraint upon power and say whether a given measure falls on one side of a line consequently drawn or on the other, and that it has nothing whatever to do with the merits or demerits of the measure. Such a function has led us all I think to believe that close adherence to legal reasoning is the only way to maintain the confidence of all parties in Federal conflicts. It may be that the Court is thought to be excessively legalistic. I should be sorry to think that it is anything else. There is no other safe guide to judicial decisions in great conflicts than a strict and complete legalism.[11]

[10]*Amalgamated Society of Engineers* v. *Adelaide Steamship Company*, (1920) 28 C.L.R. 129.   [11]Reported in (1952) 26 *Aust. L.J.* 2, at 4.

Just what a "strict and complete legalism" means to Sir Owen Dixon is amply indicated by the approach of the High Court of Australia several years back to the question of the constitutionality of the legislation of the Labour Government nationalizing the private trading banks. The High Court chose to ignore altogether the extensive economic material submitted in their briefs by the respective parties to the case, and in a decision[12] running into many hundreds of pages purported to derive the *ratio* of its decision from the past cases alone, unilluminated by any such economic evidence; although, as the Privy Council was shortly to admit when the case went up to it on appeal,[13] in constitutional cases of that nature "The problem to be solved will often be not so much legal as political, social, or economic."[14] The special character of the High Court's decision in the *Bank Nationalization Case*[15] is indicated by the fact that the nub of the decision was that the federal legislation there in question violated the guarantee contained in the first paragraph of section 92 of the Australian Constitution: "On the imposition of uniform duties of customs, trade, commerce, and intercourse among the States, whether by means of internal carriage or ocean navigation, shall be absolutely free."

Now it seems clear from an examination of the intentions of the drafters of the Constitution that this section was designed simply to eliminate the problem of border tariffs which had so plagued the six prefederation Australian colonies—the "barbarism of borderism" as it has been called;[16] a conclusion which a reading of the second paragraph of section 92[17] and also a reading of section 92 in its context in the Constitution[18] would appear to confirm. It was held originally by the courts that section 92 was addressed only to the states—that state legislation only and not Commonwealth legislation could be struck down as violative of section 92. In 1936 this view was reversed, and section 92 for the first time was held to apply to the Commonwealth as well as to the states,[19] the occasion

[12]*Bank of New South Wales* v. *Commonwealth*, (1948) 76 C.L.R. 1.

[13]*Commonwealth* v. *Bank of New South Wales*, (1949) 79 C.L.R. 497 (P.C.).

[14]*Ibid.*, 639.

[15]See generally Julius Stone, "A Government of Laws and Yet of Men: The Australian Commerce Power," (1950) 25 *N.Y.U.L.R.* 451.

[16]See generally F. R. Beasley, "S. 92: Its History in the Federal Conventions," (1948) 1 *U. of W.A.L.R.* 97 *et seq.*

[17]"But notwithstanding anything in this Constitution, goods imported before the imposition of uniform duties of customs into any State, or into any Colony which, whilst the goods remain therein, becomes a State, shall, on thence passing into another State within two years after the imposition of such duties, be liable to any duty chargeable on the importation of such goods into the Commonwealth, less any duty paid in respect of the goods on their importation."

[18]Thus the whole of c. IV of the Constitution (ss. 81–105), and especially ss. 86 to 95, appear to manifest a transitory purpose.

[19]*James* v. *Commonwealth*, [1936] A.C. 578 (P.C.).

for this judicial *volte-face* being a successful challenge to Commonwealth legislation establishing a marketing scheme controlling the production of primary products. As the Courts had previously, in terms of section 92, outlawed state legislation imposing marketing quotas, the end result by 1936 was to create a legislative no-man's land, so far as organization and control of primary production was concerned, into which neither Commonwealth nor states might enter. From the original rather modest purpose at the time of the drafting of the Constitution in the 1890's, indeed, conceptions of the content and scope of section 92 had developed sufficiently over half a century to provide by 1949, as we have noted, the doctrinal basis for the Court's invalidating Commonwealth legislation nationalizing the private trading banks. The effect has been to impose on both Commonwealth and state governments, in the name of freedom of trade, commerce, and intercourse among the states, an effective legal barrier against social and economic planning legislation. Now the elaborate superstructure of propositions which successive judges of the High Court of Australia have built over the years upon section 92 of the Constitution, with the effect of turning it into a protective umbrella shielding commerce and business generally from federal and state governmental regulation, though it may be able to be justified on broad policy grounds, can clearly, therefore, in no way be brought within the compass of a "strict and complete legalism" on the part of the judges. It is perhaps characteristic that the judges of the High Court of Australia should, in the spirit of Herbert Spencer's social statics, have converted section 92 of the Australian Constitution into an "Australian due process clause" while at the same time refusing to admit that social and economic considerations have any place in constitutional law adjudication.

II

The curiously unsophisticated attitude towards social and economic evidence that the judges of the High Court of Australia showed in the *Bank Nationalization Case* is paralleled by the judges' handling of questions of fact in the recent litigation[20] resulting from the Communist Party Dissolution Act.[21] The statute in question was introduced

[20]*Australian Communist Party* v. *Commonwealth*, (1951) 83 C.L.R. 1. This case may be compared with *Dennis* v. *United States*, (1951) 341 U.S. 494, in which the Supreme Court of the United States sustained the conviction of the eleven Communist party leaders for violation of the Smith Act. The principal constitutional issue raised in the *Dennis Case* was whether the Smith Act either inherently or else as construed and applied in the instant case violated the First Amendment; this gave the Supreme Court the opportunity also of re-examining the "clear and present danger" test as laid down by Holmes J. in *Schenck* v. *United States*, (1919) 249 U.S. 47, and subsequently developed in *Gitlow* v. *New York*, (1925) 268 U.S. 652 and later cases.
[21]No. 16 of 1950.

by a Conservative Coalition Government with the stated aim of dissolving the Australian Communist party and also of preventing communists and persons of communist affiliation from holding office in trade unions and from being employed in government service.[22] In view of the absence of any specific bill of rights under the Australian Constitution,[23] the question of a possible infringement of civil liberties as such could not be directly canvassed as a legal issue in the case. Such civil rights arguments as did come up in the case in fact could only arise interstitially and had to be subsumed under some more general non-civil rights sections of the Constitution, in this case that section of the Constitution investing the federal government with legislative power concerning the "naval and military defence of the Commonwealth."[24]

[22]For a discussion of the details of the Act and also a survey of the political events preceding its passage by the Australian Parliament, see F. R. Beasley, "Australia's Communist Party Dissolution Act," (1951) 29 *Can. B. Rev.* 490; see also Note, "Constitutional Law, Constitutions of Other Countries, Act Dissolving Australian Communist Party Held Unconstitutional," (1951) 65 *Harv. L. Rev.* 343.

[23]Note, however, s. 116 of the Constitution: "The Commonwealth shall not make any laws for establishing any religion, or for imposing any religious observance, or for prohibiting the free exercise of any religion, and no religious test shall be required as a qualification for any office or public trust under the Commonwealth"; and s. 117: "A subject . . . resident in any State, shall not be subject in any other State to any disability or discrimination which would not be equally applicable to him if he were a subject . . . resident in such other State"; and s. 80: "The trial on indictment of any offence against any law of the Commonwealth shall be by jury."

These sections have, however, only rarely been invoked in constitutional litigation. S. 80, indeed, has been rendered virtually inoperative by the High Court's interpretation of the section as requiring trial by jury only if Parliament prescribes a trial procedure which is, or which Parliament chooses to call, an "indictment": *R.* v. *Archdale*, (1928) 41 C.L.R. 128; *R.* v. *Federal Court of Bankruptcy, ex p. Lowenstein*, (1938) 59 C.L.R. 555. Parliament is thus able to evade s. 80 by prescribing some other procedure, such as summary prosecution.

The Commonwealth's power of acquisition of property under s. 51 (xxxi) from any state or any person, for any purpose in respect of which Parliament has power to make laws, is subject to the limitation that the acquisition must be "on just terms." All six judges of the High Court sitting in the *Bank Nationalization Case*, (1948) 76 C.L.R. 1, were agreed that the Commonwealth Act there in question violated the "just terms" requirement annexed to s. 51 (xxxi), the judges' unanimity on this point being quite striking in view of their conflict as to the other points raised in the legal argument. It has been held that even legislation under the defence power of the Constitution, when it involves the acquisition of property, is subject to the limitations imposed by s. 51 (xxxi); so that the Commonwealth must pay "just terms" even for property taken for defence purposes: *Johnson, Fear, and Kingham and the Offset Printing Company* v. *The Commonwealth*, (1943) 67 C.L.R. 314. And, of course, note also the operation of s. 92 of the Constitution, under the extended interpretation given to it by the High Court.

[24]S. 51 (vi). In particular it will be noted that apart from s. 116 (*supra*), there is nothing in the Australian Constitution corresponding to the First Amendment

From the federal government's viewpoint, the problem, in order to establish the relationship of the challenged legislation to its defence power, was to get the Court to take notice of such facts as might give the defence power an expanded ambit—in general, the "cold war" in Europe and Asia and more particularly the activities of the Communist party in Australia. The submission of evidence directly in the brief, in the form of affidavits and other statements, had apparently been abandoned as an effective means of persuading the Court to take judicial notice of facts, after the very scant treatment accorded to such evidence in the *Bank Nationalization Case* by both the High Court and the Privy Council.

In drafting the Communist Party Dissolution Act, the federal government relied first of all on the use of legislative recitals as averments of fact, the statute[25] making use of a series of recitals containing the following allegations of fact:

(1) That the Australian Communist Party, in accordance with the basic theory of Communism as expounded by Marx and Lenin, engaged in activities designed to assist or accelerate the coming of a revolutionary situation in which, acting as a revolutionary minority it would be able to seize power and establish a dictatorship of the proletariat;

(2) That it engaged in activities or operations designed to overthrow or to dislocate the established system of government and to procure the attainment of economic, industrial or political ends by force, violence, intimidation, or fraudulent practices;

(3) That it was an integral part of the world Communist revolutionary movement, which engaged in espionage and sabotage and activities of a treasonable or subversive nature;

(4) That certain industries were vital to the security and defence of Australia (including coal-mining, iron and steel, engineering, building, transport, and power);

(5) That the activities or operations of the Communist Party were designed to cause by means of strikes, stoppages of work, and had by these means caused dislocation, disruption, or retardation of production or work in those industries.

In a preliminary hearing Mr. Justice Dixon referred to the Full Court of the High Court two questions for consideration: (*a*) Does the decision of the validity or invalidity of the provisions of the Communist Party Dissolution Act depend upon a judicial determination or ascertainment of the facts or any of them stated in the recitals of the preamble of that Act and denied by the plaintiffs (the Australian Communist party and

---

of the United States Constitution. Specifically, there is no guarantee of any kind in the Australian Constitution against laws "abridging the freedom of speech. or of the press," such as is found in the First Amendment of the United States Constitution.

[25]Communist Party Dissolution Act, No. 16 of 1950.

others)? and (*b*) Are the plaintiffs entitled to adduce evidence in support of their denial of the facts so stated in order to establish that the Act is outside the legislative power of the Commonwealth?

At the hearing by the Full Court of the High Court,[26] five of the six majority justices (Dixon, McTiernan, Williams, Fullagar, and Kitto) of the High Court answered both questions in the negative. These judges were all agreed that the recitals in the Act did not assist the Court. How, then, was the Court to become apprized of facts which might give the defence power an expanded ambit? Such matters, in Mr. Justice Fullager's opinion, were matters for judicial notice or they were nothing.[27] For his own part, Mr. Justice Dixon thought that members of the Court might

rely on a knowledge of the general nature and development of the accepted tenets or doctrines of Communism as a political philosophy, ascertained or verified, not from the polemics of the subject, but from serious studies and inquiries and historical narratives. We may take into account the course of open and notorious international events of a public nature. And, with respect to our own country, matters of common knowledge and experience are open to us. But we are not entitled to inform ourselves of and take into our consideration particular features of the Constitution of the Union of Socialist Soviet Republics.[28]

Mr. Justice McTiernan thought that the Court might take judicial notice of the fact that Communists of the Lenin-Marx school manifest strong sympathy with the Soviet and sharp antagonism to the existing social and political orders and are desirous of overthrowing them;[29] while Mr. Justice Kitto was prepared to take judicial notice of the fact that in October, 1950, international tension had reached a point of real danger to Australia and that the possibility of a war breaking out in the near future was by no means to be overlooked.[30] But even so, he thought, that was not enough.

As to the recitals in the Act, then, these five majority justices were agreed that these did not assist the Court. *Prima facie,* no opinion of Parliament as to the actual existence or occurrence of some matter or event which would provide a specific relation of the subject of a law with power could suffice to give that relation (*per* Dixon J.).[31] In a period of grave emergency, perhaps, the opinion of Parliament would be sufficient, but not in time of peace, or when there was no immediate or present danger of war (*per* McTiernan J.).[32] Mr. Justice Williams, indeed, thought that where the constitutional validity of an act was an issue the recitals could not be more than a statement of the reasons why Parliament

[26]*Australian Communist Party* v. *Commonwealth*, (1951) 83 C.L.R. 1.
[27]*Ibid.*, 267.   [28]*Ibid.*, 196.   [29]*Ibid.*, 210.
[30]*Ibid.*, 277.   [31]*Ibid.*, 200.   [32]*Ibid.*, 206–7.

enacted the law—they indicated to the Court what Parliament believed to be the constitutional basis of the act.[33]

These five majority justices thus restricted the range of facts to which the Court might have recourse, in determining whether the ambit of the defence power could be extended to include the present Act, to those facts of which the Court was able to take judicial notice. And beyond the limited categories of facts enumerated above, no further enlightenment was provided as to the facts of which the Court did take judicial notice in the instant case.

Three of the majority judges (Dixon, McTiernan, and Williams, JJ.) in fact proceeded to arrive at their decision by applying, in effect, a "pith and substance" test.[34] In substance, the present Act was one relating to property and civil rights and not to defence, and since property and civil rights were matters outside the powers of the Commonwealth under the Constitution, the Act was therefore unconstitutional. That was not to say, however, that such legislation could not be valid in the future: in time of war or grave emergency, an act having the nature and effects of the present Act could be upheld as valid legislation under the defence power.[35]

In this view, the decision on which side of the property and civil rights–defence dichotomy a particular piece of legislation will fall turns on the state of contemporary international and national affairs, essentially a factual question. One might say, as the Privy Council did in the *Bank Nationalization Case,* that the answer will be not so much legal as political, social, and economic.[36] But the ultimate decision that the High Court here gave, as with the decision that the Privy Council itself gave in the *Bank Nationalization Case,* proceeds on a purely verbal basis.

Somewhat curiously, two of the majority justices (Fullager and Kitto JJ.) seem to have rested their decision on the ground that the Commonwealth had not affirmatively proved the relationship of the challenged Act to a specific head of legislative power. Since Mr. Justice Fullager, in particular, at once rejected any notion of a presumption of validity for the Commonwealth Act,[37] and at the same time excluded any question of validity depending on evidence,[38] the task of a national government, forced affirmatively to justify legislation, must remain rather baffling.

---

[33]*Ibid.,* 224.

[34]See especially *ibid., per* Dixon J., 200; *per* McTiernan J., 206–7; *per* Williams J., 226–7.

[35]See especially *ibid., per* Dixon J., 202; *per* McTiernan J., 206; *per* Williams J., 227.

[36](1949) 79 C.L.R. 497, 639.   [37](1951) 83 C.L.R. 1, 262.

[38]*Ibid.,* 256.

Mr. Justice Williams in part recognized this particular difficulty by, in effect, conceding the necessity "during hostilities" of according the widest possible latitude of discretion to Parliament and the executive—in that period the Court should uphold the legislation if "the measure questioned may conceivably in such circumstances even incidentally aid the effectuation of the power of defence."[39] This may, of course, be sound public policy, but such a judicial attitude can hardly be reconciled with that "strict and complete legalism" which Sir Owen Dixon has laid down as the sole function of the High Court.

Rather different to his colleagues' views was the approach of the sixth member of the group of majority justices. Mr. Justice Webb (like Dixon, McTiernan, and Williams, JJ.) seems to have regarded the problem as one of choosing between defence and civil liberties in classifying the Act for purposes of the exertion of legislative power.[40] Like Mr. Justice Williams, Mr. Justice Webb also saw the difficulties of the Court in attempting to revise the judgment of Parliament which, in his view, probably would be made, and properly so, on materials not admissible in evidence, a task for which a court was not in any case qualified.[41] However, he thought that the onus of proving that the Act was within power was upon those affirming its validity, and that the burden of proof of constitutionality could not be shifted by resorting to recitals: by putting the evidence and argument in recitals instead of to the courts. It was for the courts to examine and determine the question of constitutionality when that was challenged, and for those who affirmed constitutionality to "prove it in the ordinary way."[42] Mr. Justice Webb was not prepared to hold that the statements in the recitals involving the Australian Communist party were notoriously true and judicially noticed, though the High Court could pay regard to a public situation of emergency, so far

[39]*Ibid.*, 223.   [40]*Ibid.*, 240.

[41]*Ibid.*, 243. Compare Jackson J. in *Dennis* v. *United States*, (1951) 341 U.S. 494, 570: "If we must decide that this Act and its application are constitutional only if we are convinced that petitioner's conduct creates a 'clear and present danger' of violent overthrow, we must appraise imponderables, including international and national phenomena which baffle the best informed foreign offices and our most experienced politicians. We would have to foresee and predict the effectiveness of Communist propaganda, opportunities for infiltration, whether, and when, a time will come that they consider propitious for action, and whether and how fast our existing Government will deteriorate. And we would have to speculate as to whether an approaching Communist coup would not be anticipated by a nationalistic fascist movement. No doctrine can be sound whose application requires us to make a prophesy of that sort in the guise of a legal decision. The judicial process simply is not adequate to a trial of such far-flung issues. The answers given would reflect our own political predilections and nothing more."

[42]*Ibid.*, 244. Contrast with this Jackson J.'s solution of the judicial "fact-finding" problem, in *Dennis* v. *United States*, (1951) 341 U.S. 494, 567–570, by

as it was judicially noticed, and its effect on the contents of the defence power.[43]

In the end result, Mr. Justice Webb felt that the decision of the question of the validity or invalidity of the Act depended on a judicial determination or ascertainment of the facts without any limitation by the recitals. He had no doubt that the plaintiffs (the Australian Communist party and others) would be entitled to adduce evidence to establish that the banning of the Communist party was outside the legislative power of the Commonwealth;[44] but in any case, in the absence of evidence by the Commonwealth in support of the Act, the Act was invalid.[45]

Mr. Justice Webb thus seems to envisage the formal submission to the Court and the examination by it of some such type of evidence as the Court chose to ignore in the *Bank Nationalization Case*. The way thus seems opened by Mr. Justice Webb for the introduction of the Brandeis Brief into Australian constitutional jurisprudence.[46] By contrast to Mr.

---

simply refusing to apply the "clear and present danger" test to the instant case: "The 'clear and present danger' test was an innovation by Mr. Justice Holmes in the Schenck case, reiterated and refined by him and Mr. Justice Brandeis in later cases, all arising before the era of World War II revealed the subtlety and efficacy of modernised revolutionary techniques used by totalitarian parties. . . . [The test's] recent expansion has extended, in particular to Communists, unprecedented immunities. Unless we are to hold our Government captive in a judge-made verbal trap, we must approach the problem of a well-organised, nation-wide conspiracy, such as I have described, as realistically as our predecessors faced the trivialities that were being prosecuted until they were checked with a rule of reason. I think reason is lacking for applying that test to this case. . . . The authors of the clear and present danger test never applied it to a case like this, nor would I. If applied as it is proposed here, it means that the Communist plotting is protected during its period of incubation: its preliminary stages of organisation and preparation are immune from the law; the Government can move only after imminent action is manifest, when it would, of course, be too late."

43(1951) 83 C.L.R. 1, 244.   44*Ibid.*, 248.

45*Ibid.* Compare Douglas J., dissenting, in *Dennis* v. *United States*, (1951) 341 U.S. 494, 589–90: "The political impotence of the Communists in this country does not, of course, dispose of the problem. Their numbers, their positions in industry and government; the extent to which they have in fact infiltrated the police, the armed services, transportation, stevedoring, power plants, munitions works, and other critical places—these facts all bear on the likelihood that their advocacy of the Soviet theory of revolution will endanger the Republic. But the record is silent on these facts. If we are to proceed on the basis of judicial notice, it is impossible for me to say that the Communists in this country are so potent or so strategically deployed that they must be suppressed for their speech. . . . This is my view if we are to act on the basis of judicial notice. But the mere statement of the opposing views indicates how important it is that we know the facts before we act. . . . On this record no one can say that petitioners and their converts are in such a strategic position as to have even the slightest chance of achieving their aims."

46As first employed by Brandeis, as counsel, in *Muller* v. *Oregon*, (1908) 208 U.S. 412. It must be noted, however, that even the employment of the Brandeis

Justice Webb's approach, the basic contradiction in the approach of the other majority justices to solution of the instant case lies in the fact that, while they refuse to apply to legislation passed by the Commonwealth government any presumption of constitutionality of the type in effect applied by the United States Supreme Court to congressional statutes, since the Court Revolution of 1937 at least,[47] and as Chief Justice

---

Brief is not without its hazards. Thus P. A. Freund, *On Understanding the Supreme Court* (1949), 82 *et seq.*, has noted that there is a risk, from the governmental viewpoint, in following the Brandeis Brief technique and offering detailed statistical and technical evidence to the Court, that the Court may be unconsciously tempted to decide the case as if the burden of sustaining the statute were upon the proponent of the statute, that is, without the benefit of any presumption of constitutionality for the statute. The dilemma of the Australian government, which, unlike the United States government, has never had the benefit in respect to its legislation of any presumption of constitutionality by the Court, is therefore proportionately increased.

[47]The operation of the presumption of constitutionality in the United States has, however, been somewhat obscured in recent years by the tendency to assume that the guarantee of freedom of speech contained in the First Amendment, and by incorporation in the Fourteenth Amendment, occupies a "preferred position" in the Constitution. The notion of the "preferred position" of the free speech guarantee seems to have stemmed from dicta by Stone J. in *U.S.* v. *Carolene Products*, (1938) 304 U.S. 144, 152 n. 4, and it is manifested in cases raising free speech considerations, by a refusal on the part of the Court to show that deference to the legislative judgment that it now normally accords to Congress, in applying the presumption of constitutionality to its statutes.

The notion of the "preferred position" of the First Amendment was attacked by Frankfurter J. in *Kovacs* v. *Cooper*, (1949) 336 U.S. 77, and again in the *Dennis Case*, (1951) 341 U.S. 494, at 526, as having been put forward in the first place in the *Carolene Products Case* "with the casualness of a foot-note." As Frankfurter J. goes on to add, in the *Dennis Case*, at 540: "On occasion we have strained to interpret legislation in order to limit its effects on interests protected by the First Amendment. . . . But in no case has a majority of this Court held that a legislative judgment, even as to freedom of utterance, may be overturned merely because the Court would have made a different choice between the competing interests had the initial legislative judgment been for it to make. In the cases in which the opinions go farthest towards indicating a total rejection of respect for legislative determinations, the interests between which choice was actually made were such that decision might well have been expressed in the familiar terms of want of reason in the legislative judgment." *Semble*, too, Jackson J., in dispensing with the "clear and present danger" test so far as his decision in the *Dennis Case* is concerned (*supra*, n. 42), is prepared on this occasion at least to apply virtually an absolute presumption of validity to the congressional legislation in question, despite the First Amendment.

For reiteration of the "preferred position" of the First Amendment, however, see Black J.'s dissent in the *Dennis Case* (*ibid.*, 580–1): "I have always believed that the First Amendment is the keystone of our Government, that the freedoms it guarantees provide the best insurance against destruction of all freedom. . . . So long as this Court exercises the power of judicial review of legislation, I cannot agree that the First Amendment permits us to sustain laws suppressing freedom of speech and press on the basis of Congress' or our own notions of mere 'reasonableness'. Such a doctrine waters down the First Amendment so that it amounts to little more than an admonition to Congress."

Latham, the lone dissentient in the present case, was apparently prepared to do,[48] they refuse also to admit or consider evidence that might serve to establish a relationship between the Commonwealth legislation and the heads of Commonwealth power in pursuance of which that legislation purports to have been enacted. For although (as Mr. Justice Fullagar himself admitted in his judgment)[49] in two constitutional cases in the past[50] the High Court did in fact admit evidence as to economic facts, it will now "normally" confine itself solely to matters of which judicial notice can be taken.[51] Yet for the question—what are those matters of which the Court can take judicial notice?—the standard formula is Dixon J.'s prescription in *Stenhouse* v. *Coleman*: "Ordinarily the Court does not go beyond matters of which it may take judicial notice. This

[48]Chief Justice Latham, in spite of a long career as a Conservative political leader prior to his appointment as Chief Justice, showed during his terms as Chief Justice, in marked contrast to his brother justices, a strong tendency to broad or beneficial construction of the federal government's legislative powers.

Thus during the recent war, in passing upon the uniform taxation laws of the wartime Labour Government of the Commonwealth, he upheld the power of the Commonwealth to withdraw the field of income taxation entirely from the states, basing the legislative competence of the Commonwealth upon its general powers, as well as upon the wartime defence power as his brother justices preferred to do, with the important consequence that in Latham's view the uniform tax laws would be valid even when continued into peace time (*South Australia* v. *Commonwealth*, (1942) 65 C.L.R. 373). And again in the *Bank Nationalization Case*, although with the rest of the Court Latham found the Labour Government's legislation to be invalid, he rested his decision upon the nature of the compensation afforded under the legislation to the shareholders in the private trading banks, being quite prepared to hold the key provisions to be within the Commonwealth's legislative powers. The importance of Latham's ground of decision lies in the fact that he did not oppose any absolute bar to nationalization, as the constitutional requirements for compensation annexed to the government's power of eminent domain (s. 51 (xxxi) of the Constitution) require the provision of "just terms," a problem that could be met ultimately by redrafting any nationalization legislation rejected on this ground (*Bank of New South Wales* v. *Commonwealth*, (1948) 76 C.L.R. 1).

In the *Communist Party Case*, Chief Justice Latham seems finally to have arrived at a presumption of constitutionality in favor of the Commonwealth. As his dissenting judgment notes, (*Australian Communist Party* v. *Commonwealth*, (1951) 83 C.L.R. 1, 154): ". . . It is not for a court (either at the present stage of these cases, or at any later stage) to ask or to answer the question whether or not it agrees with the view of Parliament that the Australian Communist Parliament Party and organisations and persons associated with it are enemies of the country. It is for the Government and Parliament to determine that question, and they have already determined it. Whether they are right or wrong is a political matter upon which the electors, and not any court, can pass judgment. The only question for a court, therefore, is whether the provisions of the Act have a real connection with the activities and possibilities which Parliament has said in its opinion do exist and do create a danger to Australia."

[49]83 C.L.R. 1, 256.

[50]*Jenkins* v. *Commonwealth*, (1947) 74 C.L.R. 400; *Sloan* v. *Pollard*, (1947) 75 C.L.R. 445.   [51]See *per* Fullagar J., 83 C.L.R. 1, 256.

means that for its facts the Court must depend upon matters of general public knowledge."[52] In fact (as, indeed, the curiously assorted range of matters of which the High Court did take judicial notice in the instant case indicates), this is a circular definition that will allow the Court to take notice of whatever it so desires.

III

As we have already noted, while the ideal of a "strict and complete legalism" as sponsored so enthusiastically by Mr. Justice Dixon could result in the High Court's refusing, as it did in the *Bank Nationalization Case,* to weigh expert economic evidence submitted by both sides as to the pros and cons of central banking in the semi-planned economy of present-day Australia, this did not prevent the judges in their end decision from giving a pure laissez-faire interpretation to that "freedom" of trade, commerce, and intercourse among the states supposedly guaranteed by section 92 of the Australian Constitution. As a result of the High Court's exclusion of expert evidence in the *Bank Nationalization Case,* the range of economic facts available to the judges was no broader than their own background and experience. It is trite to observe that, on the present specialist basis of training and recruitment of members of the judiciary in the United Kingdom and the Commonwealth countries, judicial expertise does not extend today to an acquaintance with Keynesian economics. But while, according to the doctrines of the classical economists, nationalization of the trading banks might seem to impair "freedom" of trade, commerce, and intercourse among the states, the Keynesian economist might well claim that that extension of governmental control over credit and investment that is necessarily bound up in any such nationalization legislation would, by promoting stability in the national economy, augment rather than impair the scope of the "freedom" that has been held to be guaranteed by section 92. The point is that whichever premise —Classical-economics or Keynesian-economics—is adopted by the decision-maker automatically determines the result of the case.

The Privy Council indeed seems to have partly conceded this fact, for, after making the observation that in constitutional cases the issue to be solved will often be not so much legal as political, social, or economic, its judgment in the *Bank Nationalization Case* goes on to record:

Every case must be judged on its own facts and in its own setting of time and circumstance, and it may be that in regard to some economic activities and at some stage of social development it might be maintained that prohibition with a view of State monopoly was the only practical and reasonable manner

[52](1944) 69 C.L.R. at 469.

of regulation and that inter-State trade commerce and intercourse thus prohibited and thus monopolized remained absolutely free.[53]

Though this was not in fact the basis on which the Privy Council itself ultimately proceeded in arriving at its decision in the *Bank Nationalization Case,* it is clear that it might have done so and still arrived at the same end result. But the decision would then have been based upon a full and frank consideration of the policy alternatives against a background of the available economic evidence.

Of the judges of the High Court of Australia, only Chief Justice Latham appears to have grasped the full implications of the Privy Council dicta in the *Bank Nationalization Case* as to the relevance of political, social, and economic questions in constitutional decisions; though the Chief Justice seems rather to have overshot the mark by concluding that these dicta sought to authorize a sort of general *Freirechtslehre,* instead of being directed, as, it is submitted, the Privy Council opinion clearly indicates, to the determination of the factual question whether or not the "freedom" supposedly guaranteed by section 92 of the Constitution is infringed or not.

I am aware [said the Chief Justice] that it is sometimes said that legal questions before the High Court should be determined upon sociological grounds—political, economic, or social. . . . But such a proposition as, for example, that the recent Banking case should have been determined upon political grounds and that the Court was wrong in adopting an attitude of detachment from all political considerations appears to me merely to ask the Court to vote again upon an issue upon which electors and Parliament had already voted or could be asked to vote, and to determine whether the nationalization of banks would be a good thing or a bad thing for the community. In my opinion the Court has no concern whatever with any such question.[54]

Nevertheless, in rejecting, in the *Communist Party Case,* the idea that the Court should permit the parties to adduce evidence as to political, social, or economic facts, Chief Justice Latham also rejected the suggestion that the doctrine of judicial notice was an adequate substitute means whereby the Court might become apprized of facts:

The limitation of the principle of judicial notice to facts which are notorious —which are so clear that no evidence is required to establish them—appears to me to prevent a court from ever reaching a conclusion based only upon such facts with respect to an issue of actual or potential public danger calling for the exercise of the legislative powers now under consideration.[55]

[53]*Commonwealth* v. *Bank of New South Wales,* (1949) 79 C.L.R. 497, 639 (P.C.).
[54]*Australian Communist Party* v. *Commonwealth,* (1951) 83 C.L.R. 1, 148–9.
[55]*Ibid.,* 163.

The way out of the impasse for Chief Justice Latham was, in effect, for the Court to apply a presumption of constitutionality.[56] By contrast, Mr. Justice Webb (as we have mentioned earlier), seems to have envisaged the formal submission of evidence to the Court by the parties to the case and the examination of that evidence by the Court. The remaining judges in the *Communist Party Case,* however, seem not to have been aware that a fact-finding problem existed, and to have rested on the judicial notice doctrine, with all the risks necessarily attendant thereto that the decision will turn on an inarticulate major premise.

Something very like this, indeed, seems to have taken place with the judgments of the majority justices (apart from Webb J.) in the *Communist Party Case.* Thus we find Mr. Justice Dixon declaring in the course of his judgment:

[The Constitution] is an instrument framed in accordance with many traditional conceptions. . . . Among these I think that it may fairly be said that the rule of law forms an assumption. In such a system I think that it would be impossible to say of a law of the character described which depends for its supposed connection with the power upon the conclusion of the legislature concerning the doings and the designs of the bodies or persons to be affected and affords no objective test of the applicability of the power, that it is law upon a matter incidental to the execution and maintenance of the Constitution and the laws of the Commonwealth.[57]

And again in the same portion of his opinion Mr. Justice Dixon refers to the "legislature's characterization of the persons and bodies adversely affected, and no factual tests of liability."[58]

Mr. Justice Dixon's reference to the rule of law is of course an invocation of that principle which Professor Dicey, writing at the end of the nineteenth century, thought to be a basic characteristic distinguishing English constitutional law from that of the countries of Continental Europe.

We mean . . . that no man is punishable or can be lawfully made to suffer in body or goods except for a distinct breach of law established in the ordinary legal manner before the ordinary courts of the land. In this sense, the rule of law is contrasted with every system of government based on the exercise

[56]*Supra*, n. 48.

[57](1951) 83 C.L.R. 1, 193.

[58]*Ibid.* It is trite to observe at this stage that, though the Australian Constitution contains no bill of rights and in particular no constitutional guarantee of any kind against laws "abridging the freedom of speech, or of the press," the High Court decision in the Australian *Communist Party Case* in its end result appears to accord greater deference to such a principle than does the United States Supreme Court decision in the *Dennis Case,* this notwithstanding the presence in the United States Constitution of the express guarantee of the First Amendment.

by persons in authority of wide, arbitrary, or discretionary powers of constraint.[59]

In fact, running through the opinions of the majority justices of the High Court in the *Communist Party Case* is the notion that the Communist Party Dissolution Act, insofar as, in its provisions, it operates to attach obligations or incapacities on individuals independently of any objective standards of responsibility or liability, runs counter to fundamental principles inherent in the common law. It is clear that Mr. Justice Dixon, in thus specifically embracing the rule of law concept, and also, in common with his brother justices, in reacting against the absence in the contested legislation of any objective standards of responsibility and liability, is entering upon a policy interpretation, the policy here being the preservation so far as possible of the traditional common law conception of individual liberties.[60] In the absence of a bill of rights, these traditional liberties if they are to be protected by the judges must perforce be protected through the devices of statutory interpretation. There are already, in the High Court's constitutional jurisprudence, sufficient indications of a pattern of harsh judicial construction of statutes derogating from civil liberties[61] to make this latest venture by Mr. Justice Dixon and his colleagues not so novel in itself,[62] though we have certainly come a long way from Mr. Justice Dixon's ideal of a "strict and complete legalism."

[59]A. V. Dicey, *The Law of the Constitution* (9th ed., 1939), 188.

[60]This emphasis on individual liberties would seem to owe much to the continued use in legal education in the Commonwealth countries of Professor Dicey's masterly expositions. For a grudging tribute to Professor Dicey's work as "an evangel accepted reverently and without criticism or question in our schools," see the Introduction by Chief Justice Kennedy of the Irish Free State to Leo Kohn, *The Constitution of the Irish Free State* (1932), xii; see also W. Pollak, "The Legislative Competence of the Union Parliament," (1931) 48 *So. Afr. L.J.* 269, 286.

[61]See, for example, *R.* v. *Wilson, ex p. Kisch*, (1934) 52 C.L.R. 234, where the issue involved was the exercise of the Commonwealth's powers to control immigration and entry of aliens into Australia; in the *Kisch Case*, the ingenious administrative device of a literacy test in the form of a dictation test in a "European language" (as specified by the Immigration laws) was held to be ineffective where the "language" employed for the test was the almost extinct Scottish-Gaelic, which, the High Court ruled, was not a "European language." Again in *O'Keefe* v. *Calwell*, (1948) 77 C.L.R. 261, deportation proceedings against an Indonesian woman who had come to Australia as a wartime refugee and who had obtained British citizenship by marriage immediately prior to the deportation proceedings against her, were quashed by the High Court on a very strict reading of the Commonwealth Immigration Act.

It will be noted that both these cases concerned the application of the Commonwealth's immigration laws, a vexed question at any time but frequently suffering from the additional handicap of inept administration.

[62]In one sense, the High Court decisions in the *Bank Nationalization Case* and in the *Communist Party Case* are both applications of the philosophical ideas of

It is submitted, however, that the further objective stated by Mr. Justice Dixon—"To maintain the confidence of all parties in Federal conflicts" —would better be attained by the High Court's abandoning altogether the purely mechanical conception of the judicial office, the fiction that judges never make law but simply apply it, and recognizing frankly the essentially creative role of a supreme court exercising judicial review under a written and rigid constitution.[63] That this would necessitate some far-reaching changes in the Court's techniques of inquiry, and indeed in its whole approach to the task of adjudication in constitutional cases, is clear. Informed policy-making is dependent ultimately on acquaintance with all the facts. It would seem, as the starting point, that the High Court must be prepared to admit, and when admitted to weigh, evidence of the type that the United States Supreme Court has become familiar with since the Brandeis Brief was first employed. What would happen then must depend finally upon the judges themselves. It seems clear that the prevail-

---

the English Liberal school with the dual theme of economic laissez-faire on the one hand and the extension of political freedom on the other. This is in many respects parallel to the pattern of judicial interpretation prevailing in the United States from the period after the Civil War down to 1937, so far as the maintenance of economic laissez-faire is concerned; it might be argued, however, that the United States Supreme Court majorities prior to 1937 lacked that bias in favour of political freedoms which now seems manifested by the High Court of Australia.

[63]As to s. 92 of the Australian Constitution, Lord Wright who, as a member of the Board of the Privy Council sitting on that occasion, wrote the opinion of the Board in 1936 in *James* v. *Commonwealth*, [1936] A.C. 578 (P.C.), has recently gone on record in favour of a revision of existing holdings as to the scope and operation of s. 92: see "Section 92—A Problem Piece," (1954) 1 *Sydney L. Rev.* 145. After noting (at 145) his own "great diffidence in approaching questions arising under s. 92 of the Australian Constitution. The Constitution was the creation of the Australian people and its meaning and its application are matters for Australia and the Australian Courts . . . ," Lord Wright went on to observe (at 155): "It seems to me that it is a simple matter of construction that this clause is a limited *laissez-passer* clause, not a *laissez-faire* clause. It contains no guarantee against Government intervention in the ordinary general sense, but it does deal with the passage and repassage of trade and commerce across the border, and when it says that that is to be absolutely free it does, according to the ordinary rules of construction, as I understand it, refer back to the opening words of s. 92, 'on the imposition of uniform duties of customs.' In future trade is to be free of them. . . . Here, as I think, reading the section as a whole, giving full effect to the opening words and also to its general purpose and quality, everything points to the definition which I have suggested. In other words, the view which has been expressed that s. 92 deals with fiscal matters alone gives sense and efficacy to s. 92."

See also Lord Wright's recent remarks as to the leading case on the Canadian treaty-making power, *Attorney-General for Canada* v. *Attorney-General for Ontario*, [1937] A.C. 326 (P.C.), in (1955) 33 *Can. B. Rev.* 1123, and the ensuing assorted comments in (1956) 34 *Can. B. Rev.* 114, 115, and 243.

ing methods of legal education in the United Kingdom and the Commonwealth countries fall far short of giving the legal decision-maker the
broad training in the social sciences that is so necessary in handling the
complex public law issues of present-day society.[64] But it would at least
be a marked step forward to be spared, in the High Court's adjudication
of constitutional cases in the future, what Holmes has called a typical
natural law manifestation—the lawyer's unawareness that he is taking
sides on burning questions.

[64]See M. S. McDougal and H. D. Lasswell, "Legal Education and Public Policy:
Professional Training in the Public Interest," (1943) 53 *Yale L. J.* 203.

6

THE CONSTITUTION AND RACE RELATIONS
IN THE UNION OF SOUTH AFRICA

Apart from the so-called "entrenched clauses,"[1] the South African Constitution contains no formal limitations on the powers and competence of the legislature, and specifically nothing corresponding to a bill of rights or other systematic scheme of fundamental guarantees on the American or, for that matter, the Continental model. With questions directly bearing on the entrenched clauses of the South Africa Act alone excepted,[2] the Supreme Court of South Africa is not able to make the

[1]South Africa Act, 1909, ss. 35, 137, and 152:

"35. (1) Parliament may by law prescribe the qualifications which shall be necessary to entitle persons to vote at the election of members of the House of Assembly, but no such law shall disqualify any person in the province of the Cape of Good Hope who, under the laws existing in the Colony of the Cape of Good Hope at the establishment of the Union, is or may become capable of being registered as a voter from being so registered in the province of the Cape of Good Hope by reason of his race or colour only, unless the Bill be passed by both Houses of Parliament sitting together, and at the third reading be agreed to by not less than two-thirds of the total number of members of both Houses. A Bill so passed at such joint sitting shall be taken to have been duly passed by both Houses of Parliament.

"(2) No person who at the passing of any such law is registered as a voter in any province shall be removed from the register by reason only of any disqualification based on race or colour."

"137. Both the English and Dutch languages shall be official languages of the Union, and shall be treated on a footing of equality, and possess and enjoy equal freedom, rights, and privileges; all records, journals, and proceedings of Parliament shall be kept in both languages, and all Bills, Acts, and notices of general public importance or interest issued by the Government of the Union shall be in both languages."

"152. Parliament may by law repeal or alter any of the provisions of this Act: Provided that . . . no repeal or alteration . . . in sections thirty-five and one hundred and thirty-seven, shall be valid unless the Bill embodying such repeal or alteration shall be passed by both Houses of Parliament sitting together, and at the third reading be agreed to by not less than two-thirds of the total number of members of both Houses. A Bill so passed at such joint sitting shall be taken to have been duly passed by both Houses of Parliament."

[2]Such questions have arisen only twice since the establishment of the union in 1909: in 1937 and again during the constitutional crisis of 1951–2.

basic inquiry posed by courts, like the Supreme Court of the United States, possessing the power of judicial review: Is this enactment of the legislature "constitutional"? Instead, the Supreme Court of South Africa's attentions have had to be confined, as is the case with the courts in the United Kingdom, to the discovery of legislative "intent"—how far and to what extent Parliament has made use of its plenary law-making powers either directly, or else indirectly in the form of a conferment of part of its own law-making powers on an administrative authority—this latter being the field of delegated legislation.

A major difficulty in any attempt at empirical analysis of the Supreme Court of South Africa's work is that, in accordance with the conventional theory of the proper role of the common law judges in England, the Supreme Court of South Africa adopts, or purports to adopt, an essentially positivist conception of its own task. Thus in the course of his recent opinion for the court in *Harris* v. *Minister of the Interior*,[3] a case, incidentally, involving the entrenched clauses of the South Africa Act, and therefore one in which it can be argued most strongly that the Supreme Court is able to exercise an affirmative role, Chief Justice Centlivres declared:

The court in declaring that a Statute is invalid is exercising a duty which it owes to persons whose rights are entrenched by Statute; its duty is simply to declare and apply the law, and it would be inaccurate to say the Court in discharging that duty is controlling the legislature. See Bryce's American Constitution.[4] It is hardly necessary to add that courts of law are not concerned with the question whether an act of Parliament is reasonable or unreasonable, politic or impolitic. See *Swart N.O. and Nicol N.O.* v. *De Kock and Garner and others.*

The case referred to by Chief Justice Centlivres in this quotation was one in which he himself had, twelve months before, passed on the question of the validity of a provincial ordinance. On that occasion he had taken the opportunity of enunciating a positivist conception of the judicial office, asserting that "a court of law is not concerned with the question whether a provincial ordinance is reasonable or unreasonable, politic or impolitic."[5]

Though the Supreme Court of South Africa, therefore, according to its announced conception of its office, is not concerned with the "merits" of any legislation it may be passing upon, it is intended in this survey of the Court's work in the field of race relations, not merely to analyse its decisions in terms of the extent to which they flow logically from the pre-existing corpus of South African case law and English common law

---

3[1952] 2 S.A.L.R. 428 (A.D.).
4Third ed., I, 582.   5[1951] 3 S.A.L.R. 589, at 606 (A.D.).

generally, but also to appraise those decisions in terms of their end results, that is to say, their tangible effects upon the course and development of legislative programmes in South Africa.

THE CONSTITUTIONAL CRISIS OF 1951-2 RECONSIDERED

Formal constitutional authority in the Union of South Africa stems from the South Africa Act, 1909. Juridically speaking, this was an enactment of the United Kingdom Parliament: practically, however, the United Kingdom's action served to ratify the work of a convention that had met in 1908 and had consisted of delegates from the two original British colonies in South Africa, the Cape and Natal, and also from the two former Boer Republics (the Transvaal and Orange Free State) which had been defeated in the Boer War (1899-1902) and then annexed to the British Crown as British colonies. The South African Constitution to this extent represents in its historical origins something in the nature of a treaty or compact between the two main European peoples in South Africa.

Because the new Union of South Africa was still in a position of political inequality vis-à-vis the United Kingdom, in so far as South Africa was a Dominion within the British Empire, it could be argued without fear of contradiction that the South Africa Act was a form of "higher law" in South Africa, beyond the possibility of any legally effective action by the South African Parliament contrary to its express terms. But with the progressive development of the conventions governing the relationship of the United Kingdom with the self-governing Dominions, and finally the passage by the United Kingdom Parliament of the Statute of Westminster in 1931, accepted views as to the boundaries of the legislative powers of Dominion parliaments began to change also. It was in this vein that the South African Parliament in 1934 passed the Status of the Union Act, which expressly affirmed that henceforward "the Parliament of the Union shall be the sovereign legislative power in the Union." In *Ndlwana* v. *Hofmeyr* in 1937,[6] Acting Chief Justice Stratford had declared on behalf of the Supreme Court of South Africa:

Parliament's will . . . as expressed in an Act of Parliament cannot now in this country, as it cannot in England, be questioned by a Court of Law, whose function it is to enforce that will, not to question it. In the case of subordinate legislative bodies, Courts can of course be invoked to see that a particular enactment does not exceed the limited powers conferred. It is obviously senseless to speak of an Act of a sovereign law-making body as ultra vires. There can be no exceeding of power when that power is limitless.[7]

[6][1937] A.D. 229.   [7]*Ibid.*, 237.

The Acting Chief Justice went on to comment, in relation to the entrenched clauses of the South Africa Act and the special procedures required under it:

The question then is whether a Court of law can declare that a Sovereign Parliament cannot validly pronounce its will unless it adopts a certain procedure — in this case a procedure impliedly indicated as usual in the South Africa Act? The answer is that Parliament, composed of its three constituent elements, can adopt any procedure it thinks fit: the procedure express or implied in the South Africa Act is so far as Courts of Law are concerned at the mercy of Parliament like everything else.[8]

When Prime Minister Malan announced in 1951 that the special arrangements in the entrenched clauses of the South Africa Act were no longer to be regarded as binding on the South African Parliament, he was able to rely on an array of authoritative English and Commonwealth juristic opinion from the time of the Statute of Westminster onwards.[9] As a further precaution, before proceeding to enact his controversial Separate Representation of Voters Act in 1951, Prime Minister Malan took the step of obtaining counsel's opinion from the eminent English constitutional authority, Professor E. C. S. Wade of Cambridge, who expressed the view that the entrenched clauses were no longer binding on the Union Parliament.[10] It is not clear whether Professor Wade was aware, at the time he gave his opinion, of the exact nature of the legislative proposals being prepared by Prime Minister Malan: of course, according to the accepted approach to statutory construction in the United Kingdom (and *semble,* according to the South African Supreme Court's remarks, in South Africa

[8]*Ibid.,* 238.

[9]See, for example, W. Pollak, "The Legislative Competence of the Union Parliament" (1931) 48 *So. Afr. L.J.* 269, 286; K. C. Wheare, *The Statute of Westminster* (1931), 108; Berriedale Keith, *Governments of the British Empire* (1935), 47; W. P. M. Kennedy and H. J. Schlosberg, *The Law and Custom of the South African Constitution* (1935), 100; Sir Ivor Jennings, "The Statute of Westminster and Appeals to the Privy Council," (1936) 52 *Law Q. Rev.* 173, 187; Sir Ivor Jennings and C. M. Young, *Constitutional Laws of the British Empire* (1937), 265; and E. C. S. Wade, Introduction to A. V. Dicey, *Law of the Constitution* (9th ed., 1939), li–liii.

For a representative South African opinion given before the inauguration of the Malan Government's apartheid programme, see E. Kahn, "The 'Entrenched' Clauses of the South Africa Act," *Annual Survey of South African Law,* 1948, 9: "In strict law there can be no doubt that the entrenched clauses can be repealed by simple majority. Section 152 of the South Africa Act obtained its legal efficacy only from the Colonial Laws Validity Act of 1865, Section 2, and the Statute of Westminster, Section 2, has put an end to the application of this Act. The Privy Council decision of *Moore* v. *Attorney-General for the Irish Free State* [[1935] A.C. 484] puts the issue beyond doubt. . . . The Courts no longer have the testing power and there is no 'fundamental law' in the South African Constitution." And see also H. J. May, *The South African Constitution* (1949), 26.

[10]Published in the *Cape Times,* March 24, 1952.

too) the wisdom or merits of contested legislation are irrelevant to the question of validity. If this essential premise be granted, then Professor Wade's legal opinion to Prime Minister Malan can no doubt be readily justified, based as it is on a progressive and developing conception of inter-Commonwealth relations. Notwithstanding the fact that the constitutions of the member countries of the present Commonwealth were all (the new Constitution of the Republic of India alone excepted) "made in England" in terms of their formal, juridical origins, it no longer seems possible politically to justify their continued binding force today in those terms alone, more especially in the case of countries like Canada and South Africa which have a plurality of legal traditions, both English and non-English.

Dean Erwin N. Griswold and the present writer have elsewhere suggested[11] a way out of the impasse, but it involves a putting to one side of English constitutional concepts in favour of notions of fundamental law more normally postulated by American and, sometimes, Continental jurists: instead of looking to the sovereignty of the United Kingdom Parliament as the explanation of the continued binding force of the constitutions of the member countries of the Commonwealth, those constitutions can be considered as having local, or popular, roots; and they are "fundamental law" in their countries on that account, without the necessity of further support. This idea of a local root, or *Grundnorm,* for the constitutions of the various countries of the Commonwealth bears, it is true, some of the elements of a legal fiction; but it is still true that most of those constitutions were preceded, so far as their enactment by the United Kingdom Parliament was concerned, by representative local conventions, which had substantially agreed on the final provisions of the proposed constitutions before the enactment.[12] Though necessarily more significant in its long-range implications for those constitutions which have a plethora of "fundamental" provisions in them—especially the constitutions of the federal countries of the Commonwealth—the legal fiction, if it be such, comes closest to paralleling political facts in the case of South Africa,[13] since the South Africa Act bears all the hall-marks of a

[11]See, for example, the author's article, "The Union Parliament, the Supreme Court and the 'Entrenched Clauses' of the South Africa Act," (1952) 30 *Can. B. Rev.* 692, 718–20; E. N. Griswold, "The Demise of the High Court of Parliament in South Africa," (1953) 66 *Harv. L. Rev.* 864, 870–1. The problem, so far as it affects the Commonwealth countries as a whole, is treated in greater detail in the author's article: " 'Sovereignty' in the United Kingdom and the Commonwealth Countries at the Present Day," (1953) 68 *Political Science Quarterly* 511.

[12]Apart from this, of course, long-time popular user and acceptance of a constitution may well enroot it locally, custom and convention being accepted sources of constitutional law: (1953) 31 *Can. B. Rev.* 52, 61.

[13]And, *semble,* Canada too.

treaty between the two rival European peoples, the "entrenching" of the special franchise rules of the Cape Province and of the equality of the English and Dutch languages on this view representing the minimum elements of a successful modus vivendi between the two peoples. It is perhaps significant that where, in the first *Harris Case,* Chief Justice Centlivres and, in the second *Harris Case,* all the other justices writing opinions chose to rely on essentially English legal arguments stemming ultimately from the original enactment of the South African Constitution by the United Kingdom Parliament as a justification for the continued binding force of the entrenched clauses,[14] Mr. Justice van den Heever, who alone of the present justices of the South African Supreme Court would appear to have had a predominantly Roman-Dutch legal training,[15] would base that continued binding force on the notion that the South African Constitution has a local root, quite apart from the question of any imperial root.[16]

I have pointed out that the only matters "entrenched" in the South

[14]A fact, it is suggested, that weakened those judicial opinions, politically, in view of the weight of English juristic opinion against them; n. 9 *supra.* For a further South African opinion given after the inauguration of the Malan Government's apartheid programme, see D. V. Cowen, "Legislature and Judiciary: Reflections on the Constitutional Issues in South Africa," (1952) 15 *Mod. L. Rev.* 282.

[15]A quick survey through the South African *Who's Who* indicates that, of the six members of the Appellate Division of the Supreme Court concerned with the two *Harris Cases,* two, Centlivres C.J. and Schreiner J.A., had their legal education in England, at Oxford and Cambridge respectively; three others, Justices Greenberg, Hoexter, and Fagan, were trained at English universities or institutions in South Africa. Nothing could be discovered in *Who's Who* concerning Mr. Justice van den Heever's formal legal training, but he is referred to (somewhat euphemistically) in the *South African Law Journal* as the "latest but it is to be hoped not the last of the Roman-Dutch Barons," (G. A. Mulligan, (1952) 69 *So. Afr. L.J.* 25, 26)—a fact which points towards a predominantly Roman-Dutch legal orientation.

[16]Professor Wheare, whose views deserve respect, has recently indicated his repudiation of the position he had maintained in the first four editions of his book, *The Statute of Westminster and Dominion Status,* that the entrenched clauses were no longer, after the Statute of Westminster, 1931, legally effective in South Africa. Relying to a considerable extent on arguments made by D. V. Cowen, Professor Wheare contends now that the entrenched clauses are still binding, and derives this proposition from the "logic" and "nature" of the South African Constitution: (5th ed., 1953) 339 *et seq.* In the present writer's view, however, the continued binding force of the entrenched clauses at the present day is better justified pragmatically in terms of the "contractual" thesis of the South African Constitution already advanced (see in this regard also Mr. Justice van den Heever's special concurrence in the second *Harris Case*) especially since that thesis does not require a concomitant rejection of the authoritative South African and English opinions (including Professor Wheare's original opinion), which were formulated in general before the Malan Government first came to office in 1948 and therefore independently of the bitter partisan political events in South

African Constitution are the franchise laws of the Cape Province and the equality of the English and Dutch languages. Within these two special areas, if the present dispute between court and legislature remains resolved in the court's favour, the court can exercise judicial review after the American fashion and effectively maintain the fundamental character of the two provisions. In view of the absence of any bill of rights or other comprehensive guarantees in the constitution, the prospect that the South African Supreme Court can exercise an affirmative role in relation to the legislature, in race relations, might on first sight seem small. That the courts in South Africa have been able, in spite of this, to play some significant part in controlling the exercise of legislative policy in the field of political and civil rights in general, and race relations in particular, is a proposition that it is now proposed to advance.

POLITICAL RIGHTS IN THE UNION OF SOUTH AFRICA

Franchise Rights and Representation Generally

Each of the four South African colonies, before the effecting of the union of 1909, had prohibited, or else severely limited, the possibility of exercise of the franchise by non-whites. Thus the Transvaal specifically denied the vote to non-whites; the Orange Free State affirmatively conferred voting rights on whites and on no others; the colony of Natal, and to a certain extent also the Cape of Good Hope, used indirect methods, notably property restrictions and the requirement of literacy standards, as a veiled means of controlling the exercise of the franchise by non-whites. Nevertheless in the Cape of Good Hope, in contrast to the Transvaal, the Orange Free State, and also Natal, it had been possible by 1909 for a small but still significant number of non-Europeans, both natives and "coloured" persons (that is, persons of mixed blood) to obtain the vote under the Cape Colony's franchise laws. Under the union of 1909, the franchise provisions in force in the Cape Colony at 1909 were, as noted already, preserved by being specially "entrenched" in the new Constitution.

In the 1920's a movement began among the Europeans in South Africa to remove the natives from the common roll of electors in the Cape Pro-

---

Africa of 1951–2, and which were largely prompted by a progressive conception of inter-Commonwealth relations.

For further authoritative discussion of this question, see generally D. V. Cowen, "The Entrenched Sections of the South Africa Act: Two Great Legal Battles," (1953) 70 *So. Afr. L.J.* 238; H. ver Loren van Themaat, "Die Soewereiniteit van die Unie-Parlement," (1954) 71 *So. Afr. L.J.* 60; G. W. F. Dold and C. P. Joubert, *The Union of South Africa. The Development of its Laws and Constitution* (1955), 82–101. And see the penetrating comments by H. W. R. Wade, "The Basis of Legal Sovereignty," [1955] *Camb. L.J.* 172.

vince, and a number of bills for this purpose were introduced into the lower house of the South African Parliament. But marked increases in the numbers of European voters, without any corresponding increase in the proportion of native voters, caused these moves to lose some impetus: the grant of the franchise to European women in 1930 had the net effect of doubling the number of eligible European voters, a situation that was augmented by the grant of the vote in 1931 to all European men and women without qualification, while the number of non-European voters remained static. In 1936 the Hertzog-Smuts Coalition Government passed the Representation of Natives Act.[17] This Act, among its more general provisions, removed all natives in the Cape Province from the common electoral roll and established instead a separate Cape native voters' roll: those "coloured" persons who were on the common electoral roll of the Cape Province, however, were not affected by the new Act. Henceforward all natives of the union were given the right to elect four senators to the Union Parliament.[18] This new form of representation of natives in the Senate was necessarily to be indirect, since the senators so chosen must be, under the general qualifications for members of Parliament set out in the South Africa Act, of "European descent" and must possess the qualifications required for ordinary senators. Apart from this provision for representation of natives in the Senate, natives in the Cape Province were now given the right to elect three representatives to the lower house of the Union Parliament (the House of Assembly), all of whom, however, once again were to be European.[19]

[17]No. 12 of 1936. General Hertzog, when he was Prime Minister, had made it a policy to draw a complete distinction between natives and "coloured" persons: in 1926, he had introduced a bill into the Union Parliament to give the franchise to "coloured" persons in provinces of the Union other than the Cape, although the bill itself seems to have lapsed.

[18]There were electoral colleges to select the senators, the electoral colleges in general consisting of chiefs, head men, local councils, native reserve boards of management, the native advisory boards, and special electoral committees to represent natives not otherwise represented. The voting units in each electoral college were to represent the native taxpayers domiciled within their areas and each voting unit was to exercise a number of votes according to the number of its taxpayers. The act also provided that if at any time after the expiration of seven years the Governor-General was satisfied that the natives had progressed to such a stage as to justify an increase in their representation in the Senate, he might by proclamation increase the number of electoral colleges to six, each of which would have the right to elect one senator. The senators elected under the act were to hold their seats for five years, notwithstanding any dissolution of the Union Parliament.

[19]In 1935 there had been 10,628 natives on the undifferentiated electoral roll of the Cape Province: after their removal from the common electoral roll to the special native voters' roll, the number of native voters increased slightly by 1945 to 24,084 (*Handbook on Race Relations in South Africa* (1949), 29). In the province of Natal, though natives in theory had the right to a direct vote and to

Side by side with these changes, the Representation of Natives Act of 1936 also made provision for the creation of a Natives Representative Council, in which natives might sit in their own right.[20] This council, which had a majority of elected native representatives, exercised purely advisory functions, however, and in August, 1946, with its native members openly voicing dissatisfaction at their lack of concrete powers, adjourned *sine die* as a protest against what it termed the government's failure to meet the urgent need of the native people. Tentative suggestions for changes, made by the then Prime Minister, General Smuts, proved unacceptable to the native representatives and the council did not meet again,[21] being finally abolished by the Bantu Authorities Act of 1951,[22] which established general machinery for the administration of native affairs.[23]

The Representation of Natives Act of 1936, particularly its provision removing the native voters in the Cape Province of the union from the common electoral roll, has been extensively debated. It has been described enthusiastically as "the most deliberate attempt yet made in Africa south of the Sahara to give Africans of various types a place in the political machinery of their country. It must be considered as a beginning, not an end, in facing the problem of democracy in Africa."[24] A more restrained appraisal has suggested:

While it be rightly ordered that the principle of the communal franchise [for natives] for which the Act provides, is open to the gravest objections as being another step towards segregation and the entrenchment of white

be put on the ordinary electoral rolls, since the death in August, 1946, of the last remaining native voter, there have been no Africans on the common electoral roll (*ibid.*). There are no natives on the ordinary electoral rolls in the Transvaal or the Orange Free State.

[20]The Natives Representative Council consisted of some twenty-two members— the Minister for Native Affairs who presided, the five chief native commissioners as official members, four natives nominated by the Governor-General, and twelve members (who must be natives) elected by natives under an electoral college system. The functions of the Council were to consider and report upon proposed legislation affecting the native population, to advise on matters referred to it by the Minister of Native Affairs and on all matters especially affecting the interest of natives, and to recommend to Parliament or to any provincial council any legislation which it might consider necessary in the interest of natives. If the Minister of Native Affairs certified that any bill or draft ordinance introduced into Parliament or a provincial council contained conditions especially affecting the interest of natives, it must be referred to the Natives Representative Council for report.

[21]See, generally, *Handbook on Race Relations in South Africa* (1949), 513–16.
[22]No. 68 of 1951.
[23]See, generally, *Annual Survey of South African Law*, 1951, 16–19.
[24]Julius Lewin, *Political Representation of Africans in the Union* (South African Institute of Race Relations, 1942), 14.

domination, it has meant that the representatives of Africans have no longer to represent both Europeans and Africans and thus to consider a variety of divergent and often conflicting interests in one constituency. They can devote themselves to the interests of a single group. On the other hand, it has also meant that the 150 representatives elected by the white voters have shown a marked tendency to devote themselves exclusively to promoting the interests of Europeans and to ignore African needs and interests.[25]

The Representation of Natives Act of 1936 had been passed by the Parliament of the Union of South Africa in the apparent belief that it was an act of the nature defined in section 35 of the South Africa Act, for the Hertzog-Smuts Coalition Government proceeded to have it passed at a joint sitting of the two houses of the Union Parliament in compliance with section 35. The Act was challenged in the Supreme Court of South Africa on the ground that, although passed by a joint sitting of the two houses of the Union Parliament, as required by section 35, it was not such a law as is contemplated by the section. When the case came to the Appellate Division of the Supreme Court, the Court treated the question simply as involving the proof of an act of Parliament before a court of law and held that the Court could not go behind the formal record that the Act has been passed by Parliament—an application of the so-called "enrolled bill rule." The challenge to the constitutionality of the Act was therefore dismissed by the Court.[26]

Under a statute passed by the Smuts Government in 1946, the Asiatic Land Tenure and Indian Representation Act,[27] provision was made, among other things, for the representation of Indians on a communal basis in the Union Parliament. Indians in Natal and the Transvaal might now be represented in the Senate of the Union Parliament by two senators (European), in the House of Assembly by three members (European), and in the Natal Provincial Council by two members (Indian). Every male Indian who was a union national over twenty-one years of age, and possessed certain minor property qualifications, was to be entitled to be placed on a special Indian electoral roll. One of the Indian senators was to be nominated in the province of Natal and the Transvaal by the Governor-General, "on the ground mainly of his thorough acquaintance by reason of his official experience or otherwise with the reasonable wants and wishes of Indians," and the other was to be elected by the newly established Indian electors. Indian women, as distinct from males, were not, however, made eligible as electors under the new provisions; nor could they become entitled to vote under the existing union legislation establishing female suffrage, since this provided for European women only. From the time

[25]*Handbook on Race Relations in South Africa* (1949), 511.
[26]*Ndlwana* v. *Hofmeyr*, [1937] A.D. 229. [27]No. 28 of 1946.

of its introduction by the Smuts Government, the provision for political representation of Indians in the Asiatic Land Tenure and Indian Representation Act was never put into operation, for it was consistently boycotted by the Indian community, which objected strongly to the fact that representation was secured on a communal basis only, and through European representatives. The Indian community insisted throughout on being admitted for voting purposes to the common roll. The Union Parliament finally, under the Asiatic Laws Amendment Act of 1948,[28] repealed the provisions of the Act of 1946 providing for Indian representation, but without making provision for any alternative form of representation.[29]

In 1951 the Malan Government brought forward the Separate Representation of Voters Act,[30] designed, as its preamble declared, "to make provision for the separate representation in Parliament and in the Provincial Council of the Province of the Cape of Good Hope of Europeans in that province, and to that end to amend the law relating to the registration of Europeans and non-Europeans as voters for Parliament and for the said Provincial Council."[31] The main purpose of the bill, as introduced by the Minister of the Interior, was to remove the "coloured" voters from the common electoral roll in the Cape Province, to place them instead on a separate roll, and to allow them to vote for four special representatives.[32]

As a further objective, and parallel to methods used in the old Representation of Natives Act of 1936, the Separate Representation of Voters Act, 1951, established a Board of Coloured Affairs under the chairmanship of a Commissioner for Coloured Affairs. This was to consist of three

[28]No. 47 of 1948.

[29]See generally, South African Institute of Race Relations, *17th Annual Report 1945–1946*; *Handbook on Race Relations in South Africa* (1949), 30; *Annual Survey of South African Law*, 1948, 8.

[30]No. 46 of 1951.

[31]As the Minister for the Interior, Dr. the Hon. T. E. Dönges, acknowledged in introducing the bill in Parliament—(1951) 32 *Journal of the Parliaments of the Commonwealth* 601—it constituted part of the Government's apartheid policy. There were 9,000,000 natives in South Africa; 1,000,000 "coloured"; 300,000 Indians; and about 2,275,000 whites. Ever since the introduction of representative government in South Africa, the fear of political domination by the non-Europeans had hung like a dark cloud over the country. The "coloured" vote in the Cape had always been a sham and fraud. During election time the "coloured" vote had been canvassed in an improper manner and promises were made which, after the elections, were completely forgotten.

[32]The ratio between European and "coloured" representatives in the House of Assembly would thereby have become 150 to 4. Although, as an Opposition member, Mr. Davis, pointed out in the house, it is true that of the 1,030,000 "coloured" persons in South Africa only about 50,000 had a vote, nevertheless, because of their concentration in the Cape Colony, the "coloured" voters were able to take part in the election of some 55 members to the house, and indeed in 25 constituencies their vote enabled them to have a substantial say in the final outcome (*ibid.*, 607).

nominated non-European members from Natal, the Orange Free State, and the Transvaal, and eight elected non-European members, two to be elected from each of four special electoral divisions established under the Act for the Cape Province. The functions of the Board of Coloured Affairs were to advise the government, at the government's request, on matters affecting the "coloured" population of the union, to make recommendations regarding their interest, and also to act as intermediary between them and the government.

Since the Separate Representation of Voters Act, 1951, was passed by the Union Parliament by a simple majority of each house of Parliament sitting separately, the Act was immediately challenged in the Appellate Division on the ground that, though it was an act falling within the provisions of section 35 of the South Africa Act, it had not been passed in accordance with the special procedure outlined in section 35, that is to say, by a two-thirds majority at a joint sitting of the two houses of Parliament.

In *Harris* v. *Minister of the Interior*,[33] the Appellate Division held the Separate Representation of Voters Act, 1951, invalid, overruling *Ndlwana* v. *Hofmeyr*, the 1937 decision of the Court upon which the Government's counsel had relied. The attempt by the Malan Government (through the device of a High Court of Parliament having power to override the decisions of the Appellate Division) to circumvent the decision in the *Harris Case* met the same fate as the Separate Representation of Voters Act, the Appellate Division unanimously ruling that the High Court of Parliament Act was invalid too.[34]

The significance of the two *Harris Cases* for the abstract question of the nature of South Africa's government, and especially the relationship of court and legislature, has been canvassed already in this chapter. It remains to consider the practical implications of the two decisions for the franchise rights of non-Europeans in the union. While the Supreme Court maintains its present stand, the "coloured" voters in the Cape Province cannot be taken off the common electoral roll. But there are only 50,000 "coloured" voters on the common electoral roll anyway, a mere fraction of the "coloured" population of the union, and an even smaller percentage of the total adult non-Europeans. There is nothing in the entrenched clauses, and *a fortiori* nothing in the remaining sections of the South African Constitution, which would appear to buttress judicial moves directed towards the progressive extension of the common franchise to "coloured" persons beyond the present token representation; and nothing that would appear to offer any support to

[33][1952] 2 S.A.L.R. 428 (A.D.).
[34]*Minister of the Interior* v. *Harris*, [1952] 4 S.A.L.R. 769 (A.D.).

judicial moves on behalf of the as yet unrepresented[35] native and Asiatic groups within the union. There are practical limits to what courts can do if the constitutional machinery is lacking. To this extent, the quest for a representative legislature in South Africa must fall ultimately on the shoulders of the legislature itself, not on the courts; and the prospects here are singularly unpromising, for the record of past legislative action (and legislative inaction) since the establishment of the union in 1909 suggests that none of the major political parties has been much disposed to take affirmative action.

Entry to, and Exit from, the Union of South Africa

The key legislative provision in the field of entry and exit is the Immigrants' Regulation Act of 1913,[36] which was intended to be a comprehensive code on the subject of immigration, and which superseded most of the pre-existing legislation of the four provinces of the union. The nub of the Act is contained in section 4(1)(a), which defines those persons who are to be "prohibited immigrants" for purposes of the Act, these categories including "any person or class of persons deemed by the Minister on economic grounds or on account of standard or habits of life to be unsuited to the requirements of the Union or any particular Province thereof." When the Act came into force in 1913 the then Minister of the Interior, General Smuts, published a notice declaring every Asiatic person to be "unsuited on economic grounds" to the requirements of the union and of every province, with the result that immediately all Asiatics became "prohibited immigrants." The Minister's power under the Act to issue the notice was soon challenged in the courts. After conflicting decisions by intermediate courts, the Appellate Division of the Supreme Court of South Africa finally ruled in *Rex* v. *Padsha* in 1923,[37] by a three-to-two majority, that the notice issued by the Minister was *intra vires* and therefore valid. As Mr. Justice Solomon noted in his majority opinion:

The main argument advanced on behalf of the appellant was that the classification in question was made by the Minister not on economic but on racial grounds and was in consequence not justified under the powers conferred upon him. . . . The Minister has himself stated that it is on economic grounds that he deems every Asiatic person to be unsuited to the requirements of the Union. Are we justified in refusing to accept that statement? The mere fact that a similar classification might have been made on racial grounds is not in itself sufficient for that purpose.[38]

[35]So far, anyway, as the common roll is concerned.   [36]No. 22 of 1913.
[37][1923] A.D. 281.
[38]*Ibid.*, 288. This view was supported by de Villiers J.A. and Juta J.A. in specially concurring opinions, in which they took notice of the economic motives behind legislation concerning Asiatics in the various provinces of the union as supporting the view that the Minister had exercised his discretion on economic

In consequence of the Supreme Court's decision in *Rex* v. *Padsha*, this provision of the Immigrants' Regulation Act of 1913 has been the main legal means employed to prevent Asiatics from entering the union. There has been a certain amount of case law upon other sections of the Act of 1913, and in general it can be said here that the Court has not been disposed to uphold actions against the government by aliens, and especially Asiatics, who have entered or sought to enter the union.[39] On the other hand, the Court will apparently adopt a more beneficial attitude towards an applicant for entry who is the wife, or child, or similar close relative of a person already lawfully resident in the union.[40]

So far as persons who are actually citizens of the union are concerned, it is to be noted that the Supreme Court has shown a marked hostility towards apparent attempts by the government to place restrictions on the departure of its political opponents from the country. In *Sachs* v. *Dönges*,[41] where the government had attempted to revoke the passport of the well-known trade union leader, Sachs, and he alleged that the government's decision was actuated by ill-will towards him personally and by party political considerations, the Appellate Division of the Supreme Court, by a three-to-two majority, held that a subject who had been granted a passport by the Crown could not be deprived of it by an executive revocation. The majority, through Chief Justice Watermeyer, with Justices Greenberg and Schreiner concurring, in effect equated the granting of a passport to a contract. The minority judges, Justices Centlivres and van den Heever, denied that a passport was a contract and held, mainly on a broad view of prerogative powers stemming from

---

grounds. However, the two dissenting justices (Innes C.J. and Kotzé J.A.) rested their arguments on the ground that the basis of classification specified in the notice published by the Minister was racial and not economic, and that the regulation therefore, as issued, was *ultra vires* the Minister.

[39]See *Arononwicz* v. *Dönges N.O.*, [1950] 1 S.A.L.R. 568 (A.D.), no obligation on the Minister, in deporting a prohibited immigrant, to remove him to his country of origin; *Jaga* v. *Dönges N.O., Bhana* v. *Dönges N.O.*, [1950] 4 S.A.L.R. 653 (A.D.), no obligation on the part of the Minister to state reasons for deeming a person to be an undesirable inhabitant of the union; and, *similiter, Jeeva* v. *Dönges N.O.*, [1950] 3 S.A.L.R. 414 (A.D.). And see also *Khan* v. *Principal Immigration Officer*, [1952] 1 S.A.L.R. 371 (A.D.), a person alleged to have entered the union illegally must prove affirmatively that he did not contravene the act; but compare *Holden* v. *Minister of the Interior*, [1952] 1 S.A.L.R. 98 (T.P.D.).

[40]See, for example, *Minister of the Interior* v. *Ebrahim*, [1950] 1 S.A.L.R. 54 (T.P.D.); *Principal Immigration Officer* v. *Brey*, [1950] 4 S.A.L.R. 207 (C.P.D.). But compare *Latiefa* v. *Principal Immigration Officer*, [1951] 2 S.A.L.R. 589 (C.P.D.); *Harneker* v. *Jail Superintendent*, [1951] 3 S.A.L.R. 430 (C.P.D.); *Dönges N.O.* v. *Bhana*, [1953] 1 S.A.L.R. 30 (T.P.D.).

[41][1950] 2 S.A.L.R. 265 (A.D.).

United Kingdom practice and authorities, that a passport is a mere licence, which may be revoked by the Crown at pleasure.

Sachs v. *Dönges* was applied in another case the same year, *Dönges N. O.* v. *Dadoo*.[42] In this case, Dr. Dadoo, the Indian Nationalist leader, who was in possession of a valid Union of South Africa passport, had been deprived of it by a government official, allegedly by subterfuge, and the passport had then been impounded. On the authority of *Sachs* v. *Dönges*, Mr. Justice Centlivres ruled that the government had no right under the royal prerogative to obtain by judicial process the delivery of a passport. It is to be noted that, following on the decision in *Sachs* v. *Dönges*, the form of passports has been changed, and they are now expressed to be issued under the following conditions: "This passport remains the property of the Government of the Union of South Africa, and may be amended, withdrawn or cancelled at any time at the pleasure of the Minister of the Interior on behalf of the Government, and shall, upon the request of the Minister or an officer authorized by him, be forthwith surrendered by the holder to the Government." In this way, the effect of the ruling in *Sachs* v. *Dönges* appears to have been avoided by the government, though some doubt arises whether *Dönges* v. *Dadoo* is also avoided.[43]

Freedom of Speech, Assembly, and Association

In the only major case that has arisen in recent years on the second of the two matters "entrenched" under the South Africa Act, equality of the English and Dutch languages ("entrenched" in section 137 of the Act), *Swart N. O. and Nicol N. O.* v. *De Kock*,[44] the Supreme Court refused to accept as violative of section 137 a Transvaal ordinance compelling the use, as a medium of instruction, of that official language in which the pupil is the more proficient, which had been applied to compel the education of a child in Afrikaans rather than (as the school authorities and also the child's parents preferred) in English. The decision was given through Chief Justice Centlivres, with Justices van den Heever and Fagan concurring specially, over a strong dissent by Justices Hoexter and Schreiner. The basis of the majority decision was that a law which did not "discriminate" against either language did not violate the section: it was not necessary that every individual be given a free choice to use whichever language he pleased.[45]

Again, in a number of cases on the Suppression of Communism Act,

42[1950] 2 S.A.L.R. 321 (A.D.).
43See *Annual Survey of South African Law*, 1950, 3.
44[1951] 3 S.A.L.R. 589 (A.D.).
45See van den Heever J.A., *ibid.*, 623: "If an Ordinance distributes restrictions

1950, the Court has refused to diminish the full operation of statutory enactments. In *Garment Workers' Union and Sachs v. Minister of Justice*,[46] where a notice served on the trade union leader Sachs under the Suppression of Communism Act, 1950, as amended, was attacked on the ground that the notice was too wide, the Court unanimously refused to uphold the argument. The notice in question had followed the language of the Act in prohibiting a person within a specified area from attending any gathering in any place, certain kinds of meetings only being excepted in the notice. The Court, through Mr. Justice Schreiner,[47] noted: "The section does not in terms require the Minister to limit his notice to particular gatherings or gatherings of a particular type. . . . It is gatherings in the sense in which that phrase is used in the section that the notice debars Sachs from attending." In other words, since the legislature had, under the Act, authorized notices of a sweeping and unqualified nature, a notice issued under it could not effectively be attacked on the ground that it was too wide. In a further case, *Rex v. Sachs*,[48] Sachs had been given an order by the Minister of Justice under the Suppression of Communism Act, as amended, in the following terms: "You are hereby prohibited from attending any gathering whatever within the Union of South Africa and the Territory of South West Africa for a period of two years from the date hereof other than gatherings of a *bona fide* religious, recreational or social nature." At the same time Sachs had been served with notice under the Act requiring him to resign within thirty days as an office holder or member of his trade union and he had also been prohibited, under the Act, for a period of two years from being in any province in the Union of South Africa other than the Transvaal. It was argued by counsel before the Appellate Division of the Supreme Court that the orders relating to the prohibition of attending meetings and the resignation from the union were too wide. In giving judgment for the Court, which incidentally was unanimous on this point, Chief Justice Centlivres[49] conceded that statutes invading the liberty of the individual should be subjected to the closest scrutiny by courts of law, whose function it is to protect the lives and liberty of the individual. But "where the statute under consideration in clear terms confers on the Executive autocratic powers over individuals, courts of law have no option but to give effect to the will of the Legislature as expressed in the statute." The statute being clear, the orders of the minister must be upheld. The Court did, however, somewhat mitigate the

---

on or enlargements of personal liberty without disturbing the balance [between the two official languages] it cannot be said to be in conflict with section 137."

46[1952] 4 S.A.L.R. 384 (A.D.).   47*Ibid.*, 389.
48[1953] 1 S.A.L.R. 392 (A.D.).   49*Ibid.*, 399.

full effects of its ruling by holding further, by a three-to-two majority,[50] that the fact that Sachs had acted on counsel's advice was a mitigating circumstance, and the term of imprisonment with hard labour imposed on him was reduced to a suspended sentence.

If it is remembered that the Suppression of Communism Act defines Communism in part as the "encouragement of hostility between the European and non-European races in South Africa the results of which are likely to further the achievement of a despotic Government based on the dictatorship of the proletariat," the upholding by the Supreme Court, in the two cases just discussed, of the broad powers exercised by the executive under the Act could have important implications in the field of race relations. But it is also possible to view these two cases in the same light as decisions upon internal security powers in other countries during the "Cold War" period;[51] and in that light the two *Sachs Cases* in South Africa can be regarded as in a special category distinct from the race relations cases. Nevertheless, as a question of pure judicial interpretation, the limitations placed by the Court upon executive powers in the passport cases are in striking contrast to the broad, virtually unfettered discretion conceded to the executive in the Communism cases.

SOCIAL RIGHTS

Marriage and Other Personal Relations

The most interesting cases in the field of personal relations concern the Prohibition of Mixed Marriages Act[52] of 1949 and the Immorality Act of 1927 (as amended in 1950).[53] The former statute is designed to prevent marriages between Europeans and non-Europeans; the latter, its logical concomitant, proscribes, under heavy penalties, extra-marital intercourse between Europeans and non-Europeans. The courts have been able to mitigate and soften the full application of both statutes, largely by exploiting the difficulties inherent in any attempt at the legal definition of race and colour. Both the statutes in question make use of a statutory presumption. Thus the Prohibition of Mixed Marriages Act states: "Any person who is in appearance obviously a European or a non-European, as the case may be, shall for the purposes of this Act be deemed to be such unless and until the contrary is proved."[54]

[50]Centlivres C.J., Greenberg and van den Heever JJ.A. concurring: Schreiner and Hoexter JJ.A. dissenting.
[51]See, for example, *Dennis* v. *United States*, (1951) 341 U.S. 494.
[52]No. 55 of 1949.
[53]No. 5 of 1927, as amended by the Immorality (Amendment) Act of 1950, No. 21 of 1950.
[54]Prohibition of Mixed Marriages Act, 1949, s. 3.

In *Rex* v. *Gill*,[55] the first case on the Prohibition of Mixed Marriages Act, Mr. Justice Fagan held, for the Cape Provincial Division of the Supreme Court, as follows:

I need not for the purposes of our present decision attempt to indicate what percentage of mixture would be such as to "prove the contrary" in the case of a person who is in appearance a European. Suffice it to say that neither on the authorities I have referred to, nor in the ordinary acceptation of the term in South Africa, would a "slight mixture" make a non-European of one who is European in appearance. In addition we have here the evidence of association . . . all one way that at present [the bride] consorts as a European with Europeans.[56]

Mr. Justice Fagan thereupon quashed the conviction of a marriage officer based on his having performed a ceremony for a European bridegroom and a non-European bride, the evidence showing that, although the marriage officer knew there was a slight mixture of blood on the bride's father's side, the bride had the appearance of a European and had always consorted as a European with Europeans.

In *Pedro* v. *Tansley, N.O.*,[57] the widow of a non-European applied for a declaratory order that she was a coloured person and entitled to marry a non-European. The applicant was predominantly European in appearance, but was able to show that she was of mixed descent and that she habitually consorted with non-Europeans, by whom she was accepted as one of themselves. The Cape Provincial Division held that the applicant had "proved the contrary" in terms of the Prohibition of Mixed Marriages Act of 1949 and granted the order asked for.

The interesting point about *Pedro* v. *Tansley, N.O.* is that apparently the applicant, had she wished, could also have entered into a lawful marriage with a European for, being a European in appearance, she was, under the Act, deemed to be a European until she herself chose to prove the contrary.[58] Since the coming into force of the Prohibition of Mixed Marriages Act, it has become clear that the main difficulty in applying it is the number of persons who can pass equally well as European or non-European: racial tests being inconclusive in cases of this kind, upbringing, association, and "choice" tend to become the decisive factors, with the individual taking the colour of his environment.[59]

In *Rex* v. *Ormonde*,[60] there was a prosecution under the Immorality Act as amended. One of the accused was a European by race and a Muslim

[55][1950] 4 S.A.L.R. 199 (C.P.D.).
[56]*Ibid.*, 206.   [57][1951] 4 S.A.L.R. 182 (C.P.D.).
[58]See de Villiers J.P., *ibid.*, 187; and also H. R. Hahlo, "European or non-European," (1952) 69 *So. Afr. L.J.* 7.   [59]Hahlo, *op. cit.*
[60][1952] 1 S.A.L.R. 272 (A.D.).

by religion, and he and the second accused were married by a Muhammedan priest according to Muslim rites. A prosecution was subsequently launched on the ground that, being a European male, the first accused had had illicit carnal intercourse with a non-European female. On appeal to the Appellate Division of the Supreme Court, the convictions of the first accused, and also of his wife, the second accused, for a corresponding offence under the same Act were set aside. The only point at issue in the case was whether the wife was a non-European. As Mr. Justice Fagan, for the Appellate Division, noted: "Different criteria or bases for discrimination have been adopted by the Legislature in different statutes dealing with racial descriptions. It follows that a judicial decision on the test to be applied for determining a person's racial qualification for the purposes of one statute is not necessarily a guide in the consideration of another statute."[61] According to the Immorality Act, "European means a person who in appearance obviously is, or who by general acceptance and repute is, a European: non-European means a person who in appearance obviously is, or who by general acceptance and repute is, a non-European."[62] It is further provided that: "Any person who seems in appearance obviously to be a European or non-European as the case may be, shall for the purposes of this Act be deemed to be such until the contrary is proved."[63] Mr. Justice Fagan found on the evidence that it could not be said that the second accused was in appearance obviously a European or that she was a European by general acceptance and repute.

It was, however, not sufficient for the prosecution to negative the tests laid down by the Act for proving her to be a European. In order to obtain a conviction the Crown had to prove a positive, to wit, that she is a non-European in terms of the definition of that word in the Act. The definition is so framed that there must be a great number of people who cannot be proved to be either European or non-European for the purposes of the Act. No doubt that framing was intentional, taking due note of the fact that there is a doubtful class, with one foot on each side of the colour line, in respect of whom a rigid classification or a compulsory choice would be artificial and unreal and therefore likely to cause grave injustice. Indeed, cases are quite conceivable in which a person may according to the one branch of the definition, that of "obvious appearance," fall in the one group and according to the other branch, that of "general acceptance and repute," in the other. In such a case too there can be no conviction on a charge under the Immorality Act based on a classification of this person in either the one or the other of the two groups.[64]

In other words, the Crown had to prove either that the second accused was in appearance obviously a non-European or else that she was a non-

61*Ibid.*, 275.   62Immorality Act, 1927 (as amended), s. 7.
63*Ibid.*, s. 7 *bis.*   64[1952] 1 S.A.L.R. 272, at 277 (A.D.).

European by general acceptance and repute. As regards appearance, though the second accused was not obviously a European in appearance, neither was she in appearance obviously a non-European; and as regards general acceptance and repute, although there was evidence that she was accepted in some communities as a non-European, there was also some evidence to show that she was accepted in some communities as a European, which "must at the least, cast a doubt on the generality of her acceptance and repute as a non-European."[65] The Crown therefore had failed to discharge the onus of showing that the second accused was a non-European for purposes of the Immorality Act.[66] The trend of the courts in recent years, therefore, has been to treat each definition of race or colour in the context of the particular statute in which it occurs. It seems also, so far in any case as criminal prosecutions are concerned, that the courts have been disposed to construe the statutory definitions against the prosecution and in favour of the accused.

Use of Public Transport, Public Buildings, and Public Places Generally
The work of the present bench of the Appellate Division in cases on segregation in public places must be viewed in the light of a long history of interpretation. In a 1916 case, *George* v. *Pretoria Municipality,*[67] *a* prosecution of a coloured person for boarding a tram car reserved for the use of white persons in Pretoria and refusing to leave, at a time when no separate tram cars were provided for the use of natives, Asiatics, or other coloured persons in Pretoria, the Transvaal Provincial Division of the Supreme Court of South Africa had upheld the conviction over the argument that it was *ultra vires* for the Pretoria Town Council to make by-laws appointing separate tram cars for the use of white persons and of non-white persons. The Court had also ruled that the failure to provide separate accommodation for coloured persons is no defence, dismissing the proposition that there must be equality between white and coloured until such provision is made.

In *Minister of Posts and Telegraphs* v. *Rasool,*[68] the Court ruled that merely because a by-law divided the community for the purpose of its operation into white and coloured did not render the by-law *ultra vires* on the grounds of unreasonableness, the question here concerning a division of post-office accommodation into European and non-European sections. Since it was conceded that the services rendered at the non-European counter in the post office were equal to those rendered at the European counter, the only question was the reasonableness of making a

[65]*Ibid.,* 278.
[66]See generally Hahlo, "European or non-European," (1952) 69 *So. Afr. L.J.* 117.
[67][1916] S.A.L.R. 501 (T.P.D.).   [68][1934] A.D. 167.

distinction between European and non-European. The Court applied the test of Lord Russell in the well-known English case, *Kruse v. Johnson,*[69] which laid down the criteria under which by-laws may be held invalid because unreasonable. The tests Lord Russell had advanced were whether the by-laws were found to be "partial and unequal in their operation as between different classes; if they were manifestly unjust; if they disclosed bad faith; if they involved such oppressive or gratuitous interference with the rights of those subject to them as could find no justification in the minds of reasonable men." In such cases, according to Lord Russell, the court might well say, "Parliament never intended to give authority to make such rules; they are unreasonable and *ultra vires,"* the test here of course proceeding in terms of the actual authority conferred by Parliament on the inferior law-making authority concerned—ultimately the question of legislative "intent." The Appellate Division in *Rasool's Case,* through Acting Chief Justice Stratford, held: "If [it were] decided that a by-law is invalid on the sole ground that it divides the community for the purpose of its operation into White and Coloured, I cannot agree with it, for such conclusion runs counter to accepted principle and good sense. A classification by a by-law, if it presumably is to serve a useful purpose, is not invalid on that ground alone whether the line of division be race, colour, religion, or any other."[70] Mr. Justice de Villiers, in a concurring opinion, noted: "A discrimination (coupled with equality) on grounds of race or colour may or may not be unreasonable, but in my opinion it cannot be held to be unreasonable *per se* on the mere ground of being made on lines of race or colour. . . . Here we have a discrimination, coupled with equality of treatment, as between Europeans and non-Europeans, and such a discrimination is not, *per se* and without more, unreasonable."[71]

In effect, then, the majority of the Court held that racial discrimination in the form of separation on a racial basis is valid, so long as the facilities afforded to the different races are equal. One of the concurring justices, Mr. Justice Beyers, appears however to have based his opinion on rather broader grounds, in effect denying the contention that in the eyes of the law all men are equal, a proposition that was advanced in the same case by Mr. Acting Justice Gardiner in a very strong dissent. Mr. Justice Beyers pointed out that separation ran through the whole fabric of social life in the union, in hospitals, cemeteries, public baths and conveniences, play grounds, tram-cars, and elsewhere. The Appellate Division thus in effect attained, in *Rasool's Case,* the American constitutional law doctrine,

69[1898] 2 Q.B.D. 91.
70[1934] A.D. 167, 175.   71*Ibid.,* 182.

stemming from the race relations cases in the southern areas of the United States, of "separate but equal," though, be it noted, without any reference whatever to American cases.

The same principle was later applied by Mr. Justice Davis in *Rex* v. *Carelse*,[72] a decision in the Cape Provincial Division of the Supreme Court on the use of bathing beaches.[73] The holding of the Court involved the proposition that, before a regulation or by-law discriminating between white and coloured is held invalid on the ground of unreasonableness, it must be shown that the discrimination is coupled with an inequality of treatment that is, in all the circumstances, manifestly unjust or oppressive. Mr. Justice Davis referred, in the course of his opinion, to Lord Russell's dictum in *Kruse* v. *Johnson*. When Lord Russell referred to rules partial and unequal in their operation, Mr. Justice Davis conceded, he might quite possibly have meant that actual equality is necessary for validity.

In England, however, there may well have been no discrimination among different classes of the community such as was in fact to be found in South Africa. South African law, Mr. Justice Davis observed, was honeycombed with differential legislation as between white and coloured. After noting, from Dönges and van Winsen's *Municipal Law*, "It stands to reason that in a country whose statute-book is honeycombed with differential legislation as between white and coloured, and in which colour distinctions in churches, schools, sports, places of amusement and in society generally are carefully observed, it can scarcely be said that in delegating legislative powers to municipalities the Legislature could not possibly have contemplated that these subordinate law-making bodies would follow its own example as well as the settled social and colour differentiation," Mr. Justice Davis concluded that the test of the reasonableness or unreasonableness of by-laws must, when applied in South Africa, require an inequality strong enough to be "manifestly unjust or oppressive." His opinion, remembering that judicial interpretation in this field ultimately involves discovery of legislative "intent," raises certain important questions to which reference will be made later.

Rex. v. *Abdurahman*[74] concerned a regulation reserving a portion of all trains for the European race but without restricting them to it. Non-Europeans were not permitted to use the reserved portion on pain of a criminal sanction. It was held in a unanimous decision of the Appellate Division that the regulation, as applied, resulted in partial and unequal treatment to a substantial degree as between Europeans and non-Europeans and therefore that the action taken under it was not authorized

[72][1943] S.A.L.R. 242 (C.P.D.).

[73]*Ibid.*, 252.   [74][1950] 3 S.A.L.R. 136 (A.D.).

by the enabling act.[75] Mr. Justice Centlivres, for the Court, directly applied Lord Russell's test in *Kruse* v. *Johnson:* "It is one thing to authorize discrimination and quite another thing to authorize discrimination coupled with partiality and inequality in treatment."[76] Mr. Justice Centlivres found it impossible to assume that the legislature had intended, in its enactment of 1916 conferring the general power to make regulations on the railway administration, that one section of the community could be treated unfairly compared with another section:

The State has provided a railway service for all its citizens irrespective of race and it is unlikely that the Legislature intended that users of the railways should, according to their race, have partial or unequal treatment meted out to them. The conclusion at which I arrive is that the regulations have been improperly applied by the Administration in the circumstances of this case. As in my view the regulation can be applied with impartiality and equality between members of different races, it cannot be said that the regulation itself is *ultra vires* the enabling act.[77]

In consequence of the challenge made in *Abdurahman's Case* to the principle of segregation on a racial basis, the Malan Government had in 1949, during the pendency of the case, amended the Railways Act of 1916 so as to confer express powers to

(a) reserve any railway premises (including conveniences) or any portion thereof, or any train or any portion of a train for the exclusive use of males or females or persons of particular races or different classes of persons or natives;
(b) reserve all or certain trains travelling over a particular route for the exclusive use of persons of particular races or different classes of persons or natives.[78]

In *Rex.* v. *Lusu,*[79] the accused, a native, had been charged with a breach of the Act of 1916, as amended in 1949, in that, being a native, he had entered the European waiting room in the Cape Town railway station, although the room had been exclusively reserved by the railway administration for the use of Europeans. The Appellate Division, in an opinion written by Chief Justice Centlivres, with Justices Greenberg, Schreiner, and Hoexter concurring, applied *Rex* v. *Abdurahman,* in which, it will be remembered, the Court had ruled on the 1916 Act in its unamended form. The Court felt that the new section inserted in the 1916 Act by the

[75]Railways and Harbours Regulation Control and Management Act, 1916 (No. 22 of 1916), s. 4.
[76][1950] 3 S.A.L.R. 136, 149 (A.D.).
[77]*Ibid.*
[78]Railways and Harbours Regulation Control and Management Act, 1916, as amended by Act No. 49 of 1949, s. 7 *bis* (1).
[79][1953] 2 S.A.L.R. 484 (A.D.).

amending Act of 1949 could not authorize the administration to discriminate among different races and classes on a footing of partiality and inequality.[80] If this were not so, it would follow that the administration could, under the new section inserted by the amendment of 1949,

reserve conveniences on railway premises for members of a particular race only and provide no conveniences for members of any other race. This could not in my opinion, have been the intention of Parliament, for, as was stated in *Abdurahman's* case, at page 149: "The State has provided a railway service for all its citizens, irrespective of race, and it is unlikely that the Legislature intended that users of the railway should, according to their race, have partial or unequal treatment meted out to them."[81]

However, in a strong dissent, Mr. Justice van den Heever contended that the new provision inserted in the 1916 Act by the 1949 amendment authorized the administration

to reserve railway premises (including conveniences) for the exclusive use of different classes of persons, which implies discrimination. In the last resort the question whether such discrimination must be on a basis of equality depends upon the intention one must impute to the Legislature. Considering the multitude of activities in which the Administration is authorized to engage on business principles and the diverse objects to which railway premises may be devoted, I cannot imagine that it could possibly have been the intention of Parliament to entrust the Administration with a power from exercising which it must either refrain or exercise it in a manner which will satisfy the reasonable requirements of all sections of the community, but have no relation to the economic consequences or to the value of any particular section as clientele.[82]

Mr. Justice van den Heever's dissent, of course, raises the basic problem behind these decisions by the Supreme Court. If all the rulings upon reasonableness or unreasonableness in by-laws are ultimately to be related by the judges to legislative "intent," the question finally is reduced to one of the policy of the legislature. The "separate but equal" formula, though it does not challenge one of the major premises upon which the legislature in South Africa seems to have proceeded over the years, that is to say, that separation between the races must be carried out, at least allows the Court, in passing upon the factual question whether or not the separate facilities that are provided are actually equal, to ensure relative parity outside the question whether or not separation *per se* involves disparity. But what if the legislature itself intends not merely that there will be separation but that, under the separation, substantial inequality of treatment will exist? If, as Mr. Justice van den Heever's dissent in *Rex* v. *Lusu* implies, this is the general case, then the inter-

[80]*Ibid.*, 489.
[81]*Ibid.*, 491.   [82]*Ibid.*, 498.

pretations the Court has actually given in the cases involving separation in public transport and other public places, and similar questions, would seem to have proceeded on something of a fiction—that the legislature intended to provide equality of treatment.

The Court has thus been able, in the process of scrutinizing delegated legislation according to Lord Russell's test of reasonableness or unreasonableness, to give what might conventionally be labelled a strong civil liberties bias to those areas of South African public law touching on race relations. It is always possible, of course, for the legislature in South Africa to "correct" the Court's decisions by re-defining legislative "intent" in more explicit terms, but there will be, necessarily, a time-lag because of the difficulty of getting Parliament to pass a bill every time a small segment of its race relations policy is checked by the Court.[83]

ECONOMIC RIGHTS IN THE UNION OF SOUTH AFRICA

There have been, up to the time of writing, no major decisions by the Appellate Division of the Supreme Court in the area of economic rights proper, especially on the important Group Areas Act of 1950.[84] In the field of licensing, however, the Court has acted with firmness to prevent a granting or withholding of licences on racially discriminatory grounds. In *Tayob* v. *Ermelo Local Road Transportation Board,*[85] the Court intervened to prevent discrimination against a non-European (here an Asiatic) in the granting of taxi-cab licences. In *Bindura Town Management Board* v. *Desai,*[86] the Court intervened over the issue of revenue licences, finding as a matter of fact that the licence had been refused because the applicants were Indians: this case was actually an appeal from a decision of the High Court of Southern Rhodesia from which, under the statutes governing its jurisdiction, an appeal apparently lies to the Appellate Division. The language of the Appellate Division's decision in this case, together with the decision in *Tayob's Case,* though both decisions turned on the use of delegated powers by administrative authorities, suggests that the Court may be prepared in future to apply more openly a policy against discrimination on racial grounds.

[83]Julius Lewin, "Apartheid Comes to Court," *Forum* (Johannesburg), Dec., 1952.

[84]Group Areas Act, 1950 (No. 41 of 1950), as amended by the Group Areas Amendment Act, 1952 (No. 65 of 1952). As to the provisions and potential implications of this legislation, see generally, Hiemstra, *The Group Areas Act* (1953); Johnson, "The Group Areas Act: Stage One," (1951) 68 *So. Afr. L.J.* 286; *Annual Survey of South African Law,* 1950, 24–5 and 102–9; *Annual Survey of South African Law,* 1952, 55 and 126–8; *Survey of Race Relations,* 1949–1950, 26–7.

[85][1951] 4 S.A.L.R. 440 (A.D.).   [86][1953] 1 S.A.L.R. 358 (A.D.).

THE COURT'S DILEMMA: SOCIO-ETHICAL LIMITATIONS ON THE
EFFECTIVENESS OF JUDICIAL ACTION

The apartheid programme introduced by the Malan Government after it was first elected to office in 1948 is not, it is clear, an overnight phenomenon, representing a sharp break in the continuity of South African public law. It has its roots in the laws of all four of the present provinces (the Cape, Natal, Orange River, and Transvaal) passed up to the union in 1909, and also in the legislative programmes of the successive governments of the union since 1909. Doctrinally, the basic premises of the Malan Government and its opponents may not be too dissimilar:

The opposition of a majority of the South African electorate seems largely to be a matter of tactics rather than of principle. It is evident from the debates in the Capetown Parliament and the speeches of the most influential members of the [anti-Malan] United Party that the principles adopted or tacitly respected by that party as such differ from those of the National Party . . . only in degree, and one might almost say tact in their application. The majority of members of the United Party are politicians who seem to have the same traditional attitude to colour as the National members of the legislature. This traditional attitude has recently been strengthened by the Europeans' growing fear that they may be submerged by the non-whites even in the towns. Thus, during his recent electoral campaign, Mr. J. G. N. Strauss, the leader of the United Party, implicitly accepted the underlying conceptions of such recent legislation as the Group Areas Act and the Prohibition of Mixed Marriages Act. He stated only that if his party won the election, it would amend a number of points in the Acts in question.[87]

It is true that disagreements over techniques or degree may become so great at times as to amount to disagreements over principle. Yet by and large there would seem to be this "agreement as to fundamentals" by both Government and Opposition parties today—that the key concepts of South African society involve the principle of differentiation between the European and non-European races, with the concomitant of the existence in South Africa today of widespread inequalities in access to, and sharing of, power, wealth, respect, well-being, skill, enlightenment and other community values, as between Europeans and non-Europeans. The Supreme Court thus faces the problem that it is carrying out its

[87]Report of the United Nations' three-man political commission, Oct. 13, 1953, 164–5. In a speech at Queenstown on Sept. 9, 1952, Mr. Strauss defined the foundations of the non-European policy of the United Party (in terms curiously reminiscent of the Malan Government's programme) under four heads: (1) social separation of the races, with separate facilities for all; (2) no miscegenation; (3) separate residential areas; (4) use of the work and energy of the non-Europeans for the benefit of the South African community as a whole "in our farms, kitchens, factories and mines" (*ibid.*). And see also "Dr. Malan's Roll Call," *Economist*, July 18, 1952, 158–9.

duties in a community where the "living law"—the climate of opinion in which all positive law must operate—does not admit full social, political, and economic equality for non-Europeans. As Chief Justice de Villiers declared in *Moller* v. *Keimoes School Committee:*

As a matter of public history we know that the first civilised Legislators in South Africa came from Holland and regarded the aboriginal natives of the country as belonging to an inferior race, whom the Dutch, as Europeans, were entitled to rule over, and whom they refused to admit to social or political equality. . . . These prepossessions, or, as many might term them, these prejudices, have never died out, and are not less deeply rooted at the present day among the Europeans in South Africa, whether of Dutch or English or French descent. We may not from a philosophical or humanitarian point of view be able to approve this prevalent sentiment, but we cannot, as judges, who are called upon to construe an Act of Parliament, ignore the reasons which must have induced the Legislature to adopt the policy. . . .[88]

These factors, representing as they do the socio-ethical limitations on the effectiveness of legal action, must present real obstacles to any court policy of arresting, or at least mitigating, the Malan Government's apartheid programme. And any such problems for the Court must be accentuated, as we have noted, by the technical consideration that the South African Constitution (apart from the entrenched clauses) is lacking in any bill of rights upon which courts of law might rely to implement their policy preferences and is lacking even in any generally accepted power of judicial review. It is the more striking, therefore, that the Supreme Court has been able to introduce (necessarily as the product of considerable mental and verbal ingenuity in view of the absence of any bill of rights provisions) the principle of "separate but equal," this, be it noted, without any reference to American constitutional law practice.[89]

The "separate but equal" principle, as applied by the South African Supreme Court, would accept, as a working basis, the principle of separation between the races. It would permit the granting of separate facilities to the various races, but it would insist that, where facilities are provided

[88][1911] A.D. 635, 643–4.

[89]The principle of "separate but equal" in relation to accommodation of whites and negroes on passenger trains was approved by the United States Supreme Court in *Plessy* v. *Ferguson*, (1896) 163 U.S. 537, the court thus departing from an earlier, contrary view that it had expressed some years before in *Railroad Company* v. *Brown*, (1873) 17 Wall. 445. The "separate but equal" formula was finally outlawed by the United States Supreme Court (at least so far as it had been applied in the field of public education) in *Brown* v. *Board of Education of Topeka*, (1954) 347 U.S. 483. And see generally E. McWhinney, "An End to Racial Discrimination in the United States? The School-Segregation Decisions," (1954) 32 *Can. B. Rev.* 545.

for one race, they must be accompanied by facilities for all others, and that those facilities when provided must be equal as between the different races. In examining the question whether the facilities provided for the different races are equal—essentially a factual question—the Supreme Court obviously has great scope; and it has been disposed to be active, particularly since the introduction of the apartheid programme in 1948, in insisting on the provision of facilities that really are equal for the different races. But the acceptance by the Court of the "separate but equal" principle, and its enforcement, still leaves unanswered the more basic question of whether separation *per se,* even without inequality of facilities, is not discrimination on racial grounds.

Honestly applied (as it unquestionably has been applied by the Supreme Court) the "separate but equal" formula represents something of a compromise choice among the rival theories on race relations policies that have been advanced in South Africa.[90] In the United States the "separate but equal" formula represented something of a retreat from the post–Civil War enthusiasm that had led to the drafting of the Thirteenth, Fourteenth, and Fifteenth amendments to the Constitution;[91] but it would also seem to have been based partly on policy factors—the somewhat intuitive recognition by the Supreme Court of the United States that positive law decisions, if they are to have any meaning in practice,

[90]See generally, Quintin Whyte, *Apartheid and Other Policies* (1948). Whyte identifies three basic long-range "solutions" of the racial situation in the union: (i) total assimilation involves the complete fusion of the races, physically, socially, and politically, as the ultimate means of eliminating race prejudice and conflict; (ii) parallelism, or differentiation without territorial segregation, would recognize the fact of race difference and make the acceptance of such difference a matter of voluntary organisation, through separate schools, churches, clubs, commercial undertakings, industries, and professional groups, and with no intermarriage between the races; (iii) total segregation would involve the setting aside of sufficient land within the union for the eventual accommodation of the entire native population—in effect the development of a "Bantustan" able economically to support the native population—with eventual relinquishment of political control by Europeans and the attainment of native independence.

Two further policy approaches to race relations, Christian trusteeship (formerly associated with the late Jan Hofmeyr and now with the newly formed splinter Liberal party) and apartheid, seem to be variants of the basic "solutions," Christian trusteeship appearing to fall between total assimilation and parallelism, and apartheid between parallelism and total segregation.

[91]See Frank, "Can the Courts Erase the Color Line?" (1952) 21 *Journ. Negro Educ.* 304: "Segregation, or the device of so-called 'separate but equal' treatment of the races, is a by-product of the Civil War Amendments. It is a device for escaping the force of the mandate that all shall be entitled to equal protection. Before that provision was written into the basic law, there was nothing to escape and hence no need for segregation. . . . The conception of segregation, separate-but-equal style, was an intellectual wrinkle to escape the simple command of equality."

must be buttressed by a sufficiency of popular acceptance.[92] As the Supreme Court of the United States slowly approached the overriding of the "separate but equal" formula in favour of an "unseparated" equality,[93] the South African Supreme Court accepted the "separate but equal" formula (however inmperfect it may be) as a distinct step forward. Against the background of present-day South African society, it may be that the "separate but equal" formula, especially if applied by legislative assemblies without prior compulsion by the courts, represents the best prospect of some short-range solutions for the racial situation in that country. In such an approach, however, the prime obligation would be to see that, where the facilities are to be separate, any "equality" of facilities should be real and not merely notional.

Some significant currents of thought on race relations in South Africa today should not be overlooked. There is clearly an increasing awareness of the economic interaction and interdependence of the various racial groups within the union. The *Fagan Commission Report*[94] was the first really authoritative recognition of these economic facts of life in South Africa, but recently the European trade union movement has shown an awareness that the social and economic well-being of European workers may be dependent to a considerable degree on the social and economic well-being of the non-European workers too.[95] How far the fact of the economic interdependence of Europeans and non-Europeans in South

[92]*Ibid.*, 304: "In 1873 [in *Railroad Company* v. *Brown*] the Court sensed that the dominant element of the country wanted real equality. By 1896 [in *Plessy* v. *Ferguson*] the Court very accurately recognised that this was no longer so."

[93]See, for example, in relation to segregation in transportation, *Morgan* v. *Virginia*, (1946) 328 U.S. 373 (segregation on inter-state buses); and *Henderson* v. *Southern Railway Company*, (1950) 339 U.S. 816 (segregation in railroad dining cars).

The "separate but equal" principle, in matters of education, became very much attenuated in its effects by the Court's mounting disposition to scrutinize rigorously the alleged equality of any separate facilities provided—see, for example, *Missouri ex rel. Gaines* v. *Canada*, (1938) 305 U.S. 337; *Sweatt* v. *Painter*, (1950) 339 U.S. 629; and *McLaurin* v. *Oklahoma*, (1950) 339 U.S. 637. It was finally outlawed by the Supreme Court: *Brown* v. *Board of Education of Topeka*, (1954) 347 U.S. 483.

[94]*Report of the Native Laws Commission*, 1946–8, presided over by Mr. Justice Fagan. The report notes, *inter alia*, at 50, para. 67: "A course of events that can no longer be changed has made South Africa the common home of races differing so radically from each other that there can be no question of assimilation, yet economically and territorially so intertwined that they are simply compelled, from moment to moment, to regulate their contacts, to bridge their differences, and to settle their disputes."

[95]Thus the evidence presented by the trade unions to the Industrial Legislation Commission of Enquiry of 1951 was overwhelmingly against the introduction of legislation compelling the segregation of the various races in separate unions. Sachs, the General Secretary of the Garment Workers' Union of South Africa,

Africa can be reconciled with avowed legislative objectives directed towards political, social, or economic separatism as between the different races is one of the great problems to be worked out in the union in the immediate future. It seems clear, however, that the Supreme Court of South Africa, by the course of its decisions, has provided a lead for the rest of the world in a field where countries with vastly more settled political, social, and economic conditions have (no doubt with some wisdom, from the policy viewpoint, if the difficulties in maintaining a continuing background of public approval and co-operation are considered) displayed at times a noticeable caution in moving towards a final solution.

---

records the financial and organizational assistance accorded by the South African Trades and Labour Council to native workers, in his book, *The Choice before South Africa* (1952). On the other hand, Hatch, *The Dilemma of South Africa* (1952), 126, sees a principal design of the trade union movement in South Africa as being to protect the European worker from competition by the non-European.

7

CONSTITUTIONALISM IN
THE REPUBLIC OF INDIA AND IN
PAKISTAN

The actual drafting of the Constitution of the Republic of India occupied three years. A constituent assembly to draw up a constitution was first convened in December, 1946, and its members (numbering three hundred in all after the withdrawal of the Pakistan representatives), did not finally reach agreement until November, 1949, the new Constitution coming into force on January 26, 1950.

It had been expected, when the United Kingdom government announced after World War II that it was withdrawing from India, that a federal union could be formed which would enable the Muslim minority of the population of India to combine peacefully and fruitfully with the Hindu majority and so preserve the essential structure of India as it had existed under British rule. Hindus and Muslims were fully represented in the Constituent Assembly convened in December, 1946, but it soon became apparent that no agreement between the rival forces could be arrived at. Under pressure from the powerful Muslim League, the Muslim delegates broke away, declaring that their cultural identity could not be preserved by their becoming a unit in a federal state with a Hindu majority. Instead, they formed the independent, sovereign, Muslim state of Pakistan;[1] while the rump of the original Constituent Assembly continued their deliberations and eventually in 1949 established the predominantly Hindu Republic of India. Partition, not federation, was therefore the solution in India; and it was achieved in the teeth of geography and also of demography. Pakistan, for example, is really two territories, the main part located in the northwest of the sub-continent of India, and the other part isolated hundreds of miles away in Bengal, over in the east, with no direct physical communication between the two territories; while both the Republic of India and Pakistan contain respectively sizable

[1]See *infra*, pp. 141–9.

Muslim and Hindu minorities within their territorial boundaries, a situation that brought much rioting and bloodshed in its wake on the attainment of Indian independence and hence the partition.

The new Hindu Republic of India, which came legally into operation in 1949, is expressed in its constitutional instrument to be federal in form, and provision is made under the Constitution both for a union (national) government and for member states. In general, these states correspond in their boundaries to the administrative divisions existing historically in the era of British rule in India. They are divided for administrative purposes into a number of categories, with different institutions and powers pertaining to each category. Part A States are the former governors' provinces which had some extended experience in parliamentary government under British rule; Part B States are the former princely (Indian) states, or else unions of such states, whose experience with representative political institutions was fairly limited or else fairly new; while Part C States (the former chief commissioners' provinces) and also a fourth category, the territories (the Andaman and Nicobar islands) are units without prior experience in representative government.

The problems of introducing representative, democratic government for the first time into a country as vast and administratively complex as India no doubt explain the elaborateness and detail (even to the point of prolixity) of the federal-state arrangements actually made in the constitutional instrument. Yet when one examines also the drastic powers vis-à-vis the states that are conferred upon the union government by the Constitution itself,[2] it may be wondered to what extent federalism in India (meaning by this the federal form of the constitutional instrument) proceeds primarily from considerations of administrative expediency commending themselves as such to a nationally minded Constituent Assembly, rather than from well-articulated sentiments in favour of local autonomy stemming from definite and ascertainable minority groups located in reasonably distinct territorial areas. This question of the historical forces ultimately directing the choice of a federal union, rather than a unitary or some other non-federal form, becomes important when we come to consider the special role of the member states within the federal union in question. If the original pressures for federal union were closely accorded to the special interests and demands of some such minority groups as these, then we can expect considerations of states' rights to bulk large in the day-by-day working of the federal constitution, whether it is the federal executive, legislature, or judiciary that we happen to be dealing with. Correspondingly, if the pressures of local sentiment

[2]See *supra*, p. 7.

are weak, or alternatively if they become attenuated with the passage of time, then we can expect to see a federal union in which the division of power between the national government and the member states becomes subjected more and more to centripetal strains. However, the working experience under the Constitution of the new Republic of India has necessarily been too slight, since its adoption in 1949, to enable us to rule finally upon its claimed federal character.

Perhaps in consequence of the exhaustive three-year deliberations of the Constituent Assembly, the new Indian Constitution is elaborate and prolix. It is easily the lengthiest constitutional instrument ever drafted. It consists of 395 articles, plus 9 schedules, and the whole instrument, in the official version published by the Government of India Press, runs to 254 pages. It must also be the most eclectic constitutional document that has been adopted—its articles echo the phrases of the constitutions of many countries, for the Indian constitution-makers have borrowed copiously, and perhaps not always discriminatingly, from earlier constitutions, particularly those of the English-speaking federations, the United States, Canada, and Australia. In this sense, the Indian Constitution bears some parallel to the Weimar Constitution and to the other post–1918 European constitutions whose drafters have sought to construct a constitution by the dry light of reason and by assiduous culling of the positive law texts. Part IV of the Indian Constitution (articles 36-51), for example, is devoted to a detailing of the "Directive Principles of State Policy," principles which "shall not be enforceable by any court, but . . . are nevertheless fundamental in the governance of the country and it shall be the duty of the State to apply these principles in making laws."[3] Now the notion of including a statement of Directive Principles in the Constitution was apparently derived from the Constitution of Eire of 1937; Eire in its turn owed the same notion to the Spanish Republican Constitution of 1931. Lacking the teeth of a bill of rights, and yet at the same time intended to be more substantial than the gusty recitals normally included in the preambles to constitutions, the Directive Principles of State Policy have been right from the outset an anomalous portion of the Indian Constitution;[4] it is perhaps not surprising therefore that they have not been utilized or invoked at all up to the present day. This particular outcome is of course not a unique situation in the day-by-day working of constitutions—many provisions in the United States Constitution, for example,

[3]Constitution of India, 1949, s. 37.

[4]See, in this regard, the forceful criticisms advanced by Sir Ivor Jennings, *Some Characteristics of the Indian Constitution* (1953), 33–5; and see also the reservations as to the utility of the Directive Principles advanced by a thoughtful Indian observer, Dean R. U. Singh, (1947) 1 *The Federalist* (no. 5) 78–9 (Lucknow).

had become dated soon after the adoption of the Constitution and are now generally forgotten. Yet it may be regretted that the Indian constitution-makers, in spite of their undoubted erudition, have not profited from the worst errors of the "professional" constitutions of post–1918 Europe. We can observe, indeed, all through the Indian Constitution, the same key characteristics as are to be found in those constitutions: a notable heaviness of construction in conjunction with complicated rules which attempt to provide for all foreseeable contingencies, in a word the attempt to rationalize power, to replace the extra-legal facts of power by rigid and extensive rules of positive law.

In certain significant respects, however, the new Indian Constitution differs from many of the post–1918 European constitutions. Where the latter tried to disarm the executive branch of government at a time when economic and political conditions all pointed to the need for a strong centralized administration, the Indian Constitution clearly looks to the establishment of a strong executive at the centre. The Indian constitution-makers deliberately rejected the American presidential type of executive with the substantial separation of powers that that necessarily implies, in favour of the English parliamentary type of executive. They also took the further step of arming the executive with drastic powers, on its being "satisfied that a grave emergency exists," to suspend or modify the normal constitutional provisions, including the very elaborate Bill of Rights section of the Constitution—a provision that recalls the drastic emergency provisions of the old Weimar Constitution. Indeed, when it is remembered that the normal restraint upon a parliamentary-type of executive of an effective two-party system is not present in India, in view of the absence of any real parliamentary Opposition to the present Congress Party Government, it may be wondered whether the desire for a strong executive has not been carried too far, and too much of effective power under the Indian Constitution located at the centre.

Here, however, another important characteristic distinguishing the Indian Constitution from the post–1918 European constitutions comes into play, namely, the presence of a Supreme Court exercising judicial review on the model of the Supreme Court of the United States. The Indian Supreme Court will be peculiarly able, if it so chooses, to prune away much of the verbal foliage in the Constitution and to look rather to the essential purposes that the Constitution was intended by its drafters to embody. The Court starts on its work with all the advantages that Chief Justice Marshall possessed when he wrote his seminal opinions on the United States Constitution, of having a clean slate. It is thus able to make virtually its own course. In the first few years, it must be noted, the Indian Supreme Court has moved with extreme caution. With notable exceptions such as Mr. Justice Fazl Ali, its members have tended to eschew the frank, policy-making type of approach favoured by the United States Supreme Court at the present day, and to confine themselves to a baldly positivist approach. This is no doubt due mainly to the continued dominance in Indian jurisprudence of English judicial traditions and patterns of thought; the Privy Council's approach to constitutional interpretation in the era of the old British Empire, and of the Commonwealth that succeeded it, was to treat Dominion constitutions as mere statutes and to subject them to the "ordinary" (restrictive) rules of statutory construction, with a reading-down of the provisions of those constitutions as the inevitable result. The high-water mark of legal positivism on the part of the Indian Supreme Court was attained in one of that Court's first opinions, *Gopalan* v. *State of Madras,*[5] when, over a very strong dissent by Mr. Justice Fazl Ali, the Supreme Court rejected any notion of a "purposive" interpretation of the Constitution and insisted instead on strict and literal interpretation as the guiding principle of construction, with a consequent very restrictive ruling upon the protections conferred under the elaborate Bill of Rights contained in the new Constitution.

In *Gopalan's Case,* the Supreme Court had to rule on the meaning and effect of the "fundamental rights" section (part III) of the Constitution. Now the intentions of the Constituent Assembly that drafted the new Constitution seem clearly to have been to give some sort of primacy to the fundamental rights section, for right at the outset of part III of the Constitution it is declared:

Article 13 (1) All laws in force in the territory of India immediately before the commencement of this Constitution, in so far as they are inconsistent with the provisions of this Part, shall, to the extent of such inconsistency, be void.

(2) The State shall not make any law which takes away or abridges the rights conferred by this Part and any law made in contravention of this clause shall, to the extent of the contravention, be void.

It had already been declared in article 12 that in part III, unless the context otherwise required, "the State" should include *inter alia* the government and Parliament of India, and the government and the legislature of each of the states.

The legislative provision in question in the *Gopalan Case* was section 3(1) of the Preventive Detention Act (No. IV of 1950) passed by the Parliament of India. Section 3(1) provided:

[5](1950) XIII Supreme Court Journal 174.

The Central Government or the State Government may:—
(a) if satisfied with respect to any person that with a view to preventing him from acting in any manner prejudicial to
  i) the defence of India, the relations of India with foreign powers, or the security of India, or
  ii) the security of the State or the maintenance of public order, or
  iii) the maintenance of supplies and services essential to the community, or
(b) if satisfied with respect to any person who is a foreigner within the meaning of the Foreigners Act, 1946 [XXXI of 1946], that with a view to regulating his continued presence in India or with a view to making arrangements for his expulsion from India, it is necessary so to do,
—make an order directing that such person be detained.

Section 3(1) of the Preventive Detention Act of the new Indian Republic thus clearly recalls the famous (or infamous) regulation, 18 (B) of the Defence (General) Regulations, 1939, of the United Kingdom, which was discussed by the House of Lords in the case of *Liversidge* v. *Anderson*.[6] Regulation 18(B) had allowed the Home Secretary to issue a detention order if he "has reasonable cause to believe" that a person came within certain classes specified in the regulations. The central problem in *Liversidge* v. *Anderson* of whether the Court could examine the Home Secretary's "belief" and pass upon its "reasonableness" was paralleled in the *Gopalan Case* to this extent, but section 14 of the Indian Preventive Detention Act went a further step beyond the English Defence (General) Regulations by seeking positively and expressly to exclude judicial control altogether.[7]

The Supreme Court of India had little difficulty over this latter provision (section 14), holding unanimously that in prohibiting the disclosure of the grounds of detention it was directly in conflict with one

[6][1942] A.C. 207.

[7]Preventive Detention Act, 1950, section 14:
"14(1) No Court shall . . . allow any statement to be made, or any evidence to be given, before it of the substance of any communication made under [the Act] of the grounds on which a detention order has been made against any person or of any representation made by him against such order; and notwithstanding anything contained in any other law, no court shall be entitled to require any public officer to produce before it, or to disclose the substance of, any such communication or representation made, or the proceedings of an advisory board or that part of the report of an advisory board which is confidential.

"(2) It shall be an offence punishable with imprisonment for a term which may extend to one year, or with fine, or with both, for any person to disclose or publish without the previous authorisation of the Central Government or the State Government, as the case may be, any contents or matter purporting to be contents of any such communication or representation as is referred to in sub-section (1):

"Provided that nothing in this sub-section shall apply to a disclosure made to his legal adviser by a person who is the subject of a detention order."

of the fundamental rights provisions of the Constitution, namely article 22(5), which declares:

When any person is detained in pursuance of an order made under any law providing for preventive detention, the authority making the order shall, as soon as may be, communicate to such person the grounds on which the order has been made and shall afford him the earliest opportunity of making a representation against the order.

The Court, however, ruled that section 14 might be severed from the rest of the Preventive Detention Act, so that the holding that section 14 was invalid would not affect the constitutionality of the remaining portions of the Act. The Court then went on to hold (with Justices Fazl Ali and Mahajan dissenting) that the balance of the Preventive Detention Act was valid and constitutional.

The dissenting opinion by Mr. Justice Fazl Ali forms an interesting contrast to the attitude of the majority of the Court. In giving his opinion he placed great emphasis on article 19 of the Constitution, which establishes (subject to certain defined exceptions) that all citizens shall have the right:

(a) to freedom of speech and expression;
(b) to assemble peaceably and without arms;
(c) to form associations or unions;
(d) to move freely throughout the territory of India;
(e) to reside and settle in any part of the territory of India;
(f) to acquire, hold and dispose of property;
(g) to practice any profession, or to carry on any occupation, trade or business.

Preventive detention, Mr. Justice Fazl Ali held, amounted to a deprivation of the right guaranteed by article 19 (1)(d) of the Constitution. Freedom of movement, in his view, was the essence of personal liberty, and any restraint on freedom of movement must be held to amount to an abridgment or deprivation of personal liberty as the case may be, according to the nature of the restraint.[8] The proper juristic conception was that personal liberty and freedom of movement connoted the same thing, and the words used in article 19 (1)(d) must accordingly be construed in this light.[9] The right guaranteed under article 19 (1)(d) was really a right to personal liberty, and preventive detention was a deprivation of that right.[10] Mr. Justice Fazl Ali also relied on the guarantee contained in article 21 of the Constitution: "No person shall be deprived of his life or personal liberty except according to procedure established

8(1950) XIII Supreme Court Journal 174, 200.
9*Ibid.*, 208.   10*Ibid.*, 211.

by law." On the one hand, it had been, in effect, contended in argument by the Attorney-General that the words "procedure established by law" meant simply any procedure established or enacted by statute: on the other hand, it had been contended in reply that the expression "procedure established by law" should be interpreted in a wider sense as meaning what is understood in American constitutional law as "procedural due process." In ruling upon this point, Mr. Justice Fazl Ali noted:

... in America, the word "law" does not mean merely State-made law or law enacted by the State and does not exclude certain fundamental principles of justice which inhere in every civilised system of law and which are at the root of it. The result of the numerous decisions in America have been summed up by Professor Willis in his book on Constitutional Law at p. 662 in the statement that the essentials of due process are:
(1) notice, (2) opportunity to be heard, (3) an impartial tribunal, and (4) orderly course of procedure. . . .
The real point however is that these four elements are really different aspects of the same right, viz., the right to be heard before one is condemned. So far as this right is concerned, judicial opinion in England appears to be the same as that in America. In England, it would shock one to be told that a man can be deprived of his personal liberty without a fair trial or hearing. Such a case can happen only if the Parliament expressly takes away the right in question in an emergency as the British Parliament did during the last two world wars in a limited number of cases.[11]

Mr. Justice Fazl Ali then went on to consider specifically whether the "principle that no person can be condemned without a hearing by an impartial tribunal, which is well-recognized in all modern civilized systems of law" could be regarded as part of the law of India.[12] In answering his own question in the affirmative, Mr. Justice Fazl Ali found that that principle,

being part of the British system of law and procedure which we have inherited, has been observed in this country for a very long time and is also deeply rooted in our ancient history, being the basis of the panchayat system from the earliest times. The whole of the Criminal Procedure Code . . . is based upon the foundation of this principle, and it is difficult to see that it has not become part of the "law of the land" and does not inhere in our system of law. If that is so, then "procedure established by law" must include this principle, whatever else it may or may not include.[13]

Mr. Justice Fazl Ali's conclusion is the more striking because as he himself conceded in his judgment[14] the original draft of article 21 of the Constitution had conformed exactly to the American constitutional

[11]*Ibid.*, 214–15. [12]*Ibid.*, 217.
[13]*Ibid.* [14]*Ibid.*, 212–13.

formula "without due process of law"; but this version was deliberately dropped in the Constituent Assembly in favour of the present phrasing "except according to procedure established by law." Mr. Justice Fazl Ali's suggestion here, however, was that the reason for the change was that the Constituent Assembly wanted to avoid the "very elastic meaning" given to the due process clause by the United States Supreme Court in its "substantive" as distinct from "procedural" aspect.[15]

By contrast, the majority of the Court was not disposed to accept this interpretation of article 21. As Chief Justice Kania observed:

No extrinsic aid is needed to interpret the words of Article 21, which, in my opinion are not ambiguous. Normally read, and without thinking of other Constitutions, the expression "procedure established by law" must mean procedure prescribed by the law of the State. If the Indian Constitution wanted to preserve to every person the protection given by the due process clause of the American Constitution there was nothing to prevent the Assembly from adopting the phrase, or if they wanted to limit the same to procedure only, to adopt that expression with only the word "procedural" prefixed to "law". However, the correct question is what is the right given by Article 21? The only right is that no person shall be deprived of his life or liberty except according to procedure established by law. One may like that right to cover a larger area, but to give such a right is not the function of the Court; it is the function of the Constitution.[16]

Likewise the majority justices disagreed strongly with Mr. Justice Fazl Ali's views as to the meaning of article 19 (1)(d). In this regard, Chief Justice Kania commented:[17]

. . . in my opinion, reading sub-clause (d) as a whole the words "territory of India" are very important. What is sought to be protected by that sub-clause is the right to freedom of movement, i.e. without restriction, throughout the territory of India. Read with their natural grammatical meaning, the sub-clause only means that if restrictions are sought to be put upon movement of a citizen from State to State or even within a State such restrictions will have to be tested by the permissive limits prescribed in clause (5) of that Article.[18]

In particular Chief Justice Kania rejected Mr. Justice Fazl Ali's assimilation of the guarantee of freedom of movement contained in article 19 (1)(d) to a guarantee of "personal liberty." In fact Chief Justice Kania thought that the concept of the right to move freely

[15]*Ibid.*

[16]*Ibid.*, 186.   [17]*Ibid.*, 180–1.

[18]Constitution, article 19 (5): "Nothing in sub-clauses (d), (e) and (f) of the said clause [19 (1)] shall affect the operation of any existing law insofar as it imposes, or prevents the State from making any law imposing reasonable restrictions on the exercise of any of the rights conferred by the said sub-clauses either in the interests of the general public or for the protection of the interests of any Scheduled Tribe."

throughout the territory of India guaranteed by article 19 (1)(d) was an entirely different concept from the right to "personal liberty" which he saw as being contemplated by article 21.[19]

"Personal liberty" covers many more rights in one sense and has a restricted meaning in another sense. . . . There is no conflict between Articles 19 and 21. The contents and subject matter of Articles 19 and 21 are thus not the same and they proceed to deal with the rights covered by their respective words from totally different angles. As already mentioned in respect of each of the rights specified in the sub-clauses of Article 19 (1) specific limitations in respect of each is provided, while the expression "personal liberty" in Article 21 is generally controlled by the general expression "procedure established by law."[20]

Of course the major difficulty with this statement by Chief Justice Kania is that, if the right to "personal liberty" is not to be included within the rights guaranteed by article 19, the safeguards to "personal liberty" will then apparently be no stronger than those contained in article 21; and by his holding in the *Gopalan Case* itself that "procedure established by law" meant merely any procedure prescribed by the legislature, Chief Justice Kania has reduced the safeguards in article 21 to mere verbiage.

The importance of Chief Justice Kania's holding in the *Gopalan Case* should not be under-estimated. The decision, it will be noted, was given in the first year of the new Republic of India, and was one of the first decisions of the Supreme Court of India sitting in its new capacity of final appellate tribunal for India after the abolition of the appeal to the Privy Council. The judges of the Supreme Court of India, therefore, in sitting on the *Gopalan Case,* were in a real sense charting out a course of interpretation for the future. The methods of interpretation variously employed by the judges in the *Gopalan Case* and their own individual conceptions of the scope of their office thus assume an importance transcending the importance even of such drastic legislation as the Preventive Detention Act. If Mr. Justice Fazl Ali may have seemed to look to the spirit or purpose of the fundamental rights provisions rather than to the letter of the Constitution, Chief Justice Kania and the majority justices for their part, it is submitted, have surrendered too easily to the ideal of a strict and literal construction.

The key to Chief Justice Kania's whole approach is to be found in his declaration:[21]

There is considerable authority for the statement that the Courts are not at liberty to declare an Act void because in their opinion it is opposed to a spirit

[19](1950) XIII Supreme Court Journal 174,182.
[20]*Ibid.*, 182–3.
[21]*Ibid.*, 191.

supposed to pervade the Constitution but not expressed in words. Where the fundamental law has not limited, either in terms or by necessary implication, the general powers conferred upon the Legislature we cannot declare a limitation under the notion of having discovered something in the Constitution which is not even mentioned in the instrument. It is difficult upon any general principles to limit the omnipotence of the sovereign legislative power by judicial interposition, *except so far as the express words of a written Constitution give that authority.*[22]

And in the same vein, Chief Justice Kania attempts (quite inaccurately, it is submitted) to characterize Mr. Justice Fazl Ali's contention that "procedure established by law" in article 21 is equivalent to procedural due process, as a resort to "natural law": "To read the word 'law' as meaning rules of natural justice will land one in difficulties because the rules of natural justice, as regards procedure, are nowhere defined, and in my opinion the Constitution cannot be read as laying down a vague standard."[23] The Chief Justice's definition of the meaning of "procedure established by law," uttered in the same breath as his strictures on "natural law," is, it is to be noted, purely circular: "The correct question is what is the right given by Article 21? The only right is that no person shall be deprived of his life or liberty except according to procedure established by law."[24]

In truth, as an English commentator quite correctly infers,[25] Chief Justice Kania's opinion in the *Gopalan Case* simply goes to show that the establishment of the Supreme Court of India free from any right of appeal to the Privy Council has not in any way meant a departure from "well established rules of law" and "a rejection of all things English." The same interesting condition that can be observed in connection with the judicial interpretation of the Canadian and the Australian constitutions, therefore—the treating of the Constitution in the same light as an ordinary statute, to be construed restrictively and without regard to the policies that the instrument is intended to embody—seems present in Chief Justice Kania's approach in *Gopalan's Case.* Notwithstanding the attainment of political and juridical independence, then, the old patterns of legal thought remain in India.

The contrast between the majority and the minority approaches to the Constitution in the *Gopalan Case* is strikingly re-emphasized in the case of *Keshavan Madhava Menon* v. *The State of Bombay*[26] which came to

[22]Italics are mine.
[23]*Ibid.*, 186.   [24]*Ibid.*
[25]L. C. Green, "The Preventive Detention Act," (·1950) 4 *Indian Law Review* 304, 309. However, compare the criticisms of B. Schwartz, "A Comparative View of the Gopalan Case," (1950) 4 *Indian Law Review* 276.
[26](1951) XIV Supreme Court Journal 182.

the Supreme Court of India in 1951, a year after the *Gopalan Case*. In this case, a prosecution had been launched for an offense punishable under the Indian Press (Emergency Powers) Act, 1931, and during the pendency of the prosecution the Constitution of the new Republic of India came into force. It was contended in argument that the relevant provisions of the Indian Press (Emergency Powers) Act, 1931, were invalid as being in conflict with article 13(1) of the new Constitution, which provided: "All laws in force in the territory of India immediately before the commencement of this Constitution, insofar as they are inconsistent with the provisions of this Part [i.e. part III of the Constitution, Fundamental Rights], shall, to the extent of such inconsistency, be void." The fundamental right which the Indian Press (Emergency Powers) Act, 1931, would, it was contended, infringe if article 13(1) applied to the present case, was article 19(1) (a)—"freedom of speech and expression."

When the case came to the Supreme Court of India, this argument as to the operation of article 13(1) did not impress the Court. As Mr. Justice Das observed,[27] the Court could find nothing in the language of article 13(1) which might be read as indicating an intention to give it retrospective operation. On the contrary, the language clearly pointed the other way. Before the Constitution came into force there was no such thing as fundamental right. What article 13(1) provided was that all existing laws which clashed with the exercise of the fundamental rights (which were for the first time created by the Constitution) should to that extent be void. Article 13(1) did not in terms make the existing laws which were inconsistent with the fundamental rights void *ab initio* or for all purposes. On the contrary, it provided that all existing laws, in so far as they were inconsistent with the fundamental rights, should be void to the extent of their inconsistency. They were not void for all purposes, but they were void only to the extent they came into conflict with the fundamental rights. Article 13(1) had the effect of nullifying all inconsistent existing laws or rendering them ineffectual or nugatory and devoid of any legal force or binding effect, but only with respect to the exercise of fundamental rights on and after the date of the commencement of the Constitution. If, therefore, an act was done before the commencement of the Constitution in contravention of the provisions of any law which, after the Constitution, became void with respect to the exercise of any of the fundamental rights, the inconsistent law was not wiped out so far as the past act was concerned, for to say that it was would be to give the law retrospective effect.

[27]*Ibid.*, 185.

Mr. Justice Fazl Ali, who again dissented from the majority judges' views, conceded that article 13(1) of the Constitution would have no retrospective operation and that transactions which were past and closed and rights which had already vested would remain untouched. Nevertheless he could not agree with the majority as to inchoate matters which were still not determined when the Constitution came into force, and also as to proceedings either not begun or else pending at the time of the coming into force of the Constitution and not yet prosecuted to a final judgment.[28] In these cases, if the law which made the conduct in question an offence was inconsistent with the Constitution, then, in Mr. Justice Fazl Ali's opinion, neither a charge could be framed nor an accused convicted. If, therefore, the relevant portions of the Indian Press (Emergency Powers) Act, 1931, were inconsistent with article 19(1) of the Constitution of the new Republic of India, the accused was entitled to a declaration that he could not be convicted under that Act.[29]

It is interesting to note that Mr. Justice Das, in giving his majority opinion, echoed Chief Justice Kania in the *Gopalan Case,* and characterized the minority attitude as representing an

argument founded on what is claimed to be the spirit of the Constitution . . . always attractive for it has a powerful appeal to sentiment and emotion; but a Court of law has to gather the spirit of the Constitution from the language of the Constitution. . . . The Court should construe the language of Article 13(1) according to the established rules of interpretation and arrive at its true meaning uninfluenced by any assumed spirit of the Constitution.[30]

In fact, however, Mr. Justice Fazl Ali's opinion relies on a close historical analysis of the effects of repeal of statute law in England, the United States, and in India,[31] and upon a detailed survey of the intentions of the framers of the new Constitution of India as to the meaning and operation of article 13(1).[32]

The major difficulty in connection with the majority views in the *Keshavan Madhava Menon Case* is that, granted the premise that article 13(1) of the Constitution was intended to have no retrospective operation, the majority judges proceed to jump very quickly to the conclusion that to apply article 13(1) to strike down proceedings either not begun, or else still pending at the time the new Constitution came into force, is to give that article retrospective operation. That the majority judges felt some difficulty on this point is indicated by the fact that Mr. Justice Das,[33] and also Mr. Justice Mahajan[34] who specially concurred with him, felt

[28]*Ibid.,* 190.
[30]*Ibid.,* 185.
[32]*Ibid.,* 189–90.
[34]*Ibid.,* 198.

[29]*Ibid.,* 191.
[31]*Ibid.,* 187–9.
[33]*Ibid.,* 185.

it necessary to refer at this stage to the powers of the President of the Republic of India under article 372(2) of the Constitution, *inter alia* to repeal by decree any law (including in this case the Indian Press (Emergency Powers) Act, 1931) "for the purpose of bringing the provisions of [such] law in force in the territory of India into accord with the provisions of this Constitution."[35] In such a situation the provisions of the General Clauses Act would have been attracted to the situation and the pending prosecution of the appellant would have been able to be continued in view of that Act. All this, Mr. Justice Das and Mr. Justice Mahajan felt, made it "clear that the idea of the preservation of past inchoate rights or liabilities and pending proceedings to enforce the same was not foreign or abhorrent to the Constitution of India."[36] Mr. Justice Das, indeed, went a step further and speculated that on the basis of the minority arguments it would be equally repugnant to article 13(1) that "men who have already been convicted under such repressive law before the Constitution of India came into force should continue to rot in jail."[37]

These are all, of course, policy considerations, and as such, according to the "established rules of interpretation" preferred so strongly by Mr. Justice Das,[38] are strictly inadmissible unless the constitutional provision in question is ambiguous, a finding that the majority judges in fact refused to make here. The problem is not, therefore, whether or not the judges of the Indian Supreme Court should have recourse to policy in arriving at their decisions in constitutional cases, but in the last resort whether it shall be an informed conscious policy-making, or a vague, impressionistic resort to policy factors as in the majority opinions in the *Keshavan Madhava Menon Case.* It will probably be true, however, while Indian legal education continues to be closely tied to English positivist methods and certainly while the present group of English-trained judicial decision-makers remains on the bench, that the mechanico-positivist approach will prevail over the more consciously purposive, policy-oriented methods. Though the very specificity and detail of the new Indian Constitution in comparison to the constitutions of some of the other countries of the Commonwealth, therefore, may perhaps serve to fill in some of the gaps that have been left by judicial interpretation in those other countries, it seems likely that the Indian Constitution will be subjected to some stress and strain in the future unless the Indian Supreme Court is prepared to adopt a more consciously creative role. One point

---

[35]Article 372.(2).
[36]*Per* Das J., (1951) XIV Supreme Court Journal 182, 185.
[37]*Ibid.*   [38]*Ibid.*

must, however, be mentioned here. The Indian Constitution makes mandatory the retirement of Supreme Court judges at the age of sixty-five: this provision seems to have been included in the Indian Constitution on the assumption that elderly judges are conservative judges, a proposition which, of course, in the light of American experience must be taken with some reserve. Sutherland, Van Devanter, McReynolds, and Butler were, certainly, while members of the United States Supreme Court, elderly men, but so also were Holmes, Brandeis, Hughes, and Stone. One unfortunate result of the Indian retirement rule is likely to be that men will be removed untimely from the bench just as they are beginning to find their feet as constitutional judges and approach their period of greatest intellectual usefulness. Mr. Justice Fazl Ali, for example, recently removed from the Indian Supreme Court bench on attaining the age of sixty-five, was forthwith appointed by the Indian Government to the responsible and presumably physically arduous post of Governor of a state within the Indian federal system.

II

Upon its attainment of independence after World War II, recognized by the Indian Independence Act, 1947,[39] Pakistan[40] began functioning as a self-governing country formally operating under the provisions of the old Government of India Act, 1935, until such time as the Pakistan Constituent Assembly should complete its deliberations and arrive at a draft constitution. It will be remembered that a constituent assembly for undivided India (with one representative, roughly, for each million of population) had first convened in December, 1946, but that the Muslim delegates had broken away to form an independent state. The first meeting of these Muslim delegates functioning as a Constituent Assembly for Pakistan was held in the middle of 1947 and the Constituent Assembly continued to meet from that time onwards until peremptorily dissolved by the Governor-General of Pakistan on October 24, 1954. For most of the seven years during which it actively met, it was deadlocked by disagreement over what should be the key concepts of the new society and what expression, if any, the constitution should give to them. The deadlock essentially involved a conflict between Western secularism and Muslim fundamentalism—between those who would give Pakistan a

[39]10 & 11 Geo. VI, c. 30.
[40]See generally Sir Ivor Jennings, *Constitutional Problems in Pakistan* (1957); Alan Gledhill, *Pakistan: The Development of Its Laws and Constitution* (1957); Keith Callard, *Pakistan: A Political Study* (1957), Herbert Feldman, *A Constitution for Pakistan* (1955).

liberal democratic constitution along Western secular lines and those who would maintain, instead, an essentially Islamic, theocratic organization for the government of the new state.[41] The incorporation of the basic moral principles of Islam into the constitution in the form in which this incorporation was then projected, involved, amongst other things, the proscribing of legislation repugnant to the Quran and the Sunnah, with a related problem whether the Supreme Court alone or a committee learned in Islamic law should decide such repugnancy.[42]

During all this time the Constituent Assembly was also functioning as a legislature for Pakistan, and it did give its attention to a number of critically urgent problems, including the resettlement of the refugees resulting from the physical partition of India brought about by the creation of Pakistan in 1947. Nevertheless, beyond the creation of certain special committees on fundamental rights and matters relating to minorities, the passing of a resolution broadly defining the objects of the new constitution, and the appointment of a committee to work out in detail the main principles of the constitution, little progress was made after 1947 towards resolution of the controversy over the nature of the new state.

Meanwhile, it became clear that, in spite of attempts to adjust the divergent interests of West Pakistan and East Pakistan through the adoption of a federal form of constitution, the Constituent Assembly had under-estimated the extent and depth of the separatist feelings (to a considerable degree based on economic grounds) among the left-wing

[41]"Meeting on October 27, in the Parliament building in Karachi, the Constituent Assembly declared itself in favour of making Pakistan a Republic. It was argued, however, as the late Prime Minister Liaquat Ali Khan had contended not long ago that in view of the differing concepts of democracy as demonstrated and exemplified by the Western powers on the one hand and Soviet Russia and the People's Democratic Republics on the other, it would be advisable to qualify the democratic basis of Pakistan's republic. It was resolved, therefore, that Pakistan will henceforth be known as the Islamic Republic of Pakistan.

"This was an expression of the keen desire of the people of Pakistan to build their politico-social institutions on spiritual and moral grounds, and a clear rejection of Machiavellian philosophy as a state policy." *Pakistan Affairs* (Embassy of Pakistan), (vol. VII, no. 7), Nov. 20, 1953.

[42]". . . The Constituent Assembly approved and adopted the Directive Principles of State Policy which laid down that no legislature would legislate any law repugnant to the Holy Quran (the revealed Book of the Muslims) or the Sunnah (traditions of the Prophet Mohammed). It was also decided that a full bench of the Supreme Court 'alone' can hear and decide cases challenging the validity of legislations on the grounds of repugnancy to the Quran and the Sunnah. This was a clear triumph of the progressive forces over the conservative wing which originally had proposed that a committee of the learned in Islamic Law nominated by the Head of the State should consider such cases." *Ibid.* (vol. VII, no. 26), Aug. 14, 1954.

parties of East Bengal. In April, 1954, the Muslim League went down to a surprising defeat in the elections for the East Bengal Provincial Assembly at the hands of a United Front amalgam of its opponents, who openly espoused the cause of Bengal separatism. Rioting flared up shortly afterwards in East Bengal, and the central Government in Karachi used this as a pretext early in June for dismissing the provincial government of East Bengal under Chief Minister Fazlul Huq.[43] Thereafter, a complicated series of events ensued. In September, 1954, the Constituent Assembly voted unanimously to strip the Governor-General of the powers inhering in him under the Government of India Act, 1935, as adapted for Pakistan, by amending that Act to vest the powers in the Prime Minister, who was made responsible to the legislature. On October 24 Governor-General Ghulam Mohammed, during the absence of Prime Minister Mohammed Ali in the United States, issued a proclamation of a state of emergency throughout Pakistan, dismissed the Constituent Assembly which he declared had lost the confidence of the people, and ordered general elections for Pakistan, subsequently directing the Prime Minister to make certain changes and appointments to his cabinet, including appointments to the key ministries of defence and of the interior (including police).[44] In the substantial constitutional vacuum existing until a new constitution was adopted for Pakistan, the Governor-General's actions might no doubt have claimed support by analogy from the sweeping powers possessed (and also successfully exerted) by the old viceroys of British India, the arrangements contained in the Government of India Act, 1935, being after all formally operative for Pakistan until the drafting and successful adoption of a new constitution. However, a decisive factor in the whole situation (apart from the fact that the Governor-General was on the spot, while the Prime Minister was thousands of miles away) may well have been the support of the civil service and of the army for the Governor-General. This would be a situation, of course, where ultimately "naked power" is controlling.[45]

The Prime Minister seems to have acquiesced after the event (whether willingly or otherwise) in the Governor-General's actions, and he announced a reshuffle in his cabinet. However, the President of the dissolved Constituent Assembly, Tamizuddin Khan, reacted more vigorously

[43]In July, 1954, the central Government of Pakistan outlawed the Communist party in East Bengal, and shortly afterwards in West Pakistan also, as a danger to public peace. In making its announcement of the ban, the Government linked its action to the labour riots in East Bengal in April and May. *Ibid.* (vol. VII, no. 25), July 30, 1954.

[44]*Ibid.* (vol. VIII, no. 5), Nov. 5, 1954.

[45]Cf. H. D. Lasswell and A. Kaplan, *Power and Society* (1950), 139–41.

and proceeded to test the legality of the Governor-General's directives in the courts. In February, 1955, a four-judge bench of the Provincial Court of the Sind Province, in a unanimous decision, declared the Governor-General's dismissal of the Constituent Assembly, and also his appointment at that time of the new ministers to the key cabinet posts, to be illegal and of no effect.[46] This decision necessarily invalidated also actions taken by the cabinet after October 24, 1954, including re-organization of the territorial divisions of West Pakistan into a single governmental unit,[47] as well as the completion of the final draft of a constitution modelled rather closely on that of the United States (especially as to the area and scope of executive power) instead, as heretofore, on that of the United Kingdom. The Advocate-General of Pakistan promptly announced an appeal by the Government to the Federal High Court, and at the same time Tamizuddin Khan summoned a meeting of the old Constituent Assembly, despite the Government's warning that the Assembly would not be allowed to reconvene.[48] Further ventures in constitution-making in Pakistan thus seemed to turn on the resolution of this power conflict.[49]

On March 21, 1955, the Federal High Court, by a four-to-one majority, overturned the Provincial Court's ruling, on appeal,[50] the Federal High Court, however, in a very lengthy group of opinions in support of its decision, avoiding as far as possible the main substantive law issue of the scope of the Governor-General's powers and resting instead on a highly technical ground—that the court below did not have proper jurisdiction to grant the particular remedies asked for.[51] Since,

[46]*Maulvi Tamizuddin Khan* v. *Federation of Pakistan*, [1955] 3 P.L.D. 96 (Sind Chief Court).

[47]*Pakistan Affairs* (vol. VIII, no. 7), Dec. 10, 1954.

[48]*New York Times*, Feb. 13, 1955.

[49]See the remarks of Prime Minister Mohammed Ali on the occasion of the Governor-General's dismissal of the Constituent Assembly: "Constitution-making is important. But more important by far is the security and stability of our country. These must at all times be fully assured. Constitution-making by the present Constituent Assembly has resulted in developments which threaten to imperil our national unity. It has provoked personal, sectional and provincial rivalries and suspicions. Those have to be curbed and Pakistan's interests must be put above everything else." *Pakistan Affairs* (vol. VIII, no. 5), Nov. 5, 1954.

[50]*Federation of Pakistan* v. *Maulvi Tamizuddin Khan*, [1955] 1 P.L.D. 240 (Federal Court of Pakistan: Muhammad Munir C.J. (Muhammad Sharif J. with him), Akram J., and Rahman J. for the majority; Cornelius J. dissenting specially).

[51]*Per* Muhammad Munir C.J.: ". . . I hold that the Constituent Assembly when it functions under subsection (1) of section 8 of the Indian Independence Act, 1947, acts as the Legislature of the Dominion within the meaning of section 6 of that Act, that under subsection (3) of the latter section the assent of the Governor-General is necessary to all legislations by the Legislature of the Dominion, that since section 223-A of the Government of India Act under which

however, the Federal High Court's own ruling depended upon an ultimate proposition that the particular act conferring jurisdiction on the
court below, having been passed by the Constituent Assembly but not
formally assented to by the Governor-General, was invalid, that ruling
had the somewhat unexpected consequence that all other acts of the
Constituent Assembly that had not also been assented to by the Governor-General were likewise invalid; and there were some 44 of these
going back to 1948. Amongst other things, it turned out, this would
mean that all the provincial legislatures of Pakistan were improperly
composed, and that all orders issued by the Governor-General pursuant
to Acts of the 'Constituent Assembly were also invalid: such governmental actions as the creation of the State Bank of Pakistan, the regulation of currency and exercise of exchange control, and the carrying on
of certain types of criminal administration would consequently fall by
the way. The Governor-General responded to this new crisis by invoking
a concept of emergency powers, relying here on claimed residual,
prerogative powers to validate the legislation in question and take other
appropriate measures to carry on the administration and to call a new
Constituent Assembly into being. In the final result, these actions and
the constitutional principle of emergency powers asserted in support
thereof were upheld by the Federal High Court of Pakistan, on a special
Reference by the Governor-General for an advisory opinion, the decision
being, however, by a narrow (3 to 2) majority.[52] In its opinions in the
matter of the special *Reference* the Federal High Court ruled, in addition,
on the main substantive law issue that it had by-passed earlier in
Tamizuddin Khan's Case, and it upheld the Governor-General's power
to dissolve the Constituent Assembly.[53]

---

the Chief Court of the Sind assumed jurisdiction to issue the writs did not receive
such assent, it is not yet law, and that therefore, that Court had no jurisdiction to
issue the writs. In view of this conclusion we cannot go into the other issues in the
case whatever their general importance may be." [1955] 1 P.L.D. 240, at 315
(Federal Court of Pakistan).

   Compare the dicta of Brandeis J. of the United States Supreme Court, concurring specially in *Ashwander* v. *T.V.A.*, (1935) 297 U.S. 288, 347: "The Court will
not pass upon a constitutional question although properly presented by the record
if there is also present some other ground upon which the case may be disposed
of. . . . Thus, if a case can be decided on either of two grounds, one involving a
constitutional question, the other a question of statutory construction or general
law, the Court will decide only the latter." And see also the remarks of Warren
C.J., for the Court, in *Peters* v. *Hobby*, (1955) 349 U.S. 331.

   [52]*Reference by His Excellency the Governor General (under section 213 of the
Government of India Act, 1935)*, [1955] 1 P.L.D. 435 (Federal Court of Pakistan:
Muhammad Munir C.J. for the majority (Akram and Rahman JJ. with him);
Cornelius J. and Muhammad Sharif J. each dissenting specially).

   [53]See especially *per* Muhammad Munir C.J., [1955] 1 P.L.D. 435, at 464 *et seq.*
(Federal Court of Pakistan).

The outside observer will have little difficulty in understanding and sympathizing with the tactical principle (though not necessarily the doctrinal argument and reasoning) behind the first main decision of the Federal High Court in the recent crisis. The American doctrine of judicial restraint looks to the effective political limits to the assertion of judicial power in relation to co-ordinate arms of government, whether executive or legislative, and emphasizes the wisdom of judicial non-involvement, as far as possible, in great political controversies: general Commonwealth constitutional experience, not least perhaps in the Union of South Africa, in recent years, has also demonstrated the physical impossibility of judges' maintaining a position, for any sustained period of time, against that advanced by overweening executive or legislative power. But the wise judicial approach, in such cases, is surely to recognize frankly, in the court's opinion, that the issue at bar turns ultimately on considerations of power and not on law, and to refrain from a legal ruling altogether—this is, in effect, to postulate a constitutional category of "political questions" which are to be non-justiciable. Such an approach applied by the Federal High Court at the outset of the constitutional crisis, in *Tamizuddin Khan's Case*, would have yielded the same end result but have saved the court from the extraordinary embarrassment (as it subsequently turned out) of its having, according to the particular doctrinal argument on which it in fact decided that case, necessarily invalidated at the same time most of the constitutional and administrative structure and machinery on which any government in Pakistan must rest. It would also have avoided the necessity for the frenetic legal researches that then ensued in an endeavour to discover a doctrinal justification for holding the scattered remnants of Pakistan political and governmental authority together, and the further necessity for the upholding of the unbridled assertion of prerogative power under the principle *salus populi suprema lex* that the Federal High Court majority felt themselves inevitably constrained to in the later special *Reference*. The two dissenting opinions in the special *Reference*[54] (and especially that of Mr. Justice Cornelius)[55] had understandable reservations about

---

[54][1955] 1 P.L.D. 435: at 488 *et seq.* (Cornelius J. dissenting), and at 516 *et seq.* (Muhammad Sharif J. dissenting).

[55]"As I am clearly of the opinion that similar special powers are not available to the Governor-General, I will not further lengthen this opinion by discussing the value of these opinions which have been made available from Chalmers 'Opinions of Eminent Lawyers', whether categorically or intrinsically. Nor is it of advantage, from the viewpoint which seems to me to be the only correct viewpoint, to discuss the applicability of the Ship-Money case. These affairs belong to periods when, and to territories where, the power of the King was, in fact, supreme and undisputed. The records of these affairs are hardly the kind of scripture which one could reasonably expect to be quoted in a proceeding which is essentially one in

a majority holding that had to be rested, *faute de mieux*, on the constitutional claims of the Stuart kings of England: the rather extravagant sweep of the court's decision in the special *Reference*—both the actual holding and more especially the language of the majority opinion—may well embarrass the courts in Pakistan sorely in the future. If the court majority in the Federal High Court in the special *Reference* case might well have profited by application of the concept of self-restraint, not merely in the sense of its accepting the existence of desirable areas of non-justiciability but also in the sense of accepting the wisdom at times of moderation in judicial opinion-writing—of not going beyond the necessities of the case—by the same token the severe strictures advanced by the Chief Justice of the Federal High Court, in *Tamizuddin Khan's Case*, against the doctrinal argument and legal reasoning of the judges in the court below,[56] the Sind Chief Court, seem a little unfair, especially as the Chief Justice, in the same breath, appears to recognize that naked power, and not law, is controlling in the situation before the court when he queries whether it is a "wise exercise of discretion for the judiciary to re-install in power a deposed government by issuing enforceable writs against a *de facto* government."[57]

The new Constituent Assembly, elected in June, 1955, contained one notable surprise: the formerly dominant Muslim League was now reduced to one-third of the total membership.[58] Prime Minister Mohammed Ali, the leader of the Muslim League in the Constituent Assembly, was soon forced to resign as Prime Minister, in August, 1955, when his own party withdrew its support, Mohammed Ali retiring from politics and becoming instead Pakistan's Ambassador to the United States. Negotiations for a three-party coalition between the Muslim League on the one

the enforcement and maintenance of representative institutions. For they can bring but cold comfort to any protagonist of the autocratic principle against the now universal rule that the will of the people is sovereign. In the case of North America, the territory was lost eventually to the British Crown through the maintenance of just such reactionary opinions, as those which Senior Counsel for the Federation of Pakistan has been pleased to advance for acceptance by the Court. And in the English case, the fate of the King, and the Judges who delivered the opinion favouring absolute power in the King, stands for all time as a warning against absolutism, and as a landmark in the struggle for the freedom and eventual sovereignty of the people." *Per* Cornelius J., dissenting, [1955] 1 P.L.D. 435, at 515–16.

[56]*Per* Muhammad Munir C.J., *Federation of Pakistan* v. *Maulvi Tamizuddin Khan*, [1955] 1 P.L.D. 240, at 313.

[57]*Ibid.*

[58]*New York Times*, June 23, 1955; *Pakistan Affairs* (vol. VIII, no. 20), June 24, 1955.

hand, and the opposition Awami (People's) League and the United Front, broke down before the intense and bitter personal rivalry of the respective leaders of the latter two parties, Hussain Shaheed Suhrawardy and Fazlul Huq.[59] Finally, a non-partisan figure, a distinguished civil servant and economist, Chaudhri Mohamad Ali, was called in, and he managed to form a Government, which lasted one year, resting on a coalition of the Muslim League and the United Front, with the Awami League going into Opposition.[60] In the background, as strong man, remained the new Governor-General, Major General Iskander Mirza, who succeeded Ghulam Mohammed in that office on the latter's retirement through illness in August, 1955. Iskander Mirza, as civil service head of the Defence Department, had supported Ghulam Mohammed during the constitutional crisis of October, 1954, and had also acted at the time as Defence Minister.

Under pressure from the Governor-General and the new Prime Minister, the reconstituted Constituent Assembly pressed ahead at the preparation of a constitution, and finally, on February 29, 1956, declared passed a "Constitution of the Islamic Republic of Pakistan," which was formally assented to by the Governor-General on March 2, 1956.[61] Somewhat ominously perhaps for the chances of over-all popular acceptance of the new Constitution, both the Awami League members of the Constituent Assembly and also the Hindu members from East Bengal absented themselves from the final vote in the Constituent Assembly.[62]

The new constitutional instrument in structural organization and outline resembled the Indian Republican Constitution of 1949. It was, first of all, a lengthy, exhaustive document—234 articles and 6 schedules—though this was still rather less prolix than the Indian Constitution. It contained an elaborate Bill of Rights, and also Directive Principles of State Policy. The Constitution was expressed to be federal in form, though like the Indian Constitution again, in spite of elaborate machinery in the Constitution for the division and allocation of governmental functions between the federal government and the provinces, effective power seemed to be concentrated in the central government. Within the frame-

[59]*New York Times*, Aug. 11, 1955.
[60]*Ibid.*, Aug. 14 and 15, 1955; *Pakistan Affairs* (vol. VIII, no. 23), Aug. 29, 1955. Strife within the Muslim League forced Chaudhri Mohamad Ali's resignation in September, 1956. Mr. Suhrawardy then became Prime Minister.
[61]*Constitution of the Islamic Republic of Pakistan*, Gazette Extraordinary (Pakistan), March 2, 1956. (The text of the Constitution is reprinted in [1956] 4 P.L.D. 54.) See also *Pakistan Affairs* (vol. IX, no. 5), March 5, 1956.
[62]*Economist* (London), March 10, 1956.

work of the federal government, the system was parliamentary, along English lines, with a prime minister and cabinet responsible to the federal legislature, the unicameral National Assembly, and with a head of state, styled as president, who (remembering the drastic powers successfully exerted by Governor-General Ghulam Mohammed against the Prime Minister during the course of the constitutional crisis of October, 1954) was to exercise his functions in accordance with the advice of the prime minister and cabinet of the day.[63] There was provision for a Supreme Court exercising judicial review on the American and Commonwealth models.[64]

The controversial aspects of the new Constitution of Pakistan concerned the extent to which, in its federal form, it had been designed or would be able in the future to ensure substantial governmental autonomy to the two main geographical units of the country, the provinces of East Pakistan and West Pakistan; and the extent to which the new Constitution was Islamic in content and form reflecting the main aspirations of Muslim fundamentalism. As to the first point, the new Constitution did defer substantially to regional claims in so far as equality of representation in the federal legislature was expressly guaranteed to the two constituent units or provinces, East Pakistan and West Pakistan:[65] this was, of course, no hard and fast guarantee against centripetal tendencies in the government of Pakistan, but it should at least have ensured (and this had been the major demand of the East Bengal separatist movement of the last few years) that regional interests, especially those of the province of East Pakistan, would be taken into account in the processes of governmental policy-making at the centre. As to the second point, there was bitter criticism in the reconstituted Constituent Assembly, when the new draft Constitution first appeared, of some features that were thought to defer too much to Muslim fundamentalism—for example, the styling of the Constitution as the "Islamic Republic" of Pakistan, and also the constitutional requirement that the president of Pakistan be a Muslim.[66] On the other hand, the language issue, which the Muslim religious leaders had pressed strongly to be decided in favour of the classical Muslim language, Urdu, exclusively, was resolved amicably by declaring both Urdu and Bengali to be the state languages, while providing for the continuance of English for an interim period of twenty years after the adoption of the new Constitution.[67] And the issue

[63]Constitution, article 37 (7).
[64]Articles 148–64.
[65]Article 44 (1) and (4).
[66]Article 32 (2).
[67]Article 214.

of the nature and composition of electorates—whether there should be joint electorates for the whole population or separate for the non-Muslim minorities, with these minority communities, interestingly enough, demanding joint electorates on the score that separate electorates would relegate them effectively to the status of second-class citizens and limit their ambitions within a narrow field[68]—had at least not been decided finally (as once seemed likely) against the minorities' claims, for the new Constitution expressly left open for future decision by the federal legislature the issue of joint or separate electorates, for both federal and provincial elections.[69] It is true that some of the language and drafting of the new Constitution bears an unmistakeable Muslim character and flavour: note, in this regard, the Directive Principles of State Policy (see article 24, promotion of Muslim unity and international peace,[70] and article 25, promotion of Islamic principles[71]); and note, above all, the special "Islamic provisions" of the Constitution, articles 197[72] and 198. Article 198 (1) in fact declares: "No law shall be enacted which is repugnant to the Injunctions of Islam as laid down in the Holy Quran and Sunnah, hereinafter referred to as Injunctions of Islam, and existing law shall be brought into conformity with such Injunctions."

Any teeth that this stipulation might have, however, seemed to be promptly drawn by the succeeding paragraphs of article 198 which provide, first, that effect is to be given to paragraph (1) only through the appointment of a special commission which is to make recommendations within a period of five years to the federal legislature and to compile a list for the guidance of the federal and provincial legislatures of "such Injunctions of Islam as can be given legislative effect";[73] that nothing in article 198 is to affect the "personal laws of non-Muslim citizens, or their status as citizens, or any provision of the Constitution";[74] and, in the final paragraph of the article (styled as "Explanation"), that in the application of the whole article to the personal law of any Muslim sect, the expression "Quran and Sunnah" is to mean the Quran and Sunnah "as interpreted by that sect."

[68]*Economist* (London), Jan. 21, 1956; *New York Times*, Feb. 22, 1956.
[69]Constitution, article 145.
[70]Article 24: "The State shall endeavour to strengthen the bonds of unity among Muslim countries. . . ."
[71]Article 25 (1): "Steps shall be taken to enable the Muslims of Pakistan individually and collectively to order their lives in accordance with the Holy Quran and Sunnah."
[72]Article 197 (1): "The President shall set up an organisation for Islamic research and instruction in advanced studies to assist in the reconstruction of Muslim society on a truly Islamic basis."
[73]Article 198 (3).
[74]Article 198 (4).

This was a far cry indeed from the original proposal of the Muslim religious leaders that a Commission of Holy Men, learned in the Quran and Sunnah, should have power to pass on all laws enacted by the legislature and to determine their validity in accordance with their conformity or non-conformity to the Quran and Sunnah.[75] Lacking any enforcement agency other than the predominantly lay-educated Supreme Court, these Muslim fundamentalist provisions seemed likely to reduce to pious injunctions of purely moral significance, for individual members of the government to interpret according to their consciences. And even here the very generality of the Quran and Sunnah, and their lack of specificity and concreteness of ruling as to contemporary problems of political life,[76] should have ensured that they would be no real barrier to secularist ideas of predominantly Western-trained (especially in law) political leaders; though apparently only Iskander Mirza would have gone so far as to favour formal separation of church and state on the United States and general Western model.[77]

After the formal proclamation of the new Constitution, in March, 1956, the constitutional machinery began to be put in motion for the holding of nation-wide general elections. A polling date was announced for February, 1959, and President Iskander Mirza insisted that there would be no more delays. However, on October 7, 1958, Iskander Mirza announced that he had abrogated the constitution, and he called on the army to assume power, this *coup d'état* apparently being effected without significant public opposition.[78]

Right from the outset, though, it was apparent that Iskander Mirza's survival as President would depend on the support of the army, for he did not possess a political machine of his own. Iskander Mirza's links with the army, unfortunately for him, had been mainly developed in his erstwhile capacity as civilian head of the defence ministry, for he had not been a lifetime, professional soldier, his current military rank of Major General being an honorary appointment bestowed on him in connection

[75]*Pakistan Affairs* (vol. VII, no. 26), Aug. 14, 1954.

[76]See, in this regard, the thoughtful discussion by K. Callard, "The Political Stability of Pakistan," (1956) 29 *Pacific Affairs* 5, at 15–16.

[77]*Ibid.*, 17.

[78]"The President [Iskander Mirza] has given the assurance that after the country has been 'taken to sanity by a peaceful revolution', a Constitution will have to be devised, different from the one which has been abrogated, which may be 'more suitable to the genius of the Muslim people'. . . . General Mohammad Ayub Khan [Military Commander-in-Chief] has also emphatically affirmed that the restoration of democracy is the firm and unshakeable ultimate aim of the present régime, although it may not be of the same type as has been tried unsuccessfully in the past." *Dawn (Karachi)*, Oct. 10, 1958. And see also *Pakistan Affairs* (vol. XI, no. 16), Oct. 15, 1958.

with his heading of the defence ministry. Under these circumstances it was probably inevitable that, the base of power of the new presidential régime being the support of the army, the army should itself soon move to assume the symbols as well as the substance of political authority in Pakistan, more especially as by ridding itself of Iskander Mirza the army could dissociate itself from some of the popular odium attaching to the unconstitutional transfer of power represented by the *coup d'état* of October 7, 1958. Immediately after the *coup d'état*, Iskander Mirza had imposed martial law in Pakistan and appointed General Mohammad Ayub Khan as Supreme Commander of the Armed Forces and as administrator of martial law. On October 27, 1958, it was formally announced that Iskander Mirza had relinquished the office of President and that General Ayub Khan had become President in his place.[79] In a prepared statement issued at the time of his resignation, Iskander Mirza gave as reasons his belief that any "semblance of dual control" would be likely to hamper effective performance of the paramount task of maintaining political order;[80] but he left Pakistan immediately afterwards for residence in England. The new President, General Ayub Khan, had announced that martial law would be maintained as long as necessary to ensure "clearance of the political, social, economic, and administrative mess that has been created in the past"; and he went on to say that Pakistan must be "brought back to a state of complete health" and that there was "no intention to allow things to revert to the bad old ways."[81] He also promised reform in two important areas. As to the land, he promised a halting of the uneconomic carving up of land caused by the Muslim practice of dividing property among sons.[82] As to Pakistan's legal system,[83] he was critical of British legal influence for he

[79]*Pakistan Affairs* (vol. XI, no. 17), Nov. 1, 1958.
[80]*Ibid.*
[81]*Ibid.*
[82]"My object in setting up the Land Reforms Commission was to enable the Government to devise a rational land tenure policy which will satisfy, on the one hand, the social need for greater equality of opportunity and social status, and on the other, the economic need for increasing agricultural production and improving the standard of rural living through a more equitable distribution of income from land." Statement of President Ayub Khan, published in *Pakistan Affairs* (vol. XII, no. 4), Feb. 15, 1959. For details of the West Pakistan Land Reforms Regulation, implementing this announced programme, see *Pakistan Affairs* (vol. XII, no. 5), March 1, 1959.
[83]President Ayub Khan announced progress in plans for legislation to introduce "Basic Democracies," in which the object would be "not to impose a system from above but to cause a system to grow from below in relation to social, economic, educational, and moral realities of the situation." At the core of these plans was the Union Panchayat (Council) scheme, which would serve to "prepare a base on which upward pyramid of sound political system could be developed. Basic

regarded the British system as expensive and dilatory and good only for those who know the law.[84]

III

The countries surveyed, India and Pakistan, as a matter of history shared a common legal heritage to the extent that they were all, until the end of World War II, subject to British imperial authority. This experience of British rule left these countries with a tradition of strong government, which in terms of administration was territorially central-ized, and which, from the viewpoint of law-making power, was legally unrestricted either by constitutional checks and balances or bills of rights and similar fundamental guarantees.

In planning the constitutional arrangements to govern the exercise, on a representative, national basis, of the power transferred from the British Crown, the Indian constitution-makers agreed from the outset on a Western, secular constitution. The new Indian Republican Constitution, in its extent and depth of detail, evidences a desire on the part of the Indian constitution-makers to provide a blue-print in government for

---

Democracies would, in due course, replace purely official agencies and would reflect representation of the people obtained at the most intimate level, become the nerve centre of their areas where all local problems of development and civil responsibilities could be studied at close range and their solutions discovered and applied." *Pakistan Affairs* (vol. XII, no. 16), Sept. 3, 1959.

The Basic Democracies, as a distinctive and original Pakistan constitutional and governmental concept (the elections to Basic Democracies being viewed in the same light as general elections in Western countries), are envisaged, optimistically, as serving as a model for under-developed countries to establish their own types of democracy. *Pakistan Affairs* (vol. XIII, no. 4), March 7, 1960.

[84] On February 17, 1960, President Ayub Khan announced the formation of an eleven-member Commission headed by Mr. Justice Muhammad Shahabuddin, to draft a new constitution within the shortest possible time. The Commission was charged, *inter alia*, with examining the "progressive failure of parliamentary government in Pakistan leading to the abrogation of the Constitution of 1956." It was to submit constitutional proposals for ensuring at the same time "a democracy adaptable to changed circumstances and based on the Islamic principles of justice, equality, and tolerance; the consolidation of national unity; and a firm and stable system of government." *Pakistan Affairs* (vol. XIII, no. 4), March 7, 1960.

In addressing himself to the constitutional Commission, President Ayub Khan commended the exercise of "realism and originality of thought": "When applying your minds to constitutional affairs, I beg of you, not to be dogmatic and go by what is being done in other countries. Such examples are all right as guides, but their blind imitation in our own environments has proved suicidal in the past and can do so again in future. So, when making your suggestions to the Constitutional Commission, please look at the Book of Pakistan and not follow blindly somebody else's text books. Study the circumstances in our own country and ask yourselves: 'What is it that will really suit us?' " *Ibid.*

a population only a small proportion of whom were yet experienced and trained in democratic political processes. To this extent also the new constitutional instrument is a definite break-away from the rather Spartan, skeletal, British approach to constitutional law and government hitherto dominant in India. The most notable provisions in this regard are the Bill of Rights and the Directive Principles of State Policy, and also the institution of judicial review; and yet the new Indian Supreme Court, in actually exercising judicial review, has tended to cut down and confine the broad sweep of the various provisions and guarantees of the new Constitution. Partly, no doubt, this particular judicial approach reflects an awareness on the part of the judges that if the prolix, exhaustive, constitutional instrument of 1949 is to be given meaning in action, some pruning away of its more obvious excess detail is required, and that harsh judicial construction is the best available means to this end; partly it may be an unconscious reversion by the Indian judges (resulting from their essentially English type of legal training) to concepts of dominant executive and legislative power, unhampered by constitutional checks and balances, carrying over from the era of British rule. In any case, when it is remembered that the new Indian Constitution preferred to adopt the British system of a parliamentary executive in preference to the classic American system of a separation of governmental powers between executive, legislature, and judiciary, there seems little prospect in the near future of any considerable degree of judicial activism to impose additional constitutional checks and balances upon the union (central) government.

In Pakistan, the internecine conflict in the Constituent Assembly between the Muslim fundamentalists and those who favoured a Western secular constitution complicated and obscured the whole debate over the structural organization and outlines of the proposed new Constitution. Nevertheless, the dominant opinion in the Pakistan Constituent Assembly tended towards the Indian approach to constitution-making—that is to say, the exhaustive blue-print in government with provision for an elaborate Bill of Rights and with the Directive Principles of State Policy to guide and also limit the use of legislative power; and this is in fact the form that the Pakistan Constitution, as finally adopted on March 2, 1956, had taken.

The new Pakistan Constitution, like the Indian Republican Constitution and other Commonwealth constitutions, allowed for the operation of the institution of judicial review, with a Supreme Court acting as watchdog of the general constitutional arrangements. The intervention by the courts in Pakistan during the 1954 constitutional crisis, to attempt to restrain the user of the Governor-General's claimed prerogative powers, met with some resistance on the part of the central Government of Pakistan; and a drastic showdown between the Government and the judges may only have been avoided by the Federal High Court's surrender to the principle of uncontrolled executive power, under the cloak of the maxim *salus populi suprema lex.* Any appraisal of the ultimate merits of the Pakistan constitutional dispute of October, 1954, when the Governor-General dismissed the Constituent Assembly and also forced the Prime Minister to make changes in key cabinet posts, will necessarily have to be a complex one. (I am not regarding the issues presented in the *coup d'état* of October 7, 1958, and its immediate aftermath, as capable of useful classification or extended discussion in essentially legal, constitutional terms.) The issue in 1954 was hardly a clear-cut one between popular sovereignty as represented by a freely elected government and legislature on the one hand, and a purely appointive, non-elective office (that of Governor-General) on the other; for the authority of a popular mandate must surely come near to the breaking point in the case of the assertion of ordinary legislative powers by a Constituent Assembly functioning for over seven years without any substantial progress towards achievement of its ultimate *raison d'être,* the drafting of a new constitutional instrument. The bitter partisan conflicts in the new Constituent Assembly, elected after the dissolution of the old, tended to confirm the Governor-General's charge at the time of the dissolution of 1954 that the leaders of the Constituent Assembly were concerned primarily with personal aggrandizement and power rather than with the completion of the task for which they were first summoned together; and in some measure the unbroken support which the senior civil service, generally conceded to be the most responsible element in Pakistan today, gave to the Governor-General throughout, tends to confirm also the further charge that the leaders of the Constituent Assembly had by 1954 long since lost popular confidence, though the support of the army for the Governor-General was no doubt the decisive factor.

The real tragedy of the Partition in India, of course, was that the politically, economically, and militarily least viable unit—Pakistan—was left much the most poorly equipped after Partition in terms of supply of trained civil servants and administrators and, for that matter, of intellectual and general commercial élites. The continuing and exhaustive debates after 1947 in the Pakistan Constituent Assembly over such tense issues as whether to have a secular or a theocratic (Islamic) constitution; or whether to have a unitary or a federal state; or whether to have a strong presidential executive of the American type or instead the rather less direct British system of a purely titular, honorific head of state coupled with a working prime minister—seem, in retrospect, to have been doomed from the outset to be just so many exercises in empty rhetoric in the absence of either a sufficient popular base to political power or a firm and continuing guarantee of honest and efficient public administration.

Some small share of the responsibility for current disasters or disappointments in Pakistan may rest on the small group of British legal and governmental advisers—from the new Commonwealth Office and the old India Office—who flitted in the background after the grant of Indian independence in 1947. With the best of motives and ideals, they tended perhaps too readily to assume that constitutional and general legal institutions and forms worked out in a purely Western European, industrial civilization complex must automatically be relevant to the special needs and problems of the newly emergent countries of South-East Asia: they made Dicey's English Constitution, so to speak, an *Idealtyp* to which all other constitutions should desirably conform, forgetting the rather special facts of late nineteenth-century English political society that served to make Dicey's classic formulation palatable in its own day—the acceptance on the part of Opposition parties and political out-groups in the state of at least the minimum "rules of the game" and of concomitant obligations of restraint in the manner and extent of actual user of rights of political opposition; and on the part of the Government forces of their own duties of self-discipline and self-restraint in the exercise of governmental powers.

But a major portion of blame must rest on honourable and upright local leaders like ex-President Iskander Mirza, at the time of writing a rather unhappy exile in London from General Ayub Khan's second *coup* in late 1958. When Iskander Mirza threw his own and the army's weight behind the then Governor-General, Ghulam Mohammed, in the crisis of October 24, 1954, with the Governor-General's dramatic dismissal of the Constituent Assembly and his rather overt pressure on the Prime Minister and the cabinet of the day—actions which an intermediate court, the Sind Chief Court, unanimously ruled were illegal and of no effect but which the Federal High Court of Pakistan finally upheld, by majority, on appeal—he served notice that "naked power," and not law, was ultimately the controlling factor in Pakistan. The later judicial sanctioning of the unbridled assertion of prerogative power—under the cloak of the principle *salus populi suprema lex*—to which the Federal High Court majority finally felt themselves constrained, in its extravagant sweep boded rather ill for the future of constitutional government in Pakistan; and the events of October, 1958, are hardly surprising in this light.

8

THE COURTS AND THE CONSTITUTION IN
CATHOLIC IRELAND

At the time of its drafting in 1937, the new Constitution of Ireland represented something of a special case in the constitutional law of the countries of the then British Commonwealth. First, in contradistinction to all other self-governing countries of the Commonwealth at that time, Ireland's Constitution did not depend for its formal authority upon any enactment by the United Kingdom Parliament. In keeping with the sharp, almost revolutionary nature of the severance of ties with the United Kingdom, originally manifested in the Constitution of the Irish Free State (Saorstat Eireann) Act of 1922, the Constitution of 1937 is expressly declared in its preamble to have an unimpeachable local, popular source. Second, and again in contrast to the other self-governing countries of the Commonwealth at that time, Ireland's Constitution is notable for the fact that it possesses a comprehensive and detailed Bill of Rights[1] plus some analogous fundamental provisions, the Directive Principles of Social

[1]Republic of Eire, Constitution, articles 40–44. The best academic text available on Irish constitutional law is L. Kohn, *The Constitution of the Irish Free State* (1932), which, though it is concerned with the Constitution of the Irish Free State (Saorstat Eireann) of 1922, presents in its opening chapters an invaluable account of the historical origins of fundamental law notions in modern Ireland. Dr. Kohn's work was hailed, at the time it appeared, in a special foreword written by Chief Justice Hugh Kennedy of the Irish Free State, as "the first scholarly treatise on our polity. . . . Political and legal constitutional studies in this Country were in practice limited to the British Constitution and the working of the British Parliament. Professor Dicey's book became an evangel accepted reverently and without criticism or question in our schools (such as they were) of political philosophy and constitutional law. . . . I see in the use of Dr. Kohn's book, written from the wide-view standpoint of current European thought, a hope for the emancipation of our schools of law and political studies from the thraldom which has made them negligible wraiths; a starting-point from which, stimulated to work in the tradition of a revitalised national culture but in a new freedom and breadth of outlook, they may become symbols of learning and philosophy of which the nation need not be ashamed. . . ." *Ibid.*, xi *et seq.* Dr. Kohn was German-born and trained. He has since become Legal Adviser to the Israeli government. No comparable academic work has appeared on the new Irish Constitution of 1937.

Policy,[2] borrowed from the Spanish Republican Constitution of 1931.

These particular features of the Irish Constitution can no doubt be attributed in part to the inclinations of the Irish constitution-makers, understandably very strong in 1937 in the full flush of Irish nationalism, to eschew English constitutional forms and patterns; in part, too, these particular features clearly stem from the fact that the Constitution of 1937 is designed for a society that is predominantly Roman Catholic in composition. The Catholic, scholastic tone of the Constitution is made clear from the very first word of the preamble:

In the Name of the Most Holy Trinity, from Whom is all authority and to Whom, as our final end, all actions both of men and States must be referred, We, the people of Eire,
Humbly acknowledging all our obligations to our Divine Lord, Jesus Christ, Who sustained our fathers through centuries of trial, . . .
Do hereby adopt, enact, and give to ourselves this Constitution.

It is also manifest on examination of the detailed provisions of the Bill of Rights. In article 44 (religion), subsection 2 of section 1 states, for example: "The State recognises the special position of the Holy Catholic Apostolic and Roman Church as the guardian of the Faith professed by the great majority of the citizens." In article 41 (the family), subsection 1 of section 1 states: "The State recognises the Family as the natural primary and fundamental unit group of Society, and as a moral institution possessing inalienable and imprescriptible rights, antecedent and superior to all positive law." This is followed by article 42 (education), section 1 of which acknowledges the family as the "primary and natural educator of the child" and states further that the state "guarantees to respect the inalienable right and duty of parents to provide, according to their means, for the religious and moral, intellectual, physical and social education of their children." According to section 1 of article 43 (private property):

(1) The State acknowledges that man, in virtue of his rational being, has the natural right, antecedent to positive law, to the private ownership of external goods.
(2) The State accordingly guarantees to pass no law attempting to abolish the right of private ownership or the general right to transfer, bequeath, and inherit property.

Taken as a whole, indeed, the Constitution of 1937 in formal outline more closely resembles the written instruments of Continental Europe, replete as these generally are with fundamental-type provisions, than the more skeletal constitutions of the various countries of the Commonwealth. Yet the differences in actual working practice between the Irish Con-

[2]Article 45.

stitution and the various Commonwealth constitutions should not be exaggerated. Thus, for example, though the Constitution of 1937 is republican in form, the president, in powers and functions, seems essentially a Doge-like character, with effective power under the Constitution exercised by the prime minister and cabinet who are responsible to the lower House, Dáil Eireann, of a bicameral legislature, Oireachtas, just as the British cabinet is responsible to the House of Commons. The Constitution of 1937 does, however, formally envisage the institution of judicial review,[3] the only instance of this in a country of the Commonwealth that is not, like Canada or Australia or the Republic of India, federal in form.[4] It is with the impact of the Supreme Court of Ireland, in exercising the role of judicial review upon an essentially Catholic, scholastic constitutional instrument, that this survey is principally concerned.

It must be said at the outset that the Supreme Court's work to date has been rather less daring and innovatory than one might have expected, granted the break with the past represented by the Constitution of 1937 and especially the novel character and comprehensive provisions of the Bill of Rights. The Supreme Court is, of course, a private-law court as well as a constitutional court of review. An overwhelming proportion of its work in fact is non-constitutional, and the Court's members appear to be selected on a basis of strict professional attainments. These factors have frequently combined, elsewhere in the Commonwealth, to produce a narrow, rather inflexible approach to constitutional interpretation, with emphasis on harsh construction and reading down of the constitutional provisions in question. The Irish courts in this respect purport to follow a strictly legalistic approach to constitutional interpretation,[5] though off-

[3]Articles 34, 3 (2) and 4 (3, 4).

[4]See *National Union of Railwaymen and Others* v. *Sullivan and Others*, [1947] Ir. R. 77, 99 (Murnaghan J.): "Constitutions frequently embody, within their framework, important principles of polity expressed in general language. In some Constitutions it is left to the Legislature to interpret the meaning of these principles, but in other types of Constitution, of which ours is one, an authority is chosen which is clothed with the power and burdened with the duty of seeing that the Legislature shall not transgress the limits set upon its powers."

[5]See, e.g., *Pigs Marketing Board* v. *Donnelly (Dublin) Ltd.*, [1939] Ir. R. 413, 418 (High Court), *per* Hanna J., remarking upon the standard "social justice" established in Article 43, 2 (1) of the Constitution: "In a Court of law it seems to me to be a nebulous phrase, involving no question of law for the Court, but questions of ethics, morals, economics, and sociology, which are, in my opinion, beyond the determination of a Court of law, but which may be, in their various aspects, within the consideration of the Oireachtas, as representing the people, when framing the law." See also *National Union of Railwaymen and Others* v. *Sullivan and Others*, [1947] Ir. R. 77, 86 (High Court), *per* Gavan Duffy J.: "I think the attack on the statute by the N.U.R. is really intended to defeat a legislative policy which it mislikes, but this Court is concerned exclusively with the legal objections raised. Policy is emphatically within the legislative, as distinct from

setting the effects of this is the very fullness of the drafting of the Irish Constitution. It may be that a policy-oriented approach to judicial decision-making is less necessary, hence perhaps less likely to occur, if the constitutional instrument itself in effect sets out the jural postulates of the society[6] than if the constitution is largely silent except for detailing the purely functional, machinery arrangements of government.[7]

The Constitution of Ireland formally envisages a separation of powers,[8] for the effect of article 6, combined with articles 34 to 37 (the courts), is to "vest in the Courts the exclusive right to determine justiciable contro-

---

the judicial, domain. The ingenious method adopted by the Oireachtas . . . seems in fact well calculated to achieve its purpose, but if that method looked most un-promising, a Court of Law would have no right to express any disapproval of the policy behind the plan. I am not concerned with the wisdom of the measure."

[6]Compare *Buckley and Others (Sinn Fein)* v. *Attorney-General and Another*, [1950] Ir. R. 67, 82 *per* O'Byrne J.: "We do not feel called upon to enter upon an enquiry as to the foundation of natural rights or as to their nature and extent. They have been the subject-matter of philosophical discussion for many centuries. It is sufficient for us to say that this State, by its Constitution [article 43], acknowledges that the right to private property is such a right and that this right is antecedent to all positive law. This, in our opinion, means that man by virtue, and as an attribute, of his human personality is so entitled to such a right that no positive law is competent to deprive him of it and we are of opinion that the entire Article [43] is informed by, and should be construed in the light of, this fundamental conception."

[7]The Irish reports contain occasional references to American cases. See, e.g., *Pigs Marketing Board* v. *Donnelly (Dublin) Ltd.*, [1939] Ir. R. 413, 415 (High Court), where the United States separation of powers cases are referred to in detail by counsel. Yet it is true to say that the Irish judges have substantially eschewed the frank policy-making type of approach to judicial review to be found among the members of the United States Supreme Court at the present day. Part of the explanation, no doubt, is to be found in the fact that the Irish picture of American case law is generally rather hazy and occasionally quite inaccurate. Thus counsel, during the argument in *National Union of Railwaymen and Others* v. *Sullivan and Others*, [1947] Ir. R. 77, 93, relied on *Lochner* v. *New York*, (1905) 198 U.S. 45, and *Adkins* v. *Children's Hospital*, (1923) 261 U.S. 525, without apparently realizing that those cases had been overruled by *West Coast Hotel Co.* v. *Parrish*, (1937) 300 U.S. 379. Note also the references by counsel, during argument in *Buckley and Others (Sinn Fein)* v. *Attorney-General and Another*, [1950] Ir. R. 67, 76, to the "right of property" that is "acknowl-edged" by the Fifth Amendment to the U.S. Constitution.

[8]"Article 6 provides that all powers of government, legislative, executive, and judicial, derive, under God, from the people, and it further provides that these powers of government are exercisable only by or on the authority of the organs of State established by the Constitution. The manifest object of this Article was to recognise and ordain that, in this State, all powers of government should be exercised in accordance with the well-recognised principle of the distribution of powers between the legislative executive, and judicial organs of the State and to require that these powers should not be exercised otherwise. The subsequent articles are designed to carry into effect this distribution of powers." *Buckley and Others (Sinn Fein)* v. *Attorney-General and Another*, [1950] Ir. R. 67, 81 (O'Byrne J.).

versies."[9] It seems generally true, however, on the cases, that the Supreme Court of Ireland has not been disposed to read the constitutional separation of powers as imposing any absolute bar on any one arm of government's exercising functions strictly appertaining to some other arm.[10] The Court has indicated that it will approach the task of judicial review of the constitutionality of legislative enactments with at least an initial presumption in favour of the legislature's assertion of its powers,[11] and that in any case it should apply a general attitude of self-restraint in passing on such enactments.[12] The Irish constitutional cases after 1937 may conveniently

[9]*Ibid.* at 84.

[10]See, e.g., *Pigs Marketing Board* v. *Donnelly (Dublin) Ltd.*, [1939] Ir. R. 413 (High Court), (no constitutional prohibition on delegation of legislative powers in respect to matters of detail and requiring expert knowledge). See also *Fisher* v. *Irish Land Commission and Attorney-General*, [1948] Ir. R. 3 (Maguire C.J.), (an administrative body, even though it may be bound to act judicially, does not administer justice or exercise judicial power in contravention of the constitutional separation of powers). Cf. *In re Art. 26 of the Constitution and the Offences against the State (Amendment) Bill, 1940*, [1940] Ir. R. 470.
However, an administrative body, though not a court, may still be bound to act judicially. Thus, where a determination in connection with compulsory acquisition of land is made dependent upon certain findings of fact, the Lay Commissioners are bound to act judicially and to hear and consider the evidence and submissions put before them: *The State (Crowley)* v. *Irish Land Commission and Others*, [1951] Ir. R. 250, 260 (O'Byrne J.). Again, a Land Commission, in issuing certificates for the purposes of subsequent institution of ejectment proceedings in the circuit courts, may be obligated to comply with the requirements of natural justice in the sense of informing the party adversely affected and allowing him to put his case before the commission: *Foley* v. *Irish Land Commission and Another*, [1952] Ir. R. 118, 149 (O'Byrne J.).

[11]"Where any particular law is not expressly prohibited and it is sought to establish that it is repugnant to the Constitution by reason of some implied prohibition or repugnancy, we are of opinion, as a matter of construction, that such repugnancy must be clearly established." [1940] Ir. R. 470, 478 (Sullivan C.J.), reaffirmed, *In re Art. 26 of the Constitution and the School Attendance Bill, 1942*, [1943] Ir. R. 334, 344 (Sullivan C.J.). The proposition is expressed in even more positive form by Murnaghan J., in *National Union of Railwaymen and Others* v. *Sullivan and Others*, [1947] Ir. R. 77, 100: "The Court will approach the question of repugnancy of Acts of the Legislature with a presumption in favour of constitutionality."

[12]"The People, by the Constitution, have provided for the setting-up of three great Departments of State—the Oireachtas, the Executive, and Judiciary—and it is essential for the harmonious working of the machinery of State that each Department should confine itself to its own constitutional functions. If the Oireachtas enacts a law within the scope of its legal and constitutional powers, it is for the Courts to construe and apply such law. Any criticism by the Courts of the manner in which the Oireachtas exercises the discretion and powers vested in it would be as much open to objection as would any suggestion, in either House of the Oireachtas, that a decision of a Court, within the scope of its authority, was not in accordance with law." *In re Art. 26 of the Constitution and the Offences against the State (Amendment) Bill, 1940*, [1940] Ir. R. 470, 481 (Sullivan C.J.).

be classified and dealt with under three general categories, corresponding to the organization of the "fundamental rights" section of the Constitution: the areas of personal or political rights,[13] of property and economic rights,[14] and of social rights,[15] this latter category including within its scope the special roles in Irish society of the family and the church and also the problem of education.

PERSONAL RIGHTS—THE "EMERGENCY" CASES

The leading cases in the area of personal rights are of a somewhat special character since they all arose out of or during the course of the emergency created by World War II. In these cases the Supreme Court of Ireland showed itself prepared to construe with very great breadth the general grants of special powers made to the executive under emergency powers legislation, thereby closely paralleling the marked restraint shown by the English courts in trenching on similar special powers granted to the United Kingdom executive during World War II.[16] In discussing the Irish emergency cases it must be remembered that Ireland was not an actual participant in hostilities in World War II, though running a constant risk, by virtue of her strategic position, of being embroiled eventually in the conflict.

The first of the three great emergency cases decided by the Irish Supreme Court, *In re Art. 26 of the Constitution and the Offences against the State (Amendment) Bill, 1940*,[17] arose as a reference by the executive to the Supreme Court for an advisory opinion under article 26 of the Constitution. The Supreme Court refused to hold invalid the so-called "preventive detention" provisions of the 1940 Bill, which provided *inter alia* that whenever a minister of state was of the opinion that any particular person was engaged in activities which, in the minister's opinion, were prejudicial to the preservation of public peace and order or to the security of the state, the minister might order the arrest and detention of such person. The Supreme Court ruled that this provision did not confer upon the minister the power to administer justice and was not, therefore, repugnant to article 34 of the Constitution specifying that justice shall be administered in public courts. Further, the Court felt that the detention of persons provided for in the Bill was not in the nature of punishment but of preventive justice, a precautionary measure taken for the purpose of preserving the public peace and order and the security of the state, and therefore did not contravene the provisions of article 38 of the Constitution

13Article 40.   14Article 43.
15Articles 41–2, 44.
16See, e.g., the House of Lords decision in *Liversidge* v. *Anderson*, [1942] A.C. 206.   17[1940] Ir. R. 470.

providing that no person be tried on any criminal charge save in due course of law. The Court also declined to find any violation of the provisions of article 40 of the Constitution (personal rights), especially article 40, 4 (1), providing that no citizen should be deprived of his personal liberty "save in accordance with law." The Court stated it was unable to find in the phrase "save in accordance with law" any meaning other than "in accordance with the law as it exists at the time when the particular Article is invoked and sought to be applied. In this Article, it means the law as it exists at the time when the legality of the detention arises for determination. A person in custody is detained in accordance with law if he is detained in accordance with the provisions of a statute duly passed by the Oireachtas. . . ."[18]

The Irish Supreme Court's refusal in this case to consider using article 40, 4, as a possible barrier against executive or legislative action trenching on personal rights is noteworthy if we consider the similarity in the language of article 40, 4, of the Irish Constitution and the due process clauses in the Fifth and Fourteenth amendments to the United States Constitution and also the marked resurgence of procedural due process concepts in the United States in recent years. Irish contact with American constitutional law cases and general trends, however, seems to be rather casual and general at best.[19]

In the second emergency case, *In re McGrath & Harte*,[20] the Court had to consider the effect of article 28, 3, of the Constitution,[21] which in effect

---

[18]*Ibid.* at 482 (Sullivan C.J.). Compare the Supreme Court decisions in *In re Philip Clarke*, [1950] Ir. R. 235, refusing to hold as violative, *inter alia*, of article 40 the provisions of the Mental Treatment Act, 1945, empowering members of the Garda Siochana, as a first step, to be followed by two separate medical examinations, to arrest a person believed to be of unsound mind, if they thought it necessary for the public safety or the safety of the person himself. "The impugned legislation is of a paternal character, clearly intended for the care and custody of persons suspected to be suffering from mental infirmity and for the safety and well-being of the public generally. The existence of mental infirmity is too widespread to be overlooked. . . . The section cannot, in our opinion, be construed as an attack upon the personal rights of the citizen. On the contrary it seems to us to be designated for the protection of the citizen and for the promotion of the common good." *Ibid.* at 247–8 (O'Byrne J.).

[19]See n. 7 *supra.*   [20][1941] Ir. R. 68.

[21]Article 28, 3 (3) reads: "Nothing in this Constitution shall be invoked to invalidate any law enacted by the Oireachtas which is expressed to be for the purpose of securing the public safety and the preservation of the State in time of war or armed rebellion, or to nullify any act done or purporting to be done in pursuance of any such law."

This section of the Constitution was amended in 1939 so as to provide that "time of war" should include a "time when there is taking place an armed conflict in which the State is not a participant but in respect of which each of the Houses of the Oireachtas shall have resolved that, arising out of such armed conflict, a national emergency exists affecting vital interests of the State."

confers on the Irish legislature a plenary law-making power, overriding express constitutional limitations, to secure the "public safety and the preservation of the State in time of war or armed rebellion." Pursuant to these provisions, a Military Court with the power to impose sentence of death was created by special emergency powers legislation passed by the Oireachtas in 1940, and an order was made thereunder for the trial of persons charged with certain specified offences. It was held by the Supreme Court that since the emergency power legislation had been passed in accordance with the provisions of Article 28, no other articles of the Constitution could be invoked to invalidate that legislation.

In passing upon the original order of 1940 establishing the Military Court and also a further order of the same year commiting two civilians charged with murder for trial before the Military Court, the Supreme Court of Ireland also refused to be influenced by the argument that, since these were measures derogating from the ordinary common law rights of the citizen, they should be construed strictly, against the government. The Supreme Court ruled that since the orders in question had been made by the government in exercise of its powers under the emergency powers legislation, it was unnecessary that the orders should show jurisdiction on their face by reciting either the resolutions passed by the Oireachtas or the opinion of the government that they were necessary or expedient for securing the public safety or the preservation of the state. Indeed, the Supreme Court went so far as to give the order of 1940 a form of retrospective operation by ruling that the government might, in terms of the legislation of 1940 and the order made thereunder, provide for the trial and punishment of persons whether the offences were alleged to have been committed before or after the making of the order.

In the case of *The State (Walsh and Others)* v. *Lennon and Others,*[22] under a further emergency powers order made in 1941, four accused persons had been ordered to be brought before a Military Court established by the order of 1940 to be tried on a charge of murder. It was contended, *inter alia,* that the order of 1941 was *ultra vires* in that it directed the Military Court, which was to try the accused, to try them together, and so precluded the Court from exercising its discretion and control over its own procedure. The Supreme Court reaffirmed its judgment in *In re McGrath & Harte,*[23] however, and ruled that the provisions of article 28, 3, of the Constitution made it quite impossible to invoke any other article of the Constitution to invalidate an order made in pursuance of an act passed by the Oireachtas and expressed to be for any of the purposes mentioned in article 28. The order of 1941 allowed the Military Court

[22][1942] Ir. R. 112.   [23][1941] Ir. R. 68.

the discretionary right to decide if it would not be bound by any statutory or common law rule of evidence. The Supreme Court considered in passing and rejected the argument that this constituted such a fundamental change in the law of evidence as to deprive the Military Court of the attributes of a judicial tribunal and prevent the Military Court from carrying out such a trial as was contemplated by the emergency powers legislation of 1940.[24]

The three emergency cases, sanctioning as they do, in terms of their end results, the broad user of executive power substantially unfettered by court control, may perhaps be seen in proper perspective as an exceptional category of constitutional cases, distinct from all other cases, in the light of the Supreme Court's concluding remarks in *The State (Walsh and Others)* v. *Lennon and Others*:

> This emergency legislation is of a temporary character, passed for the purpose of securing the public safety and the preservation of the State during a time of national emergency. During such period the duty of determining what provisions are necessary for securing that object is vested in the Government, but any such provision must be laid before each House of the Oireachtas and may be annulled by a resolution passed by either House. Many of the arguments addressed to us would be more fittingly addressed to either House of the Oireachtas when considering the propriety of, and necessity for, the Order in question. They are not matters which can properly be relied upon in a Court of law.[25]

PROPERTY AND ECONOMIC RIGHTS

The first important case involving the question of economic rights under the Constitution directly concerned article 43 (private property). In *Pigs Marketing Board* v. *Donnelly (Dublin), Ltd.*,[26] the High Court was called upon to consider certain legislation authorizing the government to fix prices of certain categories of pigs to be purchased by bacon manufacturers. It was contended, *inter alia,* that the price-fixing legislation conflicted with article 43, 1 (2), establishing a right of private property,[27] and further, that the legislation did not come within the category of exceptions established in article 43, 2 (1), authorizing the regulation of this right of private property by the "principles of social justice." As to the first question, the High Court noted that it had been argued that any

---

[24]"If, as is conceded, the Government had power to set up a special tribunal to try specified offences, and to invest it with special powers for this purpose, it is, in our opinion, quite impossible to hold that that tribunal is deprived of its jurisdiction and powers by reason of alterations in the laws of evidence to be recognised by such tribunal." *The State (Walsh and Others)* v. *Lennon and Others,* [1942] Ir. R. 112, 130 (Sullivan C.J.).

[25]*Ibid.* at 131.   [26][1939] Ir. R. 413.

[27]Article 43, 1 (2), states: "The State . . . guarantees to pass no law attempting to abolish the right of private ownership or the general right to transfer, bequeath, and inherit property."

law passed by the state that interfered with the free operation of competition and trade or interfered with the contractual or proprietorial rights of citizens was unconstitutional. In the High Court's opinion, however, it was too late in the day for this argument to prevail:

> The days of laissez-faire are at an end, and this is recognized in . . . [article 43, 2 (2)], which enacts that the State can as occasion requires delimit by law the exercise of the said rights with a view to reconciling their exercise with the exigencies of the common good. I am of the opinion that the Oireachtas must be the judge of whatever limitation is to be enacted. This law does not abolish private ownership in pigs or bacon, it only delimits the exercise of these rights by the persons in whom they are vested, and if the law is contrary to the common good, whatever that may mean, it must be clearly proved, and I repeat that an Act is deemed to be constitutional until the contrary is clearly established.[28]

Though this decision thus stems, in part at least, from notions of judicial self-restraint involving the applying of something of a beneficial presumption in regard to constitutionality of legislative enactments, it seems clear also that the Court will not be disposed to construe the right of private property guaranteed by article 43 in any absolute way. As to the other question, whether, assuming this was a regulation by the state of the exercise of the right of private property, the regulation conformed to the "principles of social justice," the High Court was more cautious, refusing finally to pass at all on the question:

> I cannot define that phrase [social justice] as a matter of law. It cannot be the old standard of the greatest good for the greatest number, for, at the present day, it may be considered proper that the claim of a minority be made paramount in some topic. . . . I cannot conceive social justice as being a constant quality, either with individuals or in different States. What is social justice in one State may be the negation of what is considered social justice in another State.[29]

The leading case of *National Union of Railwaymen and Others* v. *Sullivan and Others*[30] arose specifically under article 40 (personal rights), especially article 40, 6 (1), guaranteeing a right to form associations and unions, such right however being subject to regulation and control in the public interest.[31] This case involves the so-called "right of association,"

[28][1939] Ir. R. 413, 422–3 (Hanna J.).
[29]*Ibid.* at 418.   [30][1947] Ir. R. 77.
[31]Article 40, 6 (1), states: "The State guarantees liberty for the exercise of the following rights, subject to public order and morality:— . . . (iii) The right of the citizen to form associations and unions. Laws, however, may be enacted for the regulation and control in the public interest of the exercise of the foregoing right." Article 40, 6 (2), adds a further qualification: "Laws regulating the manner in which the right of forming associations and unions and the right of free assembly may be exercised shall contain no political, religious or class discrimination.

in the case of Ireland guaranteed by article 40 of the Constitution (personal rights). It is here being classified under the head of "property and economic rights," however, for the reason that the right of association, where it has to do with trade unions, will normally have economic or power implications, rather than implications in the area of personal rights proper. Provision had been made under the Trade Union Act of 1941 for the establishment of a trade union tribunal with power, on the application of any trade union claiming to have organized a majority of the workmen of a particular class, to grant a determination that such union alone should have the right so to organize workmen of that class. The Act further provided that where such a determination had been granted to a particular union and remained unrevoked, no other union should accept as a new member any workman of the class in question. The Irish Transport and General Workers' Union applied to the tribunal set up under the Act for a determination that it should have the sole right to organize workmen employed in the road passenger service of the statutory transport undertaking, Coras Iompair Eireann, but immediately the National Union of Railwaymen, a rival trade union, and certain workmen of the class affected brought proceedings for a declaration that the legislation in question was invalid as repugnant to article 40, 6, of the Constitution.

When the case was appealed, the Supreme Court noted that the Trade Union Act of 1941 did not prohibit all association, but purported only to limit the right of the citizen to join one or more prescribed associations, that is, the union or unions in respect of which a determination had been made. The Court felt, however, that any such limitation undoubtedly operated to deprive the citizen of a free choice of the persons with whom he associated. The Court felt that both logically and practically depriving a citizen of the choice of the persons with whom he associated was not a mere control of the exercise of the right of association but a denial of that right altogether. In the Court's view, the Constitution stated the right of the citizen to form associations or unions in emphatic terms, and it was impossible to harmonize this language with a law which prohibited the forming of associations and unions, and allowed the citizen only to join prescribed associations and unions.[32]

In the case of *Buckley and Others (Sinn Fein)* v. *Attorney-General and Another*,[33] the honorary treasurers of the Sinn Fein organization being unable, owing to controversies within the organization, to determine who were entitled to the organization's funds, had in 1924 lodged in court a sum of money representing the central fund of the organization. The honorary treasurers subsequently had died and the plaintiffs in the present

[32][1947] Ir. R. 77, 102.   [33][1950] Ir. R. 67.

case, on behalf of themselves and of all other members of the organization, began proceedings in 1942 against the Attorney-General, as representative of the people of Ireland, and also against the representative of the surviving trustee of the funds in court, for a declaration that the money lodged in court was the property of the organization and also for an order directing the payment to them of the funds then in court. In 1947, before the action had been brought to trial, the Sinn Fein Funds Act was passed by the Oireachtas, providing that all further proceedings in the action should be stayed and that the High Court should, if application were made *ex parte* by or on behalf of the Attorney-General, make an order dismissing the action.[34] The Act also established a board charged with the maintenance and management of a trust fund into which all moneys received by the board under the Act were to be paid; and it was further provided that on application of the board made *ex parte* the High Court should make an order directing that the funds in court should be paid to the board.

On the Attorney-General's application *ex parte* to the High Court in accordance with the terms of the Act, it was contended *inter alia* that the Sinn Fein Funds Act, 1947, was in conflict with the Constitution as violating the right of private property guaranteed under article 43 of the Constitution. When the case reached the Supreme Court, the Court rested its decision equally upon article 40 (personal rights) and article 43 (private property), pointing to section 3(2) of article 40 under which the state undertakes to "vindicate the life, person, good name, and property rights of every citizen." With regard to article 43, the Supreme Court noted that Ireland by its Constitution acknowledged the right to private property as a natural right, antecedent to all positive law. This, in the Court's opinion, meant that man, as an attribute of his human personality, was so entitled to the right to private property that no positive law was competent to deprive him of it. In the Court's opinion, therefore, the entire article 43 was informed by, and should be construed in the light of, this fundamental conception.[35] Though in terms of article 43, 2, the state might regulate the rights of private property according to the "principles of social justice"[36] so as to "reconcile their exercise with the exigencies of the common good,"[37] there was no suggestion here that any conflict had arisen or was likely to arise between the exercise by the plaintiffs of their rights of property in the trust moneys and the exigencies of the common good. It was only the existence of such a conflict and an attempt by the legislature to reconcile such conflicting claims that could justify the

[34]This is detailed in section 10 of the Act. [35][1950] Ir. R. 67, 82.
[36]Article 43, 2 (1). [37]Article 43, 2 (2).

enactment of the statute under review. In the opinion of the Court, therefore, the Sinn Fein Funds Act, 1947, was repugnant to the solemn declaration as to the rights of private property contained in article 43 of the Constitution.[38]

SOCIAL RIGHTS: THE FAMILY, THE CHURCH, AND EDUCATION

In connection with the advisory opinion, *In re Art. 26 of the Constitution and the School Attendance Bill, 1942,*[39] the Supreme Court was called on to consider article 42, 3(2), of the Constitution, which governs the moral, intellectual, and social education of children.[40] The School Attendance Bill of 1942, passed by the Oireachtas, had provided: "A child shall not be deemed for the purpose of this Act to be receiving suitable education in a manner other than by attending a national school, a suitable school, or a recognised school unless such education and the manner in which such child is receiving it, have been certified under this section by the Minister to be suitable." The Supreme Court held the provision in question to be repugnant to the Constitution. Assuming that the powers conferred upon the minister by the section, if passed into law, would be exercised in a reasonable, conscientious, and temperate manner, nevertheless it was clear that a minister, construing the section in a reasonable manner, might still require a higher standard of education than could properly be prescribed as a minimum standard under article 42, 3(2), of the Constitution. Further, the standard contemplated by the section might vary from child to child, and this was not such a standard of general application as the Constitution contemplated.[41]

[38][1950] Ir. R. 67, 83. In *Foley v. Irish Land Commission and Another*, [1952] Ir. R. 118, 149 (O'Byrne J.), the Supreme Court of Ireland distinguished *Buckley and Others (Sinn Fein)* v. *Attorney-General and Another*, and refused to apply article 43 of the Constitution (private property) to strike down a scheme administered by the Land Commission under which the Commission sold lands to purchasers, advancing to the purchasers the purchase money but at the same time requiring them to reside continuously on the lands. As O'Byrne J. noted for the Court, at 153: "The argument put before this Court on behalf of the appellant, when reduced to its logical conclusion, seems to involve the proposition that any limitation placed by the Oireachtas on private property, which may result in the loss of that property by the owner, is repugnant to the Constitution and, accordingly, void. If this argument be sound, the Constitution has certainly placed serious fetters upon the Legislature in dealing with property rights and the Court is not prepared to accept such a far-reaching proposition.

"The Land Purchase Acts, of which the Act of 1946 forms part, constitute a very important branch of our social legislation. As has been pointed out in this Court the object of these Acts is to create a peasant proprietorship of a certain standard."   [39][1943] Ir. R. 334.

[40]Article 42, 3 (2), states: "The State shall, . . . as guardian of the common good, require in view of actual conditions that the children receive a certain minimum education, moral, intellectual, and social."   [41][1943] Ir. R. 334, 345.

The Supreme Court also found the provision void in so far as, under it, not only the minimum educational requirements but also the manner in which a child was receiving this education must be certified by the minister. The state was entitled to require that children should receive a certain minimum education, but so long as parents met this general standard the manner in which the education was being given and received was entirely a matter for the parents and was not a matter in respect of which the state was entitled to interfere.[42]

In the leading case of *In re Frost, Infants*,[43] the Court considered both article 42 (education) and article 41 (the family). This case concerned an ante-nuptial agreement entered into by a Protestant, the prospective husband, who was about to marry a Roman Catholic, to the effect that any children of the marriage should be brought up as Roman Catholics. The children of the marriage, with the exception of the youngest child, were baptized as Roman Catholics but, under the terms of a subsequent separation agreement between the parents, the father received custody of the children, whom he placed in a Protestant Home. On the husband's death his widow applied to the Court for the custody of the children. It was contended on behalf of the widow that the normal common law rule according to which, as the Supreme Court recognized in its opinion, the father had the legal right to determine the religion in which the children should be educated, had been displaced by the Constitution of 1937, articles 41 and 42. It had been contended, as the Court expressly noted, that in terms of these articles, the Court must:

... regard the Family as a unit, the control and management of which is vested in both parents while they are both living and, on the death of either of them, in the parent who survives. As a general proposition that is un-questionable. . . . The Constitution does not define the respective rights of the parents during their lifetime. Where, as in the present case, the parents could not agree on the particular religion in which their children should be brought up and educated, the children should not be deprived of all religious education. If that be so, then the only alternative is that one or other of the parents should have the legal right to determine the religion in which the children shall be educated. The rule which the Courts both in this country and in England have consistently followed, is that the father has that legal right, and that when that right has been exercised by him, the children must be educated in the religion which he has chosen, by his wife should she survive him. In my opinion that rule is not inconsistent with any Article of the Constitution, and the Courts are entitled to act upon it.[44]

The Supreme Court expressly stated[45] that it was not considering the question whether the provisions of the Constitution of 1937 affected the established law as to the validity and effect of ante-nuptial agreements

[42]*Ibid.* at 346.　　　　　　　　　　　　　[43][1947] Ir. R. 3.
[44]*Ibid.* at 28–9 (Sullivan C.J.).　　　　　　[45]*Ibid.* at 29.

concerning the religion in which children of the marriage were to be educated, since in the present case the parents had made a further agreement as to the education of the children at the time of their separation. But the Court also made it clear that the common law right of the father to determine the religion in which his children should be educated, though it was unaffected by the Constitution, might still, according to the common law cases, be displaced by consideration of the children's welfare.[46]

These problems were considered anew by the Supreme Court shortly afterwards, in the leading case, *In the matter of Tilson, Infants*.[47] This case once again arose from an ante-nuptial agreement between a Protestant, the prospective husband, and a Roman Catholic to the effect that any issue of the marriage should be brought up as Roman Catholics. All four children to the marriage were duly baptized as Roman Catholics, but on differences arising between husband and wife, the husband removed the three elder children and placed them in a Protestant institution. The mother thereupon brought an action to obtain custody of the children. In giving its decision on appeal, the Supreme Court recognized that, putting to one side for the moment the question of the effect of the Constitution of 1937, at common law the father had complete control over the children of the marriage and the wife had no voice against the wishes of the husband.[48] Should the Supreme Court of Ireland now follow the old common law rulings in favour of the rights of the father, in the light of the provisions of the Constitution of 1937? The Supreme Court considered article 42 of the Constitution (education):

Where the father and mother of children are alive this article recognizes a joint right and duty in them to provide for the religious education of their children. The word, "parents" is in the plural and, naturally, should include both father and mother. Common sense and reason lead to the view that the mother is under the duty of educating the children as well as the father; and both must do so according to their means.[49]

[46]See especially *ibid.* at 27.　　[47][1951] Ir. R. 1 (Black J. dissenting specially).
[48]*Ibid.* at 31. The Supreme Court here relied on the English decision, *In re Agar-Ellis, Agar-Ellis* v. *Lascelles*, (1878) 10 Ch. D. 49, in which Vice-Chancellor Malins had gone so far as to rule that "by the laws of England, by the laws of Christianity, and by the constitution of society, when there is a difference of opinion between husband and wife, it is the duty of the wife to submit to the husband. . . . The principles of this Court are the principles of propriety, that the children must be brought up in the religion of the father. The father is the head of his house, he must have the control of his family, he must say how and by whom they are to be educated, and where they are to be educated, and this Court never does interfere between a father and his children unless there be an abandonment of the parental duty. . . . [The] father, however absolutely he may have promised, is at liberty to revoke it." *Ibid.* at 55 *et seq.* The case was affirmed on appeal by the Court of Appeal, (1878) 10 Ch. D. 63 (James L.J.).
[49][1951] Ir. R. 1, 32 (Murnaghan J.).

As to the English common law authorities, the Supreme Court was not disposed to hold these as binding on Irish courts of the present day.[50] The Supreme Court was at pains also to distinguish its own recent decision in *In re Frost,*[51] pointing out that although in that case it had held in favour of the father's claims, it had not decided that if an agreement had been made by the father and mother and had been put into practice for years the father alone could rescind it. In the facts of the *Frost Case,* though there had been an ante-nuptial agreement to bring up the children as Roman Catholics, the father and mother had later made a solemn agreement to the contrary and this new agreement had been acted on for years.[52] The Court concluded by declaring that the true principle under the Constitution of 1937 was that the parents, father and mother together, had a joint power and duty in respect of the religious education of their children. If they together made a decision and put it into practice, it was not in the power of either the father or the mother to revoke such decision against the will of the other party. Such an exercise of their power might be made after marriage when the occasion arose; but an agreement made before marriage dealing with matters which would arise during the marriage and put into force after the marriage was equally effective and of as binding force in law.[53]

The Supreme Court thus rested its decision upon article 42 (education), refusing to enter into a discussion of the effects of article 41 (the family), and article 44 (religion), though these latter two articles had been referred to by counsel in argument before the Court.[54]

---

[50]"The archaic law of England rapidly disintegrating under modern conditions need not be a guide for the fundamental principles of a modern state. It is not a proper method of construing a new constitution of a modern state to make an approach in the light of legal survivals of an earlier law." *Ibid.*

[51][1947] Ir. R. 3.

[52][1951] Ir. R. 1, 33.

[53]*Ibid.* at 34.

[54]"If the Court is able to arrive at a decision of the case upon the construction of Article 42 . . . alone and without reference to Article 41 (The Family) and Article 44 (Religion), nothing is to be gained by discussing these last-mentioned articles in the present case. It is right, however, to say that the Court, in arriving at its decision, is not now holding that these last-mentioned articles confer any privileged position before the law upon members of the Roman Catholic Church, and during the argument counsel for the respondent expressly disclaimed any such privileged position." *Ibid.* at 35. The opinion of the Supreme Court as given by Murnaghan J. falls short in this respect, it is to be noted, of the comprehensiveness and sweep of the opinion of Gavan Duffy P. in the High Court. See n. 56 *infra.* No doubt Murnaghan felt it desirable to cut down the sweep of some of Gavan Duffy's propositions. The single dissent in the Supreme Court, on the part of Black, is principally directed at Gavan Duffy's dicta in the Court below.

In a matter decided in the same year as the Supreme Court decision in the *Tilson Case,* though prior in point of time thereto, Gavan Duffy P. in the High

CONCLUSION

In spite of the Irish judges' insistence on the distinction between "law" and "policy," involving the notion that judges in exercising judicial review of the Constitution have no concern with "questions of ethics, morals, economics, and sociology,"[55] empirical, case-by-case examination of the Irish Supreme Court's work shows that the judges' function, in practice, has been much more than any simple law-finding role that might reduce, ultimately, to a merely mechanical "squaring" of statutes with the Constitution. It still seems true to say, however, that the approach to judicial policy-making on the part of the Irish judges has been much less sustained and, it is suggested also, much less conscious or informed than is the case, for example, with the United States Supreme Court. As a result, no doubt, of Ireland's long historical association with the United Kingdom, the influence of English judicial techniques and English methods of legal training, and the strictly professional nature of the criteria for selection for appointment to the Supreme Court bench, the Irish judges have moved rather cautiously in translating the policy norms set out in the guarantees and directives of the Constitution of 1937 into law-in-action. The positive law of the Constitution of 1937, from the opening remarks of the preamble onwards through the Bill of Rights and the Directive Principles of Social Policy, purports to represent a society whose "living law" is Roman Catholic and social democratic.[56] But the

---

Court was called on to consider the terms of a will whereby a testatrix had left property on trust to maintain and educate in Ireland and to bring up as a Roman Catholic an infant G.Q. (the son of a Protestant father and a Roman Catholic mother who had been married in a Protestant Church in Dublin). G.Q. had been baptized in the Roman Catholic Church while his parents resided under the testatrix' roof. The testatrix directed that the selection of a Roman Catholic school to be attended by G.Q. should be in the absolute discretion of the trustees, and she further directed that if G.Q. should cease to practice the Roman Catholic religion, he should forfeit all benefits under the will. Though taking judicial notice of the special position of the Roman Catholic Church under the Irish Constitution (article 44), Gavan Duffy P. held the first condition void as "overrid[ing] the sacred parental authority and defy[ing] the parental right and duty of education under Article 42 of the Constitution"; and the second condition void as "too indefinite to be enforceable as a condition subsequent." *Burke and O'Reilly* v. *Burke and Quail*, [1951] Ir. R. 216, at 221–2 (High Court).

[55]See *Pigs Marketing Board* v. *Donnelly (Dublin) Ltd.*, [1939] Ir. R. 413, 418 (High Court), (Hanna J.).

[56]The strongest expression of these sentiments on the bench is to be found in the dicta of Gavan Duffy P. in the High Court in the *Tilson Case*, [1951] Ir. R. 1, 13, 15: "We are a people of deep religious convictions. Accordingly, our fundamental law deliberately establishes a Christian constitution; the indifferentism of our decadent era is utterly rejected by us. The Irish code marks a new departure from time-honoured precedents which are not ours and gives us a polity conceived in a spirit and couched in a language unfamiliar to the jurisprudence

actual approach of the Irish judges to the cases considered in detail above has been but rarely innovatory, and in general fairly conventional throughout. To this extent it is clear that the impact of modern Catholic political, social, and economic ideas on legal development in present-day Ireland has been rather less significant or substantial than the adoption of the radically new Constitution of 1937 might have seemed at the time to foreshadow.

---

which dominated the United Kingdom of Great Britain and Ireland. . . . Thus, for religion, for marriage, for the family and the children, we have laid our own foundations. Much of the resultant polity is both remote from British precedent and alien to the English way of life, and, when the powerful torch of transmarine legal authority is flashed across our path to show us the way we should go, that disconformity may point decisively another way. . . . The cardinal position ascribed to the family by our fundamental law is profoundly significant; the home is the pivot of our plan of life. The confused philosophy of law bequeathed to us by the nineteenth century is superseded by articles which exalt the family by proclaiming and adopting in the text of the Constitution itself the Christian conception of the place of the family in society and in the State. . . ." The Supreme Court, on appeal in the *Tilson Case*, see n. 54 *supra*, though affirming Gavan Duffy's decision in the High Court, refused to follow him in basing the decision on article 44 (religion), and article 41 (the family), Murnaghan J. for the majority being at some pains to limit the official statement of the grounds of decision to article 42 (education).

9

THE UNITED STATES SUPREME COURT
AND THE DILEMMA OF
JUDICIAL POLICY-MAKING

To understand the philosophic conflicts in the United States Supreme Court at the present day, one must go back to the dilemma bequeathed to the Court by its outstanding judicial personality of modern times, Mr. Justice Oliver Wendell Holmes, Jr., on his retirement in 1932 after thirty years of service on the Court. For Holmes's conception of the judicial function (or at least so it seems in the light of re-examination at the present day) was essentially two-sided. First, there was a tradition of judicial restraint, or more properly judicial self-restraint—the notion that the Supreme Court (in Holmes's words) should defer to the popular will as expressed in the enactments of legislative majorities "unless it can be said that a rational and fair man necessarily would admit that the statute proposed would infringe fundamental principles as they have been understood by the traditions of our people and our law"[1]—this even though the judges might personally consider the enactment in question unwise and unreasonable. From the viewpoint of constitutional technology this judicial attitude is represented by the judicial "presumption of constitutionality" of legislation. Second, there was a tradition of judicial activism, involving the notion that in certain areas of subject-matter, notably the field of political and civil rights, the Court should look with a jealous eye on legislation cutting down or trenching on those rights; on the technological side, this is represented by what amounts, in effect, to a judicial presumption of invalidity (or unconstitutionality).

The first strain, stemming originally from Holmes's classic dissent in the *Lochner Case* in 1905, was an intellectual position reiterated by Holmes as a minority judge throughout his career on the Supreme Court in opposition to what amounted to a politically and economically con-

[1]See *Lochner* v. *New York*, (1905) 198 U.S. 45, 76 (dissenting opinion by Mr. Justice Holmes).

servative majority on the Court which persisted in invalidating national and state social and economic planning legislation on the score of conflict with a liberty of contract supposedly guaranteed by the Fifth and Fourteenth amendments to the Constitution. This Court majority—the "Old Court" as it is now customary to call it—was (in the terminology of the present day) attempting to maintain through judicial activism as applied to the Constitution an essentially laissez-faire organization for American economic and social life.

Now Holmes's opposition to the "Old Court" was always expressed as a technical one—an objection in effect to judicial activism, in the name of the new doctrine of judicial self-restraint. The Old Court majority, as is well known, finally yielded in 1937 under pressure of public opinion and a powerful executive, President Franklin Roosevelt, who was roused to challenge the Court's outright rejection of the main planks of the New Deal legislation. The collapse of the Old Court seems to have been due, essentially, to public reaction to the economic philosophy that the Court majority's decisions maintained; the opposition to the Old Court, however (especially in professional and academic legal circles), was verbalized in terms of separation of powers arguments and conceptions of the proper role of the court vis-à-vis legislative majorities—in a word, the Holmesian notion of judicial self-restraint. Thus, even in the overthrow of the Old Court, something of the same ambivalence that we have observed in the basic Holmesian approach to judicial review seems to be present. On the one hand, there is opposition to the Old Court on political or philosophical grounds, in terms of objections to the particular policies that the reigning majority on the Court is implementing; this type of opposition, however, necessarily rests on the basic premise that the Court has the right (which it should exercise) of passing on legislation—the objection is here not to judicial activism as such but to the particular application of judicial activism (maintenance of laissez-faire) actually being made by the Old Court. On the other hand, there is the more technically based opposition which insists that the Court has no function interfering with the enactments of the legislature, whatever the nature of those enactments—the Court should adopt a hands-off policy. It may be, in this connection, that legislative power will be abused on individual occasions, but that is no argument against its existence. "For protection against abuses by legislatures the people must resort to the polls, not to the courts."[2]

The defeat of the Old Court majority in 1937 was followed by the

[2]See *Munn* v. *Illinois*, (1876) 94 U.S. 113, 134 (opinion of the Court by Mr. Justice Waite).

rapid departure of its individual supporters from the Supreme Court Bench. Within a space of four years after 1937 only Mr. Justice Roberts and Mr. Justice Stone (the latter, indeed, a consistent judicial supporter of the New Deal programme) remained out of the nine justices who had ruled on the legislative programme of President Franklin Roosevelt; and as these justices retired their seats were filled by men who were known as supporters of the New Deal, and who indeed had frequently led the fight for the adoption of the Roosevelt programme in the political arena —Black and Byrnes as senators, and Reed, Douglas, Murphy, and Jackson as members of the Roosevelt Administration. Even without the decisive slant given to the Court by this flood of New Deal appointments, it was quite apparent after the landslide victory of President Roosevelt in his bid for re-election in 1936 and after the *volte-face* of the Old Court majority in 1937 which followed so closely and so significantly on that victory, that the New Deal had become accepted majority opinion in the United States. However, the new majorities on the Supreme Court after 1937 proceeded to follow up the overturning of the Old Court not merely by upholding the constitutionality of individual pieces of New Deal social and economic planning legislation that were challenged before it, but by developing as it were a general presumption of constitutionality in favour of enactments of Congress, whatever the subject-matter of those enactments. On only a handful of occasions since 1937 have provisions of congressional enactments been declared unconstitutional by the Supreme Court and those cases presented somewhat special examples of the user of national legislative power so as hardly to constitute substantial exceptions to the general rule. The major case, *United States* v. *Lovett*,[3] involved a rider that had been tacked on by Congress to a general appropriation bill as a rather devious device for enforcing the dismissal by the executive of three civil servants who had been under investigation by a congressional committee. President Roosevelt, faced with the choice in this situation of either approving the whole bill or else vetoing it as a whole and so delaying essential wartime appropriations, adopted the former course but noted on the Act his personal view that the rider was "not only unwise and discriminatory, but unconstitutional." It is perhaps not surprising that the Supreme Court was persuaded to vary its rule in this case, and to step in and invalidate the rider as an unconstitutional bill attainder.[4]

Yet in spite of the impressive record of the Supreme Court since 1937

[3]*United States* v. *Lovett*, (1946) 328 U.S. 303.

[4]For other examples of judicial annulment of provisions of congressional enactments, see *Tot* v. *United States*, (1943) 319 U.S. 463; *United States* v. *Cardiff*, (1952) 344 U.S. 174; *United States ex rel. Toth* v. *Quarles*, (1955) 76 Sup. C't. 1.

in upholding enactments of the national legislature, it is true to say that the Court during that same period has been more marked in its internal disagreements than any of its predecessors. This is not the first time, of course, that there have been disagreements on the Court. The Old Court before 1937 was after all, in terms of the subject-matter for which its members voted, split two ways, with a conservative majority and a liberal minority. The difference between the Old Court and the New Court lies first of all in the nature of the disagreements, with the present Court (as revealed in its practice in opinion-writing) a court not merely of frequent and sometimes multiple dissenting opinions but of multiple and diverging concurring (that is, majority) opinions too. Speaking metaphorically, an English two-party system on the Court before 1937 has now given way to a French multiple-party system in the 1940's and 1950's. The second basic difference between the Old Court and the New is in the area of subject-matter in which the internal disagreements occur. Where the Court before 1937 was concerned above all with rights of private property supposedly guaranteed by the Constitution, the Court today is concerned with the rights of man or personal liberty. The disagreements within the New Court's ranks also mark differing degrees of judicial tolerance toward legislative and executive action on the part of the states as distinct from the national government. On the technical side, the disagreement is reflected, in part at least, in a perpetuation of the Holmesian dilemma —judicial self-restraint as opposed to currently revived claims of the need for a policy of judicial activism, though this time with a rather different content than was the case with the pre–1937 Court majority formula. This latter judicial position is most prominently identified today with Mr. Justice Black and Mr. Justice Douglas (and before their recent deaths, Justices Murphy and Rutledge); it claims to derive from Holmes's position as a liberal judge—as a symbol (for present generations at least) of liberal thought in the United States. It would, to this extent, identify Holmes's opposition to the Old Court majority less with his technical challenge that the Old Court was usurping the functions of the legislature and acting in effect as a "super-legislature," than with a postulated objection by Holmes to the social and economic values that the Old Court majority was actually implementing in its decisions, the thesis that the Old Court majority was basing its rulings, as Holmes so strikingly expressed it in his *Lochner Case* dissent, "upon an economic theory which a large part of the country does not entertain."[5]

This latter conception of Holmes as a judicial activist, and in such capacity as the liberal dissenter on a reactionary Court, claims strength

[5]*Lochner* v. *New York*, (1905) 198 U.S. 45, 75.

from Holmes's opinions in free speech cases, including his enunciation of the famous "clear and present danger" test as a means of balancing the constitutional guarantee of free speech against countervailing claims of national security.[6] It would trace this liberal tradition, as seen to be established by Holmes, also in the judicial opinions of his colleague and friend Brandeis, in part too in the opinions of Mr. Justice Cardozo, and, coming more nearly to contemporary events, in the opinions of Harlan Stone who was first of all an Associate Justice of the Supreme Court in the period 1925-41, and then Chief Justice in the crucial period 1941-6 when the internal conflicts on the New Court first became marked. As applied by the two leading liberals on the Court today, Black and Douglas, judicial activism would imply that the Court should assume a watch-dog role to ensure full compliance with the letter and the spirit of the Bill of Rights in the Constitution. Not merely will legislative action that impinges on the area of political and civil rights be cut down and the constitutional guarantees of freedom of speech and religion, of fair criminal procedure, and of equal rights for racial minorities be preserved against legislative invasion; but the Court will take the initiative to ensure that the actual administration and application of national and state laws conforms fully to the spirit of the Bill of Rights. So keen indeed is the scrutiny which the two main activists of the present day, Black and Douglas, apply to the administration of justice by the individual states that at times it seems almost true to say that these judges pursue the states sword in hand.

As one further aspect of judicial activism today, reference should be made to an important and distinctive contribution made by Chief Justice Stone to modern American constitutional law. In a judicial opinion written by him in 1938, Stone suggested by way of *obiter dictum* only (and indeed in the form of a footnote to the opinion)[7] that perhaps there might be occasion for departing from the normal presumption of constitutionality for legislation in cases where the action in question by the legislature involved a restriction or curtailment of the ordinary political processes. For the presumption of constitutionality is posited, after all, on the notion that the legislature, and not the Court, represents the people —that is majority will; and that the normal working of the political processes can "ordinarily be expected to bring about the repeal of undesirable legislation." However, if the legislature, through, for example, manipulation of the electoral laws or impeding of public discussion, prevents the political processes from operating freely, then the essential

[6]See *Schenck* v. *United States*, (1919) 249 U.S. 47, 52 (opinion of the Court by Mr. Justice Holmes).

[7]*United States* v. *Carolene Products Co.*, (1938) 304 U.S. 144, 152 n. 4.

premise from which the presumption of constitutionality is derived—the notion of a representative majority—can hardly be said to be present.

Stone's "political process" concept seemed to afford, for his own purposes, something of a solution to the Holmesian dilemma—how to reconcile deference to popular will as expressed through legislative majorities with the desire of judges from time to time to intervene to correct what they might choose to regard as legislative abuses. The political process concept thus originated as a special exception to the general judicial approach after 1937 of a presumption of constitutionality in favour of legislative action. As a special category of exceptions, it is clear that the political process concept would be somewhat limited in its area of potential application, covering essentially electoral matters and probably, too, questions of free speech—this latter notion however shading off into the contemporary concept of the free speech guarantee in the Constitution as occupying a "preferred position."[8] Yet it represented the first doctrinal challenge to the new judicial orthodoxy after 1937—the presumption of constitutionality—and as such marked the first formal step towards the development of judicial activism among the members of the present Court. But the judicial activists of today go beyond Stone's modest concept. The presumption of constitutionality may remain so far as enactments of the national legislature are concerned, but no more than this.[9] Wherever issues of political and civil rights are concerned, then laws passed by the state (as distinct from the national) legislatures, the application and administration of those state laws, and even the administration of national laws will be subjected to the most rigorous judicial scrutiny.

[8]See, e.g., *Kovacs* v. *Cooper*, (1949) 336 U.S. 77, 88 (opinion by Mr. Justice Reed). But the "preferred position" concept of the free speech guarantee has been sharply criticized by Frankfurter J. as a "phrase that has uncritically crept into some recent opinions of this Court. I deem it a mischievous phrase, if it carries the thought, which it may subtly imply, that any law touching communication is infected with presumptive invalidity." *Ibid.* at 90 (concurring opinion by Mr. Justice Frankfurter). See also *Dennis* v. *United States*, (1951) 341 U.S. 494, 539 (concurring opinion by Mr. Justice Frankfurter): "Free speech cases are not an exception to the principle that we are not legislators, that direct policy-making is not our province."

For a current re-examination of Stone's political process concept that attempts to relate it doctrinally to the more recent judicial concept of the "preferred position" of the constitutional free speech guarantee, see Alpheus Mason, "The Core of Free Government, 1938–40: Mr. Justice Stone and 'Preferred freedoms,' " (1956) 65 *Yale L.J.* 597; and see generally E. V. Rostow, "The Democratic Character of Judicial Review," (1952) 66 *Harv.L. Rev.* 193.

[9]Compare Holmes's remark: "I do not think the United States would come to an end if we lost our power to declare an Act of Congress void. I do think the Union would be imperiled if we could not make that declaration as to the laws of the several States." Holmes, *Collected Legal Papers* (1920), 295–6.

The principal intellectual opposition to judicial activism on the present Court is afforded by Mr. Justice Frankfurter. Mr. Justice Frankfurter rests firmly on the first head of the Holmesian approach, judicial self-restraint; and at the same time he challenges the claim of the judicial activists that Holmes is their intellectual progenitor. Being closest of all the members of the present Court, in terms of personal associations, to Mr. Justice Holmes, Mr. Justice Frankfurter can perhaps claim to speak with some added authority on the Master's inherent philosophic attitudes. But Frankfurter would also buttress his denial of the judicial activists' link with Holmes by recourse to Holmes's decisions themselves; and indeed a careful examination of Holmes's decisions, in the free speech area at least, would suggest that like his colleague Brandeis[10] his approach to judicial review was characterized by a conscious and sustained rejection of judicial sentimentality, an intellectual attitude befitting a sceptic and relativist (as the current Holmes-revisionist school would imply is the case with Holmes, anyway), but certainly not a liberal activist.[11]

But Mr. Justice Frankfurter's approach to judicial review, with its strong rejection of judicial activism, would claim to rest on more substantial ground than the probings of the Holmes-revisionists aimed at dispelling the "legend" of Holmes as the wearer of the liberal mantle on the Court. The main doctrinal justifications of judicial self-restraint at the present day proceed from judicial acknowledgment of major limitations to the effectiveness of the Court's assuming any activist role. First is a limitation of expertise, stemming from judicial awareness that judicial review is not always a very efficient form of policy-making; judges, because of the highly specialized and concentrated education in law and the training in professional practice that they have undergone, are in this view manifestly not the best equipped persons for translating community values into constitutional policies, and the concept of judicial notice, anyway it is said, is hardly an adequate tool for the fact-finding necessary to an informed policy choice. A realization of the limitations on effective judicial fact-finding in constitutional cases gave rise directly to the so-called Brandeis Brief[12] involving as that does the direct incorporation of

---

[10]Compare an evaluation of the judicial philosophy of Mr. Justice Brandeis: P. A. Freund, *On Understanding the Supreme Court* (1949), 66 *et seq.*

[11]See generally, L. Jaffe, "The Judicial Universe of Mr. Justice Frankfurter," (1949) 62 *Harv. L. Rev.* 357, 358.

[12]As first employed by Brandeis, as counsel, in *Muller* v. *Oregon*, (1908) 208 U.S. 412. The limitations, by contrast, of the doctrine of judicial notice as a device for acquainting the Court with underlying questions of "fact" that condition the constitutionality of legislative or executive action have been demonstrated once more by the sharply conflicting answers returned by Jackson J. (concurring) and Douglas J. (dissenting), in the *Dennis Case*, on the question of the degree of threat to national security presented by the Communist party in the United States. *Dennis* v. *United States*, (1951) 341 U.S. 494.

social and economic facts into the briefs presented to the Court by the parties. And no doubt the marked tendency in recent years, in making appointments to the Supreme Court Bench, to look for men of broad experience in public life rather than technical lawyers can be explained in part by the executive's conclusion that informed policy-making requires intellectual qualities transcending the boundaries of strict professional competence.

A second limitation, which might be characterized as a limitation of techniques, stems from the fact that any policy-making role of the Court must be expressed necessarily through the medium of case-law decisions. Unlike other courts exercising judicial review, for example the Supreme Court of Canada, the Supreme Court of the United States does not choose to render advisory opinions. It is dependent in its jurisdiction, therefore, upon the existence of an adversary proceeding. Though the artificialities of Court-defined rules as to what is a real adversary proceeding—a case or controversy—have been somewhat ameliorated by the passage of the Federal Declaratory Judgments Act of 1934, it is still true to say that the jurisdiction of the Court in constitutional cases, being dependent on the whims of private litigants, turns on rather arbitrary, casual factors of time and circumstance. As Mr. Justice Jackson has so strikingly pointed out, the decision in the aftermath of the Great Depression as to whether the United States Treasury had power to lower the gold content of the dollar[13] was determined within the confines of a suit between private parties over a few paltry dollars.[14] And Mr. Justice Frankfurter has summed up the problem in a recent opinion:

Courts are not equipped to pursue the paths for discovering wise policy. A court is confined within the bounds of a particular record, and it cannot even shape the record. Only fragments of a social problem are seen through the narrow windows of a litigation. Had we innate or acquired understanding of a social problem in its entirety, we would not have at our disposal adequate means for constructive solution.[15]

It is patent that in comparison with the legislature and the executive, the Court lacks the flexibility in timing of announcement and also application of rules essential to a really effective policy-making role.[16]

[13]See *Norman* v. *Baltimore & Ohio Railroad Co.*, (1935) 294 U.S. 240.

[14]See Jackson, *The Struggle for Judicial Supremacy* (1941), 103.

[15]See *Sherrer* v. *Sherrer*, (1948) 334 U.S. 343, 365–6 (dissenting opinion by Mr. Justice Frankfurter).

[16]The writer does not, however, accept Professor Freund's interesting suggestion that the greater procedural flexibility of Canadian and Australian courts in comparison to the United States Supreme Court—the power of the Canadian Supreme Court to render advisory opinions and also the comparative readiness of the High Court of Australia to concede standing to sue in constitutional cases—is responsible for the admittedly much greater abstractness of Canadian and Australian

A third limitation may be labeled a limitation of prestige. If the Court essays an activist role it cannot avoid taking sides in the political conflicts of the age. The end product of this must be to embroil the Court in undignified partisan controversy, and there may be a risk too, as happened with the Old Court majority before 1937, of the Court itself going down with a lost political cause. "In times of political passion, dishonest or vindictive motives are readily attributed to legislative conduct and as readily believed. Courts are not the place for such controversies."[17]

But there are further and perhaps more basic objections to the Court's assuming a policy-making role. The so-called limitation of democracy[18] accords with the first strain of the Holmesian conception of the judicial function. It contends that majority rule is denied in principle by judicial review, for in application judicial review means ultimately the imposition of the will of the "nine old men" on the prime representatives of the people, the legislature. The situation tends to arise inevitably, then, as indeed was the case up to the Court Revolution of 1937, that those who are no longer able to control the legislature look to the courts to preserve their special interests. In counter to these contentions it may be pointed out, of course, that the supremacy of legislative majorities, unchallenged by the courts, may itself deny democracy, especially where a transient legislative majority should seek to perpetuate itself by manipulation of the machinery of government established for the effectuation and determining of popular will, for example the laws governing the procedure and conduct of elections. This is a restatement of Stone's political process concept, but it is to be noted that the Court has been notoriously inactive

---

constitutional decisions. See P. A. Freund, "A Supreme Court in a Federation: Some Lessons from Legal History," (1953) 53 *Col. L. Rev.* 597, 613. This contention, it is submitted, does not give full weight to intellectual factors—legal education and professional training, criteria for selection and appointment to the bench—conducing to the final form of judicial decisions in the Commonwealth countries, whether decisions of the Privy Council or of local appellate tribunals in the various Commonwealth countries.

[17]*Tenney* v. *Brandhove*, (1951) 341 U.S. 367, 378 (opinion of the Court by Mr. Justice Frankfurter).

[18]Note, in this regard, the remarks of Mr. Justice Jackson, in *The Supreme Court in the American System of Government* (published posthumously, 1955), 57–8: "A cult of libertarian judicial activists now assails the Court almost as bitterly for renouncing power as the earlier 'liberals' once did for assuming too much power. . . . I may be biased against this attitude because it is so contrary to the doctrines of the critics of the Court, of whom I was one, at the time of the Roosevelt proposal to reorganise the judiciary. But it seems to me a doctrine wholly incompatible with faith in democracy, and in so far as it encourages a belief that the judges may be left to correct the result of public indifference to issues of liberty in choosing Presidents, Senators, and Representatives, it is a vicious teaching."

in this area of subject-matter in recent years, justifying its general non-intervention to correct abuses in the electoral system on the affirmative ground that these are "political" questions properly outside the range of competence of the Court—the doctrine of political questions.[19] Again, and especially in a federal system as with the United States, it may be a question of which popular will, or more precisely which legislative majority, is to be deferred to. What if the majority will, as expressed in a particular state or states, runs counter to over-all national will, as for example the judicial activists might say is the case in respect to civil rights, matters of public morality, and especially race relations? In such instances quite apart from any question of the merits of the state action involved, it may be a matter of cutting down the state legislative action in question in deference to considerations of overriding national policy. The answer to this type of problem, of course, may be bound up also with one's essential approach to federal government. Mr. Justice Frankfurter, for example, would appear to base his general inclination to defer to the state legislative action in these cases as much on federalistic considerations of the need for a balancing of national legislative powers by state-rights claims[20] as on the more general notion of the desirability of judicial self-restraint vis-à-vis legislative majorities, whether national or state.

One final limitation has been suggested to the effectiveness of any policy of judicial activism on the part of the Supreme Court judges. Closely linked as it is to the limitation of democracy already referred to, we may perhaps identify it, for want of a better term, as a sociological limitation, being based on a judicial recognition of the socio-ethical limitations to the effectiveness of any legal action. This view, which has undertones of Mr. Justice Holmes and also of Judge Learned Hand,[21] is once again closely associated with Mr. Justice Frankfurter,[22] and as

[19]See, e.g., *South* v. *Peters*, (1950) 339 U.S. 276; *Colegrove* v. *Green*, (1946) 328 U.S. 549.

[20]See generally, Jaffe, *supra* n. 11, at 381 *et seq*. It is to be noted, however, that in the recent public school segregation decision, *Brown* v. *Board of Education of Topeka*, (1954) 347 U.S. 483, Mr. Justice Frankfurter was prepared to abandon his usual deference to state action to be part of a unanimous Court ruling (against the arguments of the states of Kansas, South Carolina, Virginia, and Delaware), that segregation in public education violated the 14th Amendment to the Constitution.

[21]See generally, *The Spirit of Liberty: Papers and Addresses by Learned Hand* (Dilliard ed., 1953). See also, E. Cahn, "Authority and Responsibility," (1951) 51 *Col. L. Rev.* 838.

[22]Though echoed also by Mr. Justice Jackson. See Jackson, *The Supreme Court in the American System of Government*, 80: ". . . I know of no modern instance in which any judiciary has saved a whole people from the great currents of intolerance, passion, usurpation, and tyranny which have threatened liberty and free institutions. . . . No court can support a reactionary regime and no court can

expressed by him in the course of his writings and his legal opinions amounts to an attempted rebuttal to the judicial activists. Its central theme is the idea that a people must make their own salvation and not expect it to be served up to them by the judges: "Self-discipline and the voters must be the ultimate reliance for discouraging or correcting . . . abuses."[23]

It is to be noted that this approach manifests something of a distrust in fundamental law guarantees and written constitutions, at least where these are not rooted in general community attitudes: "It is highly significant that not a single constitution framed for English-speaking countries since the Fourteenth Amendment has embodied its provisions. And one would indeed be lacking in a sense of humour to suggest that life, liberty or property is not amply protected in Canada, Australia, South Africa."[24] It is also an attitude strongly reminiscent of the writings of the great English constitutional lawyer, Professor A. V. Dicey, which reveal consistently a marked distaste for the paper constitutions of Continental Europe together with a belief that the best guarantee of personal liberties is the self-restraint of legislative majorities operating in a sovereign, legally uncontrolled Parliament, as in the United Kingdom.[25] This is not the only example of an English influence in Frankfurter's approach. His approach to the states, which we have already examined, with its consciously federalistic impulse, bespeaks a conviction (which has undertones of his close friend Laski's liberal pluralism and, more obviously, of Jeffersonian democracy) that in territorial dispersion of authority lies the best insurance of group autonomy and the maintenance of personal liberty. Frankfurter's own personal background as, in his own words, "[o]ne who belongs to the most vilified and persecuted minority in history . . . ,"[26] must make him alive to the merits of a pluralist approach to governmental organisation, even though he may not always appear

---

innovate or implement a new one. I doubt that any court, whatever its powers, could have saved Louis XVI or Marie Antoinette. None could have avoided the French Revolution, none could have stopped its excesses, and none could have prevented its culmination in the dictatorship of Napoleon."

[23]See *Tenney* v. *Brandhove*, (1951) 341 U.S. 367, 378 (opinion of the Court by Mr. Justice Frankfurter).

[24]"The Red Terror of Judicial Reform" (editorial), (1924) 40 *New Republic* 110, 113 (Oct. 1). See also *Law and Politics* (MacLeish ed., 1939), 16. There is perhaps today a certain irony in the reference to South Africa—see *supra*, 96 *et seq.*

[25]See, for example, Dicey, *The Law of the Constitution* (1885); Dicey, *Law and Public Opinion in England during the Nineteenth Century* (2d ed., 1914). It is clear that Mr. Justice Frankfurter is well acquainted with Dicey's writings—compare *Law and Politics*, 7.

[26]See *West Virginia State Board of Education* v. *Barnette*, (1943) 319 U.S. 624, 646 (dissenting opinion by Mr. Justice Frankfurter). These are the opening words of Mr. Justice Frankfurter's opinion.

consistent in applying such a principle.[27] And dominating everything is Frankfurter's belief that American preoccupation with questions of legality involves the equation of constitutionality with morality and the destruction of any sense of popular responsibility for the Constitution and its working:

It must never be forgotten that our constant preoccupation with the constitutionality of legislation rather than its wisdom tends to preoccupation of the American mind with a false value . . . the tendency of focusing attention on constitutionality is to make constitutionality synonymous with propriety; to regard a law as all right so long as it is "constitutional." Such an attitude is a great enemy of liberalism. . . . Only a persistent positive translation of the liberal faith into the thoughts and acts of the community is the real reliance against the unabated temptation to straitjacket the human mind.[28]

The Frankfurterian rebuttal to the judicial activists rests, as we have stated, on the notion of judicial self-restraint. It does not involve however, in Frankfurter's case, a mere mechanical application of the presumption of constitutionality to legislative enactments. Judicial self-restraint, according to Frankfurter, is predicated on the rule of reason—unless the Court can say that reasonable men could not possibly have passed the legislation in question, the Court, irrespective of its own views on the legislation, must uphold it. In respect to national legislation, Frankfurter has gone along with his colleagues on the Court in overruling challenges to the legislation. In respect to state legislation, the problem as Frankfurter sees it is a rather different one—how to apply the rule of reason criterion in individual cases without yielding to purely subjective considerations and thus falling backwards into judicial activism. To eliminate the subjective elements from judicial decision-making Frankfurter resorts at times to proceduralisms and purports to rest his decision on technical rules; more frequently he seems to base his hopes for objective certainty on what would amount to the formulae for legal relativism. To determine such matters as whether a state can, consistently with the free speech guarantee of the First Amendment, ban motion pictures on the score of "sacrilege," he resorts to history, lexicographic and general.[29] To determine whether a state may, consistently with due process of law as guaranteed by the Fourteenth Amendment to the Constitution, utilize

[27]See, e.g., *ibid.*
[28]"Can the Supreme Court Guarantee Toleration" (editorial), (1925) 43 *New Republic* 85, 86–7 (June 17). See also *Law and Politics*, 197. These remarks are substantially repeated by Frankfurter J. in his specially concurring opinion in *Dennis* v. *United States*, (1951) 341 U.S. 494, 555–6, though without any formal acknowledgment of their original source in the *New Republic* editorial.
[29]See *Burstyn* v. *Wilson*, (1952) 343 U.S. 495, 507 (concurring opinion by Mr. Justice Frankfurter).

in a criminal prosecution evidence obtained through an illegal search and seizure, he turns to comparative law and makes a survey of practice in the forty-eight states and also in "the United Kingdom and the British Commonwealth of Nations."[30] Or he may look for the meaning of due process of law, as guaranteed by the Fourteenth Amendment, in the "canons of decency and fairness which express the notions of justice of English-speaking people. . . ."[31]

The difficulty with all these tests seems clear. "History," as the *Adamson Case* indicates,[32] may yield different answers to different judges or may be otherwise quite inconclusive, as the examination of the background history of the Fourteenth Amendment in the recent public school segregation cases clearly showed.[33] Recourse to comparative law in search of examples to be applied by American judges, apart from the risk that the examples taken may be selective rather than representative, demands first a demonstration of a certain identity of political, social, and economic conditions before the examples from comparative law can really be regarded as relevant to American experience. Frankfurter seems to assume too easily such an identity of political, social, and economic conditions on the part of the United States and the "English-speaking" world; though for one who is acquainted, as he is, with Dean Roscoe Pound's teachings, this is hardly sound sociological jurisprudence.[34] It may be, rather, that

[30]See *Wolf* v. *Colorado*, (1949) 338 U.S. 25, 29–30, 39 (opinion of the Court by Mr. Justice Frankfurter; appendix to opinion, Table J.).

[31]See *Adamson* v. *California*, (1947) 332 U.S. 46, 67 (concurring opinion by Mr. Justice Frankfurter).

[32]*Ibid.* Note the conflict manifested in the opinions of Frankfurter J., concurring specially at 59; and of Black J., dissenting at 68. See also the detailed historical Appendix attached by Black J. to his opinion. *Ibid.* at 92–123.

[33]See *Brown* v. *Board of Education of Topeka*, (1954) 347 U.S. 483, 489–90 (opinion of the Court by Mr. Chief Justice Warren):
"Reargument was largely devoted to the circumstances surrounding the adoption of the Fourteenth Amendment in 1868. It covered exhaustively consideration of the Amendment in Congress, ratification by the states, then existing practices in racial segregation, and the views of proponents and opponents of the Amendment. This discussion and our own investigation convince us that, although these sources cast some light, it is not enough to resolve the problem with which we are faced. At best, they are inconclusive. . . .
"An additional reason for the inconclusive nature of the Amendment's history, with respect to segregated schools, is the status of public education at that time [footnote omitted]. In the South, the movement toward free common schools, supported by general taxation, had not yet taken hold. Education of white children was largely in the hands of private groups. Education of Negroes was almost nonexistent, and practically all of the race were illiterate. . . . As a consequence, it is not surprising that there should be so little in the history of the Fourteenth Amendment relating to its intended effect on public education."

[34]See, e.g., Pound, *Social Control through Law* (1942). Professor Cahn has commented pungently on this same tendency in *Supreme Court and Supreme Law*

by virtue of the homogeneity of their racial and social composition, the "English-speaking" countries (apparently the United Kingdom and the Commonwealth countries) have frequently much less meaningful lessons to offer the United States than have other countries which may more nearly approach the United States' cultural diversity.[35] And what, for example, of the "canons of decency and fairness which express the notions of justice of English-speaking peoples" and for that matter, of the "concept of ordered liberty"?[36] Concepts such as these, indeed, are so vaguely and loosely worded as to allow almost any content to be poured into them.[37] It seems almost that Mr. Justice Frankfurter, in questing after absolute purity from subjective factors, has left the door open for what Holmes himself has called the "inarticulate major premise."[38] Judicial self-restraint insofar as, in the application of the rule of reason, it involves the resort to legal relativism, may run the risk of too frequently reducing to an unconscious and therefore (since the weighing of policy alternatives requisite to an informed decision is necessarily absent) rather inefficient form of policy-making.

We have seen that the philosophic division in terms of judicial self-restraint *versus* judicial activism on the present Court stems from the Holmesian dilemma bequeathed to the Court in the 1930's. The emotional intensity of the division has been heightened during the Cold War period — for the national security crisis, in multiplying the occasions for the Court's being called on to balance constitutional guarantees of free speech with considerations of national security, increases, on the one hand, the demands of the judicial activists that the Court should step

---

(Cahn ed., 1954), 63: "It may appear to you as somewhat peculiar that, in a country which contains such a high proportion of individuals who do not share Anglo-Saxon origins, the only history regarded as relevant, not merely for the purpose of defining specific terms like 'jury' but likewise for the purpose of defining basic national traditions, should be Anglo-Saxon history. It is assumed that the Volksgeist the Supreme Court is supposed to consult is Anglo-Saxon."

[35]Compare in this regard Mr. Justice Frankfurter's reliance in his dissenting opinion in *Sherrer* v. *Sherrer*, (1948) 334 U.S. 343, 356, on the practice of "the English-speaking world" and also on a "consensus of opinion among English-speaking courts the world over" as to the "domicile" necessary to base jurisdiction in divorce proceedings, as authority for the state of Massachusetts' refusal to accord "full faith and credit" in terms of the Constitution to a divorce decree granted by a court in the state of Florida.

[36]The phrase seems to have been first used by Cardozo J. for the Court in *Palko* v. *Connecticut*, (1937) 302 U.S. 319, 325; it was adopted by Frankfurter J. for the Court in *Rochin* v. *California*, (1952) 342 U.S. 165, 169.

[37]Stone, *The Province and Function of Law* (1946), 185 *et seq.*, classifies judicial concepts such as these under "The Legal Category of Indeterminate Reference."

[38]The phrase stems from Mr. Justice Holmes's dissenting opinion in *Lochner* v. *New York*, (1905) 198 U.S. 45, 74.

in to preserve constitutional liberties and, on the other hand, the arguments of the advocates of self-restraint (the judicial passivists, as we may now call them) that the delicate balancing of interests involved in these cases is properly conducted by the legislature, and that the Court must not interfere with the legislature's resolution of the conflict. The dilemma is by no means yet resolved, though, since the deaths of Murphy and Rutledge have reduced the ranks of the avowed activists on the Court to only two (Black and Douglas) out of a total of nine justices, the balance on the Court must be regarded as having been tilted rather strongly now towards the passivists.

At the same time, too, there has been some tendency to conclude recently that the judicial activists' approach, with its announced preference for a "civil libertarian" result, may run some dangers of oversimplifying the solution of legal problems by producing, in effect, a sort of "label thinking" in which the concrete fact-settings of particular cases are ignored altogether. Such a criticism has been advanced, for example, of the "absolutistic standards" at work in Mr. Justice Black's opinion of the Court in the *Steel Case*.[39] The substance of this criticism of the judicial activists' position would be that it is not enough simply to identify one particular value as being involved in a case before the Court: it may be, all too frequently, a matter of determining how much weight that particular value should be given by the Court in that context having regard to the particular techniques used by governmental authority, legislative or executive, to achieve it there. The judicial enquiry here, on this view, cannot sensibly ignore consideration of *means* employed to achieve ends, and especially consideration of the "availability of more moderate controls than those which the state has imposed."[40]

The judicial scales have oscillated violently before this. Judicial self-restraint was a reaction, after all, to a strong court before 1937 that many people felt had overstepped the limits of wisdom and discretion. The presumption of constitutionality applied by the New Court after 1937 to national legislation was, for practical purposes, a switch from a strong court (in national matters, that is) to a strong executive or president, the legislative programmes in question all being, of course, sponsored and initiated ultimately by the executive (President Roosevelt). In spite of its evidences of internal disagreements, the recent *Steel Case*[41] has at least

[39]*Youngstown Sheet and Tube Co.* v. *Sawyer*, (1952) 343 U.S. 579, 582 (opinion of the Court by Black J.). Criticized by C. H. Pritchett, *Civil Liberties and the Vinson Court* (1954), 249; and see also P. A. Freund, book review (Pritchett), (1954) 29 *N.Y.U.L.R.* 1164.

[40]Freund, *On Understanding the Supreme Court*, 27; judicially approved, Frankfurter J. (concurring specially), *Dennis* v. *United States*, (1951) 341 U.S. 494, 539 *et seq.*

[41]*Youngstown Sheet and Tube Co.* v. *Sawyer*, (1952) 343 U.S. 579.

seen both the activists and the passivists on the Court united against the conception of a strong executive[42] and throwing the weight of the Court toward a strong legislature, as the end of the cycle of the last generation —from strong Court to strong President to strong Congress. The difference this time is that in the *Steel Case* the activists and the passivists each voiced their objections to President Truman's seizure action, in terms of balance of powers arguments officially subsumed under the constitutional principle of separation of powers between the various arms of government. It is possible in this regard to speculate that we are now to have a new pragmatic solution to problems of the relationship *inter se* of the three main arms of government, in the Cold War period, in terms of a neo-Montesquieuan conception of an avoiding of concentration of a totality or preponderance of constitutional powers in any one set of hands as the means of preserving a liberal democratic society. Would this mean that both judicial self-restraint and judicial activism have by this time served their purpose as rationalizations of differing judicial conceptions of the proper role of courts in exercising judicial review? The strikingly novel agreement that the judges have shown in the recent public school segregation decision,[43] not merely in returning a unanimous vote on the general principle of ending segregation in public education, but also in refraining from their privilege of writing individual opinions and instead adhering as one to Chief Justice Warren's opinion of the Court, at least suggests that the polar extremes of doctrinal attitudes among the various judges that characterized the Stone and the Vinson Courts will be maintained much less dogmatically in the future.[44]

[42]Compare, for example, the opinions of Black J., *ibid.* at 582 (opinion of the Court); Frankfurter J., *ibid.* at 593 (concurring opinion); Douglas J., *ibid.* at 629 (concurring opinion).

[43]*Brown* v. *Board of Education of Topeka,* (1954) 347 U.S. 483; and see also *Brown* v. *Board of Education,* (1955) 349 U.S. 294. And see generally E. McWhinney, "An End to Racial Discrimination in the United States? The School-segregation Decisions," (1954) 32 *Can. B. Rev.* 545.

[44]For criticism of the manner and tone of the disagreements on the Court in recent years, as expressed both in the judges' approach to past decisions and also in the spawning of judicial opinions, both concurring and dissenting, see the famous dicta of Roberts J. (dissenting) in *Smith* v. *Allwright,* (1944) 321 U.S. 649, 669: ". . . the instant decision, overruling that announced about nine years ago, tends to bring adjudications of this tribunal into the same class as a restricted railroad ticket, good for this day and train only"; and see also the remarks of Professor Bischoff in Cahn (ed.), *Supreme Court and Supreme Law* (1954), 79. For linking of the current proliferation of opinion-writing to the dominance of pragmatism on the Court, see Swisher, book review (Cahn), (1954) 67 *Harv. L. Rev.* 1487; and compare the criticisms by Ben W. Palmer, "Background for Dissensions— Pragmatism and Its Effects on the Law," (1948) 34 *American Bar Assoc. J.* 1092. And see generally, E. McWhinney, "Judicial Concurrences and Dissents: A Comparative View of Opinion-writing in Final Appellate Tribunals," (1953) 31 *Can. B. Rev.* 595, 609–19.

10

LAW AND POLITICS AND THE LIMITS OF THE JUDICIAL PROCESS: COURT AGAINST LEGISLATURE IN THE UNION OF SOUTH AFRICA

The decision given in 1956 by the Appellate Division of the Supreme Court of the Union of South Africa in *Collins* v. *Minister of the Interior*[1] has apparently brought to a conclusion the long-drawn-out constitutional crisis in South Africa originally triggered by the passage by the Union Parliament, in 1951, of the Separate Representation of Voters Act.[2] The South African government's announced objective, in sponsoring that legislation, was to transfer the so-called "coloured" voters (voters of mixed blood) in the Cape Province of the Union from the common electoral rolls of the Province to a special electoral roll under which, in effect, they would vote as a special class by themselves for their own special representatives. In terms of the South African constitution—the South Africa Act of 1909, which had been formally enacted by the United Kingdom Parliament[3]—any such action in relation to the voters in the Cape Province had to be passed under a special procedure of the Union Parliament—that is, by a two-thirds majority at a joint sitting of both Houses of Parliament[4]—a procedure not followed by the Union Parliament at the time of passage of the 1951 legislation, for the reason, among others, that the government forces did not command the necessary two-thirds majorities in the Union Parliament. It had, however, been the general legal opinion of South African and also British and Commonwealth authorities that, since the attainment of Dominion status by the Union of South Africa as a result of the general political and constitutional evolution from British Empire to Commonwealth of Nations, and certainly since the enactment by the United Kingdom Parliament of the Statute of Westminster in 1931, the

[1]*Collins* v. *Minister of the Interior*, [1957] 1 S.A.L.R. 552 (A.D.), (hereafter referred to as the *Senate Act Case*).
[2]No. 46 of 1951.
[3]9 Ed. VII, c. 9.
[4]South Africa Act, 1909, ss. 35 and 152.

South African Parliament had become "sovereign" in the same way as the United Kingdom Parliament and was therefore no longer bound by the special procedure—by the so-called "entrenched clauses" of the South Africa Act—when legislating in relation to voters in the Cape Province. These authoritative legal opinions[5] had received a form of official blessing by the decision of the Appellate Division of the Supreme Court of South Africa in 1937 in *Ndlwana* v. *Hofmeyr*[6] a decision given in relation to the Hertzog-Smuts legislation of 1936 in relation to native (African) voters in the Cape Province, that the entrenched clauses were no longer, since the Statute of Westminster, binding on the Union Parliament. Having regard to the extraordinarily complex and tangled legal argument that ensued in relation to the 1951 legislation, a brief recapitulation of the successive steps in the constitutional crisis must be made here.[7] Upon the 1951 legislation being challenged before it, the Appellate Division of the Supreme Court of South Africa ruled[8] that the special procedure of the South Africa Act was still binding on the Union Parliament at the present day—that, when it was a question of legislating in relation to voters of the Cape Province of the Union, the "Parliament" of the Union in effect meant "Parliament functioning in terms of two-thirds majorities at a joint sitting of both Houses." The 1937 court decision was, as it necessarily had to be in terms of the present holding, directly overruled by the Appellate Division of the Supreme Court. The government's counter-attack against the court was in the form of a denial of any power of judicial review of legislation in the Supreme Court, the government proceeding to enact a measure

[5]*Supra*, pp. 98–102.

[6]*Ndlwana* v. *Hofmeyr*, [1937] A.D. 229.

[7]For additional discussion, reference may be made to the author's articles, "The Union Parliament, the Supreme Court, and the 'Entrenched Clauses' of the South Africa Act," (1952) 30 *Can. B. Rev.* 692; "Constitutional Law, Union of South Africa—the new High Court of Parliament," (1952) 30 *Can. B. Rev.* 734; "Court versus Legislature in the Union of South Africa: The Assertion of a Right of Judicial Review," (1953) 31 *Can. B. Rev.* 52; "La Crise constitutionnelle de l'Union Sud-Africaine," (1953) 5 *Revue Internationale de Droit Comparé* 542. For an examination of the South African constitutional controversy from the viewpoint of American jurisprudence, see the excellent discussion by Dean Erwin N. Griswold, "The Demise of the High Court of Parliament in South Africa," (1953) 66 *Harv. L. Rev.* 864. And see also D. V. Cowen, "Legislature and Judiciary: Reflections on the Constitutional Issues in South Africa," (1952) 15 *Mod. L. Rev.* 282; D. V. Cowen, "The Entrenched Sections of the South Africa Act: Two Great Legal Battles," (1953) 70 *So. Afr. L.J.* 238; H. W. R. Wade, "The Basis of Legal Sovereignty," [1955] *Camb. L.J.* 172, at 192 *et seq.*; H. W. R. Wade, "The Senate Act Case and the Entrenched Sections of the South Africa Act," (1957) 74 *So. Afr. L.J.* 160.

[8]*Harris* v. *Minister of the Interior*, [1952] 2 S.A.L.R. 428 (A.D.), (hereafter referred to as the first *Harris Case*).

establishing Parliament itself as a final appellate tribunal—a "High Court of Parliament"—with power to overrule past or present decisions of the Appellate Division invalidating legislation passed by the Union Parliament. The Appellate Division of the Supreme Court had little difficulty, however, in invalidating the legislation establishing the High Court of Parliament, ruling[9] that it was in no sense a court of law such as envisaged in terms of the South Africa Act but simply Parliament functioning under another name as a means of evading the special procedure of the "entrenched" clauses.

At this stage the possibilities of a direct, frontal assault by the government upon the courts may have seemed great. The government, however, in spite of its claims to an "electoral mandate" in terms of its victory in the general elections of 1953, in which it greatly increased its majority (though still having less than the necessary two-thirds majority in both Houses), proceeded more slowly and by somewhat indirect means. First of all it acted to increase the number of judges on the Appellate Division from 5 to 11, the extra judges, in accordance with standard South African and Commonwealth practice, being appointed by the government; and second, it reconstituted the upper House or Senate of the Union Parliament. Proceeding in the ordinary way of legislating —by ordinary legislative majorities in each of the two Houses of Parliament sitting separately—the government enacted the Senate Act of 1955.[10] This increased the number of Senate seats from 48 to 89; provincial representation, instead of being equal, was to be related to the number of voters in each province; and the senators were to be elected not, as heretofore, in direct proportion to party power in the various provincial councils but by the direct vote of the majority party. The effect of these new and complicated electoral changes was not merely greatly to increase the proportion of government to opposition supporters in the Senate, but actually to reduce the number of opposition supporters, and in any event to ensure, as the government had clearly intended, that it would henceforth have a two-thirds majority at any joint sitting of both Houses of the Union Parliament. The government then proceeded to enact, in accordance with the special procedure of the "entrenched clauses," a measure—the South Africa Act Amendment Act of 1956[11]—purporting to validate the Separate Representation of Voters Act of 1951. Since this later, *Validation* Act had thus been

[9]*Minister of the Interior* v. *Harris*, [1952] 4 S.A.L.R. 769 (A.D.), (hereafter referred to as the second *Harris Case*).
[10]No. 53 of 1955.
[11]No. 9 of 1956.

passed by a two-thirds majority at a joint sitting of the two Houses of the Union Parliament, any legal challenge would have to be directed to the method whereby the two-thirds majority was actually obtained, that is to the whole stratagem, by the Senate Act of 1955, of reconstituting the Senate for a single purpose of being able to comply with the letter of the "entrenched clauses" stipulation of a two-thirds majority for any amendment of the voting rights in the Cape Province of the Union—the constitutional requirement that had been upheld by the Appellate Division, in its two decisions in the first and second *Harris Cases*, as being still binding on the Union Parliament, and a requirement implicitly accepted by the government itself as legally binding by virtue of the government's actual mode of proceeding in enacting the South Africa Act Amendment Act of 1956.

The two decisions of the Appellate Division in the first and second *Harris Cases* provided no inevitable answer as to the way the court would decide in the matter of the *Senate Act Case*. On the one hand, the decision in the first *Harris Case*, even though it reversed a constitutional leading case of fifteen years' standing and ran in the face of South African and Commonwealth authoritative legal opinion up to the time of decision, was baldly positivist in form and tone, and rested on traditional "black-letter law" argument and reasoning, substantially unrelieved by discussion of ultimate philosophic principle. The opinion of the court in the first *Harris Case*, and especially the insistence on the part of its author, Chief Justice Centlivres, that courts of law are not concerned with the question whether an act of Parliament is "reasonable or unreasonable, politic or impolitic,"[12] might seem to have suggested that the court would be prepared to consider the various steps taken by the government in 1955–6 *seriatim* and not as a whole; to consider the Senate Act of 1955 separately from the Validation Act of 1956 and therefore independently of any consideration of legislative purpose; and thus to reject any argument that the Senate Act must be treated, in the light of the political motives sponsoring it, as yet another device (analogous to the now defunct High Court of Parliament) for evading the requirements of the "entrenched clauses." On the other hand, the judicial opinions in the second *Harris Case* (the "High Court of Parliament" case) were much less in the traditional positivist mould, seeming to offer a prospect that the court might enter into a discussion of questions of policy and of philosophic principle, involving consideration by the judges of such ultimate concepts of constitutional law and government as what are the essential nature and characteristics of a repre-

12[1952] 2 S.A.L.R. 428 (A.D.).

sentative legislature in a democratic society—or, to treat the question in its immediate South African context, "When is a Senate not a Senate?"

As it turned out, the government did not need the extra six appointees to the Appellate Division of the Supreme Court to secure the final removal of the checks to its 1951 measure represented by the court decisions in the first and second *Harris Cases*. In a ten to one decision,[13] the Appellate Division, in November, 1956, upheld the Senate Act of 1955 and the succeeding Validation Act of 1956 against legal challenge. Chief Justice Centlivres, whose own role had been dominant in the earlier, *Harris Cases* decisions, wrote the official opinion of the court in the present case. Chief Justice Centlivres recognized, frankly, in his opinion, that the government's purpose in sponsoring the Senate Act of 1955 had been to obtain the necessary two-thirds majority of both Houses at a joint sitting, but regarded this evidence of the purpose of the act as irrelevant to the question of its constitutionality: each of the two acts with which the court was now concerned (the Senate Act and the Validation Act) was, on its face, *intra vires* and each was enacted by a legislature which was competent to enact it: the whole legislative scheme which was adopted was therefore not open to attack in law. Thus, as the lone dissentient, Mr. Justice Schreiner, pointed out in his very interesting dissenting opinion,

. . . although the two Acts were parts of a single legislative plan to bring about a result which could not be brought about by a bare majority of each House, by the means adopted the bare majority of each House has been able to achieve the desired result.

The reasoning is that so long as the legislation, required to remove the Coloured voters from the common voters' roll . . . can be split up into stages, each of which taken by itself is legal, the whole is legal, even though the two or more Acts required constitute a legislative plan to create a two-third majority by introducing into the legislature persons nominated for the sole purpose of securing that majority.[14]

To the student of comparative law the most interesting question remaining after the Appellate Division's decision in the *Senate Act Case* is why the court, after resisting the most extreme public pressures in its 1952 decisions in the first and second *Harris Cases*, felt it necessary to make what is, in effect, a political *volte face* in the 1956 decision. Having marched its forces up the hill the Supreme Court had, in effect, now marched them down again and on the same side; for after five years of

[13][1957] 1 S.A.L.R. 552 (A.D.). Centlivres C.J. for the court (Hoexter, Fagan, de Beer, Reynolds, de Villiers, Brink, Beyers, and Hall, J.J.A., concurring with him); Steyn J.A. concurring specially; Schreiner J.A. dissenting.
[14][1957] 1 S.A.L.R. 552, at 574 (A.D.).

bitter controversy which had the incidental effect of focusing world opinion on South Africa and its racial policies and, generally speaking, in terms unfavourable to all major European political parties (English as well as Afrikaner),[15] the government was now in much the same position as it had been before the first court checks, administered in 1952, to its legislative programme.

The answer, I think it is clear, is not to be found in considerations of legal logic, and certainly not to be found in the South African Supreme Court's formal opinions in the three main constitutional cases. The South African cases are, in fact, another interesting demonstration of the shifting boundaries between law and politics, and the general community limits to any sustained judicial policy-making. As a first point, it is to be noted that the government which sponsored the Separate Representation of Voters Act in 1951 was then in its first term, having been newly elected to power in 1948 after a long period in opposition. The government which sponsored the Senate Act in 1955 and the subsequent Validation Act of 1956 had been re-elected to power in 1953 with a greatly increased majority in a general election fought primarily on the issues of the constitutional controversy. It would be an error to strain too much the concept of the electoral mandate, vague as that is in its contours even in a purely English setting.[16] It is significant, however, that in none of the crisis situations in the great English-speaking countries where courts have been involved in power conflicts with executive or legislative authority, have the courts for any considerable length of time

[15]The opposition of a majority of the South African electorate seems largely to be a matter of tactics rather than of principle. It is evident from the debates in the Capetown Parliament and the speeches of the most influential members of the [anti-government] United Party that the principles adopted or tacitly respected by that party as such differ from those of the National [government] Party . . . only in degree, and one might almost say tact in their application. The majority of members of the United Party are politicians who seem to have the same traditional attitude to colour as the National members of the legislature." Report of the United Nations' three-man political commission, Oct. 13, 1953, pp. 164–5.

[16]See, for example, Sir Ivor Jennings, *Cabinet Government* (1936), 388–390; H. T. Laski, *Parliamentary Government in England* (1947), 83. It may be argued, however, that to be palatable, the assertion by a government of the principle of an "electoral mandate" should properly be accompanied by its acceptance also of the parliamentary "rules of the game"—the concomitant principle of self-restraint of legislative majorities and deference to minority interests and claims. Compare, in this regard, the strictures, advanced recently in a South African context, on Dicey's central thesis of the sovereignty of Parliament—G. H. Le May, "Parliament, The Constitution and the 'Doctrine of the Mandate,' " (1957) 74 *So. Afr. L.J.* 33, 42. And see also G. W. Keeton, *The Passing of Parliament* (1952); H. R. Gray, "The Sovereignty of Parliament Today," (1953) 10 *U. of Toronto L.J.* 54; G. Marshall, *Parliamentary Sovereignty and the Commonwealth* (1957).

withstood a co-ordinate authority that has had a substantiality of public opinion behind it. Thus, the "Old Court" in the United States resisted President Roosevelt in his first four-year term when a great portion of the New Deal programme might reasonably be regarded as a species of *ad hoc*, trial-and-error planning, but the Court gave way completely after Mr. Roosevelt's sweeping electoral victory of 1936; and it seems fair to conclude, in the light of latter-day re-examination of the constitutional events of 1937, that the court might have acquiesced in this assertion of national law-making power anyway, even without the background threat of Mr. Roosevelt's controversial "court-packing" plan. And the United States Supreme Court's notable check, administered at the end of the 1956–7 court term, to overweening congressional power in the security area,[17] seems to have occurred, signiffcantly, at a time when the country at large was sick and tired of McCarthyism; the succeeding bitter protests and attacks on this assertion of judicial power against Congress, vented in some sections of the American press and in Congress itself, must be appraised in this light.

The moral here, if one be needed, is that courts can delay a co-ordinate authority (executive or legislative) and give it time for sober second thoughts; they may even be able to moderate its programme by deflecting or diverting administrative application of that programme; but they cannot ultimately defeat that co-ordinate authority so long as it retains control of the instruments of political power—in a democratic society, so long as it keeps on winning elections. The court's function, in the exercise of judicial policy-making, in this interpretation, would reduce to a Fabian role of delaying or moderating executive or legislative authority.

As a second point, a court is peculiarly dependent on the society in which it operates—that society's aspirations and ideals, its dislikes and prejudices. We are all of us familiar with the lesson—the prime illustration of the American Sociological school of jurisprudence—of the reciprocal influences of law and society to be found in the breakdown of the Eighteenth (Prohibition) Amendment to the United States Constitution, due to the rooted hostility not merely of the general public in respect to which it was expressed to operate but even of the law-enforcement officers who were sworn to enforce it. In the race relations area, American experience shows that judges and legislators have never been too far removed from public opinion. The "Reconstruction Amendments" to

[17]See, for example, *Grunewald* v. *U.S.*, (1957) 353 U.S. 391; *Jencks* v. *U.S.*, (1957) 353 U.S. 657; *Yates* v. *U.S.*, (1957) 354 U.S. 298; *Service* v. *Dulles*, (1957) 354 U.S. 363; *Watkins* v. *U.S.*, (1957) 354 U.S. 178.

the United States Constitution reflected the egalitarian aspirations of the dominant Radical Republican majorities in Congress immediately after the Civil War and were so interpreted by the courts in that period;[18] the judicially evolved "separate-but-equal" formula, with its retreat back from egalitarianism,[19] clearly reflected dominant American opinion on racial questions at the close of the nineteenth century, just as the slow but steady progress over the last generation in the chipping away of the separate-but-equal formula, culminating in the epoch-making decision in *Brown* v. *Board of Education* in 1954,[20] corresponded to a marked shift in community attitudes in the United States as a whole (although not necessarily in the Southern States particularly affected). In a South African context, now, an "activist" judicial approach, if it were to be maintained beyond the first and second *Harris Cases*, could hardly have avoided consideration of principles of political representation going beyond the 50,000 "coloured" voters affected by the Separate Representation of Voters Act of 1951, and in this regard both major contending European factions (English and Afrikaner) seemed to be agreed on fundamentals[21]—here the general principle of political non-representation of the non-European majorities in the Union of South Africa. North American observers, remembering the marked caution and slowness with which the United States Supreme Court itself has moved in the area of voting rights—much more so indeed than in the cognate areas of education, transportation, and public recreation facilities—should temper any tendency to criticize the South African court's *volte face* in the

[18]*Railroad Company* v. *Brown*, (1873) 17 Wall. 445.

[19]*Plessy* v. *Ferguson*, (1896) 163 U.S. 537. "What is important about each of these decisions is that each reflects the dominant social, moral, and political spirit of its times. In 1873 the Court sensed that the dominant element of the country wanted real equality. By 1896 the Court very accurately recognised that this was no longer so." John P. Frank, "Can the Courts Erase the Color Line?" (1952), 2 *Buffalo L. Rev.* 28, 29.

[20]*Brown* v. *Board of Education of Topeka*, (1954) 347 U.S. 483. And see generally McWhinney, "An End to Racial Discrimination in the United States? The School-Segregation Decisions," (1954) 32 *Can. B. Rev.* 545.

[21]Report of United Nations Commission, Oct. 13, 1953. These crucial "social facts" can serve to explain, in part, why the South African Supreme Court sought to eschew policy questions (necessarily, interests in voting and political representation of non-whites generally—whether "coloured" (of mixed blood), Africans (natives), or Asiatics), in the actual writing of its opinion in the first *Harris Case*. In the second *Harris Case*, by contrast, both common law (compare Dicey's Rule of Law concept) and civil law (compare the somewhat analogous Continental Rechtsstaat concept) strains in South Africa seem to be in accord as to the nature and character of an independent judiciary, and discussion of policy questions in the court opinion would present no major psychological difficulties for the judiciary. As to this latter point, compare H. W. R. Wade, (1957) 74 *So. Afr. L.J.* 160, 161–2.

Senate Act Case by recognition of the substantial absence in South Africa of any really adequate alternative policies on racial questions and general political representation among the contending European political parties.

As a final point, a court may become the prisoner of its own particular thought-ways—the special processes of reasoning, research, and argument developed in its ordinary day-by-day work. It is no criticism of the intrinsic quality of South African law school scholarship or of South African Supreme Court jurisprudence to say that South African legal thought has, until very recent years, been in general baldly positivist in tone. For, until the spate of litigation following on the two *Harris Case* decisions of 1952, South African courts and law schools were essentially confined to rather narrow problems of a private law character, there being no real occasion or need for consideration of the great policy issues that have confronted, say, the United States Supreme Court and the supreme courts of the federal countries of the Commonwealth in public law adjudication. In fact, right up to the time of the recent controversy in South Africa, the only really adequate English-language text on South African constitutional law was inspired and co-authored by a non–South African, the distinguished Canadian legal scholar, Dean Emeritus W. P. M. Kennedy.[22]

On this basis the real surprise in the three South African court decisions—the two of 1952 and the final one of 1956—would not be that they sought to apply a positivist approach to solution of great political tension-issues, but that policy considerations obtruded into the decisions at all—in the first of the three decisions rather as inarticulate major premises, but in the second of the decisions much more overtly and directly. The general Commonwealth experience with the public law decisions of the Privy Council, of course, has been that the positivist approach has amounted too often to a spurious positivism with personal predilections on the part of the judges and ultimate judicial value-preferences looming large in the final decisions. To say this is so is not necessarily to condemn the end-results of those Privy Council decisions, for many of them can be adequately defended on a number of grounds; but it is a valid criticism of the processes of judicial reasoning and decision-making actually applied by the Privy Council. There does seem, however, to be a stage at which the positivist judicial approach must break down in its attempt to handle policy issues covertly, with the only solution to the positivist dilemma then remaining being a species of

[22]W. P. M. Kennedy and H. J. Schlosberg, *The Law and Custom of the South African Constitution* (1935).

judicial abdication. The most obvious way out is to resort to one of the recognized machinery devices for judicial non-involvement in decision-making—the North American concept of "political questions," for example, which proclaims the non-justiciability of certain categories of constitutional issues.

Somewhat less directly, a court may do as the South African court now seems to have done in the *Senate Act Case* and seek to purge, henceforth, all policy considerations from its decision-making by giving ever more narrowly positivist decisions. Those of us who were privileged to meet Chief Justice Centlivres at the Marshall Bi-Centennial Conference at Harvard in 1955 and to hear him reaffirm, in clear and resolute terms, the necessity for a strict and complete legalism on the part of the courts and the eschewing by judges of any consideration of the merits or demerits of legislation—of the policy of an act[23]—could hardly fail to recognize that the confines of an essentially positivist supreme court philosophy could be stretched no further in South Africa and that the writing was on the wall so far as any further conflict there between court and executive-legislative authority was concerned. The actual 1956 South African court decision in the *Senate Act Case* must be seen as having been almost inevitable in that light.[24]

[23]Remarks of A. Van de S. Centlivres, in Arthur E. Sutherland (ed.), *Government under Law* (1956), 426–7.

On the occasion of the recent retirement of Chief Justice Centlivres from the South African Supreme Court, a South African commentator (unnamed) was at some pains to defend the Chief Justice from any aspersions of "positivism" in his juristic thought, such a characterization being spiritedly rejected as a "gross exaggeration": (1957) 74 *So. Afr. L.J.* 1, 2. In the same article, however, the same commentator goes on himself to characterize the Chief Justice's opinion in the first *Harris Case* as a "model of the positivistic analysis," *ibid.*, 4. In myself characterizing the Chief Justice's philosophy of law as by and large positivist (the qualification, here, being an acknowledgment of the strains to which it was subjected in the first and second *Harris Cases*), I am not, of course, using the term "positivist" as, *per se*, pejorative: there is, indeed, much to be said for the approbatory view of the same South African commentator that, in the special space-time context of present-day South Africa ("in a racially divided country," *ibid.*, 4) a positivist approach on the part of the judiciary is "wise" for constitutional and public law matters generally—particularly if that positivist approach can be applied with full judicial consciousness, consistency, and frankness.

[24]Liberal sections in South Africa, in default of prospects of sustained judicial intervention in the future, would thus seem to have to transfer the main focus of their energies and activities to the political arenas of government. Compare, in this regard, the remarks of Learned Hand: ". . . This much I think I do know—that a society so riven that the spirit of moderation is gone, no court *can* save; that a society where that spirit flourishes, no court *need* save; that in a society which evades its responsibility by thrusting upon the courts the nurture of that spirit, that spirit in the end will perish." Irving Dilliard (ed.), *The Spirit of Liberty* (1953), 164.

11

THE SUPREME COURT IN CONTEMPORARY SOCIETY: VALUES, TECHNIQUES, AND JUDICIAL PERSONALITIES

I. "DIGNITARIES"[1] OF THE LAW: THE NEW STATUS OF JUDICIAL POWER

That the judiciary will play an increasingly influential and decisive role in constitutional law development in the future is, I believe, both inevitable and also necessary and desirable. Our attitudes to the judiciary in general, and to judicial review in particular, have changed markedly in recent years. Not so very long ago, the judicial arm of government was held, in North America at least, in some widespread public disfavour and disrepute. In the United States, people remembered that the "old Court" majority on the Supreme Court had defied President Franklin Roosevelt and held up the New Deal legislative programme throughout the whole of his first four-year term:[2] judicial review, in this

[1]Thus Max Weber has convincingly demonstrated that it is decisive, for the character of a legal system, by what kind of *honoratiores*—special institutional or skill group, whether priestly interpreters, judges, attorneys, or professors—it is dominated. M. Weber, *Law in Economy and Society* (trans. E. Shils, ed. M. Rheinstein, 1954). Weber points out that the judge-centredness of the common law is not a general feature of all legal systems: indeed, as is suggested here, it has not always been true of the common law countries themselves, over all periods. The term "dignitaries," though somewhat awkward, at least seems preferable to Weber's own term *honoratiores*: it is suggested by Harold Lasswell. H. D. Lasswell (Book Review, Weber), (1954) 7 *J. Legal Educ.* 301. And compare R. Bendix, *Max Weber: An Intellectual Portrait* (1960), 348.

[2]The intellectual flavour of the era is reflected in the works on the Supreme Court written by leading figures in academic and public life. See, for example, L. Boudin, *Government by Judiciary* (2 vols., 1932); E. S. Corwin, *The Twilight of the Supreme Court* (1934); H. S. Commager, *Majority Rule and Minority Rights* (1943); Robert H. Jackson, *The Struggle for Judicial Supremacy* (1941). There are some analogies for the court-curbing proposals of the 1930's in some contemporary schemes for the curbing or fettering of the Supreme Court's jurisdiction: the intellectual and political limitations of these various schemes have, however, been clearly demonstrated. S. Elliott, "Court-Curbing Proposals in Congress," (1958) 33 *Notre Dame Lawyer* 597; and see also L. Pollak, "The Supreme Court under Fire," (1957) 6 *J. Public Law* 428, 429–31.

sense, was accepted by the law professors and also by a great part the general public as being vaguely undemocratic, and even reactionary. And even in the United Kingdom, people remembered the clamant left-wing charges, associated especially with Professor Laski and his disciples,[3] that the common law judges in England had been biased against the ideals of the welfare state and had done their best, by the course of their decisions, to frustrate the legislative implementation of its ideals. In retrospect, many of these criticisms seem a little unfair and overstated; but even granting their substantial validity in the special context of the politically angry 1930's, it is obviously absurd to regard them as being applicable, without more, to the political conditions of the 1950's or even more perhaps of the emerging 1960's. For one thing, the judges themselves have changed: the impact of a whole generation of the Legal Realists, iconoclasm[4] has at least ensured the destruction of any tendency to judicial self-assurance of personal infallibility: our judges, in the post-war era anyway, are usually keenly aware of the limits of judicial competence and of the dangers of yielding to their own political and economic prejudices—the "inarticulate major premises"[5] in decision-making. And on the whole they know that social security (if not the planned state itself) is politically received majority opinion and now beyond the realm of partisan controversy. But more than that, the society itself has changed, and its basic governmental administrative structure with it. The planned state, the welfare state, and the garrison state have brought with them an immense and often overnight expansion of governmental departments and agencies, and a great new army of administrators. In an age of controls, it is asked, who is to control the controllers? Traditionally, in the Commonwealth countries, checks upon proliferating administrative power—in the absence, in the common law world as a whole, of any fixed and firm tradition of a special administrative tribunal hierarchy after the fashion of the French *Conseil d'Etat* system[6] or the German *Verwaltungsgericht*—have been imposed through the operation of internal executive review, and through the indirect regulation involved

[3]See, for example, Memorandum by Professor Harold Laski, *Committee on Ministers' Powers, Report* (1932), Annex V, 135; Laski, *Studies in Law and Politics* (1932), 203; Laski, *Parliamentary Government in England* (1948), 309.

[4]See, for example, the works of the late Judge Jerome Frank of the United States Court of Appeals—*Law and the Modern Mind* (1930); *Courts on Trial* (1949).

[5]See *per* Holmes J. (dissenting), *Lochner* v. *New York*, (1905) 198 U.S. 45, 74.

[6]See generally C. J. Hamson, *Executive Discretion and Judicial Control: An Aspect of the French Conseil d'Etat* (1954); Bernard Schwartz, *French Administrative Law and the Common-Law World* (1954); A. Von Mehren, *The Civil Law System* (1957), 250–336.

in the ordinary legislative process, especially Questions in Parliament and similar conventionalized remedies; with the sphere of operation for the ordinary common law courts remaining a necessarily limited, peripheral (*ultra vires*, "natural justice") one. But this system of rather casual, unorganized, unco-ordinated control procedures in the common law world is so clearly inadequate to the realities of political power and practice in the contemporary state as to cause law experts in all of the common law countries to re-examine the rather tired clichés and invective of the 1930's directed against judicial power.[7] One thoughtful English jurist has recently seen fit to praise, publicly, the fairness and expedition and efficiency of the French *droit administratif* and its specialized court system, and to recommend close study of the relevance of French experience to current English needs,[8] thereby going far to correct, at long last, Dicey's egregious errors on this same general subject.[9] The recent English Committee on Administrative Tribunals and Enquiries—the Franks Committee[10]—considered this problem, having received authoritative testimony favouring a form of English *Conseil d'Etat*, at least for appellate purposes,[11] but after seeming to teeter on the brink the Committee finally decided to rest with the *status quo*.[12] English opinion on constitutional and public law matters carries great weight in

[7]Compare a recent study of changes in basic American attitudes towards judicial review of administrative agencies and their decisions: "Before the last war it was only those of the so-called 'right' (accused by their opponents of being concerned only with property rights and really aiming their shafts at the substance, rather than the administrative machinery, of the New Deal legislation) who were articulate in their demands for controls over agency authority. Since the war, however, proposals for safeguards have evoked a bipartisan response all but inconceivable a generation ago. . . . The tremendous expansion in administrative authority caused by the war and post-war emergencies has led people on both sides of the political party-line boundary to realise the need for safeguards. Extremists on both sides have moved towards the middle, and, that being the case, most of the controversy engendered by extremism has not unnaturally tended to abate." B. Schwartz, "Memorandum to the Committee on Administrative Tribunals and Enquiries," (1957) 35 *Can. B. Rev.* 743, 756. And see also W. R. Lederman, "The Independence of the Judiciary," (1956) 34 *Can. B. Rev.* 769, 1139.

[8]C. J. Hamson, *Executive Discretion and Judicial Control* (1954).

[9]A. V. Dicey, *Law of the Constitution* (9th ed. by E. C. S. Wade, 1939), 328 *et seq.*

[10]*Committee on Administrative Tribunals and Enquiries, Report* (1957).

[11]See, for example, Professor W. A. Robson's advocacy of a general administrative appeal tribunal with unusually broad jurisdiction. *Ibid.* at 28–9.

[12]"Where, in the light of these circumstances, it is justifiable to establish a tribunal or to entrust adjudicating functions to a Minister we are convinced that an ultimate control in regard to matters of law should be exercised by the traditional courts. We are not satisfied that a sufficient case has been made out for the establishment of a separative administrative court to hear appeals from tribunals or ministerial adjudications." Conclusion and Summary of Main Recommendations, para. 407, *ibid.* at 90.

the Commonwealth countries, but the Franks Committee's intellectual caution should not foreclose any independent initiative, outside England, to consider institution of specialized administrative law court review of governmental and administrative operations, or for that matter adoption of special administrative procedure acts or similar general codes of procedure governing operations of administrative agencies. In any case, Dicey's instinctive prejudice against a specialized administrative court jurisdiction is not the only one of his constitutional ideas to be challenged today: there are some who would even question his central constitutional law notion of the "Sovereignty of Parliament"[13] and find a power in the courts directly to limit Parliament's law-making authority in certain situations.[14]

II. The Law in Books and the Law in Action: The Role of Societal Facts

In the light of historical experience with judicial review in the English-speaking countries, several points can be made as to the likely future fate of written constitutions under judicial interpretation. Whether the constitution be lengthy and discursive on the Indian model or brief and succinct, it seems inevitable that it will be subjected to a form of selective interpretation with some provisions of the constitution assuming an over-riding, paramount importance and the rest receding into the back-

[13]See, for example, H. R. Gray, "The Sovereignty of Parliament Today," (1953) 10 *U. of Toronto L.J.* 54. And see generally J. W. Gough, *Fundamental Law in English Constitutional History* (1955); G. Marshall, *Parliamentary Sovereignty and the Commonwealth* (1957); H. W. Arndt, "The Origins of Dicey's Concept of the 'Rule of Law,'" (1957) 31 *Aust. L.J.* 117; G. W. Keeton, *The Passing of Parliament* (1952).
Of course, Dicey himself set practical limits to the extent to which legislative majorities might interfere with long-recognized claims of political minorities, in joining with Sir William Anson and the former Lord Chancellor, Lord Halsbury, in the heat of the Ulster crisis of 1914, in urging the revival of the royal prerogative power (defunct since 1707) to refuse assent to a bill passed by Parliament— in this case the Government of Ireland Bill. H. Laski, *Parliamentary Government in England* (1948), 344. And compare A. G. Donaldson, *Some Comparative Aspects of Irish Law* (1957), 62 *et seq.*; H. G. Hanbury, *The Vinerian Chair and Legal Education* (1958), 100, 133–4. Strictly speaking, the sovereignty of Parliament as defined by Dicey implied the "King-in-Parliament." Dicey, *The Law of the Constitution* (9th ed., 1939), 39.
[14]The assumption, through Dicey, that the United Kingdom Parliament could, in exercise of its sovereignty, validly amend or even abolish the terms of the Union of 1707 between England and Scotland has recently been authoritatively challenged. *MacCormick* v. *Lord Advocate*, [1953] S.C. 396; cf. Dicey and Rait, *Thoughts on the Scottish Union* (1920), 242–3. The opinions of the court, and especially of Lord President Cooper, going beyond the necessities of the case, demonstrate very strikingly both the particular space-time dimensions in which

ground.[15] Stripped down to their policy and doctrinal essentials, for example, almost all of the great American civil liberties cases could be quite readily subsumed under one or other of the Free Speech or Due Process guarantees in the American Bill of Rights:[16] indeed, we could reduce the category of really *essential* Bill of Rights provisions to only

---

Dicey's generalization was first formulated, and also the constitutional inelegance of assuming, without more, that the new Parliament of Great Britain, after 1707, must inherit solely English notions as to the validity of legislative claims to omnipotence without regard to distinctive Scottish attitudes: "The principle of the unlimited sovereignty of Parliament is a distinctively English principle which has no counterpart in Scottish constitutional law. It derives its origin from Coke and Blackstone, and was widely popularised during the nineteenth century by Bagehot and Dicey, the latter having stated the doctrine in its classic form in his *Law of the Constitution*. Considering that the Union legislation extinguished the Parliaments of Scotland and England and replaced them by a new Parliament, I have difficulty in seeing why it should have been supposed that the new Parliament of Great Britain must inherit all the peculiar characteristics of the English Parliament but none of the Scottish Parliament, as if all that happened in 1707 was that Scottish representatives were admitted to the Parliament of England." [1953] S.C. 396, 411. See generally T. B. Smith, "Two Scots Cases," (1953) 69 *L.Q. Rev.* 512; T. B. Smith, *The United Kingdom. The Development of Its Laws and Constitution: Scotland* (1955), 641–51; J. D. B. Mitchell (Book Review, Smith), [1956] *Public Law* 294; T. B. Smith, "The Union of 1707 as Fundamental Law," [1957] *Public Law* 99. And compare Dicey, *The Law of the Constitution* (9th ed., 1939), 88.

[15]For similar tendencies, in the judicial interpretation of the main civil codes, towards the development of "super-eminent principles," for example article 242 of the German Civil Code (B.G.B.), see Gutteridge, *Comparative Law* (2nd ed., 1949), 94–100; F. H. Lawson, *A Common Lawyer Looks at the Civil Law* (1953), 57. And see generally A. Von Mehren, *The Civil Law System* (1957).

Compare the debate, in the United States, over the so-called "preferred position" of the free speech guarantee in the First Amendment to the Constitution. See, for example, *Kovacs* v. *Cooper*, (1949) 336 U.S. 77, 88, opinion of Reed J. But Frankfurter J. has assailed the concept as a "mischievous phrase" (*Kovacs* v. *Cooper*, 336 U.S. 77, 90 (concurring opinion)); and as one originally put forward (by Stone J. in the *Carolene Products Case*, (1938) 304 U.S. 144, 152) "with the casualness of a footnote." *Per* Frankfurter J., concurring, *Dennis* v. *U.S.*, (1951) 341 U.S. 494, 526.

[16]Thus Edmond Cahn, in supporting the notion of the "preferred"-ness of the Free Speech guarantee in the First Amendment, United States Constitution, equates the Free Speech guarantee with the guarantee of the free exercise of religion, also contained in the First Amendment, pointing out that in Anglo-American political history the guarantee of free speech gradually emerged from the guarantee of free exercise of religion. E. Cahn, "The Doubter and the Bill of Rights," (1958) 33 *N.Y.U.L. Rev.* 903, 915. By the same token, it has been argued that the Fourteenth Amendment Due Process guarantee, applicable to the states, is merely a "shorthand" method of applying the whole of the original Bill of Rights (the first eight amendments, applicable, in terms, only to the nation) to the states. See the fierce debate in *Adamson* v. *California*, (1947) 332 U.S. 46, between Black J. and Murphy J. (dissenting) in support of this particular proposition, and Frankfurter J. (concurring) *contra*. Black J. supported his "shorthand" theory of the Fourteenth Amendment's scope by a detailed appendix to his opinion

one, if need be, by viewing the American Free Speech guarantee (compatibly with the existing American constitutional case law) as merely a more particularized form of Due Process.[17] Taken in its modern, expanded sense, as distinct from its original, more limited historical purpose as a guarantee of fair criminal procedure, the American Due Process clause stands as a high-level guarantee of "reasonableness" in relations between Man and the State, an injunction against governmental arbitrariness, intolerance, or oppressiveness.[18] In a way, this is all that,

containing a résumé of the Amendment's history. Frankfurter J., though categorically rejecting Black J.'s arguments, himself gave the Fourteenth Amendment Due Process clause sweeping definition by making it synonymous with "those canons of decency and fairness which express the notions of justice of English-speaking peoples." Reed J., delivering the Opinion of the Court in the same case, though rejecting the notion that the Fourteenth Amendment Due Process clause embraced *all* the rights contained in the federal Bill of Rights, conceded that at least some of these rights were so embraced: adopting the test advanced by Cardozo J., for the Court, in *Palko* v. *Connecticut*, [(1937) 302 U.S. 319], Reed J. held that such provisions of the federal Bill of Rights as were "implicit in the concept of ordered liberty" became secure from state interference by the Fourteenth Amendment Due Process clause. Whatever the merits of the rival doctrinal attitudes in *Adamson* v. *California*, the expansionist character of Due Process, on both views, is clear.

[17]That the Fourteenth Amendment Due Process guarantee includes the constitutional guarantee of free speech (applicable, by virtue of the First Amendment, to the national government) is clear: see *Gitlow* v. *New York*, (1925) 268 U.S. 652, especially *per* Holmes and Brandeis JJ., dissenting; *Whitney* v. *California*, (1927) 274 U.S. 357 (Brandeis J., concurring, linked with the right of free speech, as covered by Due Process, also the right to teach and the right of assembly); *Near* v. *Minnesota*, (1931) 283 U.S. 697. What is extremely interesting, however, is the tendency to use the concept of Due Process as an independent test, in its own right, of constitutionality, in situations where the concept of free speech is as readily available: see the constitutional standard of "vagueness," applied especially in cases involving alleged obscenity or sacrilege, worked out in such cases as *Winters* v. *New York*, (1948) 333 U.S. 507; *Beauharnais* v. *Illinois*, (1952) 343 U.S. 250; *Burstyn* v. *Wilson*, (1952) 343 U.S. 495.

By the same token, the Fifth Amendment Due Process guarantee, applicable to the nation, has been held, in effect, to include a guarantee of Equal Protection of the Laws (such as contained, in terms, in the Fourteenth Amendment and, as such, otherwise applicable only to the states). This particular holding was vital if the major 1954 decision ending segregation in education in the grade schools—*Brown* v. *Board of Education*, (1954) 347 U.S. 483—was to be capable of application, also, to the special case of schools in the federal territory of the District of Columbia. *Bolling* v. *Sharpe*, (1954) 347 U.S. 497; and see generally McWhinney, "An End to Racial Discrimination in the United States? The School-Segregation Decisions," (1954) 32 *Can. B. Rev.* 545, 561–2. And see also S. Kadish, "Methodology and Criteria in Due Process Adjudication: A Survey and Criticism," (1957) 66 *Yale L.J.* 319.

[18]Note a recent formulation by Judge Learned Hand: "We may read [the Due Process clauses in the Fifth and Fifteenth Amendments] as admonitory or hortatory, not definite enough to be guides on concrete occasions, prescribing no more than that temper of detachment, impartiality, and an absence of self-directed bias that is the whole content of justice: *constans et perpetua voluntas*

in a substantive sense, the English Rule of Law implies,[19] or, correspondingly, the French *notion de légalité*[20] or the German *Rechtsstaat* concept—that is, a philosophic duty of self-restraint among administrators in their dealings with the public, an over-riding obligation of fairness on the part of governmental officials.[21]

As a second point, it is clear that the meaning and working content of the constitution is going to change as the society that it represents

---

suum cuique tribuendi." Learned Hand, *The Bill of Rights* (1958), 34. And as to Learned Hand's approach, see also E. V. Rostow, "The Supreme Court and the People's Will," (1958) 33 *Notre Dame Lawyer* 573, 583 *et seq.*; E. Cahn, "The Doubter and the Bill of Rights," (1958) 33 *N.Y.U.L. Rev.* 903, 909 *et seq.*

[19]Compare Learned Hand's explanation of the foundations, in mediaeval English legal history, for the American Due Process formulation: "It is my understanding that the 'Due Process Clause', when it first appeared in Chapter III of the 28th of Edward III—about a century and a half after Magna Carta—was a substitute for, and was regarded as the equivalent of, the phrase, *per legem terrae*, which meant no more than customary legal procedure. I believe that it had never been construed otherwise before Coke's gloss upon it in Bonham's case, which did say that 'when an Act of Parliament is against common right and reason, or repugnant, or is impossible to be performed, the common law will control it and adjudge such Act to be void.' " Learned Hand, *The Bill of Rights* (1958), 34. And see also H. W. Arndt, "The Origins of Dicey's Concept of the 'Rule of Law,' " (1957) 31 *Aust. L.J.* 117; Sir Owen Dixon, "The Common Law as an Ultimate Constitutional Foundation," (1957) 31 *Aust. L.J.* 240.

[20]See generally M. Letourneur and R. Drago, "The Rule of Law as Understood in France," (1958) 7 *Am. J. Comp. L.* 147.

[21]The current marked disfavour that the American Due Process clause enjoys among constitution-makers in other countries—a skill-group not usually averse to borrowing freely from existing texts—is clearly a reaction to the notoriety of the "Substantive Due Process" era of American constitutional law when the clause was used, in the name of "liberty of contract," to immunize business enterprise from governmental regulation. Although this era ended with the great changes in United States Supreme Court interpretations from 1937 onwards, the old impressions seem to die hard outside the United States. See W. Mendelson, "Foreign Reactions to American Experience with 'Due Process of Law,' " (1955) 41 *Virginia L. Rev.* 493; F. Frankfurter, *Of Law and Men* (P. Elman ed., 1956), 22. Frankfurter is, of course, an old foe of the Due Process clause, dating from his professorial days at Harvard: see his editorial, "The Red Terror of Judicial Reform," 40 *New Republic* (Oct. 1, 1924) 110, 113; F. Frankfurter, *Law and Politics* (MacLeish ed., 1939), 16. Yet though foreign constitution-makers may be at pains to avoid having, in terms, a Due Process clause in their own constitutional text, its core ideal of "fairness," as presented by Learned Hand in his modern-day formulation—Learned Hand, *The Bill of Rights* (1958), especially at pp. 56–61—tends to recur nevertheless. See, for example, Republic of India, Constitution (1949), art. 21: "No person shall be deprived of his life or personal liberty except according to procedure established by law": as to the actual record of interpretation of "procedure established by law," see, for example, *Gopalan* v. *State of Madras,* (1950) 13 Sup. C't J. (India) 174; *Keshavan Madhava Menon* v. *The State of Bombay,* (1951) 14 Sup. C't J. (India) 182; *supra,* pp. 130–9. In a Canadian context, see the decision of the Canadian Supreme Court in *Roncarelli* v. *Duplessis,* (1959) 16 D.L.R. (2d.) 689, especially the majority opinions of Martland J. and of Rand J.; and see the discussion of the *Roncarelli Case* in (1959) 37 *Can. B. Rev.* 503 (McWhinney).

changes; and that a reasonably close correlation will ensue between the law and society—the positive law of the constitution on the one hand, and the *de facto* attitudes, demands, and practices of the people in respect to whom it is expressed to operate, on the other. I am speaking here not merely of the fact, amply borne out by the experience with judicial review, through time, that constitutions drafted in a horse-and-buggy age or earlier will tend to be given a form of generic (progressive) interpretation on the part of the courts so as to adjust their terms to changed community conditions—this process, after all, can quite readily be reconciled with traditional canons of constitutional and general statutory construction. I mean that the practical ambit of the constitutional guarantees will tend to expand or contract according as the society's own libertarian impulses expand or contract. Once again, American experience provides the most dramatic illustrations. The Fourteenth Amendment "equal protection" guarantee, as we have noted, was judicially interpreted, immediately after the Civil War when Radical Republican sentiment was dominant in Congress, in the broadest sense as a guarantee against racial discrimination;[22] in 1896 it was held to permit racial segregation according to the "separate but equal" formula;[23] in 1954, the line of precedents from 1896 was reversed and segregation (even where equal facilities were provided) was held to be unconstitutional.[24] The correlation between these changing, often quite conflicting, judicial interpretations and changing popular attitudes has been clearly made by American jurists who have studied this particular period of American legal and social history;[25] but indeed the difficulties in concrete application, in all parts of the American South, of the 1954 Supreme

[22]See, for example, *Railroad Company* v. *Brown*, (1873) 17 Wall. 445, where the device, through state statute, of segregating white and negro passengers into separate but identical railroad cars on the same train, was held to be unconstitutional as a violation of the Fourteenth Amendment "equal protection" clause.

[23]*Plessy* v. *Ferguson*, (1896) 163 U.S. 537. The opinion of Brown J., for the Court, reflects the changed community attitudes on the ambit of the "equal protection" clause: "The object of the [Fourteenth] amendment was undoubtedly to enforce the absolute equality of the two races before the law, but in the nature of things it could not have been intended to abolish distinctions based upon color, or to enforce social, as distinguished from political, equality, or a commingling of the two races upon terms unsatisfactory to either. Laws permitting, and even requiring their separation in places where they are liable to be brought into contact do not necessarily imply the inferiority of either race to the other, and have been generally, if not universally, recognised as within the competence of the state legislatures in the exercise of their police power." *Ibid.* at 544.

[24]*Brown* v. *Board of Education*, (1954) 347 U.S. 483; and see generally R. Bischoff, "One Hundred Years of Court Decisions: Dred Scott after a Century," (1957) 6 *J. Public Law* 411.

[25]Thus in commenting, during the pendency of *Brown* v. *Board of Education*, on the two earlier United States Supreme Court decisions [*Railroad Company* v.

Court decision ending segregation in the public schools are ample enough demonstration of this process of interaction between law and society.[26] Recognition of this proximate relationship or symbiosis between positive law and societal facts is the beginning of judicial wisdom; it does not, however, involve any necessary surrender to judicial fatalism and a policy of judicial self-abnegation on the theory that the relationship is an automatic, mechanical one which the judges are powerless to deflect or influence. Rather, it involves an acceptance by the judiciary of the political limits within which they must operate in implementing any activist, civil libertarian role. The court is a dependent institution, and, for this reason, if the judges wish to set themselves against the course of society as a whole or for that matter even of political authority in the executive-legislative arenas of government, theirs must tend to be a Fabian, delaying role rather than to involve the employment of direct, frontal assault tactics. It is often a fine equation how much the weight of judicial authority and prestige can tilt the scales against popular prejudice and mass injustice,[27] particularly where executive-legislative authority feels unable or unwilling to intervene or act. Criticism of the United States Supreme Court for its failure effectively to intervene to protect civil liberties in the United States against the more irrational Cold War security drives, at the height of the McCarthy era, should be tempered by realization of these truths. The moral is that there may be occasions, in the future, when the courts will be unable to intervene to protect constitutional liberties; in such cases, though the cause of judicial activism should not be abandoned, it must be recognized that self-discipline and vigilance on the part of the general public remain the ultimate sanctions for preserving the liberal democratic way.[28]

Brown (1873), and *Plessy* v. *Ferguson* (1896)], a leading constitutional historian, John P. Frank, correctly noted: "What is important about each of these decisions is that each reflects the dominant social, moral, and political spirit of its times. In 1873 the Court sensed that the dominant element of the country wanted real equality. By 1896 the Court very accurately recognised that this was no longer so." J. P. Frank, "Can the Courts Erase the Color Line?," (1952) 2 *Buffalo L. Rev.* 28, 29.

[26]The general problem of the operation of positive law in shaping and conditioning social attitudes, and correlatively, of social attitudes in so far as they themselves shape and condition positive law, is canvassed in greater detail by the present author in "An End to Racial Discrimination in the United States?," (1954) 32 *Can. B. Rev.* 545. And see also, as to the Union of South Africa, *supra*, chap. VI.

[27]The late Mr. Justice Jackson of the United States Supreme Court was aware of the problem, though perhaps unduly pessimistic as to possibilities of its solution in concrete cases. Robert H. Jackson, *The Supreme Court in the American System of Government* (1955), 80.

[28]Learned Hand, *The Spirit of Liberty* (I. Dilliard ed., 1953), 164.

As a third point, it is highly unlikely that any of the guarantees in a constitution, unqualified and unlimited though they might be in their terms, will ever be judicially interpreted in an absolute form. I know of no society, for example, that has consistently interpreted its guarantees of free speech or free practice of religion in absolutistic terms. Considerations of public order and even good manners must necessarily limit and condition the actual exercise of the verbally unqualified prescriptions of a constitutional Bill of Rights. The business of judicially determining whether an invalid infringement of constitutionally sanctioned interests in speech and religion has taken place thus becomes a matter of balancing these particular interests against other, countervailing interests.[29] Not every purported user of a constitutionally sanctioned interest will be of equal weight and value, and equally deserving of judicial protection. We may need to know more as to the exact manner and form in which the particular interest has been sought to be exercised, and any such judicial inquiry may well yield the answer that the occasion has been trifling or insubstantial, and undeserving of special judicial advancement.[30] In particular, I suggest, the claims of aggressive, proselytising groups that they are engaging in activities involving free speech interests need careful judicial scrutiny in the specific fact-context of the cases in which they arise:[31] whatever else it may do, a constitutional Bill of Rights should not be regarded as automatically and in all circumstances conferring a legal licence for deliberately abusive and insulting attack by any one political or social out-group on other out-groups or minorities within the community. What can be said, in such cases, is that when it is the majority that is thus selected for attack, deference to the ideal of the Open Society with its necessary free flow of ideas (even of unwanted ideas) may warrant the court's asking the majority to show meekness in the face of rudeness or public contumely on the score that the democratic way of life requires, for its successful carrying on, a certain muscularity and strength and

[29]Thus the "clear and present danger" test, as enunciated by Holmes J.—the classic formula for the determination of the ambit of the constitutional guarantee of free speech, under the United States Constitution—itself necessarily presupposes that any absolutist claims to free speech must be qualified by consideration of countervailing interests in national security. See *per* Holmes J., for the Court, *Schenck* v. *United States*, (1949) 249 U.S. 47, 52; and see also Jackson J. (concurring specially), *Dennis* v. *United States*, (1951) 341 U.S. 494, 567-70.

[30]Holmes J. himself noted: "The most stringent protection of free speech would not protect a man in falsely shouting fire in a theatre, and causing a panic." *Schenck* v. *United States*, (1949) 249 U.S. 47, 52.

[31]Compare, for example, the American cases *Cantwell* v. *Connecticut*, (1940) 310 U.S. 296; *Chaplinsky* v. *New Hampshire*, (1942) 315 U.S. 568; *Kunz* v. *New York*, (1951) 340 U.S. 290; *Feiner* v. *New York*, (1951) 340 U.S. 315.

power of self-restraint.[32] In any case it is clear that the facts will be all-important[33] in the judicial balancing of interests and the consequent judicial determination whether or not to protect the interests in speech and religion in particular cases: and in this regard we badly need to develop more efficient fact-finding techniques in Commonwealth constitutional jurisprudence.[34]

[32]"What is the spirit of moderation? It is the temper which does not press a partisan advantage to its bitter end, which can understand and will respect the other side, which feels a unity between all citizens—real and not the factitious product of propaganda—which recognises their common fate and their common aspirations—in a word, which has faith in the sacredness of the individual. If you ask me how such a temper and such a faith are bred and fostered, I cannot answer. They are the last flowers of civilisation. . . . But I am satisfied that they must have the vigor within themselves to withstand the winds and weather of an indifferent and ruthless world; and that it is idle to seek shelter for them in a courtroom." Learned Hand, *The Spirit of Liberty* (I. Dilliard ed., 1953), 164–5.

[33]The Canadian Supreme Court's rejection, in the *Saumur Case* in 1953, of the ambitious attempt by counsel to employ the technique of the Brandeis Brief as a means of introducing social facts in the record before the court is not, I suggest, one of the happier performances of the court. See *per* Kerwin J., concurring, *Saumur* v. *City of Quebec and Attorney-General of Quebec*, [1953] 4 D.L.R. 641, at 666: ". . . the appellant is entitled to his costs of the action and of the appeal to the Court of Queen's Bench (Appeal Side). He is also entitled to his costs of the present appeal except that nothing should be allowed for the preparation of a factum. Rule 30 of the Rules of this Court provides for the contents of the factum or points of argument of each party, Part 3 whereof is to consist of 'A brief of the argument setting out the points of law or fact to be discussed.' This Rule was not complied with by the appellant filing two volumes containing 912 mimeographed pages together with an appendix thereto of 86 mimeographed pages."
Although the Brandeis Brief, as first used in *Muller* v. *Oregon*, (1908) 208 U.S. 412, is now a normal feature of American constitutional law practice, as late as 1923 a Court majority could dismiss such material as "interesting but only mildly persuasive." *Adkins* v. *Children's Hospital*, (1923) 261 U.S. 525, 560, Sutherland J. for the Court.

[34]The limitations of the concept of judicial notice as a means of acquainting final appellate courts with social facts become, I suggest, increasingly and glaringly manifest. The conflict in the *Dennis Case* between Jackson J. (concurring) and Douglas J. (dissenting), as to what extent the Communist Party constituted a threat to national security in the United States, is notorious: *Dennis* v. *United States*, (1951) 341 U.S. 494. On the question whether, in the *Saumur Case*, interests in religion were actually involved in the case before the Court (viewed by the Court as the question whether the Jehovah's Witnesses are in fact a religion), compare the assorted remarks of Rinfret C.J.C., dissenting, with those of his brother justices, [1953] 4 D.L.R. 641, at 655: "Most ironically, Jehovah's Witnesses who, in their publications, affirm categorically not only that they do not constitute a religion, but that they are opposed to all religion and that religions are an invention of the demon, are now before the Canadian Courts to ask protection in the name of religion." And at 656–7: "The difficulty that the appellant is experiencing here results from several reasons: First: His right to distribute religious pamphlets does not constitute the exercise of worship or religious profession. . . . The first point above depends on a question of fact. . . . Now in all these publications it is affirmed that Jehovah's Witnesses are not a religion;

As a final point in this particular context, it must be borne in mind that there will be many areas of social behaviour, involving both individual and group conduct, raising issues that would conventionally be categorized as civil liberties issues, but which may only with difficulty be brought within the area of operation of a constitutional Bill of Rights. I am thinking here, especially, of such matters as the refusal of hotel accommodation on racial grounds,[35] and the operation of restrictive covenants prohibiting the sale or lease of property to persons of particular religious affiliations.[36] Even in the case of the United States, with its constitutional guarantee of freedom of religion and with its quite specific prohibitions, also, of racial discrimination, there have been considerable problems in imposing legal regulation of these practices since they have traditionally been regarded as affecting "private," and not "public," interests.[37] Though the limits of legal ingenuity in bringing

---

that, to the contrary, their aim is to fight all religions and that religion is an invention of the demons. . . . Under the circumstances, it is impossible for me to see in virtue of what Jehovah's Witnesses could invoke the freedom of religion."

However, contrast with Rinfret C.J.C.'s finding of fact as to the nature of the Jehovah's Witnesses, the conclusions in this regard by Kerwin J., concurring, at 663; Kellock J., concurring, at 681; Locke J., concurring, at 708.

[35]Note, for example, *Constantine* v. *Imperial Hotels Ltd.*, [1944] K.B. 693,—strictly speaking, a case concerning the innkeeper's obligation, at common law, to receive all travellers regardless of race or colour; in that case, an action was held to lie for breach of the obligation even in the absence of proof of special damage.

[36]See the landmark decision of Keiller Mackay J., of the Supreme Court of Ontario, holding void, as contrary to public policy, a covenant in a deed of land that the land was not to be sold to "Jews or persons of objectionable nationality." *Re Drummond Wren*, [1945] O.R. 778; and see generally D. A. L. Smout, "An Inquiry into the Law on Racial and Religious Restraints on Alienation," (1952) 30 *Can. B. Rev.* 863.

In *Noble and Wolf* v. *Alley*, [1951] 1 D.L.R. 321, the Supreme Court of Canada had to pass on a restrictive covenant in a conveyance of summer resort property, the covenant stipulating that the property should not be sold, transferred, or leased to any person "of the Jewish, Hebrew, Semitic, Negro or coloured race or blood, it being the intention to restrict the ownership, use, occupation and enjoyment to persons of the white or Caucasian race not excluded by this clause." The Supreme Court of Canada, reversing the Supreme Court of Ontario, held (with Locke J. dissenting) *first* that the covenant was not one which would run against subsequent purchasers of the burdened land since it did not touch or concern the land within the meaning of the doctrine of *Tulk* v. *Moxhay*; and *second* that the covenant was void for uncertainty since there was nothing in it to enable a Court to say in all cases whether a proposed purchaser came within the prohibited classes.

[37]See, in this regard, *Dorsey* v. *Stuyvesant Town Corporation*, (1949) 299 N.Y. 512, where the court of Appeals of New York held that the corporation in question, in spite of its receiving certain tax exemptions and other benefits under the state laws, was still not indulging in state action so as to attract the operation of the Fourteenth Amendment Equal Protection clause: in effect, then, the

this class of matter within the definition of public law should not be regarded as having been exhausted,[38] it is likely that there will remain a large number of civil liberties cases that must be dealt with, so to speak interstitially, in the course of ordinary private law decisions given by the ordinary common law courts. Such traditional private law concepts as the "public policy" concept[39] urgently require intensive and sympathetic study by both the academic and practising profession if they are to meet the demands likely to be placed upon them in the future in the cause of legal solution and alleviation of social tension issues.

III. JUDICIAL SELF-RESTRAINT AND JUDICIAL ACTIVISM: PROFILE OF A LIBERAL JUDGE

The fate of a constitution will turn, as I have said, in the ultimate on the judiciary and on the particular philosophic attitudes and outlook that the individual judges care to take to its detailed provisions. We know, of course, that a Supreme Court opinion is an "orchestral and not a solo performance."[40] Since the Supreme Court judges function as a collectivity and not as isolated units, there is necessarily a considerable amount of give-and-take in the informal judicial conference, and so the exact measure of contribution of each judge to a particular decision of the court can never be completely isolated, even with courts like the United States Supreme Court and the Canadian. Supreme Court that indulge in the practice of separate opinion-writing, both specially con-

---

Stuyvesant Corporation enjoyed the privilege, possessed by private landlords, of excluding negroes as tenants. Review of this decision was formally denied by the United States Supreme Court, with the notation—"Certiorari denied. Mr. Justice Black and Mr. Justice Douglas are of the opinion certiorari should be granted. . . ." *Dorsey* v. *Stuyvesant Town Corporation,* (1950) 339 U.S. 981.

[38]Compare *Shelley* v. *Kraemer,* (1948) 334 U.S. 1, where the United States Supreme Court, through Chief Justice Vinson, held that restrictive covenants attaching to land, since dependent for their enforcement in the ultimate upon judicial application in the courts, were no longer "private" action, but "public" in character and as such violated the Fourteenth Amendment Equal Protection clause.

[39]For a valuable survey essay hearing on a number of aspects of this problem, see, for example D. Lloyd, *Public Policy: A Comparative Study in English and French Law* (1953). By the same token, though a "Due Process" clause in a formal Bill of Rights might have simplified judicial solution of the problem-situation in *Roncarelli* v. *Duplessis,* (1959) 16 D.L.R. (2d) 689, in the absence of a Bill of Rights in the Canadian Constitution the Canadian Supreme Court resolved the case by recourse, in effect, to general principles of common law jurisprudence. See the majority opinions, especially of Martland J. and Rand J., *ibid.*; and see the discussion (McWhinney), (1959) 37 *Can. B. Rev.* 503.

[40]F. Frankfurter, *The Commerce Clause under Marshall, Taney and Waite* (1937), 43.

curring and dissenting opinions.[41] Nevertheless, it is possible to identify widely differing, and often conflicting, judicial philosophies or conceptions of the judicial office; and it is the interplay and interaction of these rival viewpoints as to the proper functions of a final appellate judge exercising judicial review, that are the life-blood of constitutional jurisprudence. A constitution, especially where it is equipped with a Bill of Rights, Directive Principles of State Policy, and similar formalized guarantees, may supply the jural postulates or high-level values common to a civilization: but what the judges choose individually to do with those postulates or values may vary very considerably. The more positivist-minded[42] judges may feel that it is their duty to interpret a constitutional Bill of Rights harshly, insofar as the Bill constitutes an interference with and abridgment of governmental legislative powers; that strict and literal interpretation should be the key-note in judicial review, and that care should be taken not to expand the Bill's operation beyond its express terms. On the other hand, a different type of judicial personality may choose to regard a constitutional Bill of Rights as no more than an authoritative starting-point and as a general licence for a judicially elaborated civil liberties jurisprudence.

On the first of these two broad views of the judicial office, the court should, for example, insist on the observance of strict jurisdictional requirements before giving a ruling;[43] it should decide cases narrowly[44]

[41]See generally my article "Judicial Concurrences and Dissents: A Comparative View of Opinion-Writing in Final Appellate Tribunals," (1953) 31 *Can. B. Rev.* 595; and see also K. Nadelmann, "The Judicial Dissent: Publication v. Secrecy," (1959) 8 *Am. J. Comp. L.* 415.

[42]I stress (repeating a warning given earlier—see, for example, (1958) 33 *N.Y.U.L. Rev.* 775, at 780) that the term "positivist" is used here for purposes of jurisprudential classification, only, and that I do not regard the term as *per se* pejorative, in a North American context anyway: some of the recent writings by members of the contemporary English neo-positivist school have seemed to me unnecessarily apologetic and defensive, perhaps in reaction to the strong criticisms, in Continental European legal circles after World War II, of the consequences in action of positivism, as a philosophy of law in the era of totalitarian dictatorship.

[43]"The fact that it would be convenient for the parties and the public to have promptly decided whether the legislation assailed is valid, cannot justify a departure from these settled rules of corporate law and established principles of equity practice. On the contrary, the fact that such is the nature of the enquiry proposed should deepen the reluctance of courts to entertain the stockholder's suit. . . . The Court has frequently called attention to the 'great gravity and delicacy' of its function in passing upon the validity of an act of Congress; and has restricted exercise of this function by rigid insistence that the jurisdiction of federal courts is limited to actual cases and controversies. . . ." (Footnotes omitted.) *Per* Brandeis J. (concurring), *Ashwander* v. *T.V.A.,* (1935) 297 U.S. 288, 345.

[44]"The Court will not 'formulate a rule of constitutional law broader than is required by the precise facts to which it is to be applied.'" (Footnote omitted.) *Ibid.* at 347.

and where possible avoid ruling on the constitutional (usually, Bill of Rights) issue;[45] and it should be at pains to avoid striking down legislative or executive action on the ground of existence of some conflict with the constitution's substantive provisions—it should start out, in effect, with a presumption of the constitutionality of legislative (and executive) action. This is the doctrine of judicial self-restraint; and it looks to the substantial limits, both institutional and political, to the exercise of any sustained policy-making role by the court.[46] The doctrine of judicial self-restraint takes note of the fact that the court is an appointive, non-elective body that can make no valid claims to having a popular "mandate"; that its members' prestige and public standing depend, in certain measure, on their political non-involvement and the extent to which they in fact stay aloof from the exigent here-and-now; that its members, though experts, are highly specialized experts, and not always, or even usually, well equipped for wise community policy-making; that the court, in any case, has only the most rudimentary executive powers to implement and enforce its decrees, and is therefore dependent, in the ultimate, in the giving of decisions on great tension-issues, on the full

[45]"The Court will not pass upon a constitutional question although properly presented by the record, if there is also present some other ground upon which the case may be disposed of. This rule has found most varied application. Thus, if a case can be decided on either of two grounds, one involving a constitutional question, the other a question of statutory construction or general law, the Court will decide only the latter. Appeals from the highest court of a state challenging its decision of a question under the Federal Constitution are frequently dismissed because the judgment can be sustained on an independent state ground." (Footnotes omitted.) *Ibid.* For a recent reaffirmation of these principles, see also *per* Warren C.J., for the Court, *Peters* v. *Hobby*, (1955) 349 U.S. 331, 338.

Courts in countries other than the United States, of course, are not so consistent in application of these principles of caution, particularly the principle against the granting of "premature" constitutional rulings. Thus the High Court of Australia, for example, has not hesitated to grant a declaratory judgment at the suit of a state Attorney-General against the Commonwealth (national) government to restrain it from giving effect to an act even before it was proclaimed. *Attorney-General for Victoria* v. *Commonwealth* (*Pharmaceutical Benefits Case*), 71 C.L.R. 237 (1945); and see generally W. Friedmann, "Declaratory Judgment and Injunction as Public Law Remedies," (1949) 22 *Aust. L. J.* 446. The Supreme Court of Canada, of course, renders Advisory Opinions, on reference. An American commentator, P. A. Freund, blames this assertion of a "premature" jurisdiction on the part of Australian and Canadian appellate courts for the extraordinarily high degree of abstractness and conceptualism in Australian and Canadian constitutional jurisprudence in comparison to that in the United States. *Supreme Court and Supreme Law* (E. Cahn ed., 1954), 87–8.

[46]For a more detailed discussion of the doctrine of judicial self-restraint, and the antinomic doctrine of judicial activism, see my remarks, "The Great Debate: Activism and Self-Restraint and Current Dilemmas in Judicial Policy-Making," (1958) 33 *N. Y. U. L. Rev.* 775; and see also, *supra*, chap. ix.

co-operation of the elective (executive and legislative) arms of government for the purposes of applying sanctions for those same decisions.

The argument in favour of the second view is that the judges are an élitist group of high talents, aspirations, and ideals; that, though they may not be omniscient or for that matter philosopher-kings, they are normally far better equipped intellectually than most people in government; and that, so long as they are aware of their own limitations, there is no grave risk of abuse of their great powers. The case is made that the liberal democratic society rests, at bottom, on certain basic ideals— free speech and discussion, freedom of association, freedom of conscience —and that when these are threatened by executive-legislative authority it is absurd to rest on any abstract, academic conception of the Separation of Powers and say that the judges may not properly intervene in protection of them.[47] This is the civil libertarian activist conception of the judicial office and it bespeaks an affirmative right and even duty on the part of the judges to keep the political processes open, and free and unobstructed.[48] It posits the maintenance of the free society on the existence of an independent judiciary and the entrusting to the judiciary of the responsibility, in the ultimate, for preservation of the Open Society ideal.[49] We have already examined judicial activism in the special context of the United States Supreme Court; but the activist judicial philosophy has its representatives, also, in the history of Commonwealth constitutional jurisprudence, especially Canadian, even though the philosophy may not have been formally identified as such until the last few years. It permeates the majority opinions of Chief Justice Sir Lyman Duff[50] and Mr. Justice Cannon[51] of the Canadian Supreme Court in the *Alberta Press Case*; and it is formulated with characteristic clarity and brilliance in the special concurrences filed by Mr. Justice Ivan C. Rand in the great Canadian constitutional *causes célèbres* of recent years.[52]

[47]The concept of the "preferred position" of the First Amendment Free Speech guarantees in the United States Constitution is merely, I suggest, the most dramatic illustration of this particular judicial position, *supra*.

[48]Compare *per* Stone J., *United States* v. *Carolene Products Co.*, (1938) 304 U.S. 144, 152.

[49]The phrase itself, of course, is Dr. Popper's: Popper, *The Open Society and Its Enemies* (1st ed., 1945), though the sentiment it reflects is at least as old as the American Declaration of Independence and the mainsprings of English constitutionalism.

[50]*Per* Duff C. J. C., *Re Alberta Statutes*, [1938] 2 D.L.R. 81, 107.

[51]*Per* Cannon J., *ibid.* at 119.

[52]See, in this regard, *Winner* v. *S.M.T.* (*Eastern*) *Ltd.*, [1951] 4 D.L.R. 529, *per* Rand J. at 558; *Saumur* v. *Quebec*, [1953] 4 D.L.R. 641, *per* Rand J. at 670–1; *Henry Birks and Sons* (*Montreal*) Ltd. v. *Montreal*, [1955] 5 D.L.R.

Mr. Justice Rand has been the philosopher of Canadian constitutional law—the judge who thinks through the mass of disparate detail in the case law to the great universal, organizing principles in terms of which alone the scattered details have significance: and Mr. Justice Rand has also been the judicial innovator, the judge who is not afraid to break new ground and put forward new, experimental hypotheses for testing in action. The analogy to Lord Denning[53] among contemporary English judges is both proximate and fair, even though Lord Denning is essentially a private lawyer and Mr. Justice Rand pre-eminent in the public law above all—undoubtedly the most outstanding public law judge among the Supreme Court judges of the Commonwealth countries. When one first attempts to study Mr. Justice Rand's opinions in detailed, systematic fashion, there is a temptation to assimilate him to Mr. Justice William O. Douglas of the current United States Supreme Court bench; but Mr. Justice Douglas' opinions have had at times a touch of absolutism in them—perhaps the product of the frustrations of having to dissent too often—and consequently a certain element of acidity[54] that mark them off, as examples of libertarian activism, from Mr. Justice Rand's special concurrences: liberalism perhaps requires a certain element of kindliness to reach its full development as a working judicial philosophy. In any case when one considers how crucial the independent judiciary is in the translation of the abstract, positive law of the constitution into community "living law"—law-in-action—one can only regret the rigidities of the present rule governing tenure of members of the Canadian Supreme Court—a rule only once, to my knowledge, departed from, and then by an executive dispensation in the case of Chief Justice Sir Lyman Duff—that compelled a great liberal judge like Mr. Justice Rand, at the height of his intellectual powers, to retire in 1959 on his reaching the age of seventy-five years.[55] One wonders, in any case, who, among the present bench of the Canadian Supreme Court, will aspire to Mr. Justice Rand's mantle as the liberal judge.

(2d)321, *per* Rand J at 322; *Switzman* v. *Elbling*, (1957) 7 D.L.R. (2d) 337, *per* Rand J. at 357–8; *Roncarelli* v. *Duplessis*, (1959) 16 D.L.R. (2d) 689. And see my discussion, "Mr. Justice Rand's 'Rights of the Canadian Citizen'—The 'Padlock' Case," 4 *Wayne L. Rev.* 115 (1958).

[53]Lord Denning has conveniently summarized his personal philosophy in a number of recent monograph studies. See, for example, Denning, *The Changing Law* (1953).

[54]But Douglas J. at least has never lapsed into the pejorative dissent. Compare Clark J.'s recent dissenting opinions in such cases as *Yates* v. *United States*, (1957) 354 U.S. 298, 344; *Watkins* v. *United States*, (1957) 354 U.S. 178, 217; *Jencks* v. *United States*, (1957) 353 U.S. 657, 680. And see Pound, "*Cacoethes Dissentiendi*—the heated Judicial Dissent," (1953) 39 *A.B.A.J.* 794.

[55]The fallacy that elderly judges must be reactionary or at least incompetent seems largely to have been propagated, in modern times, by supporters of

IV. JUDICIAL VALUES AND JUDICIAL TECHNIQUES: THE COMPLEXITY
OF THE JUDICIAL TASK AS A CHALLENGE TO GREATNESS

It must not be thought that I am advocating now an undiluted judicial activism as the governing philosophy at *all* times for *all* members of a Supreme Court. In any country's constitutional history, there may be some time-periods when judicial liberalism will be the prime motive force in national constitutional and general legal development, and others (possibly the majority of instances) when caution should normally be the watchword. In any case, the balanced court will be the court that benefits by having its share of all main competing philosophies, with the Chief Justice usually acting as the moderator[56] and knowing when to tilt the scales in favour of broad policy enunciations and when to decide, narrowly, on the facts or else on some non-constitutional (for example, statutory construction) ground, or even when to decide not at all.[57] In the majority of problem-situations an intermediate solution in which the actual principle (*ratio decidendi*) of the case is formulated modestly

---

President Franklin Roosevelt's abortive "court-packing" plan of 1937: Mr. Roosevelt and his disciples conveniently forgot that at the time the plan was hatched, the oldest member of the United States Supreme Court was its most liberal member, Brandeis; and that Holmes himself, the idol of American liberals, had retired only a few years before after sitting on the court through his ninetieth year. Actually, the experience of the final appellate tribunals of most of the English-speaking countries suggests little or no correlation between age and political conservatism on the part of the judiciary.

A similar rule to the Canadian Supreme Court's compulsory retirement rule compelled the retirement of Mr. Justice Fazl Ali of the Indian Supreme Court on his attaining the age of sixty-five. Mr. Justice Fazl Ali was promptly appointed by the Indian Government as Governor of a state within the Indian federal system. Mr. Justice Rand, on stepping down from the Canadian Supreme Court, was immediately elected Dean of the newly established Law Faculty of the University of Western Ontario. Neither a state governorship nor a law deanship is normally considered a sinecure for the superannuated.

[56]As to the crucial role of the Chief Justice, see for example McElwain, "The Business of the Supreme Court as Conducted by Chief Justice Hughes," (1949) 63 *Harv. L. Rev.* 5.

[57]Foreign cases which come to mind where courts seem consciously to have postponed the arriving at, or even announcement of, a decision are such *causes célèbres* as *A.L.A. Schechter Poultry Corp.* v. *United States*, (1935) 295 U.S. 495 (the motive here apparently being to see the N.I.R.A.'s particular legislative scheme tested, as a technique of economic planning, in actual working operation —Freund, *On Understanding the Supreme Court* (1949) 109); *Brown* v. *Board of Education*, (1954) 347 U.S. 483 (the delay of several years while the cases were actually before the court—from 1951 to 1954—at least facilitating the development of a majority consensus—R. Bischoff, (1957) 6 *J. Public Law* 411, 425); the *K.P.D.* (Communist Party of West Germany) decision, (1956) 5 B. Verf. G.E. (the delay of judgment for five years, until August, 1956, being dictated, presumably, by a desire not to exacerbate relations between West Germany and Soviet Russia—McWhinney, (1957) 32 *Indiana L. J.* 295, 299–300).

(preferably in an official Opinion of the Court)[58] and the wider-ranging judicial attitudes are left for expression in the ancillary opinions only (special concurrences or dissents) will normally be most satisfactory. I have, in fact, elsewhere criticized[59] the tendency, in American constitutional jurisprudence, to think too much in black-and-white terms and insist that a judge must be able to be categorized, finally and for all cases, as either an apostle of activism or an apostle of restraint, thereby foreswearing the advantages from time to time of taking the more modest, intermediate position. In fact this two-way classification of judicial philosophy in constitutional law—judicial self-restraint/judicial activism—is not really a pure dichotomy at all: for many purposes, the opposing judicial positions may better be characterized, not as polar extremes but as points on a continuum.[60] In any case, to refuse, in the

[58]Some greater self-discipline on the part of members of the Canadian Supreme Court in terms of co-operation in the preparation of an official Opinion of the Court representing the majority judges, or as far as possible a clear majority of the court, would undoubtedly facilitate study and analysis of the court's decisions. An Opinion of the Court representing the lowest common denominator of agreement—the assured minimum views—of the majority justices, could be achieved without in any way derogating from the current complete liberty of individual members of the court to file separate and individual opinions, whether specially concurring or dissenting opinions. The Chief Justice's role would, of course, tend to be rather crucial in the actual allocation of responsibility for preparation of the Opinion of the Court. The *Roncarelli* decision, handed down in 1959, is a particularly striking example of an evident complete lack of co-operation or even consultation among individual members of the Canadian Supreme Court majority in opinion-writing: (1959) 16 D.L.R. (2d) 689; discussed in (1959) 37 *Can. B. Rev.* 503.

An earlier proposal, made in 1952 by the then Chief Justice of Canada, Chief Justice Rinfret, that the Canadian Supreme Court "follow the Privy Council's practice" and issue only a single *per curiam* opinion in each case, was decisively rejected (rightly, in the present writer's view) on the score that such a practice would unnecessarily fetter and confine the Canadian Supreme Court at a time when, following the abolition by Canada of the appeal to the Privy Council, it urgently needed flexibility and independence in judicial thinking. See generally M. Bruce, "The 1953 Mid-Winter Meeting of Council," (1953) 31 *Can. B. Rev.* 178, 181–2; and see also "Judicial Concurrences and Dissents . . . ," (1953) 31 *Can. B. Rev.* 595; "Supreme Court No-Clear-Majority Decisions: A Study in *Stare Decisis*," (1956) 24 *U. Chic. L. Rev.* 99.

Of course the "opinion of the court" practice, so developed in the case of the United States Supreme Court, rests on the regularized institution of the judicial conference which takes place each week during the Court term to discuss and vote on cases. See generally Charles Evans Hughes, *The Supreme Court of the United States* (1928), 98–9. The Canadian Supreme Court does not seem to have adopted, as yet, any regular practice of a judicial conference during term, a fact which no doubt explains the anarchical individualism of such decisions as the *Roncarelli Case.*

[59]"The Great Debate: Activism and Self-Restraint and Current Dilemmas in Judicial Policy-Making," (1958) 33 *N.Y.U.L. Rev.* 775.

[60]*Ibid.* at 786, 790–1.

words of the popular song, to accentuate the positive and eliminate the negative is not necessarily to lack judicial courage. On some great political and social tension-issues that arise for the first time for judicial decision, no clear national policy may have jelled as yet: in such cases, the path of judicial wisdom may be to refrain from any sweeping enunciation of principle and to concentrate instead on the concrete facts of the case and to give a predominantly fact-oriented decision.[61] The court, in such case, is making an ally of time and relying on the processes of community give-and-take and compromise to yield, in time, a clear policy-solution.[62]

[61]This, as I interpret it, was the governing motive behind the crucial, tie-breaking opinion of Kerwin J. (as he then was) in the *Saumur Case*, for Kerwin J. seems to have been at some pains to avoid the polar extremes of doctrinal position taken by both the four other majority justices and also the four dissenters: *Saumur* v. *City of Quebec and Attorney-General of Quebec*, [1953] 4 D.L.R. 641, *per* Kerwin J. at 665.

The same essentially "wait-and-see" philosophy is in evidence in Kerwin C.J.'s laconic, twelve-line opinion in the *Roncarelli Case*, Kerwin C.J. being with the majority in a court that was split six-to-three and his opinion seeming to be deliberately pitched in rather dry, colourless terms: (1959) 16 D.L.R. (2d) 689, 691–2. Again, in the earlier, 1957 decision in *Switzman* v. *Elbling*, Kerwin C.J. was at some pains to stress that "in cases where constitutional issues are involved, it is important that nothing be said that is unnecessary": (1957) 7 D.L.R. (2d) 337, 341. Kerwin J.'s switch of votes had been, of course, crucial in the two Canadian Supreme Court hearings in the famous *Boucher Case*, *Boucher* v. *The King*: [1950] 1 D.L.R. 657; [1951] 2 D.L.R. 369: characteristically, Kerwin J.'s *volte face*, then, as between the first and second Supreme Court rulings, was recorded in a modest, twenty-five-line opinion in which he noted, baldly, that "since the distribution of my reasons in this appeal, there has been a reargument as a result of which I have been persuaded that the order suggested by me is not the proper one to make," [1951] 2 D.L.R. 369, 379.

This particular judicial approach, though lacking in the spectacular and unlikely for that reason to draw the plaudits of the law review commentators, may, nevertheless, in its cautious pragmatism, frequently offer better prospects of a long-range synthesis of the two main streams of Canadian constitutional jurisprudence than more dynamic judicial methods. It is a method especially appropriate to a Chief Justice in a court that has the good fortune also to be endowed with one or two at least of a more activist temperament. Note, for example, the change in role, as Chief Justices, of both Hughes and Stone of the United States Supreme Court, each of these men having earlier served as an Associate Justice of the Supreme Court. See generally, McElwain, "The Business of the Supreme Court as Conducted by Chief Justice Hughes," (1949) 63 *Harv. L. Rev.* 5; A. T. Mason, *Harlan Fiske Stone: Pillar of the Law* (1956). For a delineation of the "Skills of Compromise," as a prime element in contemporary American judicial philosophy, see Edmond Cahn, *The Moral Decision* (1955), 272; and compare, as to Canada, Horace E. Read, "The Judicial Process in Common Law Canada," (1959) 37 *Can. B. Rev.* 265, 289.

[62]The court, of course, should sensibly know, also, when to decide and when not to decide: in some situations, for example the *School-Segregation* issue in the United States, it may be that the wise judicial approach is a blend of both methods—the enunciation of a broad policy as a guide for future decision-making

This is especially important in the case of a plural federal society, like Canada, in which, in contrast to most other federal systems and especially those of the English-speaking countries, two quite different and occasionally opposing sets of values operate within the same territorial frontiers. The fact that Canadian federalism is pluralistic in character means that the judicial decisions of essentially monistic federal societies like the United States, while making interesting reading in view of the clarity and directness of their reasoning and the freedom with which policy issues are discussed, must be received with some caution and certainly not treated as automatically conclusive in regard to questions of ultimate value choice.[63] Many of the problem-situations thus confronting the Canadian Supreme Court will in fact be *sui generis*. To resolve them finally may require advanced judicial thinking on problems of legal theory—on the key concepts of Canadian federalism at the present day. Recourse to history—what the Founding Fathers may have intended originally—will be useful in this regard, but should surely not be regarded as decisive, by itself, at the present day. By way of comparison, the marked centripetal action in the location of effective governmental power under the American Constitution from the 1930's onwards has latterly tended to be replaced increasingly by a new states rights, or, more strictly, co-operative federalism, approach which, as most strongly identified with Mr. Justice Frankfurter,[64] emphasizes from time to time the advantages of diversity of local rule, as distinct from over-all national uniformity.[65] And by the same token recent re-

---

and a rallying point for national opinion, but the staggering of its concrete application if necessary to take account of local facts. The actual mode of formulation of the United States Supreme Court decision in *Brown* v. *Board of Education*, (1954) 347 U.S. 483, is hailed by Edmond Cahn, rightly I think, as an example of imaginative judicial handling of the *space-time* dimension. E. Cahn, *The Moral Decision* (1955), 276–7.

[63]This same proposition applies, *a fortiori*, to the judicial decisions of an essentially simple, un-complex federal society like the Australian federal system. Rand J.'s refusal, in this regard, to regard the Australian commerce and marketing cases (based on s. 92 of the Australian Constitution) as relevant to Canadian experience, seems wise and clearly correct even if the ground of distinction might more happily have been based on the developed practice, rather than the abstract constitutional texts, of the Australian and Canadian federal systems respectively. See *per* Rand J., *Murphy* v. *C.P.R. and Attorney-General of Canada*, (1958) 15 D.L.R. (2d) 145, 151–2. And see generally McWhinney, "Federalism, Pluralism, and State Responsibility: Canadian and American Analogies," (1959) 34 *N.Y.U.L. Rev.* 1079.

[64]See, for example, his opinion of the Court in *New York* v. *United States*, (1946) 326 U.S. 572, 573; and see also Stone C.J., concurring, *ibid.*, at 586.

[65]See both majority and minority opinions in *Cloverleaf Butter Co.* v. *Patterson*, (1942) 315 U.S. 148: Reed J. (opinion of the Court) at 150; Stone C.J. (dissenting) at 170; and Frankfurter J. (dissenting) at 177. And see also G. D.

thinking of the fundamentals of Canadian political life[66] points somewhat towards new pluralistic, or more strictly dualistic (in the sense of
bi-national, English-Canadian and French-Canadian) conceptions of the
locus of governmental power in Canada. Such a dualistic approach
applied to the Canadian federal system could well involve the interesting
(if somewhat anomalous, from the viewpoint of comparative federalism)
situation[67] that identical legislation enacted at the same time by two
different provinces could be at the same time a valid exercise of legislative power by the one province though not by the other.[68] Would it be
inconceivable to apply in Canada a double standard of judicial interpretation involving, for example, in the judicial scrutiny of provincial legislation in the field of religious observance, a greater (or less) standard of
deference to a provincial legislature because the province's population
is predominantly Roman Catholic rather than Protestant? The case for
greater judicial deference would be that the province, because of its
Roman Catholic background, should be entitled to protect its established
folkways and *mores* more strictly.[69] The case for less judicial deference
(and I assume this would be Mr. Justice Rand's position) would be that

---

Braden, "Umpire to the Federal System," (1952) 10 *U. of Chicago L. Rev.* 27;
P. A. Freund, "Umpiring the Federal System," (1954) 54 *Col. L. Rev.* 561.

[66]". . . A number of new concepts about Canadian federalism seem to follow.
Canada is seen not just as one central government and ten provincial governments,
Quebec being merely one of the ten: rather is it looked upon as composed of two
races, equal in status, one of which speaks through the government of Quebec and
the other through Ottawa. Hence Quebec on this view is one of two governments.
The notion of Canada as a dyarchy, or a dual monarchy, is implicit in much of
the contemporary discussion on federal-provincial relations." F. R. Scott, "The
Constitutional Background of Taxation Agreements," (1955) 2 *McGill L. J.*
1, 10. Of course, the use of the term "dyarchy" to describe an essentially "dual
sovereignty" (the national government and the province of Quebec) situation
would be strictly a misnomer in view of the precise historical connotation of the
term in British India.

[67]*Per* Fauteaux J., *Henry Birks and Sons (Montreal) Ltd.* v. *Montreal and
Attorney-General of Quebec*, [1955] 5 D.L.R. 321, 339: ". . . la véritable question
est de déterminer la nature et le caractère de la législation ou, en d'autres termes,
de savoir si la loi incriminée est véritablement une législation tendant à pro-
mouvoir l'observance des jours de fête religieuse. Aussi bien, je ne vois pas en
quoi il serait illogique qu'à une même question se posant à l'examen d'une
législation d'une autre province, il faudrait, à raison d'éléments différents
révélés par le texte de la loi et les circonstances de faits, donner une réponse
également différente à celle qui s'impose en l'espèce."

[68]This particular possibility is adverted to, though not however welcomed, in
a shrewd and penetrating comment by F. A. Brewin, in (1952) 10 *Can. B. Rev.*
840, 843–4.

[69]*Per* Rinfret C.J.C. (dissenting), *Saumur* v. *City of Quebec and Attorney-
General of Quebec*, [1953] 4 D.L.R. 641, at 659: "Who would dare to claim that
pamphlets containing the preceding declarations, distributed in a city like
Quebec, would not constitute a practice inconsistent with the peace and safety
of the city or Province? What Court would condemn a municipal council for

the province, because of its special religious character, would be more likely to trench on the interests of minorities and cultural and religious out-groups within the province.[70]

In any case, the answer to the question whether the province of Quebec should enjoy some special status, distinct from that of the other provinces in relation to Ottawa—whether, so to speak in American terms (to take an extreme example), it is to be in Canada a Calhounian rather than a Jeffersonian thesis of federalism[71] (with corresponding provincial rights analogous to "nullification" or "interposition"[72] vis-à-vis certain categories of Dominion actions)—should sensibly, I think, be determined on pragmatic considerations, and then only case by case. The German constitutional law notion of the *Bundestreue* ("federal comity")[73] which seems to have some analogies to the French private law concept of *abus de droit* and which comes very close to being a sort of code of constitutional "good manners," may perhaps help supply the answers, here: for comity as between the individual members of a federal society surely involves certain reciprocal tolerances and also

---

preventing the circulation of such statements? And I have chosen but a few passages from the books and tracts which are swarming with such affirmations. Besides, decency would command me not to cite any more of them. And that does not appear to me necessary to demonstrate that a municipality whose population is 90% Catholic not only has the right but the duty to prevent the dissemination of such infamies."

[70]Compare Stone J., for the Court, *United States* v *Carolene Products Co.,* (1938) 304 U.S. 144, 152 n. 4: "It is unnecessary to consider now whether legislation which restricts those political processes which can ordinarily be expected to bring about repeal of undesirable legislation, is to be subjected to more exacting judicial scrutiny. . . .

"Nor need we enquire whether similar considerations enter into the review of statutes directed at particular religious . . . or national . . . or racial minorities . . .: whether prejudice against discrete and insular minorities may be a special condition, which tends seriously to curtail the operation of those political processes ordinarily to be relied upon to protect minorities, and which may call for a correspondingly more searching judicial inquiry."

[71]See generally F. R. Scott, "The Constitutional Background of Taxation Agreements," (1955) 2 *McGill L.J.* 1, 10; F. R. Scott, "Areas of Conflict in the Field of Public Law and Policy," (1956) 3 *McGill L.J.* 29, 35; McWhinney, "The United States Supreme Court and Foreign Courts: An Exercise in Comparative Jurisprudence," (1958) 6 *J. Public Law* 465, 477–8; Beetz, "Le Contrôle juridictionnel du pouvoir législatif et les droits de l'homme dans la constitution du Canada," (1958) 18 *Revue du Barreau* (Québec) 361.

[72]Compare Miller and Howell, "Interposition, Nullification and the Delicate Division of Power in a Federal System," (1956) 5 *J. Public Law.* 2.

[73]As developed, for example, in the decision of the Federal Constitutional Court of West Germany in the *Concordat Case,* (1957) 6 B. Verf. G.E. 309, discussed (McWhinney), (1957) 35 *Can. B. Rev.* 842; and also in the decision on the *Referendum on Atomic Weapons,* (1958) 7 B. Verf. G.E. 367, 374. And see also Taylor Cole, "The West German Federal Constitutional Court: An Evaluation after Six Years," (1958) 20 *J. Politics* 278.

mutual understandings not to embarrass unnecessarily the other members of the federal society by one's actions.[74]

In the meantime, while the final policy solution is being sought for by the judges, it may often turn out that the crucial factors in the particular problem-situation actually before the court are not really questions of *values* but questions of concrete *techniques* actually used to implement particular values in the particular case.[75] The court is entitled to insist on a reasonable relationship between *ends* and *means*—between postulated community values and the actual machinery devices used by governmental authority to translate the values into law-in-action.[76] The old hands-off, watchman's state may, by the inexorable pressure of economic, social, and political events of the last seventy-five years, be gone forever, but we are at least entitled to insist on a certain prudent exercise of economy in the use of power, as between government and citizen.[77]

[74]In the *Referendum on Atomic Weapons* decision, the principle of the *Bundestreue* clearly dictated that the member-states of the West German federal system should not embarrass the federal government in its conduct of defence and foreign relations by holding a popular referendum poll on whether the new West German army should be equipped with atomic weapons. In the *Concordat Case*, where the court held that even though West Germany be still bound by the 1933 Treaty between Germany and the Vatican guaranteeing "separate" schools, the member-states of the West German federal system could nevertheless, under the constitution of West Germany of 1949, require non-denominational schools for all children, the principle of federal fidelity offered the only opportunity of overcoming the conflict between Germany's obligations at the international law level and the provisions of her internal, municipal law: if the state statutes, being otherwise within state legislative power, were intended to embarrass the federal government in the conduct of foreign relations or if the states unreasonably withheld their co-operation from the federal government in this area, then the state statutes would presumably fall before the federal fidelity principle. (1957) 35 *Can. B. Rev.* 842, 843–6.

[75]Compare P. A. Freund, *On Understanding the Supreme Court* (1951), 27; and see also *per* Frankfurter J., concurring, *Dennis* v. *United States*, (1951) 341 U.S. 494, 539.

[76]Thus in the fact-situation of the *Saumur Case*, the *techniques* of control actually employed by provincial executive-legislative authority—blanket prohibition—seem to have been grossly disproportionate to the *end* sought to be attained by the province—protection of the Catholic church and Catholic values against insulting or "aggressive" proselytizing activities. Whether or not the particular *end* be regarded as a legitimate user of provincial power, a question not necessarily requiring an immediate judicial answer, a more moderate control would clearly have sufficed to attain that end—say, a system of administrative licensing with grant or retention of the licence predicated upon demonstration or maintenance of certain (judicially reviewable) standards of public conduct and behaviour. *Saumur* v. *Quebec*, [1953] 4 D.L.R. 641. Rather analogous arguments apply, I suggest also, in the fact-situation of the *Padlock Case. Switzman* v. *Elbling*, (1957) 7 D.L.R. 2d. 337.

[77]Dewey puts it thus: "The criterion of value lies in the relative efficiency and economy of the expenditure of force as a means to an end. With advance of

There may even be occasions, in a federal polity, when the desired principle of territorial decentralization of policy-making may suggest the merits of judicial deference to local or provincial action, even in cases where judges may think such local or provincial action wrong. Good federalism and good manners, in such case, may dictate that the judges go along with other people's mistakes: making mistakes is a part (albeit, if long continued, a rather expensive and socially costly part) of that trial-and-error experimentation that is central to the free society.[78]

If the problems of federalism in general and of the judicial process in particular may thus seem unduly complex and even baffling, this should be taken as a measure of the infinite variety and potentiality for experimentation of democratic society, rather than a constitutional vice or weakness. In any case it is clear that the solution of the major problems of constitutional law will require a spirit of calmness and moderation and tolerance, and a large measure of co-operation on the part of the university law faculties and the practising Bar, as well as of the judges.[79]

---

knowledge, refined, subtle and indirect use of force is always displacing coarse, obvious and direct methods of applying it. This is the explanation of the ordinary feeling against the use of force. What is thought of as brutal, violent, immoral, is a use of physical agencies which are gross, sensational and evident on their own account in cases where it is possible to employ with greater economy and less waste means which are comparatively imperceptible and refined." John Dewey, "Force and Coercion," (1916) 26 *International Journal of Ethics* 359, 363.

Even in the area of military strategy where policy-makers might be expected to operate with much less deference to ethical restraints on the application of force than is the received practice, for example, in matters of government, the principle of economy in the use of power is well accepted: "It [the principle of economy of power] prescribes that in the use of armed force as an instrument of national policy no greater force should be employed than is necessary to achieve the objectives toward which it is directed; or, stated in another way, the dimensions of military force should be proportionate to the value of the objectives at stake." Osgood *Limited War: The Challenge to American Strategy* (1957), 4. And compare M. S. McDougal and F. P. Feliciano, "International Coercion and World Public Order: The General Principles of the Law of War," (1958) 67 *Yale L.J.* 771, 797.

[78]"Another and contrasting justification for a free society must be added. Sometimes new truth rides into history upon the back of an error. An authoritarian society would have prevented the new truth with the error. . . ." R. Niebuhr, *The Children of Light and the Children of Darkness* (1946), 75–6.

[79]This particular truth is well summed up in Jeremy Bentham's remark—"The law is not made by judge alone, but by judge and company." See P. A. Freund, *On Understanding the Supreme Court* (1951), 78. The massive intellectual loneliness of the appellate judicial office, and also its immense psychological burdens, are manifest in the plea by Judge (later Chief Judge) Charles E. Clark of the United States Court of Appeals (Second Circuit), (a former Dean of the Yale Law School)—"The Dilemma of American Judges: Is Too Great 'Trust for Salvation' Placed in Them?," (1949) 35 *Am.B.A.J.* 8.

12

JUDICIAL POLICY-MAKING IN AN ERA
OF REVOLUTION

I. Legal Eclecticism: The Transplanting of Judicial Review

The continued popularity and widespread practical application of the institution of judicial review, in the constitution-making of post-War Continental Europe, and also of the "new," ex-Colonial countries, is a tribute to its viability as a prime instrument of democratic constitutionalism at the present day. It is not merely that we find judicial review of the constitution formally introduced into the positive law of the new constitutions of West Germany[1] and of Japan[2]; for these constitutions, after all, were drafted and adopted during the period of Western Allied military occupation when the overt political pressures of Western, and especially American, conceptions of democratic constitutionalism might have been expected to be pervasive. The further, indeed rather surprising, fact is that judicial review should really have taken root in these countries, acquiring, in the process, a new dimension and vitality of its own and transcending in a number of important respects even its original American model. Thus the Federal Constitutional Court of West Germany anticipated, by a number of years,[3] the United States Supreme Court's final decision (reversing earlier, "political questions," precedents) to intervene in State electoral apportionment cases.[4] The German Court reasoned, with a logic that is unmistakable, that without genuine representativeness and fairness in the electoral processes, democratic constitutionalism is hardly possible; and that if the legislature itself be unable or unwilling to police such matters, then the courts of necessity must intervene, if constitutional government is not to

[1]See, generally, my *Constitutionalism in Germany and the Federal Constitutional Court* (1962).

[2]See, generally, N. L. Nathanson, "Constitutional Adjudication in Japan," (1958) 7 *American Journal of Comparative Law* 195.

[3]*Constitutionalism in Germany and the Federal Constitutional Court* (1962), 54 et seq.

[4]See, for example, *Baker v. Carr* (1962), 369 U.S. 186.

disappear by default.[5] In the case of Japan, whatever the real motives
for the adoption of judicial review in the original, post-World War II,
constitution—the so-called "MacArthur Constitution"[6]—its retention as
a permanent feature of Japanese constitutional law and government
seems to have been agreed upon, without any real disagreement or
opposition, by the expert members of the present Japanese Cabinet
Commission on the Constitution charged with the elaboration of a draft
for a new constitutional instrument, to replace the original post-War
document.[7]

The undoubted political success of judicial review, in West Germany
and in Japan since World War II offers an alternative, Civil–Law-
derived, ideal-type or model for this institution, for purposes of its
export to and application in the newly independent and self-governing
countries of South-East Asia and Africa, some of which themselves, of
course, have Civil Law, rather than Common Law, historical legal associations. Our constitutional stereotypes for judicial review have, to date,
been derived from the English-speaking countries whose public law
systems—whether involving a Presidential-executive and formal separation of powers on the American model, or a Parliamentary-executive
on the English and general Commonwealth model—have all rested on
an essentially Common Law legal base involving, at least, the Common–
Law-derived notions of precedents, case law, and judicial reasoning. We
have tended, in the Commonwealth Countries at least, to ignore the
advantages of judicial expertise, in terms either of specialist supreme
courts or else of specialist bancs within supreme courts whose jurisdiction is limited by subject matter—forgetting that, for all practical purposes since the reforms effected by the Judiciary Act of 1925, the
United States Supreme Court has become a specialist public law or
constitutional tribunal.[8] In any case, since the work of the West German Federal Constitutional Court has become amply publicized in the

---

[5]*Constitutionalism in Germany and the Federal Constitutional Court* (1962),
54 *et seq.*

[6]See, for example, K. Kawai, "Sovereignty and Democracy in the Japanese
Constitution," (1955) 49 *American Political Science Review* 663; R. E. Ward,
"The Origins of the Present Japanese Constitution," (1956) 50 *American Political
Science Review* 980.

[7]As to the project for elaboration of the draft of a new Japanese Constitution,
see *Comments and Observations by Foreign Scholars on Problems concerning
the Constitution of Japan* (1946). (Secretariat of the Commission on the Constitution, Tokyo, 1964).

[8]See, generally, "Judicial Concurrences and Dissents: A Comparative View
of Opinion-writing in Final Appellate Tribunals," (1953) 31 *Canadian Bar Review*
595, 617 *et seq.*

comparative law literature, we have at least been exposed to an alternative (non-Common Law) convention of a court successfully exercising judicial review of the constitution that is, at once, highly specialised in terms of its formal jurisdiction; anonymous, in terms of any possible identification or association, by the general public, of any of its individual judges with particular philosophical positions on the court; and, finally, collegial, in the sense of its having a collective or group approach to court decision-making and also to court opinion-writing.[9] This may help at least to correct some of the legal absolutism encountered in the Commonwealth countries to the effect that it is only through Supreme Courts of general, non-specialist jurisdiction, and through judges who manifestly do *not* have constitutional law expertise, that one can expect to have a "strict and complete legalism"[10] rendered in constitutional cases. At the same time, it is to be noted that individual West German judges have occasionally looked with wistfulness on the Common Law-derived Supreme Courts' ability, in exercising judicial review, freely to file dissenting or specially concurring opinions.[11] It may be, in the United States and in the Commonwealth countries, that this power of individual judicial opinion-writing has sometimes been exercised too freely, even indiscriminately; so that what we have, in the end-result of a given Supreme Court decision, is less a reasoned statement of the grounds for disagreement or difference from any official opinion of the court or from the consensus of the majority opinions, than "a brilliant display of the technique of the practising advocate,"[12] or worse still a purely "pejorative" judicial dissent or disagreement.[13] Nevertheless, the proliferation of judicial opinion-writing on the United States Supreme Court and on the Supreme Courts of the various Commonwealth

[9]*Constitutionalism in Germany and the Federal Constitutional Court* (1962), 21 *et seq.*

[10]The phrase itself is that of Chief Justice Sir Owen Dixon, as reported in (1952) 26 *Australian Law Journal* 2, at 4; *supra*, 79.

[11]And in one, Advisory Opinion, proceeding, the *plenum* of the West German Federal Constitutional Court actually indicated that its final ruling had been agreed upon by a 20 to 2 vote: Resolution of December 8, 1952, 2 B Verf GE 79 (1953) (*Plenum*). One of the two dissenting judges in this proceeding later released his dissenting opinion in a private (non-official) publication: Geiger, in (1953) 2 *Der Kampf um den Wehrbeitrag* 822. And see, generally, *Constitutionalism in Germany and the Federal Constitutional Court* (1962), 23–4.

[12]Ballantine, "The Supreme Court: Principles and Personalities," (1945) 31 *American Bar Association Journal* 113. And see also "Judicial Concurrences and Dissents: A Comparative View of Opinion-writing in Final Appellate Tribunals," (1953) 31 *Canadian Bar Review* 595, 615.

[13]Roscoe Pound, "*Cacoethes Dissentiendi*—the heated Judicial Dissent," (1953) 39 *American Bar Association Journal* 794.

countries has undoubtedly helped introduce a marked element of flexibility and fluidity into the constitutional law that those courts were interpreting and expounding, since immensely increasing the opportunities for a subsequent judicial "distinguishing" of unwanted earlier precedents through multiplication of alternative, and often competing, judicial doctrinal positions and policy preferences as articulated in those opinions.[14]

II. Legal Eclecticism: The Pervasive Influence of American Legal Thought-Ways

The major influence, indeed inspiration, in the present-day practice of judicial review, in the Commonwealth countries, has been the Supreme Court of the United States. This at first sight might seem rather surprising in view of the frequently expressed, official judicial distaste, in the older Commonwealth countries, for the citation of American constitutional precedents in argument before their Supreme Courts, or *a fortiori* for any reliance on those American constitutional precedents in the actual judicial opinions deciding cases.[15] It is not such a very long time, after all, since the Supreme Court of Canada refused costs to a successful constitutional litigant in respect to that part of his *factum* containing a *Brandeis Brief*-type discussion of American constitutional decisions reaching the same general interests-complex.[16]

Yet the newer member-countries of the Commonwealth have been subject to no such inhibitions in their resort to legal eclecticism. Right from the outset, the Supreme Court of India has been prepared to admit legal argument concerning American, Canadian, and Australian federal constitutional jurisprudence as an aid to the development of its own distinctive constitutional jurisprudence.[17] And some of the most recently independent and self-governing countries of the Commonwealth may go even further: the Nigerian Law Reports reveal systematic citation by counsel in constitutional cases, and actual canvassing in their opinions by the Supreme Court judges deciding those cases, of constitutional

---

[14]Julius Stone, *The Province and Function of Law* (1946), 166 *et seq.*

[15]See, for example, the Canadian Supreme Court's peremptory refusal of counsel's attempt to cite American Supreme Court decisions, as such, in argument before it. *Saumur v. City of Quebec and Attorney-General of Quebec*, [1953] 4 D.L.R. 641,—per Kerwin C. J. at 665; and see generally *Comparative Federalism. States' Rights and National Power* (1962), 92–3.

[16]*Saumur v. City of Quebec and Attorney-General of Quebec*, [1953] 4 D.L.R. 641, at 666; *supra*, 210.

[17]See generally, for example, M. P. Jain, *Indian Constitutional Law* (1962).

precedents drawn from the United States, Canada, India, Ceylon, and Northern Ireland.[18]

The influence of American constitutional ideas in the older Commonwealth countries, in the face of the official disinclination to permit citation of American cases before the courts, has had to come more or less indirectly—through the general reception of American legal ideas, in Commonwealth law schools and by the Commonwealth law professors themselves, with the post-war wave of Commonwealth law students who have fairly generally elected to take their post-graduate legal education in the graduate law centres of the United States, rather than in England as was the pre-war habit.[19] Whatever its origins, however, the *indicia* of American legal influence in the Commonwealth countries are clear and unmistakable now in Commonwealth Supreme Court opinions—in the noticeably increased policy-orientation of judicial decision-making and the interests-balancing approach in general; in the increasing judicial sophistication as to constitutional facts and as to the extent to which underlying issues of social or economic fact may properly condition constitutionality[20]; in the increased prestige of the dissenting and the specially concurring judicial opinions, as, so to speak, "reconnaissance" ventures for the future in policy-determination[21]; in the general conception of movement and change, in law and in society correlatively.[22]

III. THE RELATION OF GENERAL LEGAL PHILOSOPHY TO JUDICIAL
REVIEW: JUDICIAL PRAGMATISM

The dominant theme in North American philosophy of law today must be the concept of change or revolution in law. In Mr. Justice Oliver Wendell Holmes' own aphorism, it is revolting to have no better reason for a rule of law than that so it was laid down in the time of Henry IV.[23] The prestige argument, from age alone, that because a

[18]See, for example, *Dahiru Cheranci v. Alkali Cheranci*, [1960] N.R. N.L.R. 24; *Olawoyin v. Attorney-General*, [1960] N.R. N.L.R. 53; *T. V. Akwule and Ten Others v. The Queen*, [1963] N. R. N.L.R. 105. (I am indebted to Sir Ian Lewis, Attorney-General of Northern Nigeria, for these references.)

[19]This switch in the preferred location of Canadian graduate legal education, and some of its practical consequences in terms of general philosophy of legal education in Canadian law schools, are discussed, in part, in *Canadian Jurisprudence. The Civil Law and Common Law in Canada* (1958), 10–15.

[20]*Supra*, 180–1, 210.

[21]Roscoe Pound, Introduction to Musmanno, *Justice Musmanno Dissents* (1956), v.

[22]*Supra*, 206–8.

[23]O. W. Holmes, Jr., "The Path of the Law," in Holmes, *Collected Legal Papers* (1920), 187.

claimed legal rule has lasted a certain length of time it must automatically be valid and binding at the present-day, regardless of changes in basic societal conditions and expectations, is no longer very persuasive. According to the basic teachings of the Legal Realist and Policy schools of law, society itself is in a continuing state of flux; and the positive law, therefore, if it is to continue to be useful in the resolution of contemporary major social conflicts and social problems, must change in measure with the society.[24] What we have, therefore, concomitantly with our conception of society currently in revolution, is a conception of law, itself, as being in a condition of flux or movement at the present-day. On this view, law is not a frozen, static body of rules, but rules in a continuous process of change and adaptation; and the judge, at the final appellate level anyway, is a part—a determinant part—of this dynamic process of legal evolution.[25]

The original great debate initiated, in American legal circles, by the Legal Realist movement, was directed to the question of whether the judge did, as a matter of law-in-action, "make" law. The original Legal Realist demand for empirically-based study of judicial behaviour called for destruction of the "basic myth"[26]—the proposition that judges do not "make" law. Once this "myth" had been shattered and the necessarily inherent law-making role of the final appellate judge recognised, the subsequent Realist demand became that the judges should exercise their legislative role frankly and openly, with full canvassing of the alternative lines of policy open to the court in any given situation. The focus of the problem had therefore been shifted from a purely *descriptive* level (whether judges *do* in fact make law in their decisions), to a *normative* level with the real questions becoming now questions as to the particular policies to be applied by the judges and also the particular legal techniques to be used for implementing those same judicial policies, once selected, in the courts' decisions.

On this basis, the process of judicial decision-making would lend itself to analysis and study on a four-fold basis[27]: first, a *logical* aspect, in which the past jurisprudence and doctrines are canvassed by the judges in search of the main relevant rules of law; second, a *fact-finding* aspect, in which the material facts in the instant case are determined,

[24]See, for example, K. N. Llewellyn, "Some Realism about Realism—Responding to Dean Pound," (1931) 44 *Harvard Law Review* 1222, 1236–8.

[25]E. W. Patterson, *Jurisprudence. Men and Ideas of the Law* (1953), 559 *et seq.*

[26]Jerome Frank, *Law and the Modern Mind* (1930), 3 *et seq.*

[27]Compare E. W. Patterson, *Jurisprudence. Men and Ideas of the Law* (1953), 300 *et seq.*

for purposes of application of the relevant rules of law to those facts; third, a *policy* phase, in terms of which the judicial conclusion is arrived at whether to apply an old rule of law, whether, instead, to modify it, whether, even, to ignore it altogether and to create an entirely new rule; finally, an *information* phase, at which the judges proceed to formal rationalisation of the policy and logical bases of their individual positions, in terms of the formal opinion-writing.

What is clear is that while the *information* phase will normally be a subsequent activity, separated temporally from the other three phases of judicial investigation, these other three in no way amount to a hierarchy of steps which are approached, so to speak, in successive stages. Indeed, a Realist examination of the actual processes of judicial decision-making would suggest that, where the judge necessarily begins with a more or less undifferentiated fact-situation, the relevant rules of law, material facts, and the over-riding social policies tend to emerge more or less simultaneously, to produce a particular end-result or decision.[28] In other words, there is a species of interaction, in the judicial mind, of rules of law, facts, and policies, and the process of choice as to each one of these interacts on and reciprocally influences the processes of choice as to the others—thereby determining which particular rules of law are to be designated as relevant, which facts as material, and which policies as governing.

In taking note, in this way, of the indeterminacy of the judicial process and the opportunities for creative judicial choice thereby involved, some jurists would contend, in the full Realist tradition, that it is the policies that are really decisive in the judicial designation of the rules of law and of the facts that are to be governing and applicable in a given case. Though legal propositions and rules, as Karl Llewellyn demonstrated, have a habit of marching in pairs, with any particular proposition invariably accompanied by its own direct antithesis—"Rule skepticism"[29]; and though facts themselves, as Judge Jerome Frank pointed out, tend so often to be "wild facts"—"Fact skepticism,"[30] it is hardly necessary, for present purposes, to embrace any such extreme instrumental theories of the extent to which policies have, in fact, dominated and controlled positive law in the development of the constitutional jurisprudence of the English-speaking countries. It will suffice to say that policy considerations have been pervasive throughout the

[28]Compare John Dewey, "Logical Method and Law," (1924) 10 *Cornell Law Quarterly* 17; Dewey, *The Theory of Inquiry* (1938), 118.
[29]See, generally, Jerome Frank, "Cardozo and the Upper-Court Myth," (1948) 13 *Law and Contemporary Problems* 369, 384.
[30]*Ibid.*

history of judicial review in the English-speaking countries and that, as a matter of law-in-action, the influences of policy seem to have been strongest upon those judges who have normally made a point, in their opinions, of denying the role of policy in constitutional adjudication, and who have by contrast insisted most strongly on the necessity for a "strict and complete legalism" in the approach to decision of cases.

IV. JUDICIAL POSITIVISM AND THE INHERENTLY POLITICAL CHARACTER OF CONSTITUTIONAL ADJUDICATION

At the time of the appearance of the first edition of this work, one of the older-generation English professors charged me, in effect, with "left-of-centre" political attitudes in suggesting that the historical record of judicial interpretation of social and economic legislation, in the United Kingdom itself and also in the Colonial Empire and the Commonwealth —not less than in the United States in the so-called "Gilded Era" (liberty-of-contract-in-the-abstract) period of American capitalism which lasted, roughly, from the end of the Civil War until the Roosevelt "New Deal" era—revealed a more or less conscious judicial preoccupation with questions of social and economic basic values, all too frequently manifested in a direct injection of judicial value preferences into the cases that the judges were deciding. In this same context, another English professor of the same era charged me with being "unfair" to the Privy Council, and in particular "unfair" to Lord Watson and Lord Haldane, in my analysis and appraisal of the detailed record of their interpretation of the Canadian Constitution.

Looking back, these particular English criticisms seem curiously dated, so much have the Legal Realist teachings of the law-making, law-creating role of the final appellate judge become received opinion since that time in Commonwealth, and not less perhaps by now, in English, law schools. On any empirically-based study, it hardly seems possible to deny that the particular decisions referred to of the English and Commonwealth judges, on social and economic legislation, were neither necessary nor inevitable in terms of the positive law as written; and that the judicial interventionism, at the value level, involved the judicial projection in positive law form of the values of an earlier, usually more *laissez-faire*-attuned, era of society in place of the rather more contemporary values of current legislative majorities.

As to the Privy Council and the Canadian Constitution, my criticisms have been directed specifically to the failure of the Privy Council frankly to acknowledge and admit, in its formal opinions accompanying its decisions, that it was engaging in constitutional elaborations that were neither expressly warranted by the text of the Constitution, nor supported by the original historical intentions of the Founding Fathers of the Constitution, in reaching the results that the Privy Council did, in the period from 1896 onwards, in relation to social and economic planning legislation and Dominion-Provincial relations generally. The judicial policy-maker surely has certain obligations of public candour, in order to expose the judicial policy choices to the democratic corrective of public discussion and criticism! The failure of the Privy Council, in relation to the Canadian Constitution, to be frank and explicit as to the policy bases of its opinions, meant that the reasons for the actual policy choices too often remained obscured and concealed, with the policy considerations necessarily operating then as "inarticulate major premises" to the final decision.[31] And the failure to articulate these same policy bases meant, in turn, that the judges were not directly assisted by counsel, through the *Brandeis Brief* or otherwise, in the building of an appropriate factual record that might inform and assist a judicial conclusion on complex social and economic issues. If we had judicial policy-making on the part of the Privy Council in relation to the Canadian Constitution, in the period from 1896 onwards, it was, necessarily, because of these very omissions, a species of policy-making in the dark —at best, impressionistic and rather hit-and-miss.

It is possible in this regard to argue that a good number of the past decisions of the Privy Council, viewed now in policy terms—whatever their relationships to particular social and economic predilections on the part of the individual members of the judiciary taking part in them— happen to make sense also (that is to say, can be justified pragmatically) in terms of the development of a community consensus in the individual countries for whom the Privy Council was deciding. In this regard, while it may be difficult to think of a more aridly conceptual decision, viewed now in strict positive law terms, than the Privy Council's *Labour Conventions* decision of 1937,[32] it is a fact that the policy consequences of the decision are at the core of the present great constitutional debate in Canada. Nevertheless, Lord Wright, one of the main judicial authors of the *Labour Conventions* decision, in his informed second thoughts about the decision, had such grave reservations as to its rationality, from the viewpoint of the black-letter law and the traditional rules of construction, that, many years after the decision, he took the unusual step, for

[31]See per Holmes J., dissenting, *Lochner v. New York*, (1905) 198 U.S. 45, 74; *supra*, 187, 201.
[32]*Attorney-General for Canada* v. *Attorney-General for Ontario*, [1937] A.C. 326 (P.C.).

a judge, of uttering his own public *mea culpa*—in effect, a retrospective dissent.[33] The Privy Council's official opinion, in the *Labour Conventions* case, is pitched in black-letter law terms alone, and singularly barren of the policy-type arguments which might serve to redeem or justify it today as a conscious value-choice among competing key concepts as to federalism and the desirable location and distribution of community decision-making power in a plural-cultural society.

V. JUDICIAL POLICY-MAKING AND THE DILEMMA OF JUDICIAL VALUE-CHOICE

There have, in the last several years, been a number of important political changes on several of the final appellate tribunals of the English-speaking countries, going to the core of the intellectual conflict between the proponents of judicial activism and the proponents of judicial self-restraint. The political changes foreshadowed, in the case of the Supreme Court of Canada, by the departure of Mr. Justice Rand on his reaching the compulsory retirement age of seventy-five in 1959, and by the voluntary retirement, a little earlier, of Mr. Justice Kellock, his closest intellectual associate on the court, have been realised. In retrospect, the period of liberal activism, on the Canadian Supreme Court—lasting about a decade—can be seen substantially as having come to an end with the *Roncarelli* case decision in 1959,[34] the last great decision in which Mr. Justice Rand participated. The explanation for this lies only partly, however, in changes in judicial personnel on the court and the fact that the successors to Justices Rand and Kellock seem to be much more in the tradition of judicial self-abnegation than to be adherents to the liberal activist credo. Part of the explanation undoubtedly lies in the practical disappearance, or at least muting, of the sort of great political *causes célèbres* that are especially ripe for sweeping judicial policy pronouncements. With the death of their political arch-enemy, Premier Duplessis of Quebec, in 1959, the Jehovah's Witnesses have apparently been directing the main thrust of their aggressive proselytising activities elsewhere than in the predominantly French-speaking, and Catholic, Province of Quebec; and in any case no major direct confrontations between the Jehovah's Witnesses on the one hand and the Quebec Provincial governmental authorities or the

---

[33]See Lord Wright's comments in the course of his tribute to Sir Lyman Duff, (1955) 33 *Canadian Bar Review* 1123; and see the discussion, *supra*, 54.

[34]*Roncarelli* v. *Duplessis*, (1959) 16 D.L.R. (2d) 689.

Quebec police have in fact taken place since that time. This all recalls, of course, Jeremy Bentham's maxim that the law is not made by judge alone, but by "judge and company"[35]—which specifically includes counsel who are prepared and competent to take cases right through to the final appellate level. Recognising that virtually all of the great Canadian civil liberties cases of the decade up to 1959 arose originally from cases involving individual Jehovah's Witnesses and providing, in effect, the vehicles for judicial legislation in an area not heretofore specifically covered in any constitutional bill of rights or other fundamental law charter, one must concede how much, practically, Canadian constitutionalism owes to the energies of a litigation-minded, minority pressure group.

The seeds of the judicial conflict originally planted in these Jehovah's-Witnesses'-derived cases remain, however. In the first place, the court split unmistakably, in these cases, along general ethnic-cultural lines, with an Anglo-Saxon, essentially (though not exclusively) Protestant, Common Law, majority deciding the cases, over the strong dissent of the two French-speaking, Roman Catholic, and Civil Law, judges.[36] In cases whose fact-complexes fairly uniformly had their origins in the public assault made by the Jehovah's Witnesses in the Province of Quebec upon the Roman Catholic Church—the religion of the overwhelming majority of the inhabitants of Quebec—and correlative attempts by the Quebec governmental authorities to control or repress this activity, the Supreme Court majority imposed, in effect, more general, national values upon more specialised, Provincial values. It seems quite clear, in any case, that in situations involving competitions or conflicts between the interests in speech and communication on the one hand and interests in public order, the Anglo-Saxon, Common Law, judges on the Canadian Supreme Court have tended in the immediate past to strike the balance of the competing interests in a quite different way to their French-speaking, Civil Law colleagues.[37] More, it seems clear, from the judicial dispositions of the Jehovah's Witnesses cases arising from Quebec, that

[35]Paul Freund, *On Understanding the Supreme Court* (1949), p. 78.

[36]The third Civil Law judge on the Supreme Court—the Supreme Court Act, 1949, requiring that three of the nine judges on the court come from Quebec—Mr. Justice Abbott, a member of the English-speaking minority within the Province of Quebec, invariably voted with the Anglo-Saxon, Common Law majority in these cases and not with his French-speaking, Civil Law colleagues.

[37]Thus the Tremblay Report, still perhaps the most authoritative, and certainly the most comprehensive, public statement of Quebec's special constitutional claims, seems to establish the Quebec commitment, in ethnic-cultural terms, to the "sense of order" as being in hierarchical superiority to its commitment to the "sense of liberty" and the "sense of progress." *Report of the Royal Commission of Inquiry*

particular fact-complexes that the Anglo-Saxon judges have characterised fairly uniformly as civil liberties situations, have been characterised quite otherwise by the French-speaking judges—presumably as simple situations involving the community protection of public safety or public morals. The role of a Supreme Court functioning as a federal institution becomes especially difficult under these circumstances when we are dealing, in effect, with two radically different judicial *Weltanschauungen*. If the conflict between particularistic, regionally-based, ethnic-cultural attitudes and values on the one hand, and national attitudes and values on the other, be not too extreme, a mutually satisfying accommodation may no doubt be reached on a Frankfurterian, federalistic principle of deference to the regional authority, and in particular of deference to the decisions and determinations of the regional authority's supreme court or other tribunals. Unarticulated philosophic considerations of this nature certainly seem to be the basis, in part at least, for the various proposals at the present time that the Quebec Court of Appeal be made the final appellate tribunal for cases arising under the Quebec Civil Code (without appeal therefrom to the Canadian Supreme Court); or that the Canadian Supreme Court should be divided into bancs or chambers specialised by subject matter, with a Civil Law banc, composed of judges trained in the Civil Law, having sole competence over the Quebec Civil Code. Where the issues involved are of the nature, for example, of parental custody of minor children and whether the mother or the father should have primacy as to this—something on which the Quebec Civil Law, and the Common Law as practised in the English-speaking provinces, might seem to reach different results,[38] the price of such accommodation, and of any consequent national

---

on Constitutional Problems, Province of Quebec (1956), vol. 2, at pp. 35–7. The Quebec judges, Justices Taschereau and Fauteux, have tended in any case, in the competition between interests in public order and interests in speech and communication, to strike the balance in favour of the interests in public order: the English-speaking judges, or at least the judicial "front-runners" among them (Justices Rand, Kellock, and Abbott), with their "Open Society" commitment, have come down almost inevitably on the side of the speech and communication interests. Others of the English-speaking judges, though generally voting with Justices Rand, Kellock, and Abbott, have been a little less categorical in their judicial opinions. Justice Kerwin, for example, shewed a preference for essentially low-level, fact-oriented opinions (*supra*, 219); and in the *Lady Chatterly's Lover* case actually dissented, together with his French-speaking judicial colleagues. *Reg.* v. *Brodie*, (1962) 32 D.L.R. (2d) 507.

[38]See, for example, *Donaldson* v. *Taillon*, [1953] 2 S.C.R. 257; L. Lalande, "Puissance paternelle—Déchéance—Droit civil et jurisprudence de Québec— Composition de la Cour Suprême du Canada," (1955) 33 *Canadian Bar Review* 950. And see also *Canadian Jurisprudence. The Civil Law and Common Law in Canada* (1958), 9, 18.

deference to Provincial values may not be felt to be oppressive.[39] Where, however, as in the case of the issue, in the United States, of racial segregation in education, the consensus eventually emerges, nationally, that tolerance to regionally-based diversity in basic values on this particular issue is no longer compatible with democratic constitutionalism, then compromise may cease to be possible any longer; and one may be left with the ultimate choice either of imposition of national values by national instrumentalities (of which, of course, the federal Supreme Court is one), or else perhaps of outright political separatism. A federal Supreme Court, with its undoubted natural prestige and authority, can certainly assist, by the course of its decisions, in promoting, in time, a genuine national consensus that will increasingly reconcile the particularist regional values with overall national values. Yet this public educational function of a Supreme Court is undoubtedly a difficult one to execute, and it will normally require making an ally of time and proceeding slowly. The ultimate result in the United States, in 1954, in *Brown* v. *Board of Education*,[40] was undoubtedly predictable, after the series of rather modest, essentially fact-oriented decisions, usually under the rubric of the "separate but equal" formula, that the United States Supreme Court had begun to give in State education cases from the late 1930's onwards.[41] But it did take a rather long time to reach the ultimate Supreme Court decision outlawing segregation in education, as such; and the practical effectuation of the 1954 decision was hardly assisted by the substantial inaction in race relations matters, during most of the 1950's, of the Presidency and of Congress—the two organs, after all, charged under the Constitution with prime responsibility for governmental activism in the major areas of community social policy. In this light, it hardly seems fair to criticise the Supreme Court too much for the frequent deference to considerations of judicial self-restraint which refined or moderated its judicial policy-making during that same time period.

VI. CHANGING LAW AND CHANGING SOCIETY. CHANGING JUDICIAL VALUES

The shifting balance between judicial self-restraint and judicial activism has been borne out once again by the record of the United

[39]Lalande, "Puissance...," (1955) 33 *Canadian Bar Review* 950; also Lalande, "Audition des appels de Québec à la Cour Suprême," (1955) 33 *Canadian Bar Review* 1104.

[40]*Brown* v. *Board of Education of Topeka*, (1954) 347 U.S. 483.

[41]*Comparative Federalism. States' Rights and National Power* (1962), 66 *et seq.*

Judicial Review in the English-Speaking World

States Supreme Court in the last several years. The current marked swing, towards judicial activism once again, has undoubtedly been assisted greatly, as it certainly was symbolised publicly, by the retirement of Mr. Justice Frankfurter, the most articulate and eloquent exponent of the theory and practice of judicial self-restraint. The high-water mark of judicial activism was probably attained in the School Prayer case,[42] and also in the literary and artistic censorship cases, where the court seems to have gone very far towards removing public censorship controls altogether.[43] The State election cases, where the Supreme Court intervened at long last to control electoral apportionment schemes for State legislatures, sweeping away old precedents that had insisted on categorising such matters as non-justiciable "political questions,"[44] aroused considerable political controversy and were undoubtedly associated in the public mind with the cause of judicial activism. I believe that such association is neither necessary nor philosophically justifiable. The main canons of judicial self-restraint, and as to the necessity of judicial deference to the popularly-elected organs of government, are posited on the assumption that these latter really are responsible, in the sense of representative, organs. Any notions that the Supreme Court, as a non-elective, appointive organ, should yield to the popular will as expressed in legislation, must surely tend to weaken in the face of a legislature chosen under a gerrymandered, or otherwise un-representative, electoral system. The then Mr. Justice Harlan F. Stone had foreshadowed the principle of judicial interventionism to correct basic abuses in the electoral laws, in his *Carolene Products* case opinion in 1938,[45] when he adumbrated the primary duty of the courts to keep the general political processes free and unobstructed.[46] The supposed technical objections to judicial intervention in election laws cases (for example, lack of practical expertise in electoral matters)—which were always asserted as supplying an additional, practical support to the old doctrinal justification for denial of judicial activism, in these cases—had in any case been satisfactorily disposed of by the record of successful and painless judicial intervention, to ensure fairness and representativeness under the electoral laws, on the part of the West German Federal Constitutional Court in a series of decisions over the decade that followed

[42]*Engel* v. *Vitale*, (1962) 370 U.S. 421.
[43]See, for example, *Manual Entreprises* v. *Day*, (1962) 370 U.S. 478.
[44]See, for example, *Baker* v. *Carr*, (1962) 369 U.S. 186.
[45]*U.S.* v. *Carolene Products Co.*, (1938) 304 U.S. 144, 152 n. 4.
[46]*Supra*, 178–9, 182–3, 215.

its inception in 1951.[47] Such is the extent to which constitutional law has now become an exercise in comparative legal science that these highly successful German elections cases had been commented on in the English-speaking countries, and were presumably not unknown to some at least of the United States Supreme Court judges at the time they took the dramatic step to throw out the old precedents and actively to scrutinise the fairness and representativeness of State electoral apportionment.

Such cross-fertilisation from other legal systems, of course, demonstrates very effectively the possibility of another community's living happily with a different ultimate policy choice than one's own; and it is thus a highly practical vindication of the non-necessity of any immutability, through time, in basic judicial values. The resolution of the value-conflicts between French-speaking and English-speaking judges in Canada, as evidenced in the great *causes célèbres* of the 1950's with their two different basic value systems already referred to, has seemed to some Quebec spokesmen, who object to the essentially Anglo-Saxon, majority judicial positions in those cases, to be so difficult as to lend itself only to the most radical remedy involving, in effect, political compromise to the point of political stalemate: it is just this sort of counsel that leads to the demand, in some Quebec circles, for creation of a special constitutional court in Canada, having jurisdiction over all federal constitutional matters, but with its membership divided equally, on strict ethnic-cultural lines, as between Quebec and the rest of Canada. There is no reason to believe that the process of resolution, in Canada, of ultimate value-conflicts stemming from the two main ethnic-cultural divisions of the country, will be achieved on other than an essentially political basis. For this reason, the Canadian Supreme Court's decisions in the 1950's *causes célèbres* are necessarily part of the great political debate on biculturalism, of our times; and whether those decisions remain law for the future must turn ultimately on the final political consensus and compromise that is reached from the biculturalism debate.

Yet the two main ethnic-cultural groupings in Canada may be closer, in fact, than the judicial divisions and conflicts on the Supreme Court indicate. For the particular *Weltanschauung* projected by the Civil Law judges in those cases of the 1950's represent an older, perhaps more conservative, set of values than those of the dominant political forces in a Quebec in the throes of tremendous and far-reaching political and

[47]*Constitutionalism in Germany and the Federal Constitutional Court* (1962), 54 *et seq.*

intellectual revolution. For while the Supreme Court of Canada divided along fairly predictable ethnic-cultural lines (granted its continuing personnel) in its recent decision in the *Lady Chatterley's Lover* case,[48] the dissenting opinions of the Civil Law judges in that case have drawn fire from some younger Quebec jurists as being out-of-date, in the sense of rather excessively or unnecessarily deferring to claimed interests in the protection of community morals, as against interests in free speech and communication. The Revolution in Quebec has, in any case, since the inauguration of the Lesage government, shown a marked break with the methods and techniques of Premier Duplessis' era. The excessive governmental assertion of claimed community interests in public order, which characterised the Duplessis administration, seems to have abated. We no longer seem to have these types of cases coming before the courts, and therefore no longer have the sharply abrasive and divisive, in ethnic-cultural terms, judicial decisions of the Duplessis period. So may executive-legislative policies, whether of affirmative governmental action or of conscious governmental inaction, condition and affect the occasions and opportunities for exercise of judicial policy-making; and they can be expected to continue to do so in the future.

[48]*Reg.* v. *Brodie*, (1962) 32 D.L.R. (2d) 507.

INDEX

www.ingramcontent.com/pod-product-compliance
Lightning Source LLC
Chambersburg PA
CBHW070616030426
42337CB00020B/3823